Tommy Kono

Tommy Kono
The Life of America's Greatest Weightlifter

JOHN D. FAIR

McFarland & Company, Inc., Publishers
Jefferson, North Carolina

LIBRARY OF CONGRESS CATALOGUING-IN-PUBLICATION DATA

Names: Fair, John D. author.
Title: Tommy Kono : the life of America's greatest weightlifter / John D. Fair.
Description: Jefferson, North Carolina : McFarland & Company, Inc., Publishers, 2023 | Includes bibliographical references and index.
Identifiers: LCCN 2022049941 | ISBN 9781476689586 (paperback : acid free paper) ∞
ISBN 9781476647272 (ebook) ∞
Subjects: LCSH: Kono, Tommy, 1930–2016. | Weight lifters—United States—Biography. | Olympic athletes—United States—Biography. | Japanese Americans—Biography. | BISAC: SPORTS & RECREATION / Bodybuilding & Weightlifting
Classification: LCC GV545.52.K66 F35 2022 | DDC 796.41092 [B]—dc23/eng/20221026
LC record available at https://lccn.loc.gov/2022049941

BRITISH LIBRARY CATALOGUING DATA ARE AVAILABLE

ISBN (print) 978-1-4766-8958-6
ISBN (ebook) 978-1-4766-4727-2

© 2023 John D. Fair. All rights reserved

No part of this book may be reproduced or transmitted in any form
or by any means, electronic or mechanical, including photocopying
or recording, or by any information storage and retrieval system,
without permission in writing from the publisher.

Front cover: Tommy Kono, 1955 (courtesy of *Iron Man* publisher Denny Kakos)

Printed in the United States of America

McFarland & Company, Inc., Publishers
Box 611, Jefferson, North Carolina 28640
www.mcfarlandpub.com

To Pete George and Walter Imahara
Tommy's Kindred Spirits

Table of Contents

Preface   1
Introduction: "Go for Broke"   5

I—Early Life   11

1. From Tule Lake to Helsinki   13
2. Ascent to Olympus   31
3. A Living Legend   55
4. Descent from Olympus   73

II—From Amateur to Professional   89

5. Olympic Coach   91
6. Public Servant   114
7. Retro Coach   134
8. Political Quagmire   153

III—Athletic Immortality   171

9. Rising Above the Din   173
10. Weightlifting Sage   185
11. A Heroic Ending   204

Epilogue and Conclusion   219
Appendix I: Tommy Kono's Record of Achievement   233
Appendix II: World Records   235
Chapter Notes   237
Bibliography   261
Index   267

Preface

"A man's life is what his thoughts make of it."—Marcus Aurelius

My first awareness of Tommy Kono dates back to the summer of 1962 after my first year of college when I was training in a small weight room in the basement of my hometown YMCA in Waynesboro, Pennsylvania. There was no Olympic set, bench press, or squat racks in this dreary facility, but on the wall was a poster titled "Guide to Weight Lifting Competition" featuring sequence photos of Tommy, Jim Bradford, Dave Ashman, Clyde Emrich, Norbert Schemansky, and Joe Pitman performing Olympic lifts in competition. What inspired me most were two panels showing Kono doing the press and the snatch. I could not comprehend how anyone could hoist that much weight overhead. That Tommy was also Asian, an unknown quantity in Waynesboro, added to the mystique. By 1963, though still in bodybuilding mode, I was picking up *Strength & Health* magazines at the newsstand and was thrilled to read about the epic battle between Kono and Louis Riecke at the national championships in Harrisburg in the October issue. After the press and snatch, Tommy trailed by 15 pounds in the light-heavyweight class, owing mainly to Riecke's superb snatching ability. His execution of a 375-pound clean and jerk to retain the national title became one of the greatest moments in weightlifting lore, which not only indelibly etched an admiration of Kono on my mind but also confirmed my commitment to be a competitive weightlifter. More importantly, this climactic event epitomized Tommy's lifelong approach and commitment to the sport he loved which was as dear to him as life itself.

All of us knew it was coming for many months, but the grief that gripped the weightlifting world was profound when we learned that the great Tommy (Tamio) Kono was no longer alive. His death on April 24, 2016, of hepatic encephalopathy caused by cirrhosis of the liver triggered an outpouring of obituaries and tributes from the news and sports media, most notably the *Honolulu Star-Advertiser, New York Times, Washington Post, NBC News, Yahoo Sports, Sacramento Bee,* and *York Dispatch*. These memorials were informed by countless colleagues, friends, and journalists who for decades recorded Tommy's extraordinary athletic feats.[1] This account aims to provide a richer narrative of Kono's life that is both retrospective and introspective, written not as an intimate friend but as an acquaintance who has observed and been inspired by his approach to sport and life. It is based not only on his personal experiences and many accounts of his life but also by original sources, including interviews and correspondence. Most revealing are the instructional and autobiographical volumes Tommy authored in later life.[2] In the spirit of those accounts, my intention is to convey a behind-the-scenes perspective that goes beyond pounds lifted, championships won, and honors bestowed during the golden years of his competitive life. It will also examine other less heralded aspects of his sports involvement and his repeated struggles with adversity. And it will provide insights into the cultural origins of his competitive spirit. Hopefully this backstory will enrich our understanding of how Kono was able to tap so much mental and physical energy during his illustrious career.

This glimpse into the life of America's (and arguably the world's) greatest weightlifting champion was facilitated through assistance and support from Tommy's best friend and fellow Olympian Peter George; both of them moved to Hawaii in the 1950s at the height of their lifting achievements. Pete, though six-time Olympic and world champion, is unduly modest about his own accomplishments and openly deferential to Tommy.[3] "We both live in Hawaii, and I can claim to be the greatest weightlifter of the Nuuanu YMCA living in Diamond Head (east side of Honolulu)," is how Pete characterizes their relationship.[4]

> Tommy tells me I was his early inspiration. I was a world champion before he entered his first contest. I kid him with, "I'm flattered when you say you wanted to be like me. But you just didn't know when the hell to stop. You broke all my records!" … Tommy and I were competitors, but we have been the best of friends for 65 years—since we first met in Philadelphia in 1950.[5]

Like Tommy, Pete has been unflagging in support of American weightlifting. Arguably Pete's greatest contribution to the sport is the critical role he played in securing the consent of the Kono family to donate Tommy's enormous collection to the Stark Center for Physical Culture and Sports in Austin, Texas, in November 2016. Subsequently, the Stark Center staff, headed by Terry and Jan Todd, have not only made Tommy's manuscripts available to students and scholars but have also created a Kono/George exhibit to memorialize America's greatest weightlifter.

Other contributors to Kono's memory are included in the *Book of Remembrance* by Walter Imahara and David Meltzer, many of whom are cited in this account. I am also indebted to many others who revealed important aspects of Tommy's life, including Wes Barnett, Clarence Bass, Isaac Berger, Ryan Blake, Shelly Brown, Gary Cleveland, John Coffee, Howard Cohen, Mike Conroy, Edward Coyle, Bob Crist, Rebecca Crowther, Jan Dellinger, Lou DeMarco, Darren DeMello, Paul Doherty. Arthur Drechsler, Joe Dube, Clyde Emrich, Leo Falasco, Sibby Flowers, George George, Jim George, Pete George, Robin Byrd Goad, Ben Green, Gary Gubner, Mike Harada, Sid Henry, Stella Herrick, Gloria Imagire, Walter Imahara, Gary Kawamura, Osmo Kiiha, Bruce Klemens, William Kutzer, Murray Levin, Jodie Mattos, Natalie Mew, Carl Miller, Pete Miller, Christopher Mixon, Brian Miyamoto, Mel Miyamoto, Mike Mizuno, Harvey Newton, Brian Niiya, Russell Ogata, Joe Puleo, John Pulskamp, Denis Reno, Louis Riecke, Mark Rippetoe, Andrew Rodriguez, Brenda Salgado, LaVerne Sasaki, Norbert Schmansky, Jim Schmitz, Jaime Schultz, Sherman Seki, Cindy Slater, Frank Spellman, Douglas Stalker, Mike Stone, Hirofumi Tanaka, Julie Thomas, Chuck Vinci, Bruce Wilhelm, Ryan Yamamoto, and John Yamauchi. To Les

Simonton, Jeremy Shepard, and members of the East Alabama Weightlifting Club I am grateful for keeping me active in the current weightlifting scene. I owe a special thanks to Tommy's widow, Florence Kono, their daughter JoAnn Sumida, son Mark, and son-in-law Gary Sumida for their friendship, memories, and support of this project. Terry and Jan Todd also deserve much credit not only for making possible the acquisition of the Kono collection for the Stark Center but also for providing me an ideal place to perform research and teach at the University of Texas and for their many acts of generosity and kindness over multiple decades. Finally, my wife Sarah played a critical role in the completion of this study by orchestrating the packaging and shipment of the Kono papers as well as creating an emotional bond with the Kono family. Her love and support for my many physical culture endeavors goes beyond what words can express.

Introduction: "Go for Broke"[1]

At the centenary celebration of the International Weightlifting Federation at Istanbul in 2005, President Tamas Ajan recognized Tommy Kono as the "Best Weightlifter of 100 Years."[2] In a competitive career spanning three decades Kono, a Nisei American, surpassed all contemporaries, amassing eight consecutive Olympic and world titles and setting 26 world records in four weight classes. He also won one bronze and two silver medals, garnered 11 National and three Pan American titles, set 37 American records, and captured four international physique titles, all prior to the advent of steroids. Afterwards, he coached Olympic weightlifting teams for three countries and the American team at the first women's world championship. As physical culturist Terry Todd famously observed, "he was the complete package." While weightlifters of Kono's era lacked superior coaching, nutritional aids, and up-to-date facilities available to later lifters, Tommy had to overcome more serious disadvantages. He suffered from asthma, so severe that he missed one-third of his schooling and weighed only 105 pounds at age 14. No less debilitating was his family's relocation to the Tule Lake Internment Camp during World War II and the pervasive racism that prevailed during his formative years. How Kono overcame these obstacles to become one of the world's greatest athletes requires an examination of the strength of character he derived from the circumstances of his cross-cultural development.

Until the civil rights movement of the 1960s there was little acknowledgment of the World War II deprivations experienced by Japanese Americans. Subsequent studies, reflecting the need to redress injustices to racial minorities, then started pouring off university and commercial presses. A casual count of titles in the University of Texas library indicates 99 such monographs, beginning with *The Spoilage* in 1946 and followed by seemingly endless penitent volumes, including *Years of Infamy, Personal Justice Denied, Legacy of Injustice, America on Trial, Prisoners Without Trial, Beyond Prejudice,* and *Concentration Camps on the Home Front,* which dwell on the cruel confinement of 126,947 Japanese Americans, 71,484 of whom were American citizens, in what were often called concentration camps.[3] Contrariwise, only two books deal with the trials and tribulations of far more numerous German and Italian Americans under the protective hue of lighter skin.[4] Even apologies by presidents Ford, Reagan, Clinton, and George W. Bush could not fend off the tide of passionate protests over indignities caused by Franklin Roosevelt's executive order 9066 which led to the War Relocation Authority.[5] But there was a silver lining implicit in virtually every tragic narrative of confinement. As Stanford professor Yamato Ichihashi noted in his *Japanese History in the United States*, Japanese labor emigration "was impelled by desire for improvement rather than by the necessity of escaping misery at home." It was a positive force.[6] The majority of first generation (Issei), by hard work and ingenuity, became successful farmers on land nobody else wanted. This enterprising spirit of surviving in an alien environment provided the cultural context for Kono's positive outlook on life.

It is rooted in his youthful search for identity and the Japanese American culture of his upbringing. As Takeyuki Tsuda states in his study of ethnicity, "it is not so much the historical experiences that individuals have as adults, but those they had during their formative years as youth that have the greatest and most lasting impact on their ethnic consciousness."[7] The culture implicit in Tommy's elders, notes Paul Spickard, was devoid of "regular religious observance beyond the burning of incense to the *butsudan*, an alcove in the home set aside for religious contemplation." Religion "was not a regular activity in the schedule of most people, but it was an important part of one's identity, linking one to a web of relationships in one's family and community."[8] Another component of that cultural experience was the retention of centuries-old values inherent in Japanese civilization. Foremost was *gaman* or enduring the seemingly unbearable with patience and dignity. It was illustrated by a Nisei, G. Sato, in describing his parents' outlook. "*Gaman?* Oh yes, we had that very much so. Well, just like when we had that fire, burned down my dad's boarding house and all we had. You know, my folks didn't say much except *shikataganai* [it can't be helped] … and *gaman* … you have to be patient 'cuz you know what happened has happened. Nothing you can do to remedy it. You just have to go on."[9]

In his 1966 ground-breaking account, sociologist William Petersen notes that Buddhist and Christian ministers concurred that Japanese Americans "are distinguished by their greater attachment to family" and "greater respect for parental and other authority. Underlying the complex religious life … there seems to be an adaptation to American institutional forms with a considerable persistence of Buddhist moral values."[10] In their 1991 study, Stephen Fugita and David O'Brien concur that

> the persistence of Japanese American ethnicity stems from elements in traditional Japanese culture that structure social relationships among group members in such a way that they are able to adapt to changing exigencies without losing group cohesiveness. These cultural principles have generated for Japanese Americans, as they have for the Japanese in Japan, a strong sense of peoplehood, allowing them to adopt major elements from other cultural systems without totally sacrificing social relationships within the group. Thus, in different but very significant ways, their ethnicity persists.[11]

An important aspect of this ancient discipline is Zen which consists of attaining enlightenment or *satori*. As fabled Buddhist philosopher Daisetz Suzuki explains, *satori* "is not something added from the outside" to one's essence. "It is in being itself, in becoming itself, in living itself." For the Japanese, it is called "a life of *kono-mama*" which means "the 'isness' of a thing. Reality in its isness." Suzuki contends that "Zen has no need of things external, except 'the body' in which the

Zen-man is so to speak embodied."[12] The extent to which Tommy Kono embodied characteristics of the Zen-man forms a basis for this study of his greatness as a weightlifter and humanitarian.

That Tommy was able to tap the power of Zen and convert it into winning Olympic gold medals and promoting the American way of life during the Cold War owes much to his Nisei generational status. Unlike his Issei parents, he was born in the United States, and his exposure to old world ways, though constant, was muted. It was a generation juxtaposed on a cultural cusp which was obliged to show loyalty and respect for elders while making its way in a society which had little respect for those traditions. Education, highly valued in tight-knit Japanese families and convergent with American social norms, became a source of cross-cultural tensions. According to authors of *Achieving the American Dream*, the Issei wanted their offspring "to become involved in the mainstream yet also to retain their ethnic roots. Nisei children were expected to attend both American schools and Japanese language schools, but very few became fluent in the Japanese language."[13] Stephen Fugita and Marilyn Fernandez observe, however, that well-educated Nisei with occupational aspirations were confronted with unpleasant pre-war realities. "They were, in the main, blocked from utilizing their education except by going to Japan or returning to the difficult situation of working for the Issei in lower-prestige, ethnic economy jobs."[14] Tommy Kono typified the generation born between 1910 and the 1940s. He spoke good English (with a slight accent) but could speak virtually no Japanese. Nor did he possess any educational or occupational attainments as a youth. Fortunately, his unique ability as a weightlifter provided him an opportunity to transcend the cultural conundrum that confronted his generation.

What propelled him to national and international fame was the Americanization of the Nisei and the strong current of homogenization in society. Unlike other oppressed minorities who adopted a "counter identity," pre-war Nisei assumed "a more accommodating, assimilation-oriented strategy," according to Tsuda, "in order to avoid discrimination and gain greater acceptance by majority society." Despite their racial differences, they "asserted their American national identities and claimed racial citizenship and membership in the nation-state." Their internment during World War II only reinforced these tendencies, as reflected by Tsuda's Nisei interviewees. Mike Oshima was explicit about its impact on his ethnic identity: "Internment made it quite clear to all of us that we weren't considered real Americans because of our Japanese ancestry, even if we are U.S.-born citizens. In that sense we had no choice but to become full Americanized, to show that we *are* Americans."[15] Overwhelmingly, despite their prolonged deprivation of freedom and loss of property, Nisei internees adhered to American values. Although their confinement behind barbed wire and denial of rights were "deeply resented," according to Bill Hosokawa, author of *Nisei: The Quiet Americans*, "most evacuees continued to be loyal to the United States."[16] Perhaps the most extreme example of this sociological oxymoron was their World War II military service. Initially excluded from the draft, Nisei volunteers (largely from Hawaii) served with distinction in military intelligence, training camps, and combat. With 21,102 enlistments, the 442nd Japanese American Regiment fought heroically (with the motto "Go for Broke") in some of the toughest battles in Italy and France. Tsuda estimates that the 442nd "became the most decorated military unit in American history for its size and length of service. It also had one of the highest casualty rates, earning 9,486 Purple Hearts."[17] Citing 1946 figures from the *Pacific Citizen*, Masayo Duus reckons that 33,330 Nisei youths of 36,000 initially eligible participated in the war effort, proportionately the highest of any ethnic group.[18]

Tommy Kono was too young to serve in that war, but he did serve proudly as private first class in the Korean conflict. In 1951, the year of his enlistment, the MGM film *Go for Broke* appeared. The moral of its message was that soldiers of the 442nd, nicknamed Buddhaheads, were willing to fight bravely at all costs, suggesting a similarity to the suicidal warrior spirit of their Japanese counterparts in the South Pacific. Even more evocative are the remarks of the wife of a 442nd veteran who took part in the famous rescue of the Texas "Lost Battalion" in eastern France in 1944. "He does not want to talk about it because it was so traumatic. It was basically a suicide charge. They were willing to sacrifice everything. That was the mentality."[19] Whether Tommy ever saw or was inspired by the film cannot be determined, but the same do-or-die spirit became internalized in his approach to competitive weightlifting and personalized as a way to defend his country. "Don't hold back" was a familiar axiom drawn from his Buddhist background that helped define his athletic career and climaxed in Harrisburg, Pennsylvania, in 1963. Kono became a potent propaganda weapon during the Cold War in the Olympics and other international sporting events.

Other factors contributing to the cultural context of Tommy's upbringing and outlook include the severance of Nisei connections with their Japanese homeland and the emphasis placed by the War Relocation Authority on assimilation and Americanization in internment camp schools. In *Growing Up Nisei*, David Yoo observes that "education became a form of indoctrination in which overtly patriotic responses from students drew high marks and praise."[20] Mess hall conditions where mothers and small children, fathers, and older children ate separately led to deterioration of family structures.[21] The impact of these conditions resulted in Issei parents spending less time with their children and losing their disciplinary power and ability to inculcate elements of their Japanese heritage. Tsuda concludes, however, that "the parents of prewar Nisei often acknowledged and even encouraged the cultural assimilation of their children to American society instead of pressuring them to retain the Japanese language and culture."[22]

It was this mentality, typical of his generation, that Kono carried into adulthood and his athletic career. The experience of the Nisei, though complemented by the economic miracle that gripped postwar Japan, was unique in America. Unlike other ethnic groups subjected to oppression in mainstream society, Japanese Americans did not exhibit what William Petersen identified in 1966 as "problem minorities" who suffered from "poor health, poor education, low income, high crime rate, unstable family pattern and so on and on." Japanese Americans, Petersen maintains, defy every existing stereotype for disadvantaged minorities. "By any criterion of good citizenship that we choose, the Japanese Americans are better than any other group in our society, including native-born whites. They have established this remarkable record moreover, by their own almost totally unaided effort. Every attempt to hamper their progress resulted only in enhancing their determination to succeed."[23] By 1960, according to historian Kaoru Kendis, Japanese Americans in California, owing largely to the enterprising Nisei, occupied 38 percent of white-collar jobs, exceeded the number of white college students, 18 to 10 percent, accounted for 56 percent of professional occupations, and were second only to white males in median income.[24] Petersen's thesis, however, has sparked a vigorous debate over the validity of what is often dubbed the "model minority myth."[25] That Tommy exhibited characteristics of this controversial racial and cultural concept would be difficult to deny. It is doubtful whether he ever heard of the term "model minority" during his lifting days or even afterwards, but he was a prime example of individual initiative and inner directedness that had cultural implications. Even if it is a mythical model and the notion of Asian American exceptionalism is a false narrative, Kono's performances were real and he was exceptional.

Although Kono and his family suffered immensely for decades from the racism that was endemic in American society, and particularly on the West Coast, he showed no resentments or desire to seek retribution for perceived injustices. Nor did he show any inclination to flaunt or repudiate his Japanese American identity. It was simply who he was. Tommy was a self-reliant individual who did not depend on race, religion, or even family to shape his destiny. Unlike many other Nisei of his time, he never sought refuge in his community or capitalized on his fame to bring attention to Japanese American grievances. In this way, he was unique among many leading sports stars who have used their popularity on the playing field or court as a platform to support a political or social agenda or to right wrongs from the past. Instead, Tommy used his amazing athletic career as a platform to try to improve the sport which had rescued him from his Japanese American enclave. As his long-time friend Lou DeMarco recollects, "he always fought not for glory or financial gain" but for "love of country" and that "at the height of the Cold War, Tommy battled and defeated the Soviets constantly as they threw everything at him."[26] His only political agenda was to defeat America's foreign foes and cure the evils of his country's weightlifting establishment. Kono's racial identity could have easily triggered a xenophobic reaction from patriotic Americans during the decade after World War II, but his repeated victories against Soviet weightlifters had much the opposite effect where his race, humble demeanor, and ardent patriotism proved to be an immense asset. He stood out as an exceptional person who defied all stereotypes and expectations.

Most inspiring in this quest for American weightlifting superiority was his positive outlook which helped him overcome all odds in his personal life and on the lifting platform. It was reinforced by popular self-help books he encountered during the 1950s, Norman Vincent Peale's *Power of Positive Thinking* (1952) and Napoleon Hill's *Think and Grow Rich* (1937), and the indomitable spirit of his Olympic weightlifting coach and mentor, Bob Hoffman.[27] Although this formula of success based on the cultivation of the mind propelled Kono through his years of greatness, it could not be sustained indefinitely. In the 1960s, age, injuries, and competitors benefiting from nationalized programs and drugs severely limited his ability to lead the world.

His generation of Japanese Americans, too, was hamstrung in its impact by the next generation Sansei which was influenced by the emergent civil rights movement and could not comprehend why their elders did not protest and resist their mistreatment in greater numbers. "The Sansei's growing awareness of the past," according to one study, "helped move the community from seeing the exclusion and incarceration as a misfortune to recognizing it as a social injustice."[28] This outlook, reflecting the cultural turn in mainstream America which was coping with issues of race, gender, and the Vietnam War, flew directly in the face of Tommy's patriotic values. It also conflicted with his approach, as the "idea man," for resurrecting American weightlifting by inculcating the Buddhist emphasis of mind over body. This modus operandi, though it served as the linchpin for Kono's entire life and physical culture career, was never embraced by weightlifting's powers that be, but it coincides with the observation of University of Texas professor Hirofumi Tanaka that the Japanese, though not a particularly creative people, are good at developing ideas, and though very few Japanese are Buddhists, that religious culture is "everywhere."[29]

I

EARLY LIFE

1

From Tule Lake to Helsinki

"Take advantage of disadvantage."[1]—Tommy Kono

Little is known about Tommy's ancestral origins, but his father, Kanichi, born on August 19, 1886, was eldest of three sons and two daughters of Keizo and Yamagata Akino Kono who resided in the Hiroshima prefecture of Japan. His emigration to San Francisco occurred soon after the earthquake of 1906 as part of the great wave of over 100,000 Japanese workers who arrived in the kingdom of Hawaii and then the United States mainland between 1885 and the Gentlemen's Agreement of 1907 with Japan which prohibited further emigration of male laborers.[2] This demographic movement was spurred in part by the Chinese Exclusion Act of 1882 by Congress and internal changes in Japan after the Meiji Restoration of 1868 which brought rapid industrialization and modernization. Another factor was the Japanese government's imposition of crippling land taxes which compelled the migration of many farmers to the burgeoning cities or to go abroad. These sociological factors, according to Fugita and Fernandez, "caused many ambitious young men to begin to dream of the exciting new possibilities they heard about in America" from guidebooks, returnee testimonies, and migrant letters which "frequently painted an idealized picture of the economic opportunities in the United States. Significantly, the Issei's initial motivation to immigrate was based upon the perceived opportunity to raise their status in Japan, the so-called sojourner orientation."[3] This "push" from the homeland was accompanied by an American "pull," first in Hawaii for sugar plantation workers and then to service California's fast-growing economy. The migratory motives of Kanichi Kono are unclear, but he was a peasant farmer with only three years of formal education.[4] According to Tommy, "he sought a better life" when he left his village of Yoshida-cho (now Akitakata) at age 20.[5] He likely was caught up in the sojourner syndrome, since he returned twice to Japan after prospering in America, presumably to establish permanent residence.

Kanichi Kono

Kanichi's arrival coincided with what historian Roger Daniels calls "a crusade against the Japanese," a xenophobic movement fanned by the city's major newspapers, the *San Francisco Chronicle* and *San Francisco Examiner*.[6] Kono soon found work with the Union Pacific Railroad on the "steel gang" installing new rails for $1.35 a day which took him to North Platte, Nebraska. After serving briefly as a house-boy for a wealthy family, Kanichi became cook and head baker at the Palace Hotel restaurant, the city's finest, for $120 a month.[7] His frugal lifestyle enabled him to buy three plots of land from William (Buffalo Bill) and Louisa Cody for $385 in 1916 and four shares of stock for $125 in the Skinner food packing company of Omaha in 1920.[8] Kanichi's 1920 tax return indicates his net income was $1,300.[9] Kanichi "worked hard and conscientiously," notes Tommy, and by 1921, he had saved enough money to return to Japan; purchase a house for his parents; make donations to the Buddhist shrine; and wed Ichimi Ohata, a 19-year-old seamstress who aspired to be a teacher.[10] Their marriage arrangement stipulated that a Singer sewing machine be purchased for her upon coming to America. The family thrived in the 1920s with the birth of twin brothers Mike (Tadao) and John (Twao) in 1922 and Frank (Yoshio) in 1929. Meanwhile the Konos decided not to return to North Platte, where there was only one Buddhist family, but to join the sizeable Japanese community in Sacramento where Kanichi became self-employed making soy sauce until 1929 when the family returned to Japan. In less than a year, with Ichimi pregnant, the village doctor and elders advised the Konos to return to America where, according to Tommy, it was less crowded and opportunities to raise a family were greater.[11] Kanichi "had succeeded well as proven by his ability to return to his village the second time and purchasing a side of a mountain over-looking his village" as a future home site. Just four months after their return to the USA, Tommy was born to a midwife, Tamaki Saruwatori, at 2 a.m. on June 27, 1930.[12]

By this time the Depression was having a devastating impact, and although Kanichi had accumulated considerable savings, he made some unwise decisions that included buying out a business with a Model T Ford and telephone, purchasing a high premium life insurance policy, and loaning a friend from his home village $2,000 to start an automobile service garage. Tommy recollects "tough times" during the thirties, "and since no one could pay their debts," his dad "worked at the cannery to make ends meet." Until 1942 Kanichi distributed empty cans for the California Packing Corporation (CPC) for $35 weekly while Ichimi filled cans with fruit for $25 weekly.[13] Despite hardships, home life for the Konos was not unpleasant. "My recollection of my dad was that he was a hard-working person ... always making something in the basement with his hands, always fixing things." Kanichi was also good at baking and cooking roasts and stews, while Ichimi did embroidery work with her sewing machine and prepared Japanese dishes. Tommy recalls that his parents "got along fine together," facilitated by almost totally speaking Japanese. Mike and John always worked together, "seldom arguing," but "Frank was a 'yan-chan kozo' in the family. I remember my father would threaten to throw him in the 'muro' (room with no window and a very heavy door) when he was 7–8 years old if he didn't behave." Life for Tommy was complicated by physical weakness and distress from eczema and asthma. He recalls "many sleepless nights" endured by his mother. It was "a frequent occurrence" that "almost always flared up at nights and lasted through until dawn. No doubt my poor health had a bearing on the health of my mother later in life."[14] After a decade of trying to escape city-wide racism and survive in various rental

The Kono family, circa 1936. Front row, from left: Tommy, Kanichi and Ichimi; back row, from left: Frank, Mike and John.

dwellings in the "Japantown" district, further hardship followed when the family was whisked away on May 15, 1942, to the Sacramento Assembly Center and on June 16 to Tule Lake, one of 10 relocation centers for Japanese Americans.[15]

Tule Lake

Historian Bruce Elleman points out that the centers provided physical security, a decent standard of living, and a locale to identify Japanese Americans who wished to return to Japan. "Contrary to popular myths equating the war relocation centers with German concentration camps, the centers were not prison facilities stuck out in the middle of a desert, let alone Nazi death camps."[16] Noted novelist James Michener concurs they were not a "hell hole of starvation or death."[17] The Tule Lake encampment in Northern California provided opportunities along with deprivations.[18] It was a fertile dry lake bed of sandy lava which, when irrigated, enabled internees to grow and sell fresh vegetables and simulate their pre-confinement lives in other ways.[19] What it denied was the most honored of American values—freedom and constitutional rights. "The Japanese at Tule Lake have everything they need for happiness except the one thing they want most—liberty," observed a 1944 *Life* article. "Their life cannot be made pleasant. It can only be made endurable."[20] Perhaps the most demoralizing aspect of their experience was the sense of incarceration. To

Nisei inmate Hiroshi Kashiwagi, it was a prison. "Physically, there were the barbed wire fence and the guard towers manned by MPs with rifles and the machine guns, many of the soldiers were veterans of the war and still quite nervous. ... But in addition to the physical confinement, there was the fence around our spirit, and this imprisonment of the spirit was the most ravaging part of the evacuation experience."[21] Tommy later reflected on his experience at Tule Lake, saying it did not prepare him for the outside world. "Those who returned to normal living did not reflect back to those days because it had a negative impact and they would rather forget it ever happened." But weightlifting had a "very positive impact" on his life. "I found an activity by accident which I excelled at and gave me a sense of worth."[22] Tommy admits that his family's three and a half years internship left "scars" and "served as a base for all things that followed after the war and its return to Sacramento" on December 3, 1945.[23] But they were far outweighed by positive developments that shaped Kono's life far beyond the confines of Tule.

Contrary to most perceptions, weight training was a popular activity at the Japanese American confinements. One of them was the Tulare Assembly Center where internees spent four months prior to their deportation to the Gila River camp in southern Arizona. On May 9, 1942, they formed a weightlifting club which, by June 17, had 60 members with instructors available 14½ hours for six days a week. On Tuesday, the 23rd, the club conducted a contest in five weight classes and selected a Mr. Tulare.[24] This kind of enthusiasm was also evident at Tule Lake where veteran lifter Emerick Ishikawa, who aimed "to create Bernarr MacFaddens out of flabby-muscled male residents," organized a club on July 11. Enrollment for classes taught by Ishikawa and Edwin Kuniyoshi reached 140 by late August in a facility equipped with an 80-pound set of dumbbells and two sets of York barbells.[25] Camp officials were totally supportive. "They gave me a whole building," Ishikawa recalled. "They made for me platforms and everything." Journalist Brian Niiya reveals that

The stark barracks of the Tule Relocation Center in Northern California where Kono spent his early teens and learned about weightlifting.

the club "attracted nearly 200 young lifters, no doubt hoping to escape the boredom of being locked up." Ishikawa charged no dues but collected a $1 entry fee which was used to buy weights.[26] Regular training and additional equipment over the next six months enabled the Tulean weightlifters to defeat an aggregation from nearby Klamath Falls Naval Air Station. At their next encounter on April 17, 1943, the former out-lifted their challengers by 664 pounds with Ishikawa unofficially breaking the world record (three-lift) total of 615 by 13 pounds.[27] The Tuleans also acquired the look of a team. "The members of the club are sporting satin jackets of yellow and dark blue," reported the *Tulean Dispatch* on July 13. "We can say that they look plenty sharp."[28] Taking advantage of an easing of restrictions, Ishikawa migrated to Chicago and then to York, Pennsylvania, where he worked for Bob Hoffman and trained with the world's best weightlifters.[29] In succeeding years he won four national championships and a berth on the 1948 Olympic team.

What Tule Lake provided was exposure to the sport that would become Kono's lifelong pursuit, an opportunity he might not have had growing up outside the camp. He remained forever indebted to Ishikawa, even giving his younger son Mark the middle name of Emerick.[30] The dry air at Tule also helped Kono overcome asthma, become robust, and engage in physical exertion. LaVerne Sasaki, who trained with Tommy, believes "this health issue possibly motivated him to excel physically, in the Japanese way to 'ganbaru' (hang in there tough or diligently). Tommy also had the competitive spirit to do well against us youngsters." His interest in developing his body, Tommy recalls, stemmed from a Charles Atlas ad he saw at age 11 showing a skinny guy getting sand kicked in his face, but he could not afford the $36 Atlas course. On March 27, 1942, he had a 29" chest, 8" arm, and 26" waist at 4'8½" height, and 74½ bodyweight. "I was so skinny I had to lean forward under a shower so that water wouldn't collect in the hollows by my clavicles."[31] Sasaki recalls that "as young teenagers with plenty of spare time, we enjoyed a variety of sports in 'camp,' including basketball, baseball, judo, sumo wrestling." They also attended American public school, Japanese language school, and Buddhist services where Sasaki's father, a Buddhist minister, held memorial, funeral, and wedding services for Sacramento church members. "As the Kono family was Buddhist and like many families traditionally Japanese, Tommy, undoubtedly, had learned and picked up many traits," such as the spirit of "Ganbaru, Gaman (self-discipline) and importance of kokoro (mind)."[32] His physical exertion began with judo, an activity created by camp authorities to occupy restless youth. Tommy became so good at breaking falls that the sensei often used him for demonstrations. "I always made their 'throws' look good," he recalls.[33]

His exposure to weightlifting began in 1943 when barracks neighbors Ben "Ace" Hara and Tod Fujioka introduced him to a set of York Big 10 barbells purchased by members of his no. 27 block. Hara became an inspiration for Tommy. "He was just a senior in high school when I first met him in the Tule Lake detention camp, yet he taught me not only how to lift weights, but how to live your life. No matter what happened, he always seemed to be able to find a positive approach to things."[34] Tommy recalls that "facilities were crowded and scant." To perform squats, he had to "clean the barbell to his chest, press it overhead and lower it back down behind his head

18 **I—Early Life**

to his shoulders."[35] At first, he followed a bodybuilding routine, according to iron game author Osmo Kiiha, working out three or four times weekly with sessions lasting a couple hours. He performed such basic exercises as presses, squats, deadlifts, and curls. Upon attempting Olympic lifting, he spent his first month on a five-foot exercise bar to develop good technique.[36] By June 1944, Tommy could negotiate a 75-pound press, 70-pound snatch, and 90-pound clean and jerk at 5'1" and 108 bodyweight.[37] He was initially intimidated by the club's Olympic set.[38] "The 45-pound barbell plates looked like train wheels! Even the collar for the Olympic set was heavy! I dismissed the idea of becoming an Olympic lifter because the heavy seven-foot bar alone was way beyond my physical ability to 'exercise' with."[39] Inspired by Hoffman's *Strength & Health* magazine, Tommy steadily improved in strength and physique. From August 24, 1943, to December 16, 1944, he gained 3⅜" in height and 10

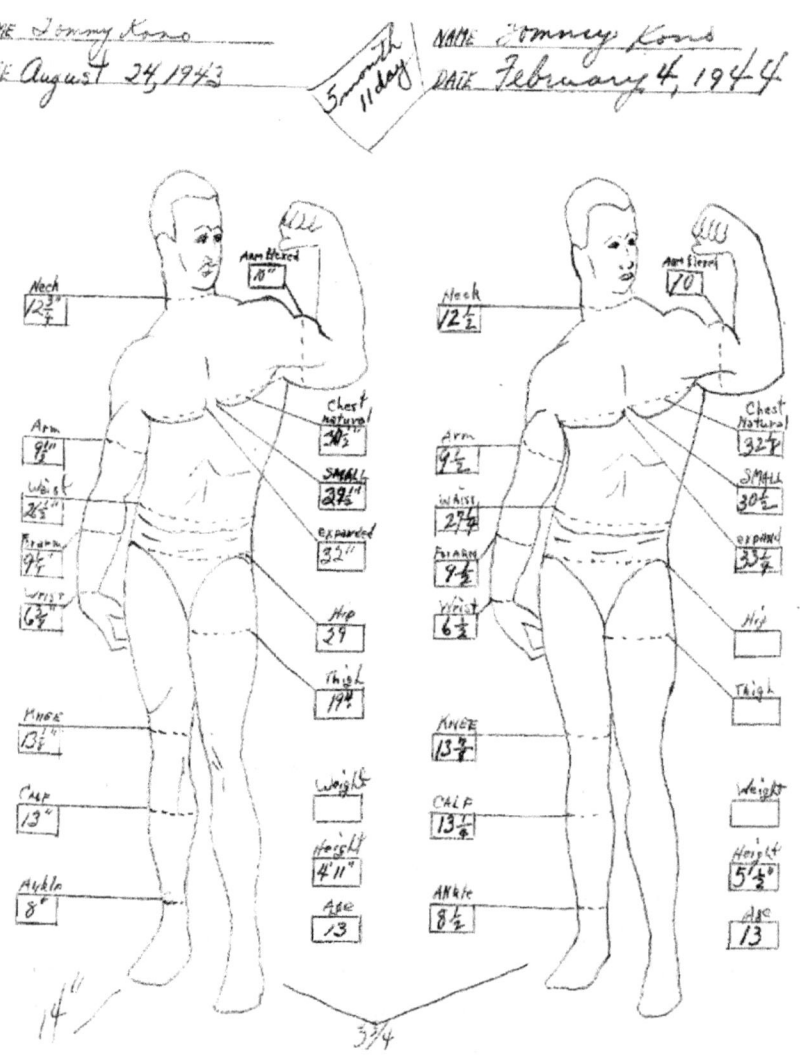

Above and opposite: **Tommy's physical progress chart.**

pounds bodyweight, adding 1½" to his arms, 1" to forearms, 5½" to chest, and ½" to thighs.[40] By practicing posing and muscle control he could display his development to maximum advantage, thereby deriving a sense of self-worth not otherwise possible in depressed camp conditions. Despite Kono's weightlifting ability, his passion for bodybuilding never subsided. Bodybuilding provided a firm foundation for his illustrious weightlifting career.

No less important to his outlook was the sanguine attitude of his confined compatriots. Contrary to expectations, Japanese Americans rarely opposed the discriminations and disabilities they experienced, even before the war. A resignation with their plight was most evident in the Japanese American Citizens League (JACL), a loyalist organization formed in 1929 to safeguard constitutional rights and promote greater Nisei participation in public life. It advised Japanese Americans to abide by Roosevelt's executive order and not despair. "We are hopeful of the future and we will jealously fight for the perpetuation of true American ideals," wrote Robert Hosokawa about his internment at Minidoka in Idaho, in the *Christian Science Monitor*. "Life in the camps was not easy. It was inadequate and morale-killing. But never in those months did we ever lose faith in America." Although their confinement behind barbed wire and deprivation of rights were "deeply resented," according to Bill Hosokawa in *Nisei: The Quiet Americans*, "most evacuees continued to be loyal to the United States."[41] Indeed, Tommy's loss of freedom only served to deepen its meaning and love for America. It enabled him to realize *shikata-ga-nai* and *arigatai*—to accept one's fate and be thankful for what you have—in an American context.

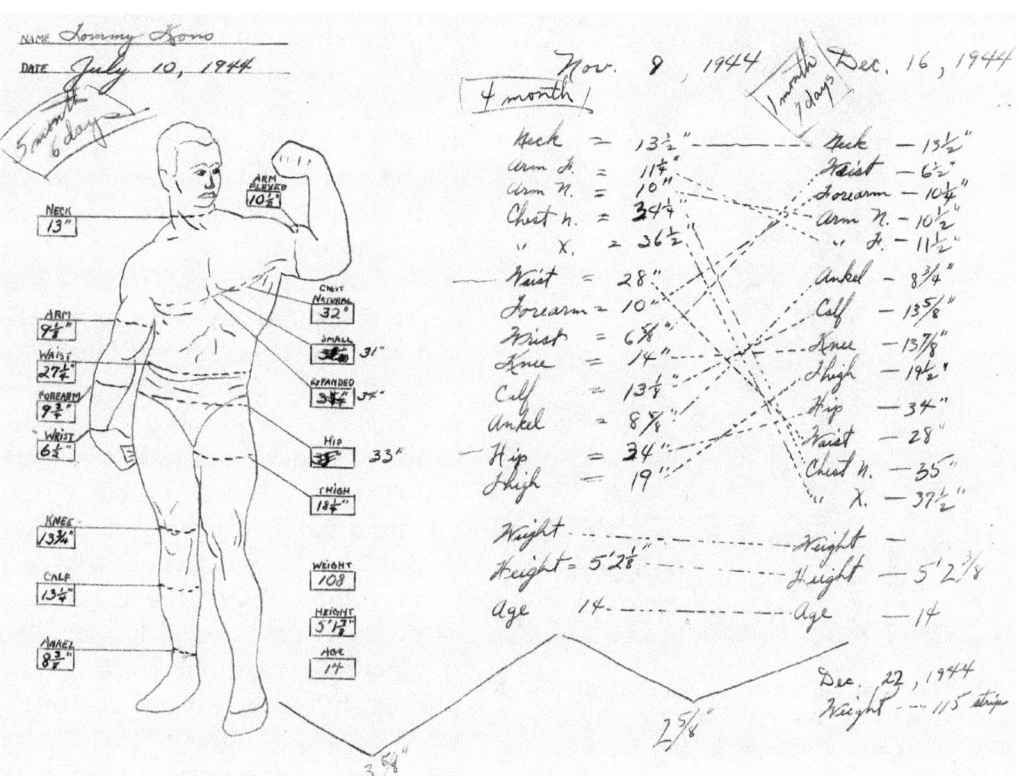

A New Beginning

On returning to Sacramento in 1945, the Kono family, mostly bereft of pre-war possessions and property, attempted to resume normal life with only about $800. Historian David Yoo calls the economic losses for displaced Japanese Americans "staggering—an estimated $370 million in wartime dollars" or in 1983 dollars at "somewhere between $2.5 and 6.2 billion."[42] Life was not easy for the Konos who worked hard to restore their economic status and earn respect from a society still unsure whether Japanese Americans deserved it. "We didn't have anything when we got out," Tommy recalled. "We checked into the Buddhist temple. They put cots in the gym. We stayed there until we found a place to live."[43] Kanichi returned to work at the cannery, along with Tommy, Mike, and John. The twins then took up auto repair at McClellan Air Force Base in Sacramento. "John and Mike endured real hard times as they sort-of took over the destiny of the Konos," Tommy recalls. "They worked together" and "found every which way to save for they were determined to succeed." Frank took off for New York with a camp friend but returned "disillusioned." He eventually became an archivist at the state capitol in Sacramento. Tommy, still in high school, lived in a three-room dwelling with flimsy walls above a garage shared by two other families. It had a community kitchen and a roof-top bathroom with an alley entrance. "At that time I didn't know how some of my classmates could afford to go bowling and have ice cream sodas at the fountain ... and even afford a girlfriend."[44] Eventually the family purchased a property on July 20, 1948, at 1130 T Street in Sacramento, several blocks south of Japantown, thereby lessening immediate access to its ancestral community.[45]

After his graduation from Sacramento High School in 1948, Tommy was a healthy, happy, and energetic teenager living in the city's Japantown.

Further distancing from his Japanese roots and exposure to American values occurred in the late 1940s with his attendance in Sacramento's integrated school and higher education system. Tommy's schoolwork was always satisfactory but rarely outstanding. At Lincoln School, just prior to internment, his performance was mediocre.[46] After the war, at Sacramento High School, he excelled in physical education, drafting, and photography but showed no interest in organized sports. "I tried high school track, basketball and football

Tommy attended Sacramento Junior College in 1948–49 where he was a member of the Japanese (Nisei) American Club. He is pictured second from left in the back row in the college yearbook.

but I was never very good," he later admitted. "They took too much energy and, if anything, I was over-trained."[47] After graduation in 1948, he attended Sacramento Junior College (now City College) majoring in mechanical engineering.[48] Unable to resume bodybuilding because of a lack of weights, Tommy played church league basketball for a year until he could afford to join the YMCA. At his training mates' behest, he competed as the youngest team member in a contest

As a college student, Kono became interested in the practical aspects of physical culture through drawing where he could use his artistic talents.

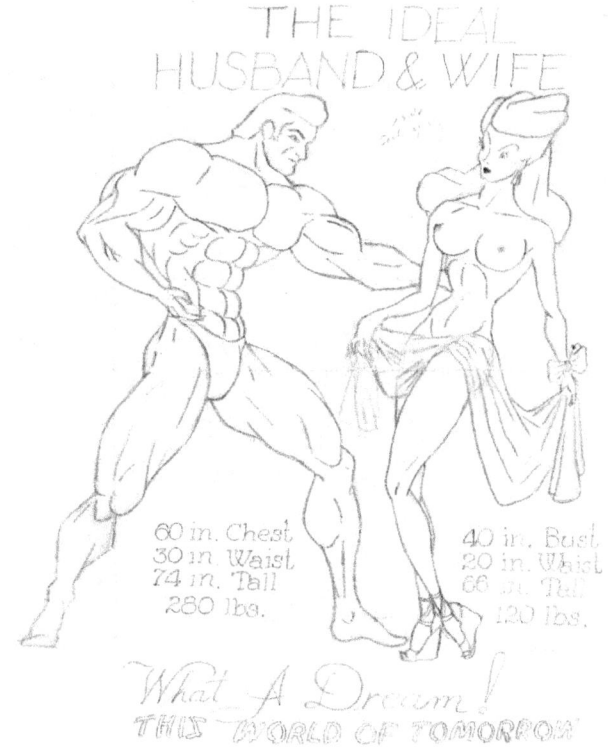

on March 6, 1948, at the San Jose YMCA where he placed second of two lifters in the 148-pound class with a 175-pound press, 185 snatch, and 225 clean and jerk for a 585 total. His attire appeared quaint. "I competed wearing 'Keds' canvas-topped tennis shoes, shorts and tee-shirt. I wore my eyeglasses and wrist-watch because I trained with them on," he recalled. "Later I added a lifting belt to this ensemble."[49] It was hardly an encouraging start, but this competition "hooked" him, and he "started training earnestly on the Olympic lifts." A fortnight later he totaled 625 pounds at a Sacramento meet and "was on his way."[50] Despite criticisms from classmates that weight training would strain the heart, cause

Membership in the Sacramento YMCA enabled Tommy to develop his weightlifting skills on a regular basis.

Kono's training was supplemented by a gym he constructed in the basement of the family's new home on T Street.

rupture, and induce muscle-binding, Tommy trained harder to disprove popular opinion. He seemed undaunted, revealing the optimistic spirit that served him so well during his illness and confinement. His obsession with barbells also opened other avenues for self-improvement that complemented the gains he was making in muscle and strength. "I studied physiology, anatomy, kinesiology to understand bodily functions so it would help me progress faster. Then I dabbled a little in psychology, chemistry and physics to get a clearer picture of some of the 'whys and wherefores' I did things which hindered or helped me in my sport."[51] As an autodidact, Tommy was learning far more about the world and himself than from the narrow mechanical engineering college curriculum which he found increasingly boring and irrelevant.[52]

Chester Teegarden

In July 1949 he put formal education aside and became a junior clerk at the driver's license division of the Department of Motor Vehicles where he performed filing, typing, chart-making and receptionist duties for $195 monthly. Here again, he had the opportunity to assimilate American values through gainful employment at a governmental institution. Tommy now had the wherewithal to interact with talented lifters at gyms in the bay area, a hotbed of physical culture. Foremost were those of Ed Yarick in Oakland and Chester Teegarden in Richmond where Kono met light-heavyweight Dan Uhalde who employed the innovative squat-style to set a California snatch record of 260 pounds.[53] "That's the reason we got to know each other so well," he explained to Teegarden. "He claims this cleaning did much to improve his snatch. I decided to follow this regime ... the outcome, terrific!" Tommy never had a coach, but Teegarden mentored him, and in April 1949, after Tommy had been competing a year, Chester told him "there is a simple but fundamental principle you do not yet understand. CONCENTRATION OF EFFORT IN LARGE MUSCLE GROUPS IS THE *BASIC* PRINCIPLE OF BAR BELL TRAINING." Until this time Kono had been doing lots of bodybuilding movements. "It is because you do TOO MANY exercises that you do not progress faster," Teegarden advised. "Do less. SPECIALIZE, and gain more."[54] Not until months later did Tommy take his mentor's words seriously by incorporating Olympic lifts and heavy squats into his routine.[55] "In those days," he recalled, "I ate, talked, and dreamed of weightlifting!"[56]

By the fall of 1949, Tommy was making dramatic gains by concentrating on leg strength. On September 5 he reported "great news" to Teegarden. Much to his surprise, he easily cleaned and jerked 290 pounds at the Sacramento YMCA. "Everyone thought that I was joking about trying to clean & jerk 300. I surprised all of them when I bounced the weight on the platform and cleaned it. I jerked this weight to everyone's satisfaction except mine. ... I was staggering around for a while. I finally planted my foot firmly and locked my arms." He also jerked 250 five times. Also gratifying were Tommy's gains in pressing and grip strength. "BOY, DOES MY BODY ACHE. ... BUT BOY THAT POWER I'M GETTING."[57] After winning the Pacific Coast Championships, he returned to bodybuilding. Seeing Tommy's potential as a bodybuilder, Teegarden suggested:

if you wish to do well BOTH in physique and in lifting you will have to have 17" arms and 47" chest and with a 30" waist.... Your great advantage now is your PAST experience and understanding of the DKB [deep knee bend]. When you learn to make your arms and chest grow as you have made your legs come out you will have a terrific physique. Build yourself up like some of those pictures you have drawn. Stop being tommy kono and become TOMMY KONO!![58]

Although he was performing multiple sets of repetition squats with heavy weights—280/12, 320/12, 350/8, 320/12 and 350/12—these results brought little satisfaction. "I seem to have lost power all over," he complained to Teegarden. "Well, well, what would Tommy do some day if he felt really strong?" the latter quipped.[59] Soon he was squatting with 420 pounds for a single repetition and utilizing the squat style for cleans as well as snatches. That formula, Teegarden proudly pointed out, "is the way Kono came up." Indeed, in just two years since his first meet in March 1948, Tommy's total increased from 585 to the 745 he registered at the Northern California Championships in Berkeley on March 21, 1950.[60]

At this point, after experimenting with other movements at a heavier bodyweight, Kono seemed conflicted over whether to become a middleweight. "I am closer to the world record in the 148 class then 165. Why take chance? I may not lift good as 148," he told Teegarden, "but as 148 I know what I can do. I'm 5'5½" remember?"[61] At the state championships at the Los Angeles YMCA on April 15, he totaled 770 pounds via lifts of 220-235-315. Teegarden records that his press was so superior that he "started lifting after every other lifter in his class had finished" and that he was allowed to snatch and clean and jerk with the two heavier classes. With regard to the best lifter trophy, "Kono took care of that little detail by so wide a margin that there was no guessing who was to get it." How important concentration was to his success was illustrated by an incident just after he requested 305 for his first clean and jerk.

> Kono took his grip on the bar, dead lifted it, set it down and walked off the platform. ... [George] Brignolo had told Kono that the door of their room was open a few moments ago when he had gone upstairs in the Y. Kono's immediate reaction was, "Wallet, money and everything gone." But before it was time for Kono's second attempt C&J Brignolo returned and said, "No, it wasn't ours, it was another door." Kono felt better so on his second with 305 he slammed it up, took 315 on his third and got it up in perfect form thus establishing a new California record by 15 lbs.[62]

An ongoing distraction for Tommy was the health of his mother who was going blind and afflicted with other problems he attributed to menopause. Caregiving at home and driving her to doctors limited his training to two hours thrice weekly. But after he posted the nation's highest lightweight total of 780 at the Pacific Coast Championships at Berkeley on April 29, the hat was passed to raise $300 for his flight to the 1950 national championships in Philadelphia a fortnight later.[63]

A Philadelphia Story

Friends predicted he would become the lightweight champion with an 800-pound total, but he managed only a lackluster 760-pound total via lifts of

220–235–305, losing by five pounds to Joe Pitman, premier lightweight of the York Barbell Club. Tommy recollected he had two attempts in the clean and jerk with 315 pounds to make a 770 total and surpass Pitman by five pounds.

> Took time, pretty sure I'll make it. Stand on end of platform like I always do before my try ... walked up to weight and tried hard. I was very nervous ... hand shaking like hell. I gave it everything I had but no timing, speed or coordination. I fell on my butt. I had the weight high enough but no soap. I was very worried now. I tried talking to myself. Walked around back stage then came out to try again. I was more nervous than the second try. I couldn't clean the wt for it was a little too forward. ... I had lost my timing.

"I must have been very disappointing to the fellas over here who were pulling for me," Tommy intimated to Teegarden. "I know I felt like hell after the contest."[64] In *Strength & Health*, however, Bob Hoffman was impressed, noting that Kono "looked powerful but a bit tired, it had been a long trip, he seemed slow, lacking in fire and drive. The muscles in his legs were tremendous, giving considerable idea of the great power he possesses."[65] *Iron Man* reporter Harry Paschall also recognized Kono's leg development, and "like all men of Oriental descent, he moves with the fluidity of water flowing. And he has not tapped his own potentialities because he pulls the weights much higher than necessary to squat with them."[66] Likewise George Greenfield of Norfolk, Virginia, who met Tommy in Philadelphia, found him to be a "swell kid and lifter, should have won the 148 class." Teegarden, observed that Tommy was "back on body building" but was consoled that his protégé had gained "a great amount of competitive experience ... with the best lifters on this continent."[67]

An unexpected benefit from Kono's visit to Philadelphia was the opportunity to mingle with some greats of the iron game he had only read about in magazines, including John Grimek, Bob Hoffman, Mark Berry, and Ray Van Cleef. It culminated in a trip to York, America's "mecca of physique stars and lifting sensations."[68] But the most eagerly anticipated and transformative encounter was with the Ohio contingent from the American College of Modern Weightlifting in Akron. He wanted to know how its leading lifter, Pete George, described in a recent *Iron Man* article as a "Wonder Boy," had improved so much in so little time.[69] Kono had already benefited from knowledge of the squat-style snatch and clean from Dan Uhalde and others on the West Coast. In Philadelphia this information was reinforced through encounters with George, Larry Barnholth, his coach, and middleweight Richard Giller who demonstrated the George-Barnholth technique. George recalls Kono first struck him as "a skinny Oriental kid with glasses who ... adopted my style of lifting."[70] That he could soon perfect it by imbibing directly the master's words became possible with the 1950 publication by George and Barnholth of *Secrets of the Squat Snatch* which Tommy annotated and tried to imitate.[71] Even more critical to his success was an awareness of the mental preparation necessary to become a champion. In a subsequent memoir titled "The 'Mind Game,'" Tommy revealed his moment of enlightenment when he sat in the audience a row behind Barnholth and George as the heavier classes lifted in Philadelphia. During a lull in the competition, he asked Barnholth when he thought improvements in world records would stop.

> I will never forget his answer. His reply was, "A one-inch diameter bone can support 10,000 pounds. When the arms are pulled out of their sockets, that's when we've reached the limit." A one inch diameter bone will not support 10,000 lbs. of weight nor will we ever get to the point where our arms are pulled out of their sockets when we try lifting; but, can you comprehend the positive message he conveyed to me?[72]

The impact of this revelation cannot be overestimated. It was soon obvious in a statement on how mental preparation induced positive thinking that appeared in a 1950 issue of Teegarden's *Bulletin*.

> I've learned that it isn't so much the size of a muscle that makes a lifter lift heavy weights, but how he thinks. ... Of course there will be a physical limit ... but only when my arms are pulled out of their socket when in cleaning a weight. I had thought about this a lot and a recent letter of Barnholth stating it a little differently convinced me that I could total just about as much as I wanted to. So don't be surprised if I total 850 to 900 next year.[73]

Tommy never broke 850 as a lightweight, but his previous performances inspired West Coast promoter Ray Van Cleef and Hoffman to find the wherewithal to fund his travel to Brooklyn to compete in the 1950 world championship try-outs in September.

To this end the latter solicited, through a letter in the *Sacramento Union*, assistance from some civic-minded individual for the sake of American prestige in the Cold War. "We have always had a League of Nations in American weight lifting," Hoffman explained, "but this year we would have two Orientals on the team, a Negro and assorted other nationalities. It would help the international situation

"Wonder Boy" Pete George from whom Kono gained much inspiration, performing a squat-style snatch with 255 pounds.

where Russia tries to show that we are fighting the yellow races to have a couple of these boys on the team." To Tommy, he argued that "it should not be too hard to get someone to look after your mother while you are away. ... If I am enough interested in America's prestige to try so mightily to produce a winning team there should be someone in your city interested enough to help you."[74] A response was soon forthcoming from Elmer Singley on behalf of the Oak Park Athletic Club who agreed to pay $375 for Kono's cross-country air fare with further aid from theater owner Ken Wright. "The Oak Park club had only $100 in its treasury," reported the *Pacific Citizen*, JACL's official organ, "but that did not deter the members who borrowed the sum from a bank."[75] While training for the last leg of his journey at the York Barbell gym, according to Lou DeMarco, John Grimek found him looking forlorn and asked what was wrong. "He handed John a telegram; his mother had passed away. Immediately Grimek said you have to go home and forget the tryout, forget lifting as family is everything. John drove him to Washington, but it was fogged in with no flights going out. Grimek turned the car around and drove to Philadelphia" and put Tommy on a plane. "Don't worry about missing out this year," Grimek later consoled him. "Just remember there will be other championships and you will get your chance if you keep training."[76] "Poor old Tommy" was Teegarden's response. "Kono was hot for 240–240–315." But none of that mattered to Tommy in retrospect. "Mom's death had a profound effect on all of us."[77]

Private First Class Kono

At the tryouts Joe Pitman gained a team berth with a 765-pound total (225–235–305) and captured the world lightweight title in Paris with a 776½, all of which were within Kono's range. Not surprisingly, a slough of despond set in for Tommy, especially with no upcoming meets. Although he "felt extremely strong" and able to press 250, snatch 240, and clean and jerk 340 at 156½ bodyweight a day after the Paris meet, he was "contemplating giving up lifting for awhile. The darn thing's getting me down," he told Teegarden. He believed he was "going stale on real heavy weights. I don't make progress at all anymore. And I think I'll forget about losing weight with Thanksgiving and Christmas so near. I want to eat [till] my stomach aches full too!!!"[78] It was not until February 24, 1951, that he competed again at the Northern California Championships in Berkeley, but he managed no more than a 760-pound total. A month later he was drafted into the U.S. Army at the heart of the Korean War, classified as 3-C because of poor vision. Although he stayed in excellent condition during the 10 weeks of basic training at Fort Ord, he had no opportunity to lift weights except occasionally with a five-foot bent exercise bar. When his company commander graciously granted him a five-day furlough to travel to the senior nationals in Los Angeles, Tommy not only had to lose 12 pounds to enter the lightweight class but also was only able to work out three times on up-to-date equipment at Muscle Beach in Santa Monica and the Los Angeles YMCA. Hungry and thirsty, he "ached all over" by the day of the competition. It was a courageous but hardly stellar performance, totaling 760 (225–235–300) and losing again to Pitman by 15 pounds. What Tommy learned from this bitter experience, befitting the Asian outlook of his upbringing, was resignation to fate. "You never can tell what the future has in store for you, but ... you have to have a strong desire to do well, no matter what." Van Cleef also recognized the encumbrances Kono had to overcome. "Under proper conditions we could expect Tommy to conquer the world in the lightweight division."[79]

Further persistence in the face of adversity was required over the next year as Tommy endured the rigors and uncertainties of his military assignment. After basic training he attended cooking school, then cooked at Fort Ord for seven months with Korea as his destination. Kono noted that army cooks were often targeted because the North Koreans believed American soldiers "moved on their stomach" and would get demoralized if not well fed. With a shortage of cooks on the front lines, he had to practice shooting and cook with a carbine slung over his shoulder. But Tommy's cooking responsibilities enabled him to eat nutritious meals and train every other day. He would hitchhike to the San Jose YMCA to use its Olympic weightlifting set. And just three weeks before he was to be shipped overseas, the Army, recognizing him as a candidate for the 1952 Olympic team, reassigned Kono to Fort Mason in San Francisco to be a gym instructor. Most importantly, he could train weekdays at the local YMCA and on weekends at Yarick's Oakland gym.[80] While waiting six months for the next major contest, Tommy acquired a feel for heavier poundages by training and competing as a middleweight. It enabled him to post a (255–240–340) total of 835 at an Oakland meet in November and an 845 total at a San Jose contest in January 1952. His 265-pound press was a new American record.[81] He also displayed versatility in an odd lift (powerlifting) contest sponsored by Yarick in December where he bench pressed 300 pounds and squatted 460 pounds but was bested by teenage sensation George Brignolo. In February Tommy competed in his first physique contest, placing seventh at the Mr. Superman Contest in San Jose amidst such national level bodybuilders as Robert Shealy of Los Angeles, Victor Nicoletti of Hollywood, and Henry Lenz and Zabo Koszewski of Santa Monica.[82] A premonition of greatness came at the California State Championships in Los Angeles in April when he lost 15 pounds in a week to compete as a lightweight and make a 780-pound total that included a state record 235-pound press. This ordeal provided "convincing proof" to Van Cleef that "he is our brightest hope for a victory in the lightweight division at Helsinki."[83]

A Path to Greatness

Further proof was forthcoming at the Junior National Championships in May 1952 at the Oakland Civic Auditorium where Tommy registered a (240–250–325) total of 815 that exceeded Stan Stanczyk's world record by five pounds. He was "the sensation of the Jr. Nationals" exclaimed Bob Hise in *Iron Man*. "We feel he is the greatest lightweight of all times as he is nowhere near his top lifts."[84] *Strength & Health* heralded it as "the greatest lifting performance ever turned in at a National Junior championship ... the first time a world's record was set in a junior championship."⁸⁵ Hoffman, however, had made the mistake of underestimating Tommy. "I never realized just how strong Kono is until he had won 35 bottles of [Hoffman's] suntan lotion from me. I offered him a bottle for each pound he lifted over 780 and I had to buy the stuff back to keep in business."⁸⁶ A month later at the Senior National Championships in New York, Kono qualified for the Olympic team with an American snatch record of 253½ and total of 799 pounds, outdistancing 1948 Olympic champion Frank Spellman and Joe Pitman by 33 and 39 pounds, respectively, and winning the "best lifter" trophy. *Iron Man* editor Peary Rader noted that "he has good style and lifts only after deep concentration."⁸⁷ Yet he seemed mystified by his extraordinary ability, admitting that "tho he is muscular still you can't see where he gets the power for his lifts. He is built for lifting however, with very good leverages and leg and trunk proportions. ... We feel it is only a matter of a short time until he will hold every world record in the lightweight class."⁸⁸ To Hoffman, "Kono's strength and ability are out of this world."⁸⁹

What neither Hoffman nor Rader could comprehend was Tommy's ability to use his mind to perform extraordinary physical feats, despite the hardships of his youth, deprivations resulting from racial discrimination and wartime incarceration, training challenges of a soldier/athlete, and frustrations from losing two major championships. When asked what accounted for his progress, Kono pointed to his head, saying, "It's all up here," meaning the ability to outlift anyone else depends on concentration and an open mind unrestricted by limits. "I recognize no limits in lifting."⁹⁰ Tommy was able to "take advantage of disadvantage." At the Helsinki Olympics in July 1952 he went on to surpass the rest of the world in his class with a 799-pound total that included a 231½ press, a 308½ clean and jerk, and a world record snatch of 259, despite having to reduce several pounds to maximize American team points and endure severe stomach cramps for two days.⁹¹ "Standing on top of the winner's stand with an Olympic gold medal hanging from my neck, I was very happy," Kono recalled. "When I heard the national anthem played.... I was thinking, 'Wow, all these people have to rise for the national anthem for me.' It was good to see the Russians standing up for me. I represented my country and I did well for them. At a time like that, you don't reflect back on what has happened to you. You can't cry over spilled milk."⁹²

In the aftermath of victory, Tommy was overwhelmed with accolades, including congratulations from the California State Assembly. He informed his father that he had been "signing autographs right and left every day but I still get a kick out of it."⁹³ Kono's achievement as a Japanese American was duly celebrated by the *Pacific Citizen* but it was somewhat compromised by his inclusion amongst numerous other minority athletes as justification for the multi-racial direction of United States foreign policy. At Helsinki "America's polyracial delegation is already providing valuable propaganda for the forces of democracy. ... The appearance of these non–Caucasians proved somewhat of a surprise to certain other delegations who had been imbued with the belief that discriminatory attitudes affected every phase and level of American life." Hoffman put Kono's achievement firmly in the context of weightlifting, observing that "winning a place in Olympic competition or the big prize of a gold medal ... is the greatest height an athlete can attain."⁹⁴ Perhaps the

Gold medalists at the 1952 Olympic Games. From left: Pete George (middleweight), John Davis (heavyweight); Norbert Schemansky (middle-heavyweight); and Tommy Kono (lightweight).

greatest accolade was bestowed on Tommy's father Kanichi when he opened the front door of his home on Christmas Day and learned that his son had been named "Athlete of the Year" by the *Sacramento Union*. "For years I have lived in America," he told his son John. "I cannot speak very well the English language. And because I am not trained, I never before was able to repay my adopted country. Tommy is my gift to Sacramento and America."[95]

2

Ascent to Olympus

"I've always thought weightlifting saved my life."[1]—Tommy Kono

Although weightlifting may not have saved Kono's life, as he sometimes speculated, by redirecting his military service from a cook's life in war-torn Korea, it enabled him to direct his energies to a future in physical culture. Barely seven months after his Helsinki triumph, Tommy prepared a memoir titled "Weightlifting Paid Off." "In 1948, after my first weightlifting contest, if someone told me I would be an Olympic Champion 4 years later I would have thought him crazy. ... With each passing year I became more sold on the value of weight training and what its practice had done for me." Most obvious were improvements in his health, appearance, strength, and poise, allowing him to live a "fuller life." Weightlifting also provided "a free ticket to many of the places and countries I would never have dreamed of seeing." What Tommy could not foresee from his 1953 perspective was that weightlifting would facilitate an escape from the underclass status and humdrum lives of his Nisei compatriots and that respect for him as a talented athlete would henceforth neutralize any demeaning gestures and attitudes. Life now had meaning. "Each awaking moment started off a day of eventful happenings. No long[er] was my life dull with boring usual run of the day."[2] His Helsinki victory enabled him to embark on a trajectory of national and international fame.

German Victory Laps

This outcome was by no means obvious in light of the restrictions of Army service. Three days before his Olympic triumph, Tommy was confronted with "bad news" from Washington stating that he and teammate Clyde Emrich were to go directly to Zweibrucken, Germany. He had hoped to return home to "enjoy the fruit of my victory (I'm only human), then return to Germany and finish out my Army term." But the Army had other ideas that would have a three-fold benefit—allowing Tommy to fulfill his military obligations, solidify his newfound celebrity status, and contribute to pro–American public opinion.[3] Thus his European tour of duty became a "profitable and enjoyable one." Soon he and Emrich were popular personalities in German cities, performing before 8,000 persons in Berlin and 12,000 in Frankfurt. "Between these exhibitions we were also sandwiching in posing and strength feats at

Service Clubs" in various bases.⁴ These outings "made us real performers," Tommy recalls. "We 'delivered' on almost every occasion and the audience knew this from our exertions." They "never disappointed them."⁵ The Army provided a training environment conducive to these goodwill shows. In Heidelberg, Emrich was in charge of tennis courts, swimming pools, and a steam bath, and in nearby Mannheim, Kono managed a large stadium. "We would travel back and forth," Emrich recalls, where they would train together. "What he loved to do, if we were going to lift somewhere, the day before he would go to some local bakery and get the most creamy bun or biscuit that he could get, and then after the meet he would get back to the hotel and couldn't wait to eat his biscuit. We had a lot [of] fun."⁶ Their celebrity status, however, did not exempt them from military responsibilities. Tommy, having to perform guard duty, trained as early as 4 a.m. and as late as midnight, sometimes in an attic where he could not drop weights or a basement with drafts and no heat. Often he could only train 15 minutes at a time or lay off for several days. Traveling to exhibitions presented additional hardships, where he was expected to perform at his best with less than five hours of sleep. "In the Army one can never plan a set schedule with certain days and times to train." Everything was so uncertain that he had to "make the best of everything at that particular time." It was the kind of solace redolent of his Japanese cultural heritage—*shitaka-ga-nai* or acceptance of circumstances that cannot be helped. He "made use and profited by the experience of disadvantage" by being "able to do so well wherever I appeared." The quietude of his Buddhist-borne outlook always enabled him to "take advantage of disadvantage."⁷

His exhibitions were punctuated by frequent competitions, the first occurring on October 11 in Copenhagen. Much to Kono's dismay, since the event was designed for him

Tommy Kono's favorite photograph, showing him performing a 225-pound snatch at an outdoor swimming pool in Berlin, Germany, shortly after the 1952 Olympics. He is wearing sunglasses to protect his eyes.

to break a world record, he weighed 6½ pounds over the class limit. By the time of the contest, he weighed 148¾, but the question remained whether this reduction would weaken him. Any doubts were quickly dispelled in the press where he hoisted 248½ pounds, surpassing the world record by 2½ pounds. His 253 snatch was six pounds less than what he did in Helsinki, but his first clean and jerk of 314 exceeded his Olympic mark by 5½ pounds.[8] Tommy recorded (in third person) that "some 600 people that night had been thrilled to the record shattering performance of this 5 feet 5½ inches, 148½ pounder, and to prove their appreciation by rounds of applause, waves of cheers, and a bedlam of noise and confusion for congratulations followed. Bows after bows were made by Kono to quiet the crowd down." Afterwards he was led through "throngs of milling people trying to shake his hands for his accomplishments of a few minutes ago to his dressing room."[9] On November 8 in Karlsruhe, Germany, at a pound over the class limit, he hoisted 242–264–341 for an 847 total,

Clyde Emrich and Tommy became training partners and close friends while serving in the Army in Germany where they competed and performed exhibitions.

then made identical lifts two weeks later in Heidelberg. Tommy had long considered moving up a class, and being an Army cook had tested his resolve to remain a lightweight. Tommy admits to being "fond of eating rich foods in large quantities." It had always been easier to move up than down in weight classes, but when he was able to achieve neither his desired bodyweight nor total in his last two outings, he "kissed the lightweight class good-bye."[10]

His introduction to the higher class proved spectacular. What perked up Kono's morale was a letter on December 1 from 1948 British Olympic coach Oscar State about a "big deal" coming up in Halluin, France, a fortnight later. "Can't horse around," Tommy reckoned. "Got to start banging away & improve." In addition to strenuous workouts, he discovered a new source of mental stimulation to incentivize his training. "Determined to take a good w/o but have to alter plan to decide to train in gym when people are around," he recorded on December 8. "All goes well. Lots of people." He had a "red letter day," maxing at 259–248–319. In his middleweight debut on the 14th, he posted a 270 press, 264 snatch, and 347 clean and jerk for an 880 total that equaled Pete George's 1952 Olympic total and added 33 pounds to his own best. "With slight urge of State (Oscar) I took 347 & did it perfectly."[11] "It was a memorable affair," Tommy recalled, "for I had been honored the privilege of carrying the American flag." He wrote to Oakland gym owner Ed Yarick that "he was happier over this opportunity to carry the American flag than ever winning the Olympic games."[12]

Suddenly "lifting became serious business," he recalled. "We were representing the U.S. and this was not just another contest like in Germany as guest lifters during a league competition."[13] On December 16, at Robert Cayeux's gym in Paris where the great Charles Rigoulot had trained, Kono pressed a 270-pound antique globe barbell, then clean and jerked it and dumbbell pressed 241 pounds with 118.8 in his left hand and 122.2 in his right. "I had

Tommy performing a 330-pound jerk at an exhibition on September 27, 1952, in Ziegelhausen, Germany, where he also pressed 220 for three repetitions and snatched 231 at 155 pounds bodyweight.

read and heard so much about the spherical barbells that I wanted to try myself on them. What was supposed to be a work out with these bells turned out to be an impromptu exhibition. ... To please the crowd we tried our hands on just about every globe bells they had in the gym."[14] Although he did mostly cleaning and pressing movements, Tommy complained afterwards that "knees are sore from jars of jerk," a portent of future physical challenges. But at subsequent exhibitions in Germany, he was able to overcome this annoyance to total 880 and 891 pounds.[15] By year's end, Tommy placed third in a *Strength & Health* photo contest, was voted Most Outstanding Athlete of the Year by the Pacific Coast AAU, and was named to the

Olympians Clyde Emrich (left) and Tommy (weightlifting) with Sammy Lee and Pat McCormick (diving) at the swimming pool in Heidelberg supervised by Emrich.

Strength & Health All-American Weightlifting Team. Tommy concluded that "all the previous training I had done would serve as a fuse to the shattering of records that was to come in 1952."[16]

In 1953, he went on a record-setting rampage as a middleweight. In succeeding months he unofficially exceeded world record totals repeatedly, though usually not under official conditions. On February 21, a week before being shipped home, he put on an exhibition in Mannheim, hoping to make "a lasting impression on the German students of lifting." Kono arrived in peak condition weighing 162½ pounds after training "hard and conscientiously" for 10 days. "In the past I had taken exhibitions and contests more or less as a part of my work out." Rarely did he get over 6½ hours of sleep, and his training was often haphazard. For his final performance, he adhered to a rigid program to prove for himself "that a 900-plus was possible for a middleweight."[17] His 280½ press, 275 snatch, and 352 clean and jerk for a 907½-pound total became a source of pride not only as an unprecedented feat but for his manner. Under a thin veil of modesty, he referred to qualities of conduct he wanted to epitomize. "He has left a lasting impression upon those who saw him perform. Mild in manner, kind in speech & conduct, we shall miss him for he has shown us sportsmanship and true friendship."[18] On March 20, Tommy was honorably discharged as private first class and transferred to active duty with the Army Reserve.[19] Four years of military service along with his international lifting experiences broadened Kono's view of the world, deepened his love for America, and further drew him away from the Japanese American community.

California and World Champion

Upon returning to California, Kono resumed his career as a draftsman with the state division of highways where he earned three promotions with salary increases from $264 to $325 per month. Civil service examination results show that he ranked first in his class with a 10,730 score.[20] Periodic performance reports show that he rated high in relationships with people, work habits, and personal fitness.[21] Unbefitting his great strength but utilizing his budding artistic talent, Tommy's duties consisted of drawing maps and charts, making ink tracings on cloth, and checking alignments of highway and city limits.[22] Needing a change of pace following his tedious transition to civilian life to regain "muscle tone," he embarked on a bodybuilding program, intending to enter the Mr. California Contest in Los Angeles on April 4. At the urging of local officials, however, Tommy consented to perform as an extra lifter in the state championships. "Borrowing a lifting belt and using my regular street shoes I started with a low poundage and worked my way up. I did not know what I was capable of lifting but I didn't expect much because I had not been training on the Olympic three." Much to his surprise, he managed 270–270–350 for an 890-pound total. In the physique contest, however, Tommy encountered the likes of Bill Pearl, Zabo Koszewski, Ken Cameron, Vic Nicoletti, Monte Wolford, and Ed Holovcek to finish out of the running. At Yarick's "Big Show" in Oakland a week later, however, he again displayed his versatility by pressing 260 twice,

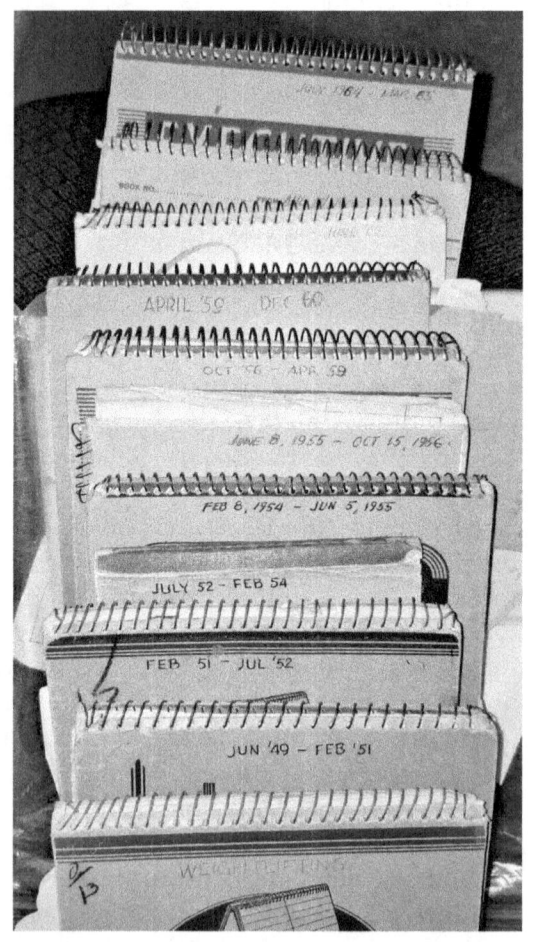

Training logs kept by Tommy from 1949 to 1965 where he recorded virtually every training and competitive lift along with comments about his diet, mental state, and physical condition.

snatching 255 twice, and clean and jerking 340 pounds. He then entered the bench press/squatting contest where he won his weight class with 330 and 440 pounds, respectively.[23]

What followed was a period of lassitude when Kono believed he could sustain peak condition "without any strict training on the lifts" or "use of heavy weights." Consequently, his lifts dropped significantly at the Pacific Coast Championships at Oakland in May. "The power portion of my training had been neglected too long," he concluded.[24] To recover his motivation Tommy joined 1951 Mr. America Roy Hilligenn for a two-week public exhibition in Hawaii underwritten by Dr. Richard You and gym-owner Rex Reville. The pair arrived on May 10, a day after the Oakland competition, and were welcomed by You, Richard Tomita, Emerick Ishikawa, Tom Yoshioka, Ed Bailey, and other local weightlifters. They stayed at You's home, but despite the aloha hospitality of his hosts, Tommy found the "warm weather makes me feel lousy," and he still felt "no power." On May 15, at a health and strength exhibition sponsored by the Hawaiian AAU Weightlifting Committee at McKinley High School, Kono tied one middleweight Olympic record by pressing 270 pounds and exceeded another with a 350 clean and jerk. He "won plaudits of an ardent audience of lifting and bodybuilding fans," reported the *Star-Bulletin*, "for his competent and poised power. He also gave a well-received demonstration of physique posing," reminiscent of the routine of 1946 Mr. America Clarence Ross when he visited the Islands.[25] But Tommy was disappointed because he missed all of his snatches. "No

This photograph shows Tommy's exhibition at McKinley High School in Honolulu during his first trip to Hawaii in November 1953. During that visit, he met movie star Rita Hayworth on Waikiki Beach.

real drive. No enthusiasm at all" was his reaction after another lackluster showing the following day.[26]

Several days of inactivity that included a picnic at the beach and a posing and lifting exhibition at a local hospital pulled him out of his slump.[27] On May 22, the *Star-Bulletin* reported that Kono "thrilled a packed house" in the Territorial Weightlifting Championships at the Nuuanu YMCA by totaling 880 pounds with individual lifts of 270–260–350 at five pounds below the middleweight limit. "Kono missed the world's record of 362½ for the clean and jerk when he barely failed at 365 pounds." Hilligenn further delighted the audience with "a sensational posing exhibition."[28] Thus, by the time he left Hawaii, Tommy was in a different frame of mind, leading later to speculation by the *Honolulu Advertiser* that he would likely establish residence there. "He likes Hawaii. He was impressed by it when he visited here several years ago. He has been thinking of returning ever since."[29]

The immediate impact of this uplifting experience was a renewed enthusiasm for training when he reached the mainland. After making 270–270–340 at Yarick's Gym on June 3, he exclaimed that his "training went terrific. Gave me all the confidence in the world."[30] An additional wake-up call was sparked by the approaching Senior Nationals on June 6 in Indianapolis and Yarick's offer to pay Tommy's travel expenses. "I planned my training so that I could turn in my best performance at the National to prove that I would lift just as well in my 'back yard' as I can in foreign soil."[31] At 163½ bodyweight, he registered a new personal high (285–280–350) total of 915, 100 pounds higher than his record-shattering lightweight lifting at the Junior Nationals a year earlier. With a total that was "the greatest ever recorded by a middleweight," Hoffman observed, Kono combined "great strength and excellent lifting technique." He was easily the outstanding lifter of the championships. Based on the Hoffman Formula which normally favored lifters in heavier classes, Kono's rating of 689.9 exceeded that of mid-heavyweight Norbert Schemansky (668.36) and heavyweight John Davis (689.23), both of whom were Olympic champions. Hoffman pronounced him "the world's best lifter."[32]

Tommy's performance set the stage for the 1953 world championships in Stockholm. This time Hoffman funded the trip for seven lifters and himself. It included the cost of bringing the team initially to New York, the most expensive leg of which was Kono's trip from California for $277. Tickets to Sweden were $818 per man. To meet the total cost of $7,000, Hoffman allegedly "scraped the bottom of a number of barrels." But it was necessary to defend "our cherished team title." To Hoffman's "horror," however, Tommy struggled to make his first attempts of 264½ in the press and snatch. In the latter "he had been doing 275 in training, so we expected anything up to 286½." With the 264½ "Tommy tried again, and again but failed badly to get the weight up. This was his last chance. He faced the weight, while our hearts stood still. He lifted it" and saved the championships. With a 347-pound clean and jerk, Kono clinched first place, then tried 369¼. "Tommy pulled the weight to his chest, adjusted his body in readiness to come up, and then smoothly and powerfully as an elevator rose from the squat with this great weight. He jerked the weight, held it easily enough at arms' length and a new world record was created" which actually weighed 371¼. It was a prodigious effort, 208 pounds more than Kono's 163 bodyweight.³³ What made it possible, Hoffman claimed, was his company's miracle food supplement. "We had sent carton after carton of Hi-Proteen to Tommy Kono in Sacramento before the championships," but he consumed little of it owing to his need to reduce to the middleweight class. Then after the distress of nearly missing all of his snatches, Hoffman accompanied Kono to the dressing room. "I said, 'Tommy, you forgot your Hi-Proteen tablets.' He took a handful and kept munching them." When he came out for the clean and jerk, Kono was "a new man. ... Who could say that the energy-producing power of Hi-Proteen tablets did not play an important part in this great success?"³⁴ However much it satisfied Hoffman's need to claim credit for Tommy's final lift or promote his miracle supplement, it is unlikely that any dietary intervention could have had such an immediate physiologic impact.

Nor does Tommy's take on his heroic performance mention any Hi-Proteen boost or Hoffman's intervention; rather, he attributes it to anger "at myself for having done so poorly" after the first two events, the need to "redeem myself" and give the audience "something better than what I'd done so far." What he learned from his near defeat was "not to be over-trained and not push myself too much the week of the contest."³⁵ Iron game sage Harry Paschall placed "more emphasis on the mental side than on the muscles" Tommy used to execute his 371¼-pound final lift. Why, he asked, "can little (comparatively small, that is) middleweights like Tommy Kono now lift 371-lb. barbells in the clean and jerk when a 300-lb. giant like Louis Cyr had difficulty with 350 years ago?" Paschall ascribed the advancement to conditioned reflex.

> What happens, we think, is that the subconscious mind controls the nerves which put out the muscular impulse, and when the conscious mind sees somebody lift 200 lbs., it conveys the belief to the subconscious that you, too, have muscles sufficient for this task. ... Basically, the reason for constantly mounting records is about 75 per cent in the head—as Tommy Kono always maintains.

Suspecting "the mind may have something to do with how much weight you can lift," Paschall was studying the beliefs of the ancient yogis and providing *Strength & Health* readers the opportunity to purchase a book on *The Study and Practice of Yoga* for $2.50.³⁶

These Eastern ideas were not dissimilar to the

Bob Hoffman, so-called "Father of American Weightlifting," examining a canister of Super Hi-Proteen in his office at 51 Broad Street in York where all the great American champions trained in the 1950s.

revelations Tommy published several years earlier or the pedagogy of the Barnholth brothers on mental conditioning. In a February 1954 update, he reflected on these thoughts. "The mind governs all our movements, thoughts and action," he asserted. "It is 'Mind over Mind' that we must all grasp to improve our total ... or anything worth-while in life." Unless one is able to dispel all thoughts that the barbell is too heavy, "you are defeated before you even begin the lift!" As Tommy learned from his experience with the snatch at the world championships, "your body can attempt to lift a weight well within its power but unless your mind gives it the 'go' signal that weight will be un-liftable." Auto-suggestion was the key, a "mild form of self-hypnotism whereby lifters would not only think but audibly say to themselves that they will succeed. Not one iota of the word 'failure' ever enters their mind." It would be as if life itself depended upon it. "They know from past experience that should they hold back their effort, no matter how small, it may mean the difference of a grand success or a miserable failure."[37] By this "do or die" attitude Tommy convinced himself in Stockholm to make his third attempt snatch and his record-breaking clean and jerk. It was the difference between ultimate failure and victory for himself, his team, and his country.

Mr. World

Imbued with these ideals, Tommy decided to test his capacity for success in the light-heavyweight class upon returning to California. Weighing only five pounds above the middleweight limit, his press of 296 pounds and 936 total at the San Jose YMCA on December 5 surpassed the national marks of Stan Stanczyk and came within 12 pounds of the world record aggregate set by the Soviet champion Arcady Vorobiev. Never one to hold back or fear failure, Tommy nearly jerked 400 pounds. He went on to total 940 as an extra lifter at the Northern California Championships and win an Oakland physique contest on March 6, 1954.[38] An unexpected bonus to his weight gain was his enhanced physique. On February 13, he won the Mr. Iron Man Contest as well as an "odd" lifting competition by bench pressing 360 and squatting 460 pounds at the Berkeley YMCA.[39] At Yarick's show on April 24, Kono bench pressed 380 and squatted 480, but he still came in second to Marty Orlof and Frank Spellman who hoisted 400 and 510 pounds, respectively. He was consoled, however, when his triple 350-pound overhead jerks "received a lot of applause."[40] It is also evident from his training logs that these feats were taking a toll on his body. Multiple sets and repetitions of over 400-pound squats were frequently causing sore knees.[41] Undaunted, Tommy placed second (after a tie-breaker) to future film physique star Ed (Holovchik) Fury at the Mr. Pacific Coast Contest on May 15 in Berkeley, while winning awards for best back and best legs, largely the result of muscles developed from Olympic lifting. For his bodybuilding prowess, Kono appeared on the July 1954 cover of *Iron Man* which rarely featured a weightlifter.[42]

That he exhibited such a serious interest in bodybuilding should not be surprising since it was critical to his transformation from weakness and ill health during his childhood. But even after he started performing the Olympic lifts and winning competitions, bodybuilding remained an important part of his training, mainly as a way of avoiding staleness between meets and sustaining a balance of overall fitness and muscularity. It complemented his lifting by bolstering his self-esteem. What helped him win regional physique contests in 1954 was the extra bodyweight gained as a light-heavyweight which added size and fullness to the ample muscular frame he had built in the lighter classes. Hoffman was duly impressed by Tommy's bodybuilding success which he self-servingly attributed to Olympic lifting. In an article titled "The Best Form of Bodybuilding," featuring a photo of Tommy with an impressive lat-spread, Hoffman asserts that "Kono's wonderful physique is almost entirely the product of the three standard lifts plus such exercises as heavy squats, dumbbell presses, high pulls, and supine [bench] presses."[43] Tommy seemingly gave credence to Bob's claims by winning the 1954 Plus Bel Athlete du Mond (Mr. World) title on October 16 in Roubaix, France, a week after winning the world weightlifting championships in Vienna. Tommy won the title easily with superior musculature, symmetry, and posing ability, scoring 150 points over 137 each for his nearest rivals, Antoine Boulos of Egypt and Tun Maung of Burma.[44] Despite its international status, Hoffman admitted "the general standard of physical excellence was less impressive than the contestants in a single contest in one major U.S. A.A.U. district." An *Iron Man* report agreed that the competition was "not very representative of the best in the world." Still it seemed fitting that Kono, as "champion of champions," should hold a world physique title to complement his world lifting title.[45] "The first two weeks of October were really memorable ones," he observed to Dr. You who was mentoring his progress. "In all, I broke five world weightlifting records and won one physique title—the title of (believe it not) Mr. World."[46]

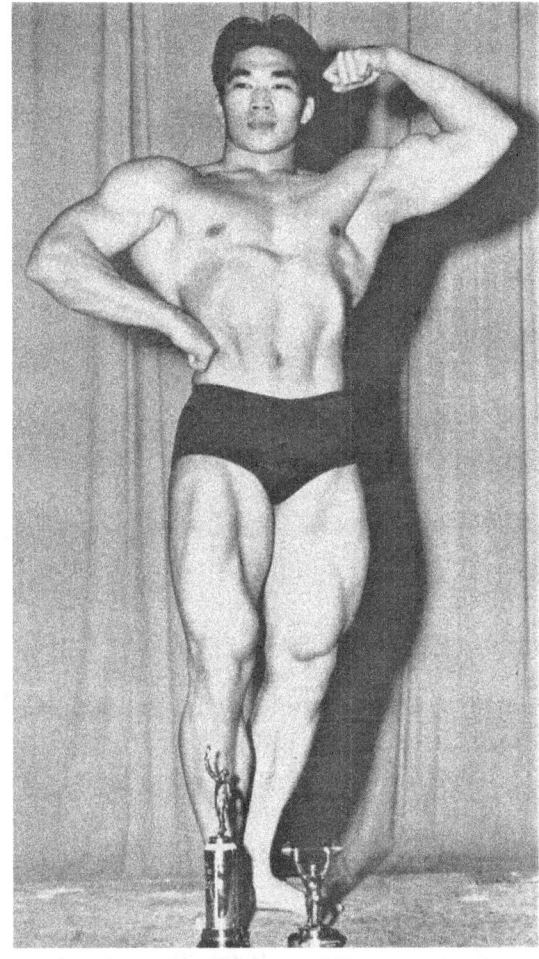

Tommy as he appeared on the cover of *Iron Man* magazine after winning the Mr. Iron Man contest in Berkeley on February 13, 1954. He also won the lifting portion of the meet with a 360-pound bench press and a 460-pound squat (courtesy *Iron Man* publisher Denny Kakos).

A year later, Kono provided a sampling of his Roubaix routine at an exhibition in Honolulu at McKinley High School where he was "a sight to behold," according to sports reporter William Metz. With his body bathed in "a slightly amber glow" from overhead lights,

> Mr. World turned and presented his back to the 1,200 spectators. He raised his huge arms slowly until they formed an inverted arch. The movement spread his back and shoulders until they presented a wedge atop his slender hips.
> Then it began.
> While the rest of his body remained immobile, the muscles of his uplifted arms came alive. They jumped and rolled and quivered and leaped. Starting at his wrists, the rippling motion swept down, and around his arms to envelope his shoulders. Then the action poured back up to his wrists and danced the length of his arms several times more. ... About 600 women squealed, and approximately 600 strong men murmured appreciatively.

On many occasions Tommy's posing would be accompanied by his blowing up a hot water bottle, driving a 60-penny nail through a two-inch board with bare hands, tearing a phone book or deck of cards in half or lifting a heavy weight. In this instance, it preceded a variety show to raise money for island athletes to attend the Olympics.[47] Kono's flair for entertaining, however, did not endanger his amateur standing. In 1954, "I got an offer to be in the Mae West Show in Las Vegas," he later told lifting friend Bill Brewer. "I was offered $200 a week and guaranteed for 6 months and then possible road show to London, Paris and New York. After debating for a day I turned it down because I would have become professional then and no more lifting competitions."[48]

Perfecting the Press

Another byproduct of his heavier bodyweight was an increased interest in the press which advanced from 296 (December 1953), to 300 (April 1954) to 308½ (October 1954) to 316¼ (March 1955), usually well below the light-heavyweight limit.[49] His motivation is partly revealed in a typescript titled techniques for "Improvement on the Press." Tommy's instructions, however, embraced virtually all aspects of Olympic lift training. It was fundamental that "to improve on anything you must do it often so that the movement becomes automatic. By movement I mean the proper movement. It must always be in the 'groove.'" He also believed it unwise to train more than four times weekly, exceed three repetitions per exercise, and press more than 30 minutes. Kono deemed it important, however, to use heavy weights. "With constant handling of heavy weights you make the muscles accustomed to the stress and strain" and "strengthen any weak muscle group to the chain of muscles used to press limit poundages." Warming up and advancing to a heavy press has the advantage of stimulating the nervous system for greater loads, but he advises against over-exertion or any training lift requiring maximum effort. "What makes a champion lifter? It is the person who can gauge his out-put of energy to the requirement at hand." To prevent staleness, he recommends a variety of routines and the "rest-pause method" heavyweights Paul Anderson of Toccoa, Georgia, and Doug Hepburn of Vancouver, Canada, used to conserve energy.[50]

Realizing that some lifters, especially Russians, used "trickery" to gain an advantage by excessive backbend to incorporate more muscles in the shoulder girdle and provide better head clearance, Tommy devised a movement to increase one's lifts without cheating. "Pressing in the strict style *with* commendable poundage," he recognized, "is only for the few!" We are not physically adapted to handle extremely heavy poundage in the strict style because of the unfavorable leverage placed upon our structure. "If we can modify our form so as to use the advantageous position of our physical make up and still follow the rules, our records will raise to a new height." He resolved the problem by experimenting with his anatomic potential after the 1952 Olympics where he had pressed 231 pounds. At an exhibition in Copenhagen in mid–August, four pounds heavier and without training, Tommy discovered the "style."

> I decided to play safe and start with low poundage of 209. It was then that I stumbled on the correct way of pressing for this weight shot to arms-length! This surprised me, so without hesitating I jumped to 225 for my second attempt. ... This weight too went up like a breeze. For my third and last attempt I elected to take 242, a weight that was 11 pounds better than what I had pressed at the Olympics two and a half weeks before, and this too successfully went over-head!

Tommy explains that having come upon this method accidently, it took two months of experimentation before he rediscovered the "style." It involved standing "as tall as you can at the beginning of your press from the chest and end up attempting to compress your body while elevating the weight over-head. You do this by throwing your chest up, consequently attempting to arch your *upper* thoracic region."[51] Unwittingly Tommy had perfected a portion of the so-called Olympic or "Russian" press that the "cheaters" had been utilizing. Missing was the lower body thrust from the hips and knees that would eventually result in the abolition of the press as a competitive lift in 1972.

At the Pacific Coast Championships on May 15, 1954, Tommy had an opportunity to test his innovative pressing technique as a light-heavyweight. But he only made his first attempt with 280 pounds, after which he missed 300 pounds twice. He admitted to an English correspondent named Reg that he pressed with too much backbend, was "over-trained," and weighed only 168 pounds. He also "made a mistake of entering the sub-divisions for the Mr. Pacific Coast before the lifting." He had expected to compete with Dave Sheppard "but got disappointed when he didn't show up. I really needed something to get me going in that meet. I didn't feel too much like lifting." But he learned a lot. "I think totaling so low in the contest was just what I needed. Physique is out! It's just lifting for me, concentration on one goal only and that is of improving my total to a new height for the Nat'l." Tommy explained that "weightlifting had become an exacting science with me and I want to study every phase of it so I can be well versed on improving the total. Every little knowledge counts!"[52] Indeed Kono would be well served by his focus on the press which would be critical to his future success. It accounted for 13 of his 18 world record lifts and contributed to his five world record totals from August 1952 to June 1961.[53]

At the 1954 national championships in Los Angeles, Tommy tested his pressing technique against Frank Spellman and Stan Stanczyk, both gold medalists at the 1948 Olympics. After making 275 pounds, he confidently pressed 290 which was rejected for excessive backbend. Still, Kono held a five-pound lead and eventually won with a 930 total despite missing his final clean and jerk of 380 pounds.[54] What most concerned the powers that be in York was Tommy's bodyweight. Though he made a respectable 950½ total on Labor Day in Monterey, California, Hoffman was dismayed that he only weighed 172 pounds. "Now that we have crossed the Rubicon," he lectured Kono, and "decided that you are lifting in the 181 … you must have more weight." Bob advised him to eat more nuts, especially walnuts, which were high in protein and aided digestion. He also suggested spaghetti and offered to send Kono his book on *Better Nutrition*. But diet, Hoffman believed, was only part of the problem. "I believe much of your trouble is being too active, work, training, the pursuit of fun. This business is serious, you must concentrate on gaining strength, muscle and weight." He advised him to get more sleep and have less fun. "I didn't really start having fun until I was thirty-eight and I have had a lot since then and have the capacity for a lot more. So get your sleep."[55] Little did Hoffman realize that Tommy's secret to success was that weightlifting always had priority over "fun," at least as Bob defined it. Though unlikely to dispel Hoffman's concerns fully, Kono proved his mettle a month later when he became light-heavyweight champion at the 1954 world championships in Vienna.

Trips to international competitions were a high point of Kono's experience. Here a team of many of America's greatest weightlifters and officials is preparing to depart for the 1954 world championships in Vienna. From left: Clarence Johnson, unidentified, John Terpak, Bob Hoffman, John Davis, Clyde Emrich, John Ziegler, Norbert Schemansky, Dave Sheppard, Pete George, Stan Stanczyk standing on his suitcase, unidentified, Tommy Kono, and unidentified.

His 308½-pound press was a critical factor. It was a "wonderful press," reported *Iron Man,* though Tommy "did appear to have considerable back bend."[56] But it helped to outdistance his Soviet counterpart by 16¾ pounds with a 958¾ total and a world record clean and jerk of 380¼. *Strength & Health* editor Jim Murray lauded this effort, observing that "Kono showed the class of a real champion in trimming Russia's [Trofim] Lomakin, who out-weighed him 181¾ to 173¼." Kono's clean and jerk and press were 207 and 135¼ pounds, respectively, over bodyweight. Harry Paschall was more circumspect. Tommy "did a splendid job in loading up with protein to lift in the 181-lb. class and seems good enough in both press and jerk to maintain his leadership. But his recent shakiness in the snatch is enough to give any American barbell bug heart failure every time he performs."[57] Hoffman concurred, noting that Kono needed to "snatch 300 to be in proportion with his other lifts" and retain his position as world's best weightlifter with a formula rating of 703.172. By the end of 1954, the United States claimed 13 of the 28 world records, five of which were held by Tommy. He was named to the All-America Weightlifting Team in two bodyweight divisions, and only the snatch seemed beyond his grasp.[58]

With the onset of 1955, accolades continued for Kono's pressing ability. Responding to a training session bet, he pressed a pair of 112½-pound dumbbells together for 10 repetitions, then at the Pan American Games in Mexico City in March, he pressed 316¼ for a world record and made a 966½ world record total. He was "by far the class of the 181-pound division," claimed Hoffman, "weighing only 169 full of food." Tommy out-pressed his nearest rival, Osvaldo Forte of Argentina, by 73¾ pounds but made only his starting snatch of 275½, just 22 pounds more than Forte.[59] At the national championships on June 5 in Cleveland he pressed 310 pounds, leading Peary Rader to wonder "where he gets such amazing power."[60] Paschall commented on his "marvelous pressing style without the usual quick shove," but he also noted that Kono negotiated only his first snatch of 270 pounds. "It is fortunate that he is equally good at the clean and jerk." Just how prodigious Tommy's pressing power had become was evident at an exhibition at a local military base where, with little warm-up and wearing street clothes, he cleaned a 275-pound barbell, then pressed it three times. After a short pause, he repeated this feat.[61] Murray explained in the August 1955 issue of *Strength & Health* that Kono's meteoric rise went beyond technique and training hours. He believed the quality that set him far ahead of other lifters his size was "thought," that Tommy "always thinks ahead of what other men are lifting." Most importantly, "he *believes* he will reach his goals, and when he starts to make a lift, he expects the weight to go up."[62] It is appropriate that Kono, fully flexed and poised to press 300 pounds, graces the cover.

Spreading Goodwill

High drama attended his participation at an invitational meet in Moscow on June 15, 1955, the first visit by American athletes to the Soviet Union since World War II. The USA weightlifting team included 340-pound Paul Anderson who startled the sports world by pressing a world record 402 pounds.[63] Also impressive but with far less fanfare was Tommy's head-to-head confrontation with middleweight Yury Duganov. As expected, he out-pressed the Russian by 17 pounds, but Duganov, world record holder in the snatch, evened the score with a 275½ success. Tommy then easily outdistanced his rival in the clean and jerk and set a new press world record of 291½ on an extra attempt. At Leningrad on June 18 he set another press record of 292½ and registered the highest ever middleweight total of 931¼.[64] But these heroics were overshadowed by the more captivating feats of the ponderous Anderson, who became an instant international celebrity.[65]

Although the six-man American team only tied the Russians in overall competition, the admiration evoked by Anderson's size and strength was a moral victory and hiatus from the acrimonious relations plaguing the two countries. It encouraged the State Department to send him and other weightlifters on goodwill tours to counter Soviet expansion in the Middle East and South Asia. It was easy to perceive Anderson as a silver bullet who could mesmerize audiences and bureaucrats and thereby win the hearts and minds of distant peoples to the American way.[66] Immediately after the Russian mission and euphoria stemming from Anderson's showing, the American team embarked on a Middle East trip at the invitation of Mohammad Reza Pahlavi, Shah of Iran, for a "command performance." Hoffman, the team coach, was passionately patriotic and anti–Communist and was unrestrained in his convictions in *Strength & Health*. "America's victory in weightlifting more than any other one thing," he believed, "depicts America's strength."[67] This hastily assembled side-trip seemed an ideal opportunity to show off America's physical strength.

Prior to its Iranian performance, however, the American contingent of Chuck Vinci, Pitman, Kono, Stanczyk, Sheppard, Anderson, Clarence Johnson, John Terpak, and Hoffman visited Egypt. A large delegation of weightlifters carrying bouquets of flowers greeted them after their marathon air journey from Leningrad. The athletes stayed at the Continental Hotel, the best in Cairo, and had a sumptuous dinner at one of former King Farouk's palaces. By the time of their exhibition on June 23, after traveling 12,000 miles, the lifters were weakening. "Strange food, strange water, and irregular living conditions were taking their toll." Anderson failed to repeat his 402 press, but Tommy pressed 280 pounds and clean and jerked 352½ twice for which he "received a great deal of applause."[68] It was much the same story in Alexandria following a trans-desert bus trip where 5,000 spectators were "greatly impressed" by the Americans, according to the Associated Press. "All were suffering from upset stomachs and fatigue from their tiring journey, yet exhibited feats never seen in this part of the world."[69]

After a brief exhibition in Beirut, the lifters arrived in Tehran to a heroes' welcome. It included "a big parade," palatial lodgings, and a multi-course feast, but the lifters were travel weary and homesick, and a stomach virus added to their misery.[70] Tommy reported that all team members feared the food, especially green vegetables and fruits, and that all water had to be boiled. As a result, he lost 15 pounds, and Anderson dropped 22.[71] Peak performance could hardly be expected from weightlifters who were dehydrated, undernourished, and losing weight. Yet they not only had to exhibit their athleticism but compete with a contingent of Iranian strongmen. With Mohammad Reza presiding over the competition, the Americans bested their Iranian counterparts in all classes despite their diminished strength. Tommy posted a respectable 281 press, 253 snatch, and 341 clean and jerk, just missing 358. But he was quite overwhelmed by the royal ambiance. "Can't sleep after that."[72] Anderson, on the other hand, who lost 25 pounds and could only press 363 pounds, was underwhelming. Sickness also prevented him, to the disappointment of fans, from accompanying the team to the ancient capital of Esfahan where the best performer and crowd-pleaser was Vinci, who not only fended off an Iranian champion but also impressed the crowd with his physique. What enabled Vinci to perform so well was his ability, unlike his colleagues, to eat the food. "He had been sick," Hoffman explained, "but he would lose it like the ancient Romans and eat again."[73] Kono, touted as the world's greatest weightlifter, complained to his father in Sacramento on July 3 that he was "still stuck out here" for several more days due to airline snarls. "I'm tired of the trip."[74] On returning in July, Pitman, Sheppard, and Anderson accompanied Hoffman to Washington for a personal welcome by the chief executive at the White House and Richard Nixon in his office. They said "we were the best ambassadors America ever had," Hoffman reported. "We showed the way."[75]

Always seeking recognition from high places, Hoffman was gratified by Nixon's support for another expedition in the fall to more countries on the Soviet southern perimeter, although his athletes were still recovering from sickness and fatigue. Furthermore, it was imperative that the Americans be in top condition for the world

Tommy being greeted by Mohammad Reza Pahlavi, the Shah of Iran, during a 1955 weightlifting goodwill tour to the Middle East. Others in the background included (from left, beside the shah) Clarence Johnson (assistant coach), Bob Hoffman (coach), John Terpak (assistant coach), Chuck Vinci, Joe Pitman, Stan Stanczyk, and Dave Sheppard.

championships in Munich. Even if Hoffman had to pay for the trip, "we can't let the Russians win, it is worth millions in propaganda value for most nations admire strength more than any other one thing."[76] Although the Russians narrowly defeated the Americans at Munich, Kono handily won his class with lifts of 314, 281 and 363¾ for a 958¾-pound total and added to American prestige by winning the IWF Mr. Universe Contest over Arthur Robin of France.[77] Yet media attention focused again on Anderson who executed a 408-pound world record press and posted a resounding 1129½ total.[78]

As their recognition reverberated through the media, the propaganda potential for the lifters' next goodwill tour in mid–November increased dramatically. The team consisted of Vinci, Kono, Jim George, Emrich, and Anderson, along with Johnson and Hoffman. The first leg of their 8,000-mile journey took them to Baghdad, Iraq. Here, observed Hoffman, they found "an odd and ancient land. It is just the same now as it was a thousand years ago." At their first exhibition in Basra, the lifters performed well, including Anderson who repeated his 402-pound press and hoisted a modified 451-pound clean and jerk. Despite a "dead bar," Tommy did 292–264–352, and the next day he and Vinci wowed a high school audience with posing and muscle control exhibitions.[79] Later the team was treated to a "unique" dinner called a Kuzi, consisting of three whole lambs that everyone ate with their fingers.[80]

The lifters journeyed next to the northern city of Kirkuk where Anderson again was the star attraction. People on the streets were "fascinated" by the Dixie Giant, observed Hoffman. "At one spot a crowd gathered around us, and Paul happened

An informal gathering of one of America's greatest weightlifting teams outside the Munich Sports School at the 1955 world championships. Pictured here from left are Jim Bradford, Jim George, Paul Anderson, Clyde Emrich, Pete George, Tommy Kono, Olympic coach Bob Hoffman, Chuck Vinci, and John Terpak, all of whom won at least one national championship.

to give away a photo of himself, and immediately the people went wild—everybody wanted a picture!" The weightlifters found refuge in the local USIA office. Anderson highlighted their final exhibition by executing a modified clean and jerk of 457 pounds, but as a victim of sand fly (Pappataci) fever, it was the last lifting he would do on the tour.[81] Reaction from Iraq was encouraging. In an open letter in *Al Yaqdha* to Ambassador Waldemar Gallman, "Sportsman" Hussain Al-Zubaida expressed appreciation for the visit of Anderson and Kono, leading embassy officials to conclude that the weightlifters "brought about closer understanding between the Iraqi and American peoples."[82]

On November 10 the Americans arrived in Afghanistan. At Kabul, Hoffman learned it was served by no railroads, only two planes weekly, and a trickle of trucks crossing the Khyber Pass, despite war-like conditions, from Pakistan. The lifters received a warm welcome from the Afghans whom Hoffman described as "handsome" and "fierce-looking." Although team members were able to savor some American food, largely from cans, their living quarters were Spartan.[83] Conditions for their lifting exhibitions were hardly better. Emrich recalls they had "55-gallon barrels in a roped off place where we lifted. Why we lifted in Afghanistan I don't know, cause' they advertised us as strongmen and we'd be lifting cows or something. It was the only country where they didn't know what weightlifting was."[84] George remembers Afghanistan as "one of the most backward civilized countries in the world." The only available weights were a "mix-matched set of plates and bar. We made up what we thought were the poundages. We were breaking world records right and left."[85] With poundages he considered "approximate," Tommy, feeling "very weak all over and run down," could manage only 247–225–286 on November 12.[86] Meanwhile the estimated crowd of 10,000 expected the "world's strongest man" would fulfill the "real program" organizers had arranged for him, more in keeping with their cultural conditioning. "They wanted to test his pulling power against a horse, they wanted to see him pull a string of cars and wanted him to lift a car or truck." Unfortunately, Anderson stayed in bed during the team's six days in Kabul. "He had a touch of sand fly fever, a headache, and indigestion. Perhaps his main trouble was homesickness," Hoffman speculated. George believed Anderson's nonappearance stemmed from Afghan perceptions of weightlifters as strongmen who lifted rocks, cars, and objects to which people could relate. "My understanding is that's why Anderson left. ... We were all sick."[87]

Again, Vinci compensated for the big man by staging what Hoffman called a "phenomenal display" of muscle control. With "the best back in the world," he was "called back time after time to show his wonderful muscles."[88] Uppermost in Hoffman's thoughts, however, was his lifters' impact on public opinion and America's strategic goals. Some Afghans told a group of visiting congressmen, who witnessed the exhibition, how they were grateful to see ordinary Americans, not just officials and engineers. The goodwill tour had arrived at an opportune time since a plebiscite would soon determine whether the country would favor Russia or America; a group of tribal chiefs and headmen told Hoffman that "our visit might be a deciding factor which would sway the people of Afghanistan more strongly toward the West."[89] These concerns were reflected in an October 1955 USIA intelligence report of continuous anti–Western propaganda stressing "Soviet friendship and cultural ties with countries of the area." In Afghanistan, there was "no let-up in personal appeals to Muslims" by Soviet officials, "utilizing slanderous references concerning Americans and their world policy."[90]

Much the same strategic considerations confronted the tour in India. At New Delhi, embassy and USIA representatives escorted Hoffman and his lifters to a trade fair "dominated by displays of the communist bloc," mostly of machine tools. Obviously, those countries "had gone to great lengths to make a favorable impression." While Anderson departed on the next plane, the others arrived in Bombay where they stayed in a comfortable hotel with palatable food. Hoffman was disappointed, however, that the 800 people at their first exhibition, though enthusiastic, were "more interested in the physique part of the show than the lifting." Later in a large stadium, the Americans performed well, but again the main attraction, in lieu of Anderson, was Vinci, who "lifted splendidly and showed his muscles well," according to Hoffman.[91] Tommy did his best, with 280–265–330 lifts and a posing routine, but he was diagnosed with bronchitis.[92] Next morning, to Hoffman's chagrin, newspaper headlines exclaimed, "*Vinci wins the heart of the crowd.*" The Indians were more enthusiastic about Vinci, who had never won a world championship, than Kono, who had won three and an Olympic gold medal. No less disconcerting, the Indian press was "leaning very strongly to the communist countries." It intrigued Hoffman that their goodwill tour was being followed by "the Russian Rover Boys," Nikita Khrushchev and Nikolai Bulganin, dual heads of the Soviet state. Whereas the weightlifters attracted huge crowds, "they had millions to our thousands." Prime Minister Jawaharlal Nehru also declared a long holiday to welcome the Russians, bringing countless rural residents to the cities "ready to be enthusiastic about anything, particularly 'kings' from another land." It signified the Indian leaders' desire to work more closely with the Kremlin.[93]

The weightlifters could hardly escape this harsh Cold War reality. Soon after arriving in Calcutta on November 20, they learned the Russian Rover Boys had received a "great welcome" in Bombay. "Few foreign dignitaries have cottoned on to our people as did Mr. Nikolai Bulganin and Mr. Nikita Krushchev," reported *The Times of India.* Heading the American coverage was the "hard luck" story of the world's strongest man whose Indian visit was cut short either because "his health failed" or he had "a mild affliction of home-sickness."[94] While the article focused mainly on Kono, Vinci received the greatest approbation from crowds. "Mighty Mouse was always ready at the drop of a hat ... to show his muscles," noted Hoffman.[95] By this time, Tommy's fever was "running high" at 102 degrees, and he was only capable of posing.[96] In Burma, the final country on their tour, Hoffman again seemed at odds with local sentiment. Although Tun Maung had placed third at the Munich world championships, young men seemed disinclined to weightlifting. At a clinic in Rangoon, Hoffman observed "a good many skilled lifters, but unfortunately as in other eastern countries, the bodybuilders, the aspirants of Mr. This and That, outnumbered the lifters." The Americans' weightlifting, hampered by intense heat and flying bugs, was lackluster, but the spectators enjoyed it, particularly when Kono and Vinci displayed their muscles.[97]

Jim George (third from left), Tommy, and Chuck Vinci (right) at an instructional gathering with Indian weightlifters in Calcutta on the penultimate leg of their South Asian journey.

In Mandalay, the farthest destination on their tour, Hoffman observed that they were near the Communist China border, and people in one remote village were "hard at work putting up decorations for the visit of the Russian leaders" a few days later. Geographically, he reckoned they were half way around the world from York. Kono was the only lifter who circumnavigated the globe by going east to his new home in Honolulu. "Those who saw us at the airports regretted they did not have the opportunity to see the great Paul Anderson." Despite his many sacrifices, Tommy had been upstaged by Anderson and Vinci throughout the tour. For Hoffman, it was "a wonderful trip to strange and wonderful places," but questions remained about its impact on public opinion.[98]

The Ugly Americans?

Initial responses were not encouraging. There were no crowds, especially with Anderson's absence, awaiting team members in New York, Chicago, or Honolulu. Nor were there White House invitations or State Department commendations. "There was none of that," observes Emrich. "There was no response at all. I don't recall any coverage in the Chicago papers. Just friends asking how it was." George recalls the trip "ruined my life. After returning I was down for a couple months with hepatitis. I lost about 40 pounds. Was I congratulated for serving my country or given any sort of accolade locally? No. No ticker tape parades."[99] A Honolulu newspaper, however, reported the return of Kono who uncharitably referred to the Middle East as "backward countries" with "weightlifters 15 or 20 years behind the latest methods."[100]

Meanwhile, Hoffman and Johnson rushed back to Louisville on December 2 to attend the annual AAU national meeting, as Johnson was on the Executive and Foreign Relations Committee. They encountered unpleasant news. Hoffman was not confirmed as a delegate to the International Weightlifting Congress prior to the Melbourne Olympics. Then AAU president Carl Hansen and a committee of past presidents discussed complaints about the overseas goodwill trip. Johnson duly conveyed their views to Hoffman.

> First and foremost was correspondence from the State Department setting forth complaints from officials of Foreign Countries objecting to articles that appeared in Strength and Health Magazine and certain actions that occurred on our tours.
> From Iraq alone came a voluminous letter stating that references to their country, customs, and people appearing in Strength and Health Magazine were very objectionable. … The State Department takes the position that we were on a good will tour for them and that articles such as this has undone all the good that was accomplished while we were there and in addition has created an animosity which is very difficult to overcome. They bring up incidents that happened in other countries and statements that were made.

Johnson explained that the committee was inclined to believe these complaints because of numerous improprieties by Hoffman at other AAU events, most recently at a Mr. Universe Contest at Virginia Beach. It was imperative that he address these objections to "get things ironed out in time for the Olympics."[101] Tommy suffered much discomfort, disappointments, and culture shock, but there is no indication that he became disillusioned or that the tours lessened his resolve to represent his country in the best possible way on the front lines of the Cold War.[102]

Considering this fiasco, it is not surprising that a subsequent trip to East Asia projected during the euphoric days following the first tour never materialized.[103] But Hoffman's insensitivities and his lifters' unfamiliarity with local customs only partially explain the lack of further weightlifting tours. Sickness and exhaustion were pervasive on both trips. Ultimately it was unrealistic expectations that doomed this promising strategy to make friends and check Communism. The State Department and Vice President Nixon placed too much confidence in Paul Anderson after his stunning performance in Moscow and popularity in Egypt and Iran in June 1955, leading them to believe he could excite the peoples on the southern borders of the Soviet Union into thinking the United States was the strongest nation with a superior culture. His illness and inability to live up to those expectations dampened these assumptions. When Anderson failed to appear for an exhibition in Kabul, some doubted that he was as strong as reputed.[104] A tone of resentment is evident in Hoffman's report on the team's condition in Calcutta where he contrasts Anderson's lassitude with Kono's fortitude. Though also "sick and just hanging on," Tommy, after touring the world for weeks, was "breaking world records while the strongest man in the world had long before gone home sick."[105] Such lapses of duty could easily be interpreted by State Department officials as lack of patriotism. Displays of strength by Kono and Vinci's physique were no substitute for the world's strongest man.

Dr. Richard You

By this time, Tommy had moved from Sacramento to Honolulu through Richard You, a physician of Korean descent who was a keen admirer of Bob Hoffman and supporter of Hawaiian athletes. You was born in Honolulu on December 23, 1916, and became a wrestler for the University of Hawaii in the late 1930s as a middle and light-heavyweight.[106] After graduating in 1939, he earned a medical degree from Creighton University in 1943, then served as a medical officer in the Pacific theater through the end of World War II. Afterwards he returned to Honolulu to establish a medical practice where he took a special interest in treating athletes and administering vitamins and minerals, often free of charge.[107] His early efforts were devoted to distance runners, then after establishing the Hawaii Athletic and Physical Culture Association, he expanded to multiple sports, including boxing, swimming, football, Tae Kwon Do, and women's track and field and served as an American team physician at the 1952 and 1956 Olympics. Possibly owing to a surfeit of local talent, weightlifting held a fascination for You, especially since the sport was undergoing a resurgence on the mainland. Emerick Ishikawa, who figures prominently in You's success stories, recalled him saying that "he was going to form a team that could beat the York Barbell Club who had a monopoly in weightlifting in those days.... *'Hey, we're going to win.... We're going to beat them for the first time. Let's work up a strategy.'* ... He pushed to the end."[108] Subsequently six Hawaiian weightlifters, led by Dr. You, traveled to New York City to beat the best lifters in North America in the 1952 national championship.[109]

Kono's contacts stemmed from 1952 when You provided emergency treatment for his stomach ailment in Helsinki. "We have a Hawaiian doctor, Dr. You, taking care of the Olympic team," he told his brothers, "the one that brought the Hawaiian 6 men weightlifting team over. His first love is weightlifting so he's taking special care of us. He's got me taking his own formulated vitamin & minerals pills so I should be in the best shape at the Olympics."[110] Tommy's impressive performance led You to invite him to Honolulu in November 1953.[111] A 1957 article states that he

> planned to stay for a week, was here for 15 days, and left with a vow that he would return to make his home.
>
> Back to Sacramento the world looked different, and Kono wondered if he had been "up in the clouds" when he thought of moving. He stayed where he was, went to work every day, and dreamed of Hawaii.
>
> Furthermore, Dr. You continued his campaign to make Kono an Islander.
>
> In 1955, the doctor and the weightlifter both went to the Pan-American games in Mexico City, Kono's resistance weakened. Finally, Dr You made a trip to Sacramento to talk to him again, and Kono decided on the move.
>
> He never has regretted it, he says.[112]

Kono recalls that each time he encountered You on the mainland "he would say, 'you belong in Hawaii. Finally, I thought this guy is serious," so serious that You and his wife "went to Mexico City and then they flew over to Chicago or Detroit and picked up a car and they drove to Sacramento."[113] In Honolulu, Tommy was provided living quarters at the You home on Emma Street and employment, along with Ishikawa, at You's York Health Food Store where he would serve as president of the York Athletic Company on Fort Street near the Nuuanu YMCA.[114] To what extent Kono subscribed to You's X-D-R (exercise-diet-rest) training system is uncertain, but it was owing to You that he settled in Hawaii and found a livelihood that enabled him to travel and compete on the highest level.[115] You later expressed pride in his investment, calling Tommy "the MOST REMARKABLE ATHLETE of them all."[116]

3

A Living Legend

"The best moments in our lives ... usually occur when a person's body or mind is stretched to its limits in a voluntary effort to accomplish something difficult and worthwhile."[1]—Mihaly Csikszentmihalyi

The significance of Kono's relocation to Hawaii cannot be exaggerated. In addition to the nurture and wise counsel by Dr. You at a critical juncture of his weightlifting career, he quite unintentionally severed his few remaining links with Sacramento's Japanese American culture and redefined himself as a Hawaiian American. Not unlike his acquisition of allegiance to America, it occurred through a process of osmosis. Although Hawaiians of Japanese descent have always been a sizeable minority on the islands, there is no evidence that Tommy sought to cultivate any special relationship with them outside weightlifting. It was fortuitous that his training and coaching at the Nuuanu YMCA was founded in 1912 by B.M. Matsuzawa of the Tokyo YMCA who came to Honolulu to open a facility catering to Asians.[2] By the outbreak of World War II it was a hotbed of weightlifting, popularized by 1948 Olympian Harold Sakata, a Japanese American from Kona.

Tad Fujii

Kono quickly found the Nuuanu YMCA ambience along with the climate and lifting atmosphere of the islands conducive to progress. At first, he was unsure of his future beyond the upcoming Melbourne Olympics, but he was thinking of going to college, he told a local reporter. "Once he dreamed of being a doctor so he could help others. Now he hopes to become a physical education teacher."[3] Soon, however, he settled into his regular training routine with even loftier goals. It could easily be assumed that Dr. You became his coach or that Kono simply coached himself. Shortly after following Tommy to Hawaii, Pete George asked him if there were any good coaches on the islands. He said, "yes, there is one of the best here, a guy named Tad Fujii." But when Tommy introduced Pete to Tad at the Nuuanu YMCA, he was not impressed. He had met many famous weightlifting coaches, "men like Bob Hoffman and others, who come on strong, are loud, act very authoritative and like to take charge. Tad wasn't like any of them. He acted very humble, was soft spoken, and wasn't trying to take anything." But it didn't take Pete long to see that he was "a very exceptional man" and that he was "a keen observer, a quick analyst, and a good communicator—everything needed in a great coach." What's more, Fujii "gave freely of his time" to improve weightlifters, George concluded. In doing so, he was "expressing mankind's noblest quality—the desire to help his fellow man. The Hawaiians call it Aloha." George observes that Fujii "helped coach every champion weightlifter that ever trained at the Nuuanu YMCA."[4] Evidence of Fujii's influence on Tommy comes from Gary Kawamura who was coached by both of them. Tad was "a connoisseur of weightlifting." Unlike Dr. You, Fujii became a technical expert. "Tommy would say, 'Tad knows what he's talking about. Listen to him. Tad used to come down when Tommy was there. And Tad would be coaching, and Tommy would respect and not butt in. I thought that was something, that someone as great as him would have that respect.'"[5]

Russell Ogata also had extensive experience with both coaches during his lengthy career. He recalls that Tad was lifting prior to the appearance of Richard Tom and Harold Sakata on the national and international lifting scene. "He supported lifting and would coach all lifters at the Nuuanu Y before during and after meets." Fujii was "a mainstay during a time when Olympic lifting was not as popular or good instruction not as readily available."[6] How much he helped Tommy is uncertain, but he coached many other lifters and quietly contributed to the Nuuanu lifting culture from the 1940s to the 1980s.[7] More explicit was Kono's impact on the Hawaiian weightlifting scene. "Through his inspiration," noted E. Fullard-Leo of the *Honolulu Advertiser*, "our Olympic old-timers—Ishikawa, Yoshioka, Tom, and Tomita—are staging a comeback and every island in the Territory is forming its own barbell clubs."[8]

The Elevator Man

After winning the 1955 Mr. World contest, Kono embarked on a record-setting romp in early 1956 where he repeatedly exceeded world middleweight press poundages—293½ (Honolulu, January 20), 295½ (Honolulu, February 17), and 300 (Kauai, February 25). Then he broke the light-heavyweight record at the Oahu Open on March 9 with a 317½-pound press at a bodyweight of 173½. Hearsay had it that he snatched 300 pounds and jerked 400 in training the following month, seemingly set for another record-breaking performance at the nationals at Philadelphia in June.[9] His training logs, however, reveal a somewhat different scenario. Tommy divulged that he constantly struggled to maintain a positive outlook and regular routine. Inadequate sleep was always a concern. "Feel I could use more sleep" is a frequent entry. Another nagging issue was aching knees. "Knees are sore," he wrote after squatting on January 16. "Scared of knee jars," he admitted after doing clean and jerks on the 30th. Stress was compounded by his standing a lot at work, his rigorous training routine, and the prospect of upcoming competitions and exhibitions. These pressures culminated with the visit of British Mr. Universe Reg Park for a "Big Show" at Farrington High School on April 7. After pushing himself to keep up with Reg in a workout the next day by doing doubles in the squat with 430 and the bench press with 335, he succumbed to overtraining. "I believe I need good rest from lifting," he concluded. That night "I either drink, smoke too much or had lousy food—upset system & throw up, head ache for two days."[10] For the next four weeks he decided to "do a little bodybuilding" while conducting clinics and exhibitions on Maui and at Hilo. Then he embarked on "serious training" for the Territorial Championships on May 19 where he hoped to total over 1,000 pounds with lifts of 318½, 301, and 382½. The most he could manage, however, was a 900 total via lifts of 285. 265, and 350 at 174 bodyweight.[11]

Such unrealistic expectations were not unusual for Tommy who always, in the positive mode, set his sights high. At the national championships on June 1 he intended to make 300, 295, and 375 for a 970 aggregate.[12] He started with a 300-pound press, but the judges disallowed it for excessive backbend. Still, with his 280 snatch he seemed on course to set a world record total. He hoped to exceed Fyodor Bogdanovsky's recent mark of 914 which had broken Kono's previous record of 903½ set in 1954. "Tommy wanted to get that record back," Hoffman explained. He seemed poised to attain it going into the clean and jerk after pressing 290 and snatching 280.

> To our surprise and consternation he missed 350. This would have given him 920 and a world record total. But he was not satisfied, he wanted 365, which would have broken his previous best record. To make a long, long sad story short, he missed twice with that weight, three misses in all, lost the championship, lost the world's record, lost the best lifter award.[13]

It was likely overconfidence stemming from the string of records he had set in previous months that marred his judgement, but the Philadelphia setback did not dampen his enthusiasm.

It is evident in responses to questions about his training practices from V.M. Kasyanov, editor of the Soviet magazine *Theory and Practice of Physical Culture.* After recounting his introduction to the sport, he cited Hoffman's teaching as a basis for his own trial and error to understand the finer points of weightlifting. "It is only by constant practice with the correct style that one learns to execute the lifts properly." It was imperative to rectify any mistake before it becomes a habit. His workouts consisted chiefly of the Olympic lifts for 60 to 90 minutes three or four days weekly. "I consider boredom in training as one of the chief causes of stagnation in lifting. For this reason I rearrange my training methods and program about every three weeks." He always kept "repetitions low in number because too many repetitions would create muscle fatigue. I also avoid extremely heavy weights in my training for the use of too close to limit poundage would be exhausting on the nerve." Kono attributed much of his progress to Dr. You's correction of his dietary deficiencies. Although he had previously practiced correct eating habits, "it wasn't until I placed myself under the capable hands of Dr. You that I really derived the full benefits from the correct nutritional stand point." Tommy admitted his worst deficiency was "very poor sleeping habit," a fact borne out by frequent frustrations in his training logs. "I sleep soundly and well but the hours of sleep are very short. I often go for weeks at a time with as little as 5½-hours of sleep per night." He believed he could improve faster if he could get more sleep. But a critical factor "in training and commonly over-looked detail is the discipline of the mind in relation to the lifts. The complete mastery of the mind over the body enables the body to handle heavy, limit weights."[14]

The full text of Tommy's letter was printed in the December 1956 issue of *Strength & Health,* reasoning that the Soviets "are wondering just what it takes to build a world champion weightlifter like Tommy Kono."[15] In an unpublished addenda, Tommy elaborated on the importance of Dr. You to his recent progress and that of other Hawaiian athletes who had benefited from his tutelage. Most critical was a high protein, vitamin and mineral diet. The result was "something short of amazing," he observed. "What normally takes me 3 months to get into top shape took but 6 short weeks. My recuperative power improved by approximately 400% for I was able to equal or exceed world record poundages in the lifts almost every week

Tommy was a master of single-hand lifting and often performed see-saw presses with dumbbells to improve his shoulder strength. On September 4, 1956, he pressed a pair of 135-pound Olympic barbells.

once I was in peak condition."[16] Much of his remarkable increase during the spring of 1956 he attributed to this change in diet. With his sights set on the Olympics, Kono repeated this tour de force in the fall, albeit in an unconventional way, first by setting a world press record of 322½ pounds as a mid-heavyweight weighing only 183 on September 15, followed by a clean and jerk record of 382½ as a light-heavyweight on October 12, both in Honolulu. On September 4 he pressed two 135-pound Olympic barbells that were placed on his shoulders, a dazzling display of strength and balance.[17] Kono's ability to transcend four weight classes in his career and set world records in all of them led to his cognomen of "Elevator Man."[18]

Russian Rivalries

At the Olympic Tryouts in San Jose on October 27, at 176 bodyweight, Tommy lifted well below his capacity. He pressed 290 pounds, but his attempt at 310 was ruled out because of excessive backbend. "Again," noted Yarick, "he ruined everyone's nerves in the snatch by making two failures with a 280 snatch, but made it easily on the third." In the clean and jerk he lifted 370 on his second attempt but failed with 383.[19] But with a 940 total, he still far outdistanced the competition.[20] And there was nothing lackluster about his performance at the Olympic Games on November 26. He made all nine attempts, even an Olympic record of 292 pounds in the snatch, a lift, as Hoffman pointed out, in which he "has been notoriously uncertain"; often missing his first two attempts, "a habit that could easily drive a coach to both strong words and strong drink!" His second clean and jerk of 369 pounds clinched the gold medal over Russian Vasily Stepanov, and teammate Jim George set a world record of 303 on a fourth attempt snatch. "The lifting was decided," Hoffman reported, "but the greatest feat was still to come. The bar was loaded to 385¾ pounds—a new world record. *Tommy Kono came out and lifted it perfectly!* Our boys had made two new world records in this class, and the future looked very rosy to the USA."[21] A further highlight of their Olympic experience was a luau staged at Dr. You's home in Honolulu while the lifters were on route to Melbourne to celebrate Hoffman's 58th birthday. It consisted mainly of native seafood dishes highlighted by a commemorative ring presented by Pete George on behalf of team members. For Hoffman, "it was the nicest birthday party he ever had."[22] For Tommy, it brought together the two promoters who most facilitated his ascent to greatness. The 1956 Olympics culminated a banner year in which he became the world's most admired weightlifter.

The euphoria stemming from Kono's *annus mirabilis* extended into 1957, but he was uncertain at first about whether he should continue competing after winning two Olympic gold medals and setting numerous world records. "What higher achievements can I obtain in weightlifting?" he asked. "I felt my competition days should be over and that I should instead direct my concentration in improving myself in other areas such as education and finance." Dr. You, however, argued that since he was still young at 26, he should continue competing until he could no longer perform at his peak. Tommy accepted You's explanation as "wise advice" and "continued to give exhibitions and lift in local contests. My enthusiasm was fired up for

American gold medalists at the 1956 Olympics in Melbourne. From left, Isaac Berger (featherweight); Tommy Kono (light-heavyweight); Paul Anderson (heavyweight); and Chuck Vinci (bantamweight).

From left: Chuck Vinci enjoying the company of Dr. Richard You (Hawaiian weightlifting promoter), Pete George, and Tommy at the Royal Hawaiian Hotel in November 1956 during the Olympic team's stopover in Honolulu on the trip to Melbourne.

the sport because I had hit an improvement zone. In fact, my lifting during the first half of 1957 was great!"²³

On February 1 at a Honolulu meet, Kono surpassed his own world record as a light-heavyweight by three pounds with a 989 total, via a world record press of 319, a 290 snatch, and a 380 clean and jerk. "Tommy is striving to boost it to the fantastic height of 1,000 lbs.," observed journalist Ray Van Cleef. "Had he not lost his balance in his 305 snatch effort, the 1,000 or better goal would have been achieved."²⁴ A month later he followed up with a world record 321-pound press at 178½ bodyweight and performed an off-the-record bench press of 370 for two repetitions with a two second pause. Then just two weeks before the national championships in Daytona Beach, Tommy had a freak accident that injured his left hand. As Osmo Kiiha explains: "A load of five musclemen tilted the Cadillac he was seated in, causing the car door to shut on his third finger, splitting the fingernail lengthwise." Using straps, "he was able to maintain his pulling power and strength."²⁵ Sore knees and his need for female companionship, however, interfered with his concentration and training. On January 25, Florence Rodriguez accompanied him to an exhibition on Kauai. On March 20 he "didn't feel like train[ing] cause of Florence," and on the 27th he was "rushed cause I have a date with Flo."²⁶ These distractions did not deter his performance at the nationals, however, where he out-lifted his adversaries in all three lifts with a 970-pound total, including a 295 snatch, his highest in official competition. Kono, representing You's York Athletic Club, was also the only recipient of a prize offered by Hoffman to any lifter who exceeded the total made by a Soviet lifter in the same class at the USSR championships. Tommy's 970 was his best in any American competition outside Hawaii.²⁷ Hoffman cited him as "an outstanding example of proper nutrition and weight training. His diet has been supervised in recent years by Dr. Richard You, including Hoffman's Hi-Proteen."²⁸

At the world championships in November at Tehran, however, Tommy was barely able to retain his crown by tying Russia's Fyodor Bogdanovsky and winning on lesser bodyweight. While he tied the world record with a 297½-pound press, Kono faltered in the snatch, making 270 and missing twice 281 twice, while his Soviet adversary made this weight. In the clean and jerk, Tommy called for 358¼. "Things looked gloomy for the American

Tommy Kono displaying his physique outside a housing unit at the Olympic Village in Melbourne.

cause when he failed twice to clean this weight," Bob Hasse reported. For his final attempt "Kono wanted to jump to 363¾, but teammate Isaac Berger prevailed upon him to try again with his starting poundage and fortunately for all concerned except the Russians, the idol of the Hawaiian sports pages acquiesced and made his final lift with the 358¼. Kono shook, shivered, and quivered under the bar in the jerk but finally gained approval for the lift."[29] It was an electrifying moment, and when Bogdanovsky could not negotiate this weight, Kono won America's lone gold medal. For Tommy, however, the 358-pound clean and jerk was more dramatic than the 375 he hoisted six years later to win the national title in Harrisburg. "No Hoffman, no Terpak to witness it," he recalled. "I won over Bogdanovsky by being the lighter man. I was carried off the platform by the Iranians for my clutch performance."[30]

Why Tommy was unable to lift a weight that was normally within his capacity on his first two attempts is a mystery, but his final success illustrates his ability to perform when the stakes were highest. "Strict adherence to the scientific nutritional program, rigorous training and clean living have established Kono as probably the greatest weightlifter of our times," wrote Monte Ito in the *Honolulu Advertiser*.[31]

Tommy followed his victory in Tehran with a five-day stopover in Japan where he demonstrated his winning form at U.S. military bases, Japanese colleges and clubs, and on television, meanwhile "signing autographs by the hundreds," according to an Associated Press report. He liked Japan better than any country but America.[32] "I was really popular in Japan," he later declared. "A Japanese movie producer once asked me if I'd like to play a Japanese Tarzan in a film. But I turned him down because I couldn't imagine swinging from a vine."[33]

A few months later he repeated these heroics in 1958 at another standoff with Bogdanovsky at an invitational meet in Moscow where Tommy, the lone American lifter, had to overcome the disadvantages of grueling international travel, frigid weather, and an unfamiliar environment. Fortunately, he was in good shape when he received a cablegram from AAU General Secretary Dan Ferris inviting him to compete with other Americans, against their Soviet counterparts in early March. It was only on arriving

Although Kono was physically well suited to be a weightlifter, he and many others believed that the true secret of his strength was his ability to focus, stay mentally positive, and believe he would succeed in competition. In this photograph, he pauses, mentally preparing himself before attempting a heavy clean and jerk.

in New York that he learned, after a nine-hour flight from Honolulu to San Francisco and a connecting flight to Chicago, that he would be the only American competitor, mainly because the Russians refused to defray expenses for any other lifters.[34] Yet Kono persisted in less than ideal training conditions in Moscow, and in the contest he felt lost when stepping into the huge ice skating rink converted into a lifting arena. "In addition there were movie cameramen, photographers, and officials ringing the front perimeter of the platform; it was almost unnerving," Tommy recalled. Not surprisingly his total of 920¼ (via 292–270–358) with five attempts missed was not his best, but it was good enough to surpass Bogdanovsky by 11 pounds. Tommy later explained how he had to travel through 11 time zones, adapt from Hawaii's warm weather to Moscow's freezing cold, lift without a coach or team-mate, unable to speak Russian, and compete against five world-class opponents. "This trip and competition," he concluded, "were the most challenging one in my weightlifting career."[35]

What helped Kono summon sufficient courage to overcome such odds was his conviction that he was competing not so much for personal glory but for his country. As he often remarked: "When I'm competing outside the continent, I always felt like I was representing the United States and was always more emotionally involved."[36] What was "most important" to Kono, a *New York Times* report affirmed, was "the fact that he is helping his country. He is probably the nation's most tireless 'sports ambassador.'"[37] After beating the Russians for the ninth straight time, Hawaii's Bob Krauss reported, Kono "was mobbed for autographs at the end of the meet. 'I signed

In March 1958, Kono was the only American to compete in the first "Prize of Moscow" weightlifting competition which was held on an ice rink.

my name on everything from posters ripped off the wall to Kleenex,' said Tommy. Fans even gave him their Communist party membership cards to sign."[38] While Paul Anderson had stolen his thunder in his previous Moscow outing in 1955, Tommy clearly created his own thunder this time.

Meanwhile, Kono was also basking in the glory of Honolulu's sports pages and presenting scores of exhibitions, demonstrations, and lectures to civic associations. He was no less a celebrity on home turf. As sportswriter Andrew Mitsukado observed in 1958, Tommy was stimulating interest in weightlifting throughout the islands. "Weightlifting is now enjoying its greatest popularity both from the standpoint of participation and fan interest."[39] Representing the Nuuanu YMCA, he held national records in all four lifts spread over four weight classes.[40]

What few could comprehend was that his platform heroics were made more dramatic by occasional losses. They not only made him appear more human but also served to cast his great victories into bold relief. This yin-yang syndrome, redolent of his Buddhist cultural heritage, was evident in his alternating bodybuilding with weightlifting, his light/heavy training routines, and his flirtations with snatch failures in numerous meets. It was even more conspicuous in his two consecutive losses to rival Bogdanovsky during the visitation of the Soviet team for invitational matches in May 1958. At Chicago's International Amphitheatre on the 12th, expectations were high for Tommy. Hoffman noted that he "had never been defeated in international competition." He had nine consecutive wins and seemed invincible, but "this night he was off and Bogdanovsky was really on." In a do-or-die effort to

A familiar scene at weightlifting meets in the 1950s when the lifter and the barbell had to be officially weighed after a record lift. Depicted here is the certification of Kono's world record 295-pound press at 163 bodyweight on August 3, 1956, by (from left) Thomas Collazo (judge), Don Potter, Dr. Richard You (chairman), Alvin (Buzz) Brock (Hawaiian heavyweight champion), Kono, Tad Fujii (judge), Richard Tomita (referee), and Tommy Kowalski.

snatch victory from defeat, Tommy cleaned a world record 380¼ pounds but missed the jerk, thereby losing by 28 pounds. At Detroit's Masonic Temple Auditorium on the 15th it was much the same story, with Tommy missing his final clean and jerk attempts and losing by 11 pounds.[41] At stake on the 17th at the final East-West clash in New York's Madison Square Garden was Kono's reputation as world's best weightlifter. He measured up to the challenge by tying the Russian lifter and winning on lighter bodyweight. Murray Levin, later president of the United States Weightlifting Federation, recalls that it was "the largest crowd ever assembled to see a weightlifting meet" with over 10,000 spectators. "After the press and the snatch Kono needed a fantastic clean and jerk to win. John Terpak was Kono's coach at this event and he told me this story. He whispered in Tommy's ear, 'I figured out what you should take to beat the Russian.' Kono turned to him like a tiger. He said, 'don't tell me how much I need. Just put it on the bar and I'll lift it.' I was sitting up front that night and he put everything he had into that lift and won that match."[42] Hoffman concluded that "Kono's comeback victory on this occasion well illustrates that a man must be at his physical peak to beat the great Russian lifters."[43]

Becoming a Legend

With no Russians to challenge him at the 1958 national championships, Tommy "lifted pretty much alone," remarked Hoffman. His middleweight total of 890 exceeded that of runner-up Louis Riecke of New Orleans by 95 pounds. The only electrifying moment was his extra attempt 285-pound snatch, a personal best and national record. It was "nice lifting but far behind his best of 936¾."[44] At the 1958 world championships in Stockholm, however, Tommy rose to the occasion by trouncing Bogdanovsky with a 947¾ total.[45] It also provided a celebrity moment with his class attracting the largest crowd of the championships, a complete sell-out. "Tommy is very popular in Stockholm and throughout the world," observed Hoffman, "and is always a good drawing card. He had received the lion's share of newspaper publicity, for after all he was one of the two competitors in action who had previously won a world title there in 1953." Tommy did not disappoint his fans. After making a "fine press" with 297½, he made three perfect snatches with 270, 281, and 286 and then requested 294 for a world record fourth attempt. "To be honest," wrote Hoffman, "I did not expect Kono to make it, but he approached the weight, carefully planted his feet, grasped the bar with the hook grip, rocked forward as he partially straightened his legs, then back to the flat back, low hips, head up starting position. He pulled as he had never pulled before, and there, wonder of wonders, was the bar safely held at arms' length. Tommy Kono had done the seemingly impossible!"

Still in the clean and jerk, he was only five pounds ahead, and after failing his second attempt with 363¾ he returned from the platform saying his knee hurt. Nevertheless, realizing his victory was in jeopardy, he tried the same weight, and even risking injury, made it.[46] What made this championship even more memorable was an incident recalled by teammate Ike Berger whom Tommy asked to record his world record snatch.

Intense concentration enabled Tommy to shatter world records in four weight classes. He was a clutch lifter, pictured here straining to come up from the bottom position of a heavy clean.

"Here's my movie camera. Why don't you record me while I'm lifting?" I said, "sure Tommy." So he was going for a world's record, but I didn't record it. "So why didn't you do it?" … "I'm sorry. I didn't think you were going to make it, so it would have been a waste of film." He was so upset, but he took it like a man and he understood. But he didn't miss it. He broke the world's record. And I didn't record it, and he kept mentioning it, and it became a story that kept on everywhere we went. It was very funny, very very funny. It was funny to him too. It was funny to everybody.[47]

In winning the featherweight title, Berger set world records in Stockholm in the clean and jerk and total, and Tommy's snatch and total made him the only weightlifter to hold four world records.[48]

By the onset of 1959, Kono was also holder of seven national records in two weight divisions, named Hawaiian AAU Athlete of the Year, recognized as Sportsman of the Year by Honolulu Sportswriter Red McQueen, and third in voting for the AAU Sullivan Award. Again, at the Senior Nationals he was in a class by himself in an otherwise worthy field of middleweights with a 905 total, far short of his best of 947½ pounds. Likewise at the Pan American Games in Chicago, he only totaled 898 pounds, via lifts of 281–264½–352½. It took the 1959 world championships in Warsaw to bring out Tommy's best. Hoffman was concerned that America would win no gold medals, having won at least one at every world championships since 1936.

The critical moment occurred when Tommy, though leading by 5½ pounds and the lighter man, was confronted with a 286½ pound snatch that would seal his victory against erstwhile rival Bogdanovsky. For his first attempt with this weight, Hoffman was "worried as Tommy placed his hands wider apart than usual. A failure. Tommy was reaching the zenith in competitive spirit. 'I will snatch it, I must snatch it, I will make this for you, Bob.' And sure enough, he did." Tommy went on to make a 358¼ clean and jerk for a 936 total and a 16-pound victory over Bogdanovsky. It was his eighth consecutive world title, observed Hoffman. "His reign is unmatched in weightlifting history."[49]

Kono's victory was underscored just after the Warsaw championships by his winning the FIHC Mr. Universe title, leading Peary Rader to declare him "America's Greatest Athlete." With eight consecutive world and Olympic weightlifting titles and four world physique titles over the previous decade he personified success derived from "heavy, sustained training and enthusiasm" and "an ideal example for those who find it hard to train continuously."[50] Further accolades descended on him after returning from Poland when the House of Representatives of the first legislature of the new state of Hawaii passed a resolution bestowing on Tommy "its highest commendation, praise and thanks for his great achievements and contributions to the State of Hawaii."[51] He was runner-up for the 1959 Sullivan Award (won by shot-putter Parry O'Brien), the highest any weightlifter has ever placed, and his picture appeared on the cover of *Amateur Athlete*.[52] He was also the recipient of "much fan mail," according to journalist Eddie Sherman. "One 12-year-old gal from Kalihi wrote Tommy: 'I would like to feel your muscles sometime. Can I meet you downtown? I'll bring my own lunch.'"[53] But the most personal tribute to Kono's accomplishments occurred during the junior nationals in Sacramento on May 20, 1960. Much to his surprise and delight, the local YMCA staged a *This Is Your Life*–style tribute based on the popular television show hosted by Ralph

Kono on the victor's podium between Fyodor Bogdanovsky (Soviet Union, left) and Jan Bochenek (Poland).

Edwards that aired weekly on NBC. Although Edwards was not present, he prepared the script, and sportscaster Stu Nahan of KCRA affiliate in Sacramento was master of ceremonies. In addition to his father and twin brothers, Tommy was honored with recollections by Ben Hara and Tad Fujioka, his former training partners from Tule Lake, iron game journalist Ray Van Cleef from San Jose, and Sacramento mayor James McKinney who presented him with the key to the city. Included also were letters of praise from Bob Hoffman, IOC Chairman Avery Brundage, President Eisenhower, and Vice President Nixon. It was "the nicest thing that ever happened to a WEIGHTLIFTER," declared Los Angeles Coach Bob Hise.[54]

The weekend's festivities were further enlivened not only by his participation as an extra lifter but by performing several strong man stunts to illustrate the mental toughness that made him an outstanding lifter. He entertained the audience by driving nails through a two-inch plank with his cloth-covered hand, blowing up a hot water bottle until it burst, and tearing a telephone book in half. Kono's younger son Mark vividly recalls these public demonstrations. "I remember him accompanying me to a cub scouts meeting and seeing him driving a nail through a 2-by-4 to demonstrate what you can accomplish if you really concentrate and put your mind into doing something. For him, it wasn't about showing off his might. It was to show the power of the mind. He read so many books on the power of positive thinking, he believed in 'mind over matter.' But that fell by the wayside with us as kids."[55] Likewise, its meaning no doubt fell short on Tommy's audience, though many of the lifters could have benefited.

Kanichi Kono (center) beams with delight over the honor bestowed on his youngest son on the *This Is Your Life*–style tribute staged by the Sacramento YMCA on May 20, 1960. Stu Nahan, a popular sportscaster for KCRA television in Sacramento, is at right.

There is no evidence that Kono ever explained the rationale behind his strongman stunts, but he became incensed by publications that misrepresented his training techniques. He was alarmed by an article in the January 1960 issue of *Muscle Builder*, a magazine edited by Joe Weider, that used a touched-up photo of himself to advocate the overhead squat as a "new" exercise. It superimposed chains on a photo of him executing a 270-pound snatch at the 1954 world championships to illustrate its effectiveness. Kono flatly denied this allegation in a well-crafted letter to the editor in the October 1960 issue of *Strength & Health*. "I do not know whether the author of the article or the publisher of the magazine touched up the photo, but it is certainly misleading in regard to my training practices."[56] Curiously, this issue of *Muscle Builder* cannot be found in the magazine or Kono collections at the Stark Center, my own collection, or the holdings of numerous iron game aficionados. This letter was likely fabricated by a *Strength & Health* editor or York advocate to establish credibility by association with the world's greatest weightlifter. Kono had inadvertently become implicated in the ongoing feud between York and Weider, but he was also learning some of the consequences of fame. "No American lifter," observed Ray Van Cleef, "is more of a celebrity to the public at large than Tommy Kono."[57]

A behind-the-scenes glimpse at Kono's private life and training routines is hampered by his reluctance to discuss his personal habits and proclivities. So infrequently are women mentioned in his training logs that it appears he had no sex or social life. His sole means of relaxation seemed to be movie-watching. Otherwise, his focus was almost totally on weightlifting from which he had always gained a sense of satisfaction. There were virtually no career opportunities for professional weightlifters, but his expertise and fame in this activity definitely spurred his interest in

Tommy aspired to work for Bob Hoffman at the York Barbell Company where iron game luminaries often visited. From left: Vic Boff, Harry Greenstein (son of "the Mighty Atom"), Tommy Kono, Steve Stanko (seated); Norbert Schemansky; Joseph Greenstein ("the Mighty Atom"); and Leah Greenstein (the Atom's wife).

pursuing some health-related field. Tommy once "wanted to become a doctor," but it was too time-consuming.[58] The extent to which he managed Dr. You's health food store or served as his laboratory technician is uncertain, but it was his only source of income, and You also provided him with housing, funding to compete overseas, promotional opportunities to underscore his growing fame, and manifold nutritional benefits. A 1958 *New York Times* article reported that he "eats a normal diet, nothing fancy, nothing special. He smokes occasionally and takes a drink now and then. He supplements his diet with iron and protein vitamin pills. Kono practices for an hour or an hour and a half three or four times a week at the Honolulu Nuuanu Young Men's Christian Association gym."[59] What the *Times* article overlooks is the prodigious amount of energy and effort exerted in Tommy's workouts. Although he constantly complains in training logs that he is getting insufficient sleep; suffering from aches, pains, and injuries; and often feeling like he does not wish to work out, he is sustained by his positive outlook—that mind will inevitably triumph over matter. As he explained to a Polish sports editor in 1958, "there seems to be no limit to what the human being can hoist over-head. The end result will be governed by the (human) mind." He reiterated this faith in human willpower just before the Rome Olympics to the *York Dispatch*, that the fine margin between a champion and an also ran is in the mind. "Weightlifting is a mental state, he believed. ... If you think it's an impossible lift—it will be."[60] These convictions, however, would be tested during the next several years as he entered his thirties.

At the height of his popularity, Kono was beset with the consequence of so many years of hard training and stress on the body that has plagued so many seemingly indestructible world class athletes. Whether it was from overcompensating for physical weakness in his early years at Tule Lake or his patriotic fervor, he enlisted the full force of his mind to push his body to the limits. But there was no possibility of making those kinds of demands on an injured frame. The first hint of a knee injury in competition, a frequent ailment of Olympic lifters caused by jarring effect of the squat cleans and jerking motion, occurred on Kono's second clean and jerk attempt at the 1958 world championships. Achy knees, aggravated by heavy repetition squats, had plagued his training for nearly a decade, but this was more serious. At Warsaw in 1959 he injured his right knee while attempting a world record clean and jerk of 374 pounds. A premonition of this injury, according to Tommy, occurred at an exhibition he, mid-heavyweight Bill March, and Ike Berger gave at a Boy Scout jamboree in Dover, Pennsylvania. "I performed a Split-style Snatch of 135 lbs. My best Snatch at that time was 297 lbs. using the Squat-style, so you would think that a measly 135 should not bother me. Well, evidently my forward knee, the right one, must have flexed a little out of alignment for it did not feel right after I gave the exhibition." After failing with the 374 jerk at Warsaw, his right knee became stiff and swollen. This irregularity caused him to favor his left leg, resulting in a comparable injury to that leg. "I was now plagued with both knees being bad going to the 1960 Rome Olympics."[61] Tommy still won the Senior Nationals at Cleveland in June 1960 with a 865-pound middleweight total, but Hoffman noted his injured right knee prevented him from training properly and handicapped him in all the lifts.[62] Although he negotiated a respectable 290-pound press with a power clean and considerable backbend, thereby saving some stress on his joints, he missed his first attempt snatch with 260 before making it. "He then went on to unaccountably fail with 315 in the clean and jerk," reported Peary Rader, "then made it easily, but could not get 330," which was far below the 358¼ he lifted in Tehran and Warsaw.[63] Obviously, the Senior Nationals provided a chance for Tommy to sense whether his body could withstand the rigors of Olympic competition.

In its aftermath, Kono spent a week undergoing treatments with Dr. Russell Wright, an osteopath who was team surgeon for the Detroit Lions and Detroit Tigers, then recuperating in York while training for the Olympics. According to Hoffman, Dr. Wright "advised Tommy to take it easy for a time. Kono did, so easy, in fact, that it worried me a great deal. He favored his knee in training, avoiding jerking even modest weights."[64] And a month before the Olympics he joined other lifters training in York to give an exhibition at the Maryland Penitentiary in Baltimore.[65] By this time, expectations for Tommy's performance were high. "Kono virtually guarantees the U.S. a gold medal," asserted *Time* magazine.

> But in frank moments, Kono admits that he is about fed up with weight lifting. "At the start it was a joy. Now it's an ordeal. I'm a special target of the Russians. I'm always under pressure to defend a title or break a record." In fact, Kono is talking of quitting after this year. To ease his ennui in the meantime, he bends nails with his fingers, drives spikes into boards with his fist, blows up hot-water bottles until they burst and looks forward to the Olympics—when he will have the chance to become the first weightlifter in history to win gold medals in three different classes.[66]

Van Cleef concurs that winning at Rome would give Kono "the unique honor of being a champion in three different divisions at the Games." It would also enable him to fulfill "his intention to retire from competition after the Olympics."[67] Despite his injury and subpar performance in Cleveland, Rader had confidence in Kono who "is a great competitor and usually comes through when a lift is needed."[68] Rome would provide a supreme test of his ability to use his mind to conquer his body.

Knowing this competition "meant so much to him," Rader reported that Tommy used his superiority in the press to take an early lead. His controversial third attempt with 308½ was turned down by the judges but passed by the jury on appeal, allowing him to establish a comfortable 11-pound margin over Russian rival Alexander Kurinov. In the snatch, however, he made a critical strategic error. Rader "often wondered why Tommy starts his snatches and clean and jerks so high and we remarked to Dr. You who was sitting beside us that we hoped that he would start with 270 or less for his first attempt. Imagine our disappointment when we heard them announce that he was starting with 281. We believe this was where Tommy lost the title, because he started too high in the snatch."[69] Kono made 281 for his third attempt, but Kurinov did 292, and the lifters had equal subtotals, with Tommy being the heavier. In the clean and jerk, he made 352½ pounds but failed with 363¾, then 374¾, both times trying to jerk on his stressed knees. Kurinov countered with 358¼, 369¼, and 374¾ for a new world record, thereby besting Kono by 22¼ pounds and winning the gold medal. It was "one of the Olympics' notable upsets," reported *Time*, by Kurinov who had always venerated Kono "as one of the world's great athletes."[70] It was a shock for Tommy—"I experienced a real blow."[71]

Ever the sportsman, Tommy smiled afterwards and said, "I had to lose some time." Hoffman viewed his loss as a mixed blessing. His failure to earn a third gold medal not only cost Kono his best chance to win the coveted Sullivan Award for 1960 but also the likelihood that he would become a living legend and remembered in perpetuity as the greatest weightlifter of all time. He could be consoled, Hoffman mused, by future opportunities. "Tommy wanted to retire so he could spend more time at business, perhaps marry as other people do, but he said, 'I can't quit now, I'll have to beat him.' So it looks like we still have a great middleweight lifter in the U.S."[72] Indeed, he had executed a 352½-pound clean and jerk and registered a 942¼-pound total with a 308½-pound press that equaled the world record. Despite losing, it was one of his best performances. Whether drugs played a part in tapping his recuperative powers and fueling his courageous effort cannot be proven, but with his usual cargo of Hi-Proteen to boost his team's efforts, Hoffman allegedly brought some "anabolics" supplied by team physician John Ziegler. Only bantamweight Chuck Vinci and light-heavyweight Jim George are mentioned in John Grimek's reports to Ziegler that he received from Hoffman.[73] "I knew people were taking things," recalls George. "I didn't really get involved in it. Ziegler scared me. He and Doctor You scared the hell out of me. I was never really in that loop."[74] Indeed, none of George's remaining colleagues in 2016 admitted or were even aware of steroid use in Rome in 1960.[75] Although no evidence links Tommy to Ziegler's "anabolics," he was one of five lifters (of seven) who made gains over previous performances, and it was Vinci who became America's last male Olympic gold medalist in weightlifting.

4

Descent from Olympus

"Weightlifting is 50 percent mental, 30 percent technique, and 20 percent strength."[1]—Tommy Kono

At the conclusion of the 1960 Olympics, Kono had to reckon with the consequences of losing. "Tommy and I considered anything but gold a loss" is the view of Pete George who won six Olympic and world championship titles.[2] What Kono could not accept, after a decade of unparalleled success, was that his lifting career was on a downward trajectory. Neither intense concentration nor his positive and patriotic outlook had provided a pathway or the willpower to stave off the debilitating impact of age and injuries. His defeat was projected even further by Hoffman formula compilations to select the world's best weightlifter which Tommy often dominated. Not only was his rival Alexander Kourinov deemed "the top strength athlete of the present day," but Russians reigned supreme for all lifts in classes once controlled by Kono.[3]

Reckoning with Defeat

Confused at first, his inclination was to "give up the sport." But "I love weightlifting," he told himself. It had made it possible for him to visit many countries and become famous.

> I regularly receive letters from all over the world addressed simply: "Hawaian Islands, Tommy Kono." It seemed to me that I had done a lot in weightlifting and it was time for me to leave the sport. These were my thoughts as I was returning from the eternal city. I quit training and gained a little weight. Two months went by and I could no longer fight with my desire to test my strength. I resumed training—as a lightheavy.[4]

His training, under Dr. You's supervision, was done while suffering from traumatic osteoarthritis in his right knee and a more serious condition in his left knee which required an operation. He then returned to heavy weights. As Tommy explains, he "purposely avoided all leg work for three months" to let his knee heal. He compensated by doing upper body bodybuilding exercises and concentrating on heavy dumbbell presses.[5] At a post–Olympic exhibition in Honolulu, he pressed 250 pounds for 10 repetitions and two 105-pound dumbbells 20 times at 172 bodyweight. On February 3, 1961, he pressed 300 pounds for four repetitions, "tho' I could have gotten it for 5 reps," he told Hoffman, "I didn't want to back-bend and tax my back too much. ... My pull was so strong ... that if I wanted to Clean 380 I could have. My snatch pull, incidentally, is stronger than ever." He was eager to try all three lifts.[6]

A comeback opportunity soon emerged. With You's blessing, Kono entered the 1961 Prize of Moscow tournament which he had won handily six years earlier. By this time, his pressing power was so great that he "felt capable of breaking a world record in the Press ... if I could clean the weight!"[7] At 177¼ bodyweight he pressed a world record 336¼ pounds on March 8, along with a 303 snatch and 374¾ clean and jerk for a 1,014 world record total. Tommy "drew a standing ovation from the large crowd," Hoffman observed. "Many claimed it was the best heavy press ever made."[8] In a final stab at immortality, Kono hoisted a world record press of 350 pounds at the Nuuanu YMCA as a middle-heavyweight at 183½ pounds, thereby having set world records in four weight classes. At a meet on June 17 in Tokyo, he intended to set another world middle-heavyweight record, but even after eating five or six meals a day and developing a taste for Japanese seaweed and fish pastes, he could not reach the desired bodyweight. He did, however, challenge his ailing knees by performing a full squat clean on his way to a world record 338¼ press as a light-heavyweight.[9] In this second visit to his ancestral homeland, Tommy was surprised that weightlifting was a "major sport" that attracted large crowds. "They had the Japanese intercollegiate lifting championships while I was there, and one day there were 180 participants."[10] As a rebound from his less-than-spectacular Olympic performance, it seemed to be a highwater mark or afterglow of his brilliant lifting career.

Despite recent setbacks in Rome, Hoffman sought to involve Tommy, still regarded by many as the world's greatest weightlifter, in new product development, much as he had used John Grimek's physique to promote Hi-Proteen a decade earlier, to increase corporate profits and reassert America's weightlifting superiority. Kono's presence in Japan and acquaintance with distributors there and in Hawaii led Bob to suspect that American strength athletes could benefit from a superior quality of protein drawn from the sea. To satisfy his curiosity, Tommy shipped a couple boxes of fish products to York. "The question is, how many will like it," he told Tommy. "I think it will take a lot of practice for the uninitiated to get around to eating Octopus." Hoffman seemed eager to work out a deal. He believed it could be "a really big and profitable business, one that will mean a good present and a better future for you. We can tell a very glamorous story about these products and with your great success through the lifetime use of sea products. Too bad that you do not like fish too well. I will have to eat it for you, as I am very fond of most fish." The other "subject that is so close to our hearts" was the "machine" that Dr. Ziegler was employing to improve lifters' strength through functional isometric contraction. Bill March and Lou Riecke had registered impressive gains with the power rack that Hoffman would soon manufacture and market. With a recent total of 970 pounds and expecting to break 1,000, March was "rapidly becoming an international lifter." No less impressive was Riecke who had totaled 983 via 303–303–377. Hoffman wanted to send Tommy a prototype. For nearly 30 years he had been working on ways for lifters to manage heavy weights.[11] Although Kono believed the power rack would "make a difference in my cleaning and snatching," it was not until the summer of 1963, leading up to the Stockholm world championships, that he started using it. Yet Hoffman, resorting to creative chronology, concluded isometrics was a major factor to his 1961 world records in Moscow and Tokyo and Mr. Universe victory.[12] "Isometric Contraction helped make it possible for him to do all of this, for he had been having trouble with his knees."[13] Unaware that March and Riecke were likely making gains as much from steroids as isometrics, Hoffman announced his miracle machine in "The Most Important Article I Ever Wrote" in the April 1962 issue of *Strength & Health*.

Mind or Matter?

It is well known that steroids not only have a substantial influence on performance and physique but also can dramatically augment an athlete's recovery from injuries. It was exemplified in the comeback of American heavyweight Bob Bednarski after an elbow dislocation at the Pan American Games in 1967. Bednarski then became dependent on dianabol and other drugs for the remainder of his lifting career.[14] Although this never happened to Tommy, it remained a question of whether You was administering drugs that might have affected his performance during this period. In a recorded interview with two undercover agents from the Drug Enforcement Administration in 1976, You explained that he responded to bodybuilders' requests for dianabol by sending them to another doctor. "'Cause if I catch any of my athletes taking drugs, I will throw them off the team."[15] But Jim George regarded Dr. You as "an amateur magician and cardsharp who was dealing off the bottom." He was allegedly dabbling in steroids at the same time as Ziegler, and there was "an outside possibility" that Tommy was taking them.[16] Admittedly Kono, vulnerable to the recuperative power of drugs, did gain bodyweight, a frequent consequence of their use, and set world records.

But for Tommy, it was more a question of putting mind over matter.[17] It is not surprising that he and other super athletes—the likes of Paul Anderson and, in later years, Mark Henry—are suspected of deriving their strength from performance-enhancing drugs. As Tommy explained to me in March of 1992, he had tried steroids but thought he "didn't need them." They made him "nervous." Nor did functional isometric contraction work for him. And he was overly sensitive to Dr. Ziegler's isotron, which stimulated muscular contraction with doses of high frequency electricity.[18] Unfortunately I did not have the presence of mind to ask when, for how long, and under what circumstances he took steroids. Steroid use could only have occurred with the advent of the Ziegler era after 1959 when Kono's fortunes were in relative decline. In lieu of further revelations from his training logs, curiously missing from April 1959 to August 1962, some credence must be given to circumstantial evidence. Impact of steroids would be most discernable in sudden spurts of performance. The following chart shows Tommy's three-lift totals for both weight classes from February 1955 till his last meet in June 1965.

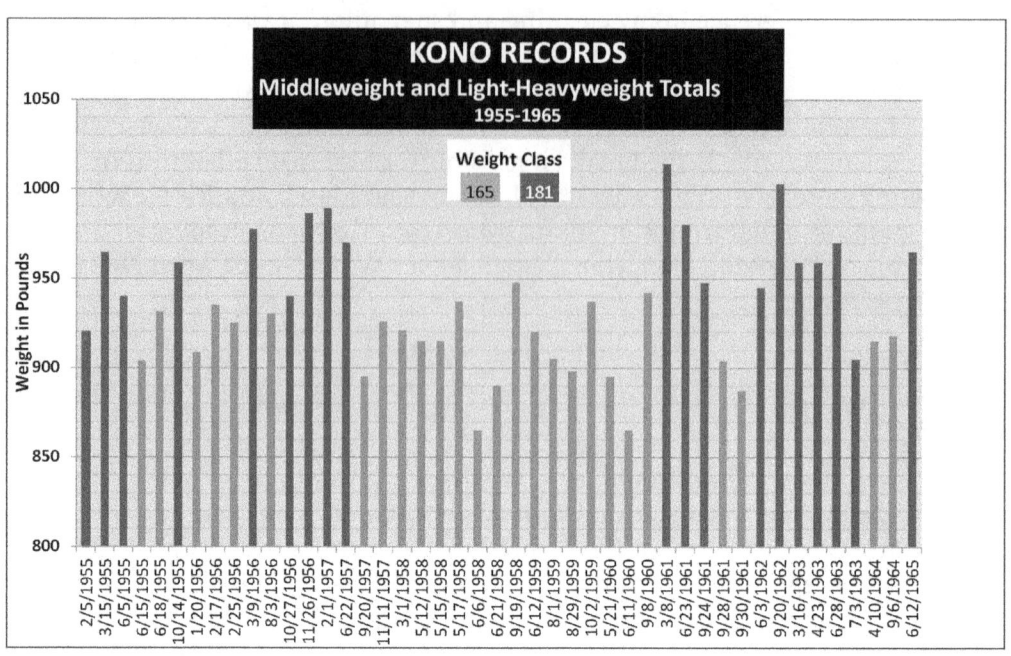

What is most revealing from these data is how impressive Tommy's performances were as a middleweight prior to 1960, averaging 915.94-pound totals for 19 meets, followed by a significant decline to 903.67 pounds for seven meets. The opposite effect is evident for his light-heavyweight years with an average of 960.69 pounds for nine meets before 1960, and a rise to 964.77 in his remaining 10 contests.[19] Bodyweight gain often accompanies steroid use, and Kono's increased weight was aiding his performance after 1959, but there is no evidence that steroids were the reason. If so, they were not benefiting him on the international stage since his competitors' totals were rising even more rapidly. Indeed, Tommy's best years in both classes preceded the drug era.

Following his prodigious output in Moscow, Honolulu, and Tokyo, Tommy returned in June 1961 to Los Angeles. Though weary from three weeks travel in Japan, he won the light-heavyweight title at the Senior Nationals with lifts of 310–290–380 for a 980-pound total. For the next three months he rested and reduced 15 pounds to reenter the middleweight class and regain his world title and world records from Kourinov. It was an encounter the weightlifting world was anticipating on September 24 at the Vienna world championships. But he did so against the advice of Dr. You who advised him against any major competitions for a year and to set his sights on the 1964 Olympics.[20] Unfortunately, Tommy held on to too much weight for too long during the recuperative phase of his training and had to lift as a light-heavyweight after desperately trying to make the 165¼ middleweight class limit. After hours of trying to recoup his strength and bodyweight, Kono weighed 169¼ pounds, the lightest in the class. Tommy also admitted that both knees were bothering him during the competition, possibly disturbing his concentration. His total of 947¾ pounds, via 303–281–363¾, was only good enough for a bronze medal behind Russian Rudolf Plukfelder's 992 and Hungarian Geza Toth's 953¼ and tied with Finland's Jaakko Kailajarvi. As Hoffman rightly reckoned, the "Scales Beat Kono."[21]

As consolation in the aftermath, Tommy won the Mr. Universe title awarded by the International Weightlifting Federation. It should be remembered, however, that bodybuilding by this time was becoming a specialized art/athletic competition distinct from weightlifting and that weightlifters who entered high-level physique contests were becoming rare. The most prestigious version, conducted by the National Amateur Body-Builders' Association (NABBA) since 1948, was dominated by such notables as John Grimek, Steve Reeves, Reg Park, and Arnold Schwarzenegger. The IWF Mr. Universe was limited to weightlifters who had competed in world championships; Tommy's main rival was American mid-heavyweight Bill March who was big, bulky, and smooth. It is doubtful whether Tommy's amateur physique, constructed largely from weightlifting movements, could have withstood competition from seasoned professionals who trained solely for bodybuilding. His early encounter with Bill Pearl, Zabo Koszewski, and Ed Holovcek in California had proven that point. The years of his IWF titles coincided with NABBA winners Pearl (1961) and French star Arthur Robin (1957). Unlike NABBA, the IWF Universe lapsed within a few years. Even less credible were the Mr. World titles Tommy won in 1954 and 1955, years dominated by Mr. America Jim Park and Canadian great Leo Robert. Unlike his approach to weightlifting, Tommy never sought the strongest competition. Yet few would gainsay that he had an outstanding built-body. Put in perspective, Tommy had the most functional physique of any strength athlete of his time.

His lifting during the next 12 months, though still world class, stagnated. At the Prize of Moscow Invitational in March 1962, he managed a credible 303-pound press as a

After winning the 1961 IWF Mr. Universe Contest, Kono's picture appeared on the cover of *Strength & Health* magazine.

light-heavyweight but missed all of his snatches. Then he won the Senior Nationals in Detroit in June with a 945-pound total, far short of the 1,014 world record he set earlier in Moscow. He further showed signs of faltering at the world championship team tryouts on September 8 when, after pressing 320 pounds, he missed 280 thrice in the snatch, relegating him to alternate status. Fortunate to lift at the world meet in Budapest in October, Tommy did 330½, 297½, and 374½ for a 1,003-pound total, only to be exceeded by the great Hungarian lifter Gyozo Veres who totaled 1,012, most likely drug-induced.[22] On that occasion Kono's teammate, heavyweight Gary Gubner, revealed in a 1992 interview that "Kono, Schemansky, and March," prior to leaving for Budapest, were injected with a steroid using the code name of vitamin B-12 which left "tennis ball welts on their butts."[23] Despite Gubner's confirmation of this incident 24 years later, it is corroborated by no further evidence. Tommy attributes his improved performances in Moscow and Budapest to concentrating on the press to lessen stress on his knees and his ability to perform best where stakes were highest. "If you review all the world records I had set, you'll find that I was never able to establish a record within the continental U.S." Another motivation was Kono's love of his country. He recalled that "patriotism plays an important part in my performance. I become emotionally worked up thinking that I am representative of the United States."[24] Frustrated with foreign adversaries benefiting from steroids, Tommy sought to enhance his own lifts by adopting the so-called Olympic or Russian press. "I'm changing my pressing style," he told Hoffman in late 1962, "so I can press as much as I can jerk. If Pluykfelder and Veres, [Louis] Martin and [Ireneusz] Palinski can get away with jerk-presses it's foolish for me to stick to the old style." Yet his average press for the remaining five meets of his light-heavyweight career was only 305.4 pounds, whereas dating back to June of 1961 it was 320.4.[25] These data suggest that the new pressing style no more than drugs was forestalling Kono's descent.

A Heroic Comeback

His next major goal in the path to ascent was the Pan American Games in Sao Paulo, Brazil, in April 1963. "Maybe I'll retire after that," he mused. "But I'll talk it over with my advisor and manager, Dr. (Richard) You, before I take any such action." You's prognosis, however, was hardly encouraging, observing that Tommy's knee ailments were not responding to treatments, and he was sometimes suffering considerable pain. "The knees swell up from time to time and it is necessary to draw fluid from them. But he does not complain. He keeps trying all the time. Kono is one of the most courageous men I have ever seen."[26] He was first suffering from osteo-arthritis in his right knee, Tommy later explained to his brother John, "and because I favored it, my left knee got bad and eventually I had to get an operation on it (1962).... They entered my left knee from behind and took out what they call a 'baker's cyst,' a sac removal which had two small pieces of cartilage floating around within the sac that was irritating the joint. I thought that cured my situation ... but it did not."[27] Andrew Mitsukado concluded that his knee ailments were "the result of constant pressure from lifting excessive weight" and that it was also taking a mental toll. When he was forced to eat four or five times daily to lift in a higher weight class, he became "awfully tired of eating." Mitsukado reckoned that Kono's "prowess and flexibility has made him the most respected and feared lifter in the world," but without a miraculous recovery, it seemed doubtful that he could retain his lead. Tommy agreed, but he wanted one last chance for a gold medal in the 1964 Olympics, if only his knees permitted. His dilemma was "whether he should retire while he is still rated among the best lifters in the world or continue until he has gone over the hill."[28] The ineluctable truth bearing down on Tommy was whether the mental courage he tapped to overcome all physical barriers was now causing injury and invoking retaliation from the body. Would he have the courage to quit?

It hardly seemed possible after he returned from Sao Paulo to a hero's welcome at his hometown of Sacramento. In the course of winning his third Pan American gold medal, he broke the last games record that eluded him when he snatched 292 pounds, exceeding the previous 281 held by Stanczyk. What "thrilled Tommy most of all in Brazil," according to journalist Pat Frizzell, "was carrying the United States flag at opening ceremonies in the jam-packed Sao Paulo stadium, with 70,000 onlookers cheering. 'This was the parade in which a lot of our athletes threw their hats to the spectators and people ran out to grab them,' Kono said. 'It was a wonderful experience.'" So exuberant was Chester Teegarden over his homecoming that he named a weightlifting meet at Sacramento High School the Tommy Kono Championships. "Kono is a lifter worth naming meets after," Frizzell concluded.[29]

Initially Tommy intended not to compete in the national championships in June 1963 and "take a long rest" before deciding whether to compete in Tokyo.[30] Hoffman alleges that Kono was not prepared to lift in the Harrisburg competition and needed a break. He had just competed in two major international championships and was suffering financially from loss of time at work. But the Japanese were sending a four-man delegation with no interpreter.[31] Tommy, who knew some Japanese, responded immediately to Bob's call for help and decided belatedly to defend his title.[32] His training logs, however, reveal a different story. On his last training day in York, three days before the meet, Tommy appeared robust. He recorded poundages of 295 press, 335 clean, 265 snatch, and 375 front squat. His press was "in groove," his snatch form was "good," his high pulls "very good," and his front squat "done rather strongly." He intended to total 1,000 pounds (via 330–290–380) in Harrisburg.[33]

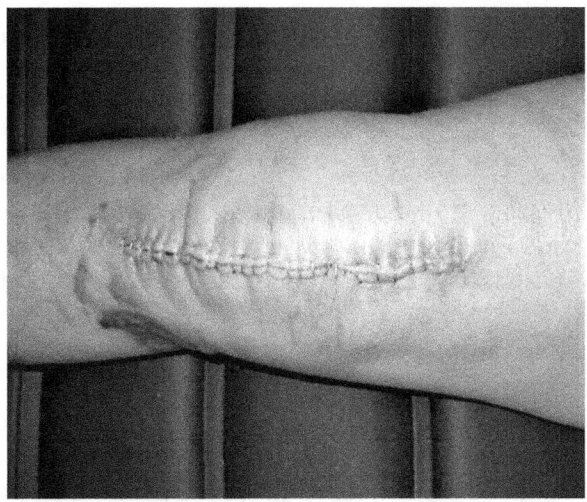

Knee problems, incurred during the climax of his lifting career, required repeated surgeries and eventually impacted his hip, which necessitated a total replacement in 1996.

Lou Riecke, on the other hand, had been preparing for this showdown for several years under the tutelage of Dr. Ziegler with his arsenal of ergogenic aids. From his New Orleans home, Riecke wrote in March 1961 that he now had "Tommy Kono's (whose name hereafter will be referred to as 'Mud') picture on the wall in my garage." A fortnight later, he "cut out of a magazine another picture of our friend, Tommy. This one I have cut down so that only the seat of his pants is left," he told Ziegler. "As I look at it, I say, 'Kono, my friend, *that's your ass!*' and I push a little harder on the bar. This is a form of whimsy on my part, but I mean it."[34] By 1963, after coming a close second in 1961 and failing to total in 1962, Riecke was primed for victory. Unlike his rival, Tommy refused the newfangled methodologies Ziegler was cranking out. He recalled visiting him once in Olney with Bill March and concluded that "Ziegler was a kook."[35]

Having experimented with the controversial expedients lifters were adopting in the early 1960s, steroids and the lean-back press, Tommy resorted to the mental resources that had proven so effective in the 1950s. Armed with confidence derived from his inner strength, he was able to stave off challenges from Riecke in 1961 and 1962 and heroically defend his national title in 1963 for the last time. As Hoffman described it, Tommy needed a 375-pound clean and jerk to tie Riecke and win on lower bodyweight.

> This did not seem possible, for he was out of condition. But what a competitor this man is. The yellow glow of the tiger showed in his eyes. He approached the bar, and three times he walked away from it. Then, with a double superhuman effort he cleaned the weight. It was too much for him. He simply could not jerk it.
>
> One more attempt. Tommy took more time to prepare for this lift than I had ever seen him take before. I was reminded of Pete George's ordeal at the 1948 Olympic Games, when the Olympic gold medal hinged on the 363¾ pounds this 18-year-old school boy weighing only 162 pounds had cleaned. Pete tried so hard to hold that jerk, but failed. Was that to be Kono's fate?
>
> As he stood at the bar, I said to him. "Tommy, you can do it!" He cleaned the bar, and I shouted, "Now jerk it, step forward, bang your feet," and he did just that and was again the champion. Those who saw this lift saw the greatest effort of Kono's long championship career. It was a never-to-be-forgotten performance.[36]

Tommy later admitted "I didn't think I was going to make it. ... But I knew I had to go for broke or else."[37] He reflected that the 1963 nationals was "the last of my good lifting. Having nursed my damaged knees for four years and being plagued by unusual injuries.... I should have realized that these were all signs that my good lifting days were over."[38] Even so, as a display of mind over matter, Harrisburg was his finest hour.[39]

Yet Tommy persisted for the next two years trying to regain his former stature. To this end, he decided on July 3 to "avoid squats to let knees recuperate," substitute front squats, and emphasize high pulls and other less leg stressing exercises. On the 26th he was encouraged that his "knees are not bad & thighs are strong." His confidence consequently increased that he could regain his world title at the 1963 championships in Stockholm. After doing double front squats with 335 pounds and double high pulls with 365 in early August, he was aiming as high as "324, 308 & 385. IT CAN BE DONE!"[40] At Stockholm on September 10, despite an injured thumb, he pressed 297½ but missed all of his snatches with 275½. "I barely squeezed through the 1963 Nationals," Tommy confessed, "but it left me nothing for the World Meet in Stockholm. I was overtrained and fizzled out completely in Sweden."[41] Hoffman attributed his failure as much to age as injury. "Too bad he did not have a flash of his 1958 form and style or the entire story of this year's championships would have been different."[42] Stark realization that his lifting career had reached a plateau must have come in 1963 when, for the fourth and final time, he was runner-up for the coveted Sullivan Award.

Marriage and Maui

Meanwhile, it was time for Tommy to move on with other aspects of life. For the past decade he had devoted himself entirely to weightlifting and was virtually devoid of a social life. Mrs. Harriet Nomura, Dr. You's secretary, whom Tommy called "Ma," stated in 1958 that "Tom has never and still doesn't find time for girls. ... I told him once he's the kind of guy who would turn down the biggest date for weightlifting. And he has agreed—for now."[43] But shortly after moving to Honolulu he met Florence (Flo) Rodriguez who was working at a downtown store in 1956 when he came in. She vividly recalls the moment she saw him. "I thought 'Whoa!' I can still see him in my mind. He was huge, at his peak. I was 17. He was very, *very* impressive. And he was very *very* nice. Very caring."[44] He was "very popular with the girls and very polite." Flo was the fifth of six children of a Portuguese family whose antecedents came to Hawaii in the late 19th century to work the sugarcane plantations. Most of these immigrants were from the Madeira and Azore islands which shared a similar climate and cane-based economy. Flo, who was born in 1937 in Makaweli, Kauai, remembers her family as very poor. Her father was an alcoholic, and her mother put some of the children in an orphanage or with relatives where abuse was not uncommon. They lived in many places. Flo's mother did not want them and even said she wished they were not alive. Flo did not seem to have any feelings about her—just memories of a horrible upbringing. She was also stricken with polio. Although Flo never had to spend time in an iron lung or wear braces, she developed a slight limp.[45] It could be argued that not unlike Tommy, she had to overcome significant disadvantages in her youth, but she became a young woman whose attractiveness Tommy found compelling.

It was not until 1963, however, that Kono was in a position to consider marriage. Since the late 1940s, his whole life centered on training and travel. His succession of Olympic and world championships during the next decade took its toll on his social life and economic well-being. As he entered on the downward course of his lifting career, his thoughts turned to marriage for which greater financial security would be necessary. Social Security records indicate that, from 1951 to 1958 (including two years in the U.S. Army), his yearly income average was $1,330, whereas from 1959 to 1961 he earned an average of $3,942.[46] Although the cost of living was higher in Honolulu than Sacramento, it was time to settle down. It took eight years from the time Tommy and Flo met, but she says they were seeing each other constantly "in between all the others." There were "too many women" for him to make up his mind. He "almost married" one of them, named Leah. "She wanted to marry him. And she came here to Hawaii." But "there were a lot of them," including Cindy Wyatt, a star athlete from Buffalo, New York, whom Dr. You recruited with two other women in 1962 for the track and field program he was nurturing at the University of Hawaii.[47] Only 18, Cindy was attractive and strong and thrived on regular weight workouts with Tommy who wrote an article on her for a 1962 issue of *Strength & Health* where she is shown jerking 225 pounds.[48] As their relationship blossomed, Flo got fed up and migrated to upstate New York where she got a job at the University at Buffalo medical school, lived with her sisters, and had a son named Jamieson.

Eventually, Tommy made up his mind, and according to Flo, while accompanying Cindy to her home in Buffalo in the spring of 1963, he reconnected with Flo. With so many ties to his native culture already obliterated, marrying a fellow Japanese American never seemed a consideration. Tommy's outlook was truly multicultural, reflecting his embrace of American and Hawaiian homogenization. By this time, Flo was residing in Tonawanda, near Buffalo, and they were married on May 4 in Kenmore, New York.[49] Hoffman instilled special meaning to the wedding by providing rings for the bride a few months later. "When I placed the rings on her finger it was such a great surprise to her that her hands were trembling. Her sister and her brother-in-law couldn't get over the size of the 'rock.' It really bowled her over." Tommy then introduced Flo to his lifting friends—Tomita, Tom, Sakata, Ishikawa, and Pete George—at a Honolulu gathering.[50] But with marriage came the realization that weightlifting could no longer be his sole focus. "Looking at my last year's earnings and with the responsibility of a family," he wrote his brothers in early 1964, "I've done some deep thinking." He determined that "my income is just a little better than our expenditure."[51] What impact age, injury, and now family would have on Tommy's hopes for a third Olympic gold medal remained uncertain.

His plans to launch a business venture on the neighboring island of Maui would either resolve or compound his financial concerns by adding another layer of responsibility to his crowded life. For several years, Kono—given his extensive physical culture background—had been thinking about opening a gym. To this end, he had been coaching weightlifters as a volunteer at the Nuuanu YMCA since 1959 and for seven months had been working at Mitsuo Kawashima's health studio (founded in 1947) to learn the business.[52] He even discussed the possibility of collaborating with Mits and Timmy Leong, Hawaii's leading bodybuilder and successful gym owner, to open a large facility jointly. But there were already 18 gyms on Oahu. Then Tommy was approached by Joe Bulgo to run his defunct health studio in Maui that he was unable to manage along with his new position on the Board of Supervisors for the island and singing career. Wary of being hustled into a business arrangement he might later regret, Tommy queried Bulgo with a barrage of questions ranging from equipment, rental fees, and maintenance. Kono estimated it would cost $5,000 to $7,000 to renovate the place.[53] Bulgo's somewhat glib response was reassuring that risk would be minimal. He would rent the facility to Tommy for $125 for the first three months, provide a part-time assistant instructor, and

4. Descent from Olympus

A gathering of great Hawaiian Olympic weightlifters at the beach. The most famous three are standing (from left): pro wrestler and 1948 Olympic silver medalist Harold Sakata, who gained fame as Oddjob in the James Bond film *Goldfinger;* Pete George, whose platform career nearly matched Kono's, and Tommy Kono. The three kneeling men are (from left) Richard Tomita, Richard Tom, and Emerick Ishikawa.

guarantee 115 students within the first two weeks. "My sincere belief is that you will do tremendously well. ... You've got nothing to lose."[54]

For reassurance, Tommy reached out to brothers John and Mike. He explained that he had visited the Valley Island many times for clinics and exhibitions and regarded it as "a 'hot bed' for lifting. I think it's the only place in the U.S. where weightlifting contests are held between high schools!" The facility once had 150 members, and there were no other gyms. Additionally, Hoffman agreed to extend Tommy a long-term loan on equipment and health foods. Bob was very encouraging, saying "he wanted to see me make money, especially after spending so much time in the game." Probably the "best thing" about the gym business, he confided to his brothers, "is that you collect the money *first* before you render service."[55] When Tommy did not hear from them for several weeks, he assumed their displeasure. "I wish that you two would show a little confidence in me," he wrote. With the blessings of Hoffman, Mits, Timmy, and You, however, he was convinced that "it would be impossible not to get at least 100 pupils a month." He decided the gym business would be his best career move. "With my back ground you might say that I was groomed for this turn of events. What other profession or business am I more adapted for?"[56] With equipment already ordered from York and advance notice provided to Dr. You of his resignation, the stage was set for his transition from amateur athlete to professional trainer.

Tommy planned a gala celebration for the grand opening of the Maui Health Center on Friday, May 1, featuring a parade in downtown Wailuku headed by local fitness celebrities and culminating with athletic and posing exhibitions, a teen talent show, and music for dancing. County Chairman Eddie Tam cut the ribbon for the facility located above Clyde's Shoes on Market Street.[57] When asked why he chose to open his business on the Valley Island, Kono responded with characteristic aplomb.

> First, I've always liked Maui. I've been here 18 times and only twice did it cost me anything. The people are most friendly and I have many friends here. Secondly, I feel Maui is ready for a program like this and I have faith in the people here. ... Thirdly I have always wanted to start a gym of my own and pass on the vast knowledge I have gained in my world-wide travels and competitions to someone who's interested. ... What good is knowledge if you can't pass it on to somebody?

He also wanted to work with the schools. Despite his celebrated career and Olympic lifting expertise, Tommy's business would be devoted solely to bodybuilding with no heavy lifting. To assist with these duties and run the center during Tommy's overseas trips, he hired Russell Elwell, a local all-around athlete and bodybuilder of note.[58]

For $37, adults could enroll for a 90-day course that would cost less than 95

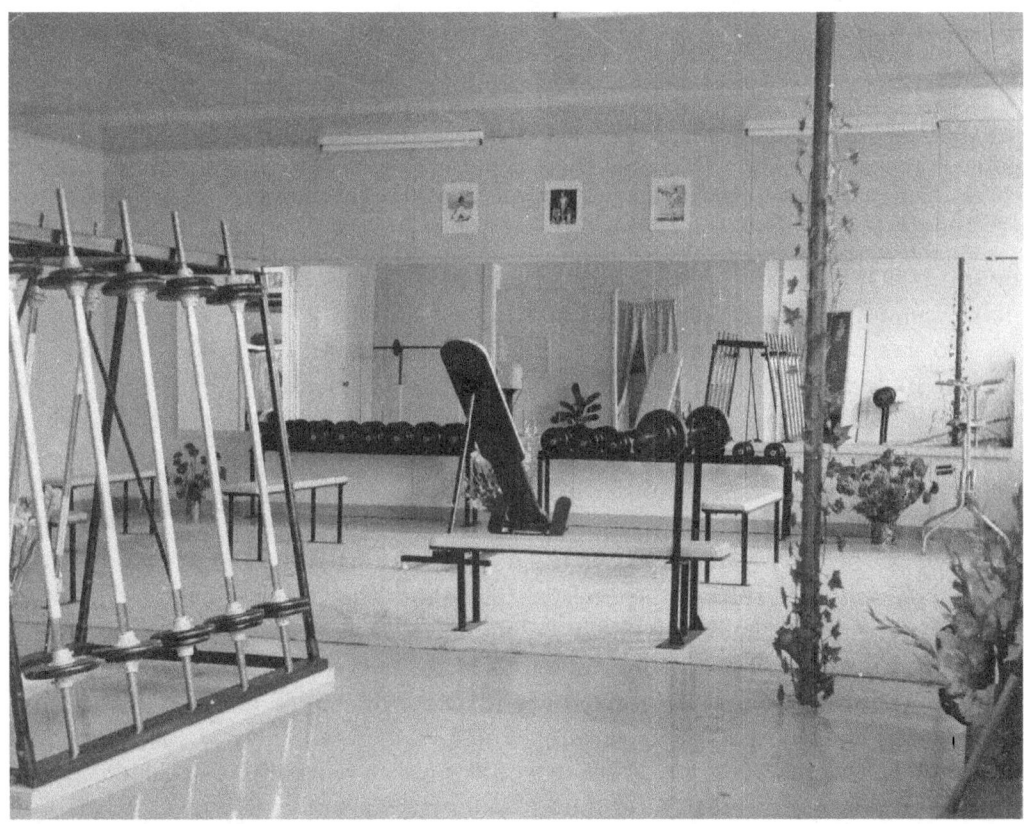

As he transitioned from competition, Tommy, like many other weightlifters, sought to apply his athletic experience to commercial advantage. With encouragement from Bob Hoffman and Dr. You, he opened the Maui Health Center on May 1, 1964. This picture shows how it appeared in September of that year.

cents for three visits a week. "You can use the facilities 6 days a week and it costs no more!" Tommy estimated. The center provided separate departments for men and women, a variety of machine and manual equipment, and supervised personal instruction. The latter included a "Figure Fitness and trim-line for the housewives and office girls overseen by Florence Kono." Tommy's promotional hyperbole was not unlike others in the fitness industry.

> You want to be ALIVE and experience the JOY OF LIVING? Spend 20 minutes at the Maui Health Center and that night you will sleep more soundly and wake up feeling more refreshed than you have in a long time. Spend 3 times out of a week with us, altogether 60 minutes, and see if you don't feel more buoyant and energetic. Spend 3 months with us and notice the DRAMATIC CHANGE in your whole personality.

Testimonials allege that a Kahului mother of five lost 35 pounds and trimmed seven inches off her waist in three months, an overweight Wailuku school girl lost 15 pounds in three weeks, and a slim Wailuku father gained 11 pounds of muscle. "Slim or skinny high school boys gain on the average of 3 to 4 pounds in 2 to 3 weeks and triple their strength in a month time."[59] The records of three Wailuku trainees over three months, however, were less dramatic. A 38-year-old secretary seeking weight reduction lost 7¼ pounds and 2¼ inches from her waist; a 50-year-old housewife seeking hip and thigh reduction, lost one inch on her hips and ¼-inch on her thighs; and a 41-year-old lino-typist seeking general conditioning registered a ½-inch arm growth and ¾-inch waist reduction.[60] Perhaps the most misleading promotional gambit was the implication that "growing exercises" at his health center, along with proper nutrition, would help boys 12 to 17 grow taller. "We have on record boys growing from ½ inch to 1¼ inches within 2 months' time."[61] No mention is made of the natural height-inducing hormones that kick in at puberty.

As a businessman, Kono, given his public-spirited nature, plunged into numerous community activities. Pointing out how similar programs benefited athletes in Honolulu and Hilo schools, he allowed members of the St. Anthony's High School varsity football team to train weekly at his club. Tommy also conducted public lifting, posing, and muscle control performances throughout Maui and neighboring islands; showed free films at the Maui Health Center; and even broadcast a radio show every Friday morning on KNUI (Wailuku) with health advice.[62] On May 1, 1965, coincident with his dedication to youth development, Kono served as chairman of the annual Scout-O-Rama at the War Memorial Center in Wailuku. Displays of traditional scouting skills were complemented by physical fitness demonstrations of Explorer Scouts led by Tommy who fondly recalled his experiences as a Cub in Sacramento prior to World War II and later as a Scout in Tule Lake's troop.[63] Arguably the undertaking that most ingratiated himself with the community and promoted his business was his chairing (with Bulgo) of the annual Community Chest fund drive in the fall of 1965. The campaign had 200 volunteers and was expected to reach $95,000 by Thanksgiving.[64] No doubt Tommy's charitable demeanor as well as his athletic fame contributed to his acceptance throughout the islands and made him a magnet for mainland celebrities. Noted nutritionist Paul Bragg, aged 84, during his three days on Maui, called Kono "the greatest specimen of physical fitness in the world today."[65] Tommy seemed satisfied with his Maui enterprise. It was

After retirement, Tommy was always available to perform impromptu lifting stunts for appreciative audiences.

"a turning point in our lives," he reflected in his 1964 Christmas letter, "the realization of a dream."⁶⁶

Unfulfilled Aspirations

Meanwhile, he was nurturing other dreams. He assured Hoffman in June 1964 that "since moving over here to this island I've developed more enthusiasm for the sport and have a better out-look on my future in weightlifting." Although he would not be attending the national championships in Chicago, he planned to compete in the Olympic tryouts at the New York World's Fair in August as a middleweight. "Busy as I am of late, even with my limited training I feel capable of lifting well. … I intend to funnel all my energy toward a gold medal."⁶⁷ On the other hand, it appears that the multiple distractions in his life were taking a toll. At the tryouts he was pitted against young Joe Puleo, a rising star from Detroit. Tommy had been training hard, noted Peary Rader, "but I feel that perhaps his knee trouble has for some time now cut down on the heavy leg work he should be doing" and that "his legs showed the lack of work both in appearance and in the drive he needed for his lifts." The lifters were nearly even after the press and snatch. With a 5½-pound deficit, Tommy gambled, after both lifters made 341½ pounds in the clean and jerk, that he could win with 352 which Puleo missed twice. Needing it for an Olympic berth, Tommy was

> confronted with the lift of his life. ... He paced the floor and concentrated a long time, then after a great fight made the clean and struggled upward and made his leg drive ... he held it and struggled for a long time to lock out his arms but slowly and surely the weight literally crushed him to the floor. It was a bitter moment for Tommy and everyone felt his disappointment.[68]

Puleo, of course, was elated, but whether he or Kono would be selected for the team was determined by a final Olympic tryout two weeks later in York. Both lifters made 352-pound clean and jerks and improved overall, with Puleo out-lifting Kono by 11 pounds, but neither of them was chosen for the eight-man team to go to Tokyo. Puleo qualified as an alternate, but for Tommy, it was the sad end of his Olympic dreams.[69]

But it did not dampen his competitive spirit. "This is the last one," he insisted during his last workout prior to leaving for the 1965 Senior Nationals in Los Angeles in June. "Tommy makes no secret about it that training alone is no fun," reported Wayne Tanaka from Maui.[70] Yet Kono showed no lack of positivity. A fortnight prior to the nationals he hoped to press 340, snatch 300, and clean and jerk 380 for a 1,020-pound total at 178 bodyweight.[71] What he actually did on June 12 was set a new light-heavyweight meet press record of 330 pounds, and he nearly made a 290 snatch. After Gary Cleveland completed his final clean and jerk with 360, Tommy, in a desperate attempt to win on lesser bodyweight, tried 380 pounds which Hoffman recalled he had made in 1954 in Copenhagen when he was 11 years younger and five pounds heavier. "Although he wanted the weight badly and although the 'tiger' was in his eyes, the determination which had brought him so many victories was not quite enough on this occasion. So, after two dramatic attempts which had the audience on the edge of their seats, Tommy had to settle for what looked like a sure second place." But Puleo clean and jerked 385 pounds, which relegated Kono to third and an announcement of his retirement. In an emotional speech, Tommy congratulated his adversaries and thanked everyone who made his career possible. "No doubt everyone had a lump in his throat at the conclusion of this message," observed Rader, who called Kono "one of, if not the greatest athlete America has produced." For Hoffman, he was "one of the greatest lifters of all time" who would "never be forgotten."[72]

That Tommy experimented with steroids and a technique that corrupted the strength ideal and ultimately changed the face of Olympic lifting should not detract from his reputation. It was an age of innocence when neither steroids nor the Olympic press were illegal or seriously stigmatized and could have had no effect on Kono's previous victories. Emphasis should be placed on his unprecedented achievement of eight consecutive Olympic and world championship titles before the advent in the U.S. of anabolic drugs. Coping with a beleaguered body—plus the inevitable age-related decrement in performance—is probably the most difficult psychological adjustment a great athlete must make, especially after a decade of euphoric triumphs. Yet Tommy faced it bravely, calling it "the realities of life."[73] He confessed, even after two decades, that he "found it difficult" to quit. "Everytime I'd hear the barbells clanging, I was like an old firehorse. I'd get all worked up and had the urge to make a comeback."[74] Tommy attributed his denouement in Los Angeles to loss of concentration, the intangible quality that had always insured victory. He came to this realization, according to reporter Ann Miller, when he "went down to pick up the bar" and "wondered where his 2-year-old son was. 'That's when I realized. Hey it's time to retire,'" he concluded.[75] It was a Zen moment.

II

FROM AMATEUR TO PROFESSIONAL

5

Olympic Coach

> "At the Olympics, the physical condition of the athletes is as close to perfect as human beings can get. The difference between a trip to the medal stand and a quiet plane ride home may be all in the mind."[1]
> —Adam Rogers, "Zen and the Art of Olympic Success"

During the mid-sixties, Tommy's career was progressing on other fronts. Training housewives, businessmen, and students had provided satisfaction for a while, but he craved the excitement of competing at the highest level. He "soon grew tired of the gym" which was not challenging enough. "I thought all of my knowledge in 16 years of weightlifting was going to go down the drain if I don't use it."[2] To this end, he began to negotiate with Mexican weightlifting authorities as early as January 1965 about coaching the national team for the Mexico City Olympics in 1968. In a letter with his resume, Tommy assured Federation president René de la Cerda that his "performance is unmatched in the sport of weightlifting by any other lifter, past or present" and that his knowledge encompassed "every facet of training and conditioning, technique and style of lifting" as well as nutritional needs. For his services, he expected a three-year contract that would include a $3,000 advance, a $1,000 monthly salary, traveling expenses (with per diem compensation) for him and his family, medical coverage, and no more than 30 coaching hours a week. Tommy felt these terms were justified inasmuch as he would be leaving "a growing business with a very good income" and uprooting his family from the comfort of their home to an unfamiliar environment. But he was confident he could "develop a powerful Mexican team capable of winning world and Olympic honors and its team members establish many world records."[3]

The Mexican Adventure

With the acceptance of Tommy's terms by Mexican authorities, he quickly put his share of the Maui Health Center up for sale for $4,500 and departed on December 1, 1965, for Mexico City. Although he had resided in Maui barely 18 months, there was no resentment over his departure from his "dream" job, just expressions of pride and joy for his continued success. He was feted to a testimonial dinner by the Sportsmen Maui club and praised by congressional representative Patsy Mink for enabling Hawaii to share this enhancement of his reputation.[4] Tommy had intended to attend the Mexican National Championships in December but encountered unexpected delays. Unable to secure an airline ticket because of holiday bookings, he bought a station wagon which was under repair for three days, then had to wait several days for his visa to be cleared in El Paso. Kono and his wife were ill-prepared for the hardships entailed by the 2,100-mile journey to Mexico City. A newspaper account captured their epic ordeal which entailed unloading and loading their luggage each night to prevent theft. "The entire Kono family, including Jamie, 3, and Jo Ann, then two months old, shared the distressing 'never again' experience as they encountered numerous problems before and during the trip drove through rain, snow and hail storm over rough, mountainous terrain, and spent 15 nights, including Christmas and New Year's Eve."[5] At the Olympic site, Tommy joined other foreign coaches, hired by the Mexican government to beef up its teams, including three Americans to coach track and field and gymnastics. The weightlifting site consisted of 20 platforms, 30 Olympic barbells, and 30 extra bars. "It is probably the most used place at the Center," he observed. "The coaches here are all very firm believers of the use of weights. The wrestlers, basketball players and both the men and women volleyball teams, gymnasts and the cyclists use weights as part of their regular training. The field men use weights too." Tommy seemed satisfied with these arrangements and "lucky" to work with two federation officials who were "ex-lifters, young and progressive thinkers. ... Whatever my needs for the Center I've been able to get." Admittedly his Mexican employment was a temporary "leave of absence," but for Kono it "was so attractive that I could not refuse."[6]

Tommy was no less pleased with his coaching responsibilities and the response of his charges to his pedagogical principles. Initially the language barrier seemed insuperable, so he compensated by using sign language and his talent for drawing pictures. "The first thing I did was request a big blackboard—classroom size," he recollected. "Then I was able to illustrate the proper lifts and form."[7] Another challenge was his lifters' lack of technique in executing the quick lifts, insufficient power in the basic muscle groups, and a mental barrier that hampered their capabilities. Kono addressed these deficiencies during two three-week courses, after which "all the lifters showed dramatic improvement." It was most evident at a Central American Games Team Trial held at Montezuma Gym in February where two lifters, bantamweight Manuel Mateos and middleweight Felipe Pacheco, established six national records. Then at an invitational meet with leading lifters from the United States in Mexico City in March, three Mexicans, Mateos, Pacheco, and lightweight Mauro Alanis, set six more national records in besting the Americans in three weight classes. "To say that all the boys from the Olympic Center did well is putting it lightly," Kono reckoned. What made it a proud moment for his coaching is that Mateos "did a rare thing in the sport of weightlifting by executing nine perfect lifts in an international contest," and Pacheco overcame a 12½-kilo deficit to defeat veteran Pete Talluto. "Probably the most difficult thing to overcome in sports is to be far behind in points and to make up the difference in an all-out effort at the very end." Progress charts Tommy kept over his first four months showed that virtually all lifters improved. Major technical faults had been corrected, strength had increased, and most importantly a "positive attitude" had emerged.[8]

5. Olympic Coach

Tommy was convinced that an important ingredient to his athletes' progress was nutrition. In a memorandum titled "Food Supplements—An Essential Part of An Athlete's Diet," he argued that unlike a normal person, an athlete "requires more energy output, speed, timing, endurance" and "should have additional vitamins and minerals in his daily diet." Kono cited numerous weightlifting powers that supplied team members with food supplements, including Japan and Russia where vitamins were injected "directly into the blood stream so their athletes are assured that all vital elements are absorbed instead of going through the slow process of digestion and assimilation." Tommy explained that concentrated food supplements promoted dietary efficiency by taking up less space in the digestive tract, taking less time to absorb, and providing an alternative to ordinary food that accumulates bodily waste and hinders performance.

> I have had the pleasure of working with Dr. Richard You, two times U.S. Olympic team physician, for almost nine years and during that time I have seen him handle many hundreds of athletes and supervise their nutritional needs. ... I do not claim to be an expert on nutrition but I know from my own personal experience that when I consume more than the necessary amount of food supplements than a *normal person* requires, I do perform much better on the weightlifting platform in both training and in competition. I find that I can train harder and longer and recuperate much faster.

Kono believed "ordinary foods are for ordinary people." The body was constantly tearing down and rebuilding cells. "To assure ourselves that we create the most

After winning the bid to host the 1968 Olympic Games, Mexican officials wanted to hire the world's greatest weightlifter to coach their team. Not able to communicate effectively in Spanish, Tommy used his drawing skills, mainly with stick figures, to instruct his charges.

efficient new cells and body we must supply it adequately and even to an excessive amount in the essential nutrients we need." For Mexico to produce super athletes, the essential ingredient was food supplements to help them "run faster, jump higher and farther and hoist more weight without unduly stressing their bodies."[9] Tommy later admitted that "one of the things that made coaching difficult here in Mexico was that the boys I had at first knew very little about nutrition" and were "not in good physiological condition." One of them took nearly a week to recover from a normal training session.[10]

Although Mexican weightlifters were no match for the super athletes of other nations at the East Berlin world championships in October 1966, Tommy was pleased that they "performed well" and brought "favorable publicity to Mexico."[11] Perhaps the most important takeaway was it allowed Mexican lifters to look and learn from some of the world's best athletes. What interested Tommy most was "the training sessions where we can learn much by watching." Therefore, he spent as much time as possible "in the large training hall which housed 10 lifting platforms observing the various top lifters go through their paces."[12] Although the totals of his six team members fell short of what they made at the national championships, his year-end charts showed improvements since he started coaching in January.[13] At the nationals, the nine boys he trained at the Centro Deportivo Olímpico Mexicano set 29 personal records, seven of which were national records and one a junior world record. He could proudly say that of the 38 contestants in the 1966 national championships in eight classes, "lifters from C.D.O.M. won 5 first, 2 seconds, 1 third and 1 fifth place."[14] What's more, future prospects looked bright, judging from the key areas of "Attitude Toward Training" and "Competitive Spirit."[15]

"The Mexican team is shaping up now," Tommy confided to Hoffman in March 1967. He looked forward to the Central American Championships in Cuba and the Pan American Games in Winnipeg where "Mexico should have a very strong team for several boys are making amazing improvements."[16] Buoyed by optimism that his coaching was making a difference, Tommy requested an increase in compensation to $1,250 per month for the duration of 1968 and return fare to Hawaii on fulfilling his contract. It was duly approved on May 26 by Dr. Josué Sáenz, president of the Comité Olímpico Mexicano.[17] Although Tommy attributed this increase to his athletes' "continued improvement" and fulfilling his contract obligations, he later admitted that the U.S. State Department was supplementing his salary with monthly deposits to his American bank account.[18] Although this might appear to be an exorbitant income, especially compared to the lower wages and cost of living in Mexico, the average monthly expenses for the Konos from January to May of 1967 were $810, which did not include $250 a month for servants.[19] It seemed imperative for Tommy to seek additional sources of income.

The Idea Man

To this end, he relied on his credibility with the weightlifting community and Bob Hoffman who had helped him climb the ladder of success. "Without your personal aid I would have never been able to accomplish any of the achievements," he told Bob in 1962. "I really thank God the day my two friends introduced me to the barbells and your courses at the relocation camp in 1944."[20] Tommy was always intensely loyal to Hoffman, and attachment to York remained the lodestar of his post-competitive ambitions. His Maui studio had always featured York equipment and supplements. To promote the health and well-being of athletes and the public and to strengthen his bond to York, Tommy devised two products—a Slim-Trim Waistband and a T.K. Knee Band in 1964.[21] The former, he explained, was "comfortable to wear, made of special quality material and built to last indefinitely. It would appeal to overweight persons who needed to reduce their waistline and need lower back and abdomen support." The knee band would give support, improve circulation, and "promote healing of injured knees."[22] Lacking the means to turn his ideas into reality, Kono worked out an agreement for York to produce and market the bands.

Many months passed, however, with no response to his queries about progress. By early 1967, Tommy was growing impatient, wondering if production had started. "If you haven't don't wait too long, Bob, for even tho' any new venture takes time, time is also money."[23] Part of the delay stemmed from Terpak's lukewarm opinion of the bands. To allay concerns about their sales potential, Tommy, calling himself "the idea man," suggested that Bob place ads in *Athletic Journal, Sports Illustrated,* and other leading publications. "Even a small ad. It would pay in the long run to be the *first* to put it on the market." Also, testimonials from use of the bands would be good advertisement. And to ensure customer satisfaction and minimize returns, Kono suggested modifications to maximize comfort and inclusion of instructions with each sale.[24] To provide more incentive and further link his fortunes to York, Tommy wrote reassuringly of his personal commitment and appreciation for all Hoffman had done for weightlifting and himself.

> I am extremely grateful for all this and in return I would like to help you and your work as much as possible. I'm a professional now so I can endorse nearly everything in the line of weight training. I've been approached in the past to endorse an Olympic set, write [a] testimonial on a certain brand [of] protein and have been approached to write articles by another muscle magazine company and have refused them all ... simply because I value my connection with you and York more than the green stuff. Loyalty is something that cannot be bought.[25]

What defined his future relationship with York Barbell was that Tommy had too much faith in Bob Hoffman, saying money did not matter. His loyalty, gratitude, and guilelessness enabled the company to appropriate Kono's ideas and capitalize on his lack of business experience.

Reminiscent of Hoffman's pitch in "The Most Important Article I Ever Wrote" when he launched isometrics in 1961, Tommy announced "A Major Breakthrough in the Field of Weight Training" in the June 1967 issue of *Strength & Health*.[26] Although it stemmed from the "sore knees" that hampered Kono's training and ended his weightlifting career, the breakthrough was no longer branded Tommy's "Slim-Trim Waist Band" and "T.K. Knee Band," but as "Bob Hoffman (BH) Knee and Waist Bands." Marketing the product was made to fit the mythical image of Bob as father of weightlifting. Hence it was Bob, whom Tommy personally, albeit inaccurately, credited for devising a cure for lifters' sore knee woes.

> The invention, or solution, resulted after many experiments and consultations with Olympic coach Bob Hoffman. If there is a new development in lifting you can be sure that Bob Hoffman either originated the idea and/or collaborated in its development. He was the first to offer to the public the Simplified System of Barbell training that has become the standard in weight training ... and, more recently, the formulator of the system of training that took the world by storm, the Bob Hoffman System of Functional Isometric Contraction. And now he is announcing the Bob Hoffman (BH) Knee and Waist Bands.

This Bob-boosting charade was enhanced by Hoffman himself in an article which traced the idea's inception back to his childhood reading about Biblical heroes, such as David and Goliath who were armored and "girded for strength" going into battle thousands of years ago. "The point of this article," according to Bob, was to tell readers "about a *new and modern way* to 'gird for strength,' the same method that is now being used by the members of the York Barbell Club." This "breakthrough" was an age-old practice still used by world champion lifters and made possible through a "wonder material" provided by modern technology. It was "so scarce for a time that one BH Knee Band was passed around from [Russ] Knipp, [Bob] Bednarski, [Bill] Starr, [Tommy] Suggs, and Bob Hoffman."[27] Bob's underlying point was that he would receive virtually all of the credit and his company most of the profits from Kono's idea.

Advertisements featuring the BH Knee and Waist Bands continued to appear in *Strength & Health* from July 1967 to January 1972 complemented by ads for these products in York's sister magazine, *Muscular Development*. From December 1968 to September 1970 York also advertised "Hoffman's Slim-Trim Waist Band," thus appropriating Tommy's original title and idea. Further promotion was provided by photos of leading lifters in contests wearing the knee bands. Bob Bednarski, Walter Imahara, and Joe Puleo were among the first to appear in the black rubberized gear. In a pictorial spread of the Empire State Invitational Meet in December 1967, five of the 16 lifters are wearing them.[28] How many knee and waist bands York sold cannot be determined, but from 1967 to 1972, roughly the time they were marketed, there was a dramatic upsurge in sales.[29] Monthly averages nearly tripled during this period.

1966—$215,243   1968—$293,078   1970—$451,813   1972—$616,972
1967—$238,032   1969—$335,068   1971—$540,835

Unfortunately, Tommy received little compensation for his ingenuity. It was only after the sale of 20,000 or 30,000, Tommy recalls, that he received a check for $800 for only one or 2 percent of total sales.[30] Use of the BH knee bands eventually tapered off. In a five-page *Strength & Health* pictorial of the 1977 Senior Nationals, 18 of the 27 lifters are wearing knee wraps but none resemble those Tommy invented.[31]

Still, as weightlifting coach for Mexico for the 1968 Olympics, Tommy remained the "idea man" for York, which he hoped would be his eventual destination. Living in Mexico required many personal and cultural adjustments, including learning Spanish and providing for his family. He explained to Hoffman that Flo was continuing her education to be a teacher, and it cost $250 every 10 weeks for classes at the University of the Americas. "Getting an American education in a foreign country is very expensive, so you can see the 'idea-man' has to keep coming up with ideas." Further ingratiate himself with York, Tommy submitted newspaper clippings on health issues for Bob's future articles and addresses of Olympic officials he believed should receive promotional copies of *Strength & Health*.[32] Also, to keep his name alive with York and the lifting community and to generate additional income, Tommy became a contributor to the magazine.

He began by writing educational articles based on knowledge acquired as a lifter and coach. As he later explained in *Championship Weightlifting*, the seeds for his coaching career were planted in the typescript he had prepared in 1953–54 on how to train for the press. Then, as an "assistant coach," he helped groom American lifters backstage at world and Olympic championships, thereby contributing to America's golden age of weightlifting not only by his performances but also by assisting others. As Mexico's national coach, he was enabled by his travels to study training methods of international teams and apply this knowledge to his charges. He also used his camera "to capture the critical moment of good technique. ... With a relatively basic background in the science of physics, some knowledge of anatomy and a smattering of kinesiology, I was able to analyze the Olympic lifting movements so it became a logical sequence of applied leverage."[33] His knowledge was reflected in articles on food supplements, the snatch and clean and jerk, Cuban weightlifting, and the 1966 world championships.[34] No doubt as a payment-in-kind, the idea-man was allowed a 2"×3" ad in *Strength & Health* for multi-color decals of hyper-muscular weightlifters and bodybuilders that could be ordered from him for $1.00.[35] What Tommy wanted, of course, was regular compensation. In March 1967 he informed Hoffman that he had not received payment for two months. "In fact, I haven't received any kind of statement from Mike [Dietz] for all the articles and photos of mine which was [sic] published in the September, October, November, February and March issues. ... I know York has always been good on its words but I'd like to see some proof of my work."[36] Despite this annoyance, Kono authored six more articles prior to leaving Mexico on the anatomy of a weightlifter, Russian lifters, and the 1967 Little Olympics in Mexico City, noting that "the Russians have surpassed the land of the red, white and blue by virtue of its number of participants in the sport and by their caliber and organization."[37] Tommy was always patriotic, but the experience of living abroad seemed to enhance a sense of loyalty to his country and York Barbell.

Manuel Mateos

Kono appeared no less loyal to his newly adopted country as expressed in his 1967 year-end report. He took special pride in Manuel Mateos who, as a 15-year-old bantamweight, twice broke a junior world press record (Mexico's first in any sport), defeated Jack Hill, Jr., in the 1966 American Teenage Nationals, and finished second to veteran Walter Imahara in the 1967 Pan Am Games as a featherweight. At the former instance, Hoffman noted that "Mateos, well coached by Tommy Kono" along with two pages of lifting and dietary instructions, forged ahead as the meet progressed.[38] Prior to the Pan American Games in Winnipeg, Tommy reminded Bob to bring some translated Russian material on nutrition for two Mexican sports physicians named Zapata and Saavedra. "These doctors here are in great need of this type of information. Incidentally, while on the subject of nutrition I hope you will take along a few extra canisters of Super H-Proteen and Energol to Winnipeg." He also wanted to "discuss further some ideas I have for York. As I said before, Bob, I'm an idea man."[39] Along with Mateos, two of Tommy's other lifters did well enough to earn Mexico ninth place overall and qualify three entrants for the 1968 Olympics.[40] In lieu of a 1967 world championships, Mexico hosted a pre–Olympics in October where Kono's entrants did well, placing sixth, seventh, 10th, and 11th against stout international competition.[41]

In preparation for the Olympics in early 1968, Kono divided his lifters into three groups where he could address such issues as balance and flexibility, body extension, positioning, pulling, paraphernalia, and pressing technique, necessarily adhering to the controversial four-part Olympic Press which enabled lifters to employ legs and hips. He advised his charges to follow a light-medium-heavy training schedule—going heavy only once a week and always working at just 90 to 95 percent capacity to ensure quick recovery. "Greatest improvement," he believed, "can be made if your workouts are scientifically arranged" and "you enjoy the training. This can be achieved only if the workout is short, fast & interesting."[42] To facilitate progress and promote the Olympics, Tommy arranged a tour of Mexican towns which he deemed "a great success. The boys learned a lot about giving exhibitions and we received a lot of publicity," he told Hoffman. He next arranged for the visits of seven leading Russians led by Vorobiev in January and escorted his own best lifter, Mateos, on a European tour of Hungary, Poland, and both Germanys in March "to groom him for the platform in October."[43] By August, Tommy reported to a weightlifting official in Curacao that "young Mateos is progressing nicely. Last month at the Mexican Nationals he made 115, 102½ and 143½ [kilos] for a 360 [792 pounds] total. ... A couple weeks later we went to Los Angeles and he came through for another world jr. Record with a Press of 119½ kilos."[44]

At the Olympics, Mateos pressed another junior world record of 120 kilos, despite strict officiating, equaled his best previous total of 360 kilos, edged out three European lifters who had previously outlifted him, and did better than all lifters from the western hemisphere in his class. Impressed by his eighth place finish, British reporter George Kirkley believed "this lad seems assured of featuring strongly in future world championships."[45] Tommy's other featherweight entry did not fare as well. Owing to strict officiating, all of Miguel Medina's presses were disqualified. But lightweight Mauro Alanis, a veteran of three Olympics, placed 15th which to Hoffman, who was head referee, "represented a great deal of improvement. The Mexican team was using the Hoffman Liver Tablets and were so enthusiastic about them that they gave me a Mexican sombrero which was so big" he had to "send it home with the team luggage."[46] Tommy, too, was pleased by his lifters' progress, and in his report to Josué Sáenz, president of the Comité Olímpico Mexicano, expressed the belief that the many thousands of dollars spent on the promotion and development of the sport had created a "solid foundation" for Mexican lifters to do well in future international competitions. "If a 4-year program is planned now and followed through, I am positive that Mexico can make a wonderful showing in weightlifting at Munich, Germany, in 1972." Perhaps the most positive result was its impression on the United States government which justified his monthly subsidy. American Ambassador Fulton Freeman expressed pride in the "outstanding work" Kono had done "not only with the National Federation but also at the National Physical Education School and at the various Binational Centers where you conducted weightlifting and physical conditioning clinics." As a representative of the American Specialist Program, Tommy had been not only an "excellent coach" but a "gentleman" who exemplified the attributes of a goodwill ambassador.[47]

Teutonic Anxieties

The possibility that Kono might extend his Olympic coaching career to West Germany prior to the Munich Olympics first occurred in a conversation with former German national coach Wolfgang Peter, who asked him at the 1966 world championships if he was willing to conduct clinics at sports centers throughout the country. Peter even secured appropriations for a month's salary equivalent to what he was making in Mexico plus airfare.[48] Although Tommy was unable to secure a temporary release from his Mexico contract, this encounter led to a brief visit to West Germany in April 1968 and substantive conversations with Siegfried Perrey, director of the German Sports Federation, who visited Mexico before the Olympics. Tommy described Perrey to Peter as "a 'go-getter' in every way," an impression that helped him become "extremely interested in trying to secure a coaching job in Europe." In recent years there were two countries he judged most desirable. "First was Japan for obvious reason," he told Peter, and the other was West Germany. "Ever since the time I was stationed in Germany I've always wanted to spend more time there. This past European trip convinced me even more that I like the country and its people." What made this proposition seem possible was his assumption that the Bureau of Educational and Cultural Affairs of the State Department in Washington would subsidize his position in Germany, much as it did in Mexico. To this end, Perrey appealed to bureau chief Edward Re for financial assistance, stressing Kono's qualifications and the "tight budget" of the German Weightlifting Federation. "We are most anxious to have him."[49]

It was a strong and logical appeal, and Tommy was anxious to assume the position.[50] His anxiety was evident in a letter to Peter where he described coaches and lifters in Germany as "very intelligent" and the sport's future as "very promising." In Mexico, on the other hand, there were "only three Mexicans who really understand the technical side of lifting. The normal schooling of the lifters are about the equivalent of the 7th grade and their trait are such that they wish to reach only a certain level and no more." But the proposal did not sufficiently weigh the Cold War international politics at stake. Mexico was a third world country on the southern border of the United States which required special assistance to stave off the threat of

Communism so prevalent in the region. West Germany, alternatively, was a Western democracy with a robust economy and site of numerous American military installations. Oblivious to strategic matters, Tommy explained to Perrey on July 30 that his salary in Mexico had increased from $1,000 to $1,250 per month and that his German compensation should be roughly the same with a State Department supplement. By November 30, he was allegedly receiving $1,450 from Mexico and was requesting $1,500 ($18,000 pa) from the Germans.[51] He deeply desired a coaching position with the German republic, but he was approved for the standard rate of only 2,500 ($9,125) Deutsche Marks per year.[52]

Nevertheless, Kono was convinced that "if Washington, D.C. is approached properly I will receive the remaining difference from them." Acting on this assumption, he accepted a one-year contract to move his family to Germany and start coaching on February 1, 1969, at the sport school in Hennef near Cologne. In succeeding weeks Tommy appealed to both governments for increased compensation, citing his family's unsettled living quarters and need to focus full attention on his lifters.[53] Especially in light of these personal and financial commitments, Tommy was surprised and dismayed to learn on March 3 that the Bureau of Educational and Cultural Affairs would not be able to assist his project. Funds, according to program officer Martha Geesa, "have been so drastically reduced that we are able to carry out only a few of the projects given high priority by our Foreign Service posts." An embassy official in Bad Godesberg confirmed this disappointing news, explaining that specialist programs were "severely cut, particularly for Europe." None were being subsidized.[54] Even an appeal to Hawaiian senator Daniel Inouye was unsuccessful. Although he was impressed by Tommy's achievements and wanted to improve German-American relations, Inouye encountered "severe pressures" by Congress to reduce government costs which were exacerbated by inflationary pressures. It was the same story at the State Department, despite repeated efforts by Tommy and Perrey to reverse the tide of government resistance.[55]

Meanwhile, Kono was buoyed by the prospects of his new coaching assignment. "The West Germans are so up to date," he told Jim Easterwood of the *Honolulu Star-Bulletin*. The coaches even meet monthly to discuss technique. "In Mexico I had to start from scratch."[56] In May 1969 he admitted to a *Stars and Stripes* reporter that unlike his previous assignment, he had "far more talent with which to work here in Germany." Especially impressive was the Turnund Sportverein in Nurnberg, he reported to Deutscher Athleten-Bund president Walter Lippold. The weightlifting area was the largest he had so far encountered in Germany with nine Olympic bars and six platforms.[57] Yet repeated appeals to German and American officials for financial relief over six months were in vain. In desperation, Kono explained his plight to Josef Neckermann, a member of the West German Olympic Committee.

> My gross income of 2,500 DM after taxes and health insurance amounts to 1,777.25 DM a month. I have two school age children, 7 and 4, who are in the Deutsche Schule because it cost over 700.00 dollars per year in the American school. In addition, my wife is five months pregnant and that means additional expenses. ... Now it is time for the renewal of my contract and I am perplexed. My sport, hobby and whole life is weightlifting and I enjoy my

coaching job but I cannot become as deeply involved as I would like if I am beset with financial problems that concerns the welfare of my family.[58]

These untoward circumstances were made less bearable by unanticipated coaching difficulties and by frequent travel and absences from home. At a lehrgang (training camp) in the resort town of St. Moritz, his lifters suffered from myriad debilitating afflictions, including sore wrists, inflamed tonsils, ripped abdominal and leg muscles, a shin laceration, a swollen ankle, toothache, and "too many dianabols." Nor did the cold weather, snow, and tourist-driven prices lift anyone's spirits. Tommy had to wear long underwear, double sox, and a warm turtle-neck sweater. "There were just too may inconveniences to make it a successful lehrgang," Tommy reported to his superiors. He was also home sick. "Last nite I dreamed of Shirley Jones," he told Flo. "I don't know how come but it was also in color! I guess I miss you that much."[59]

Nor were Tommy's lifters offering satisfaction on the lifting platform. At the European championships in Sofia in June 1971, 123 lifters from 22 nations competed. West Germany finished sixth with seven points, behind the Soviet Union (54), Poland (33), Hungary (33), Bulgaria (23), and Sweden (14). Germany's only bright spot was its talented super-heavyweight Rudolf Mang who placed third. Much the same outcome prevailed at a dual junior (ages 20 and under) competition between West Germany and Bulgaria on September 4 where the latter won seven out of nine weight divisions and outlifted the Germans by 3,187.5 to 2,900 kilograms.[60] It is not surprising that Tommy's initial excitement about his coaching assignment began to wear thin. During a brief visit to Honolulu, he admitted to a reporter that he was "tired of running. He wants to come home. 'I'm ready to settle down. My family needs a more secure place.'"[61] These feelings were accentuated by the dismal performance of the three West German lifters at the 1971 world championships in Lima, Peru, who placed 12th of 20, 12th of 22, and ninth of 18.[62]

No less disconcerting was his inability to train regularly. On November 7, he started doing technique work on the Olympic lifts with a goal of reaching a 900-pound total and possibly sparking a comeback. But his workouts stressed mainly bench presses and squats with as many as five repetitions of 253 and 352, respectively. On November 15 Tommy admitted that he "can't train as in original plan cause coaching comes first & I can't concentrate purely on my training. I need longer time for the improvement I wanted. Decide not to push myself but rather train the way I feel and use wts that are comfortable."[63] At age 40, he must have realized that neither his body nor mind could withstand the stress of heavy training, but in readjusting priorities at mid-life, he was encountering some unexpected obstacles with his coaching.

In the wake of these failures to live up to expectations, it is hardly surprising that Kono's supervisor, Otto Schumann, expressed "great dissatisfaction" on November 7 with both athletes and coaches. Tommy, however, refused to tolerate this reprimand.

> You hire two coaches [Tommy and Lothar Spitz] and tell us we have complete responsibility and then you make all the decisions. We have the title and the position but our hands are tied

because we are like puppets with members of the Vorstand and even outsiders being allowed to pull the strings. Then when something goes wrong we have to take the blame for it. ... Everybody is screaming for results but this cannot be accomplished with everyone looking for someone to blame.

Tommy complained that his superiors were too apt to rely on "book" coaching and disinclined to accept methods advocated by their coaches. "I refuse to accept the blame for the poor showing of the lifters," he told Schumann, "when I am only expected to take orders that are the result of closed meetings and discussions." He was especially upset over his loss of respect among the weightlifters and his identity as national trainer. "I am under pressure from above and below and I find that these working conditions are impossible. So impossible in fact that if it is to our mutual satisfaction I should like to make this letter one of resignation to be effective as of January 31, 1972."[64]

Underpaid and underappreciated in his West German coaching assignment, Tommy vented his frustrations on his supervisor, Otto Schumann.

York Aspirations

Meanwhile, Tommy was pursuing another form of escape that would keep his hopes and prestige alive in the international community. Although he had continued to bombard Hoffman with ideas and information, he was disappointed that York had not fulfilled its part of its knee and waist band agreement. Perhaps to induce a response, he observed to Bob on September 9, 1969, that Weider had "joined the bandwagon" and that he had been approached by "several companies to endorse their product and work with them to get percentage. In all fairness to you I have held off the decision but I will decide by the end of this month." Also, Adidas approached Tommy about designing a new weightlifting shoe. "As I have said before I get some pretty good ideas and I would like to work with you for York but sometime this becomes rough when my good nature is taxed too much."[65] Not only did Tommy not abandon York, but he continually sought closer association. In October, he proposed an experiment with the identical twins Otto and Ewald Spitz whom he had encountered in coaching. The difference in muscularity between Ewald, who had been training "hit-or-miss" with weights for six years, and Otto, who was a runner, was striking. "My project," he explained to Bob, "is to develop the skinny one to equal the muscular one in one year and get him to equal the lifting ability (770 as a lightwt.) in another year with proper technique and correct training program. In other words, develop him in 2 years what it took the other 6 years." Tommy's experiment was successful partly because he persuaded Hoffman to supply food supplements by military (APO) mail. Although Ewald also made progress, Kono reported that in "13 months of training Otto made exceptional gains." But the real story was one of commitment.[66]

At this point the big idea that had been pullulating in Kono's mind for decades finally surfaced. Although his contract with the West German team did not expire until January 1972, he was willing to resign a year earlier to be part of the York gang. "I think I can fit into any of your departments," he told Terpak in October 1970, which

> goes into a little of public relation, magazine, production, clerical and business end as well as the coaching side. Your "research and development" sounds interesting if it would be challenging and with a good future position in the company. I want to be productive, Johnny, and I want to learn about the business. I think you'd have to admit that I've always been interested in the York Barbell business-wise and my ambition has always been to work for the York Barbell Company if the salary was good. ... What would be a reasonable amount for a person of my background, 40 years old, married and with 3 kids? In Mexico I started with 13 grand a year and in my last year I was earning 15 grand. Here in Germany I started with 12½ grand per year plus per diem whenever I am away from Mannheim and the traveling cost.

Intending to be more persuasive, Tommy's estimates of his previous salaries are inflated, and for Germany greatly inflated. Knowing that 15 grand might be unrealistic, Kono suggested the slack could be made up through living expenses or a company car. "I know the wage that Hoffman wants to start off employees are low but I honestly think that I am a bargain." Tommy also raised the possibility of becoming America's first national coach, a subject much in the air in weightlifting circles. "Maybe Bob can work such a thing out so that I can become the national coach and work for York at the same time. I don't wish to take the coaching title away from him but I can enhance his Father of Weightlifting title by working under him."[67]

Terpak's response equally revealed York's mindset. "You were right," he responded, "when you referred to Bob in one of your letters as having low figures in mind." Terpak explained that nobody, except Bob, Mike Dietz, and himself, was making as much as $15,000. "I asked Bob what he thought a mutually satisfactory salary would be (this after we agreed that you could possibly do the company some good in the research and development area) and his reply was $150 per week plus bonus" which was "an intangible and could very easily vary. But even at two grand you'd be a long way from 15 total. My suggestion is that we keep working on this."[68] This response was hardly encouraging to the still young and ambitious Kono, who decided to pursue a new tack directly with Hoffman in May 1971. As a result of his myriad contacts with the international lifting community, Tommy warned that the Germans were much better organized since his arrival, the Cubans were on the verge of overtaking the United States in the Americas, and the Poles and Hungarians were vying for supremacy with the Russians in Eastern Europe. He reminded Bob of how the Russians "used to take movies of every lift made by the American team members" at Helsinki in 1952. "I think now the U.S. has to copy from them if we expect to lift at least on equal terms." Recently he had attended the Danube Cup in Yugoslavia where he spent a lot of time with Oscar State (IWF secretary-general), who shared lots of information about the Weider organization and the state of international weightlifting.

> Bob, I don't think you can just sit back and let things happen. You can't be content with your Olympic barbell plates and bars and the progress the lifters in the U.S. are making. Already Schnell here in Germany has made the 25 kg. plates out of rubber and it was officially used last month in the German Championships (Nationals). His new bar is really something too! I've told Terpak about it last year but he said that he was content with the bar you now have. ... This might be so with your business but what about your weightlifting team? Whatever happened to the "Old" York which was the mecca to visit and train in for every up and coming weightlifter in the US.... Why is it that the best lifters in the U.S. don't beat a path to your door anymore? ... I hate to write these words but at the same time it is true and if something isn't done then all the work you've done in the past will only become history.

Tommy wanted Bob to rejuvenate York and reassume the leadership it held in the world of weights during the 1950s. "I'd like to be a part of this re-construction job, Bob. I think I can offer much and be a great asset to you and York."[69] Somewhat out of touch on another hemisphere, Tommy was probably unaware that Hoffman's ego had moved to softball and powerlifting as a result of his disenchantment with Olympic lifters and that his health was declining.[70]

Even without encouraging news from York, Kono remained persistent, this time utilizing the strategy of homesickness. He complained to Terpak in October 1971 that he was in a "rut" with regard to living conditions. "Matter of fact I see my entire family in a rut over here." He was concerned that his children were "missing out on the American way of life and this is mainly on activities that stimulate the mind and activate the body." He found the school system "sorely lacking" and was "fed up with living on foreign soil and being an outsider." Tommy was "convinced that we should be back in the good ole U.S.A." Although he professed to enjoy his job and allegedly had a government guarantee of a position for life, he was willing to leave Germany prior to the 1972 Olympics if he could earn as much in America. He wanted to know, "have you and Bob come up with any new figures pertaining to my employment?"[71] Impatient after receiving no response, Tommy issued an ultimatum on November 14 with an updated resume and endorsement letters from Oscar State and Fulton Freeman. He reminded Terpak that "it's been almost 4 weeks since I wrote to you and I'd like to know what the decision is so could you telephone me this coming Friday between 4 and 5 P.M. your time."[72]

What enabled Tommy to issue such a bold ultimatum was Dr. You's assurance that a civil service position in the Honolulu Department of Parks and Recreation had already been "created sometime ago" which would "pay you a minimum of about $15,000 per year to start." Furthermore, it would "give you a lot of time in weightlifting, sports and physical fitness. Young Suk Ko has not filled that position and that job is available for you at anytime." Kono would serve as an administrator for sports and physical fitness. "You will be rapidly promoted at the right time," You assured him. With regard to his German commitment, You strongly urged Tommy to "stick it out until after the Olympic Games because it is a great prestige position for you and the knowledge you will gain will be fantastic. Andrew Mitsukado agrees with me on this matter."[73]

No record remains of what transpired, but Tommy fulfilled his contract to coach the West Germans at the Olympics. Meanwhile, he took advantage of every opportunity to solidify his connections with York and America's weightlifting hierarchy. Under the leadership of its new chairman, Bob Crist of Hampton, Virginia, the AAU Weightlifting Committee was taking steps to revive America's international standing along the lines Kono had been sharing with Hoffman. Tommy therefore eagerly accepted Crist's invitation to conduct a "master clinic" on European training programs the day prior to the national championships in Detroit in June 1972. It was important to have "someone of your stature to put on such a clinic," Crist argued. The lifters "need someone they can identify with and certainly you hold a special place in their hearts as the best we have produced in the last 20 years." Tommy graciously responded afterwards that it was "great to be back in the states" but was quite "overwhelmed" by how much traction the national coach movement had gained. Although he had always entertained the possibility of filling it, he was "a bit stunned by the reality of it all." Most problematic would be the size of the United States. "Because of the great miles existing between states the cost for this kind of program might be prohibitive" and beyond reach of American organizers unless he could "supplement my income by working for York." The only bright spot in such a scheme would be that "the facilities are already there so it wouldn't involve a great deal of expense right off."[74] But such a plan remained hypothetical, especially given Hoffman's disenchantment with Olympic lifting and support of powerlifting and softball. Indeed, funding, even to bring Tommy to Detroit, proved problematic. "We have lots of people working on Kono and his travel," Crist assured Terpak, "military, state dept etc. We may still have to fly him over if this falls through. I got a recent letter and he is well prepared and ready."[75] Funding was finally provided by Thompson Vitamins. I attended Tommy's clinic at the Zembo Mosque where, with Clarence Bass and other notables, I earned my national referee's card. Tommy's presentation was pleasantly and logically conveyed, in contrast to the browbeating we endured in Rudy Sablo's referees' clinic. I don't know how I ever passed the test!

The National Coaching Debacle

As the Olympics approached, Tommy's prospects for employment in the United States improved dramatically. Olympian Russell Knipp, representing the weightlifting component of Athletes in Action (AIA), a Christian advocacy group based in Tulsa, offered him a full-time position training local businessmen, coaching an AIA weightlifting team, and working with American lifters nationwide. Knipp assured him that the program was underwritten by Tom Weir, a real estate executive with deep pockets and that Tulsa was one of the world's "richest and loveliest cities." It would guarantee "the best possible surroundings and facilities for you and your family." Tommy responded that Flo was "very excited about living in Tulsa" and that he was pleased with AIA's goal of "seeing U.S. back on top of the weightlifting field." His terms included a minimum yearly salary of $18,000 for two years. What must have given him pause, especially as a non–Christian, was Weir's expectation that Kono would help his organization "have an impact for Christ internationally."[76]

Meanwhile, Crist was tending to last-minute details, optimistic they could seal a deal at the Olympic Games with mutually acceptable terms. The wheels were "turning" and things were "moving," he assured Tommy. To expedite the process, the executive committee approved a proposal on September 5 to offer Kono a two-year contract requiring him to visit 12 training centers for $12,000 per year.[77] At Munich, West German lifters finished a disappointing 10th place with 18 team points, behind the United States with 21 points, but this did not deter the zeal of American negotiators to hire Tommy.[78] They offered him a national coaching position, funded by Thompson Vitamins, which would provide him with a car to conduct clinics, as well as a salary and benefits, and would require him to write occasional articles for *Boys Life* magazine. But Tommy explained to Crist that he had accepted a better offer (via personal call) from Honolulu Mayor Frank Fasi to join the Parks and Recreation Department.[79]

> Prior to our meeting with you at the Holiday Inn for going over the finalization of the contract, my wife and I had entered into a series of discussions on the pros and cons of this position. When I thought of myself first, it seemed too good to be true as here was the position I'd always dreamed about holding, and I was willing to go ahead and take it. But when I thought of my family and the way we've been living for the past seven years and more importantly the last two years, I really had to think twice. During the past 8½ months here in Germany I spent approximately 6 weeks out of 37 at home. My "father" role amounted to phone calls every two days lasting 2–3 minutes and I was almost a stranger in my own home when I did get home. Added to this, my wife was having trouble with my oldest son and her nerves were shot from having to cope with three kids alone.

No less critical was the behind-the-scenes influence of Dr. You and Parks and Recreation Director Young Suk Ko. "Your confirmation of my position," Tommy explained to Young, "was vital in my final decision making because I had in my hands two contracts to coach in the U.S. one paying 15 thousand a year" for the AAU "and the other paying 18 thousand a year" in Tulsa. These figures were assumptions, but Tommy's Honolulu position was real, and it would allow him to travel to national and international meets and assist American weightlifters. "My living in Hawaii doesn't mean my enthusiasm for the sport of lifting will be any less," he assured Crist.[80]

Crist was despondent but understanding about Kono's decision. "We had to pick up the pieces and start from scratch," he told Tommy. "As you know, sponsors are hard to come by and they associate themselves with winners and those that have a name and can blend toward their products and sales." Crist suspected that Kono never really believed the AAU committee could deliver what it was offering. Carl Miller, a young and enthusiastic coach from New Mexico, seemed to be the best alternative, but he was reluctant to move to the East Coast or Midwest where most registered lifters lived. Most critically, William Thompson and his executive assistant Al Hoder were reevaluating their sponsorship intentions in light of Kono's withdrawal. "Miller does not have either the competitive record, or the credentials and name that Tommy Kono does," reported AAU Sports Administrator Jim Stevens. Additionally, Thompson, Hoder, "and most U.S. industrialists, are disillusioned by the politics and general tenor which pervaded the 1972 Olympic Games" and "reluctant to invest money as readily." Stevens wanted Tommy to write to Thompson and Hoder to stress the importance of their sponsorship and endorse Miller as "an accomplished candidate, worthy of their support, and capable of fulfilling all facets of the program."[81] But it is unlikely that Tommy knew either Thompson, Hoder, or Miller. In essence, Stevens was asking him to play the role of a ghost.

Weightlifting Mentor

Still, he remained on good terms with York. By the time Kono left Mexico after the 1968 Olympics, he had garnered a wealth of training information from over two decades of competitive and coaching experience on the highest level. No doubt to reinforce his ties with York and supplement his income, he decided to share his knowledge by authoring a series of "ABC's of Weightlifting" articles that appeared in *Strength & Health* from February 1969 to June 1974. The reason he started the series, Tommy later told Murray Levin, was "because Iron Man was publishing just anything and everything that pseudo coaches and lifters who thought they came across something good would write." He sought to counter this misinformation by "coming out with something basic and concrete."[82] Focused mainly on training and contest preparation, the series was interspersed with articles on Russian methods, personalities, and competitions. Much of this information was later distilled into his two-volume *magnum opus* on *Weightlifting Olympic Style* and *Championship Weightlifting*. In retrospect, Tommy's inability to secure employment at York and a national coaching position proved to be in his best interest with York in decline vis-à-vis the Weider organization and Olympic weightlifting failing to keep pace with the world. His situation in Honolulu, on the other hand, provided steady employment, benefits and stability for his family. An air of contentment is evident in a 1973 letter to Isaac Berger. "Flo's attending a couple of night classes so that keeps her busy. The kids are busy growing up and have become well-adjusted to their new environment. We have invitations and entertainment to do on most of the weekends so it keeps us socially active but flat broke."[83] It was one of the best decisions he ever made.

These facts of life soon became obvious to Tommy and York. In his editorial for the March 1974 issue of *Strength & Health*, Hoffman admitted his organization was "facing difficult times" and that neither magazine was doing well. He speculated that "perhaps more people want to be a Hercules, instead of a great athlete, a great Olympic weightlifter, or a person who is interested only in keeping fit." Discussions were afoot among company officials to make *Strength & Health* a bi-monthly or combining it with *Muscular Development*.[84] Responding to Bob's appeal for input from readers, Tommy and Flo attempted to revive York's sagging morale. Florence (or her amanuensis) expressed satisfaction with the magazine. The March and April issues, she noted, "contain some of the most interesting and enjoyable articles on health and strength that I've come across in a long time." She liked the broadened coverage of sport and family life and inclusion of "articles of interest to women. The articles on bicycling are especially timely and I devour all the nutritional reports." Tommy expressed "real surprise" and delight with his wife's views and encouraged York editors to "keep up the good work."[85] But in a private letter to Hoffman, Tommy expressed "shock" with the March editorial. "It is really unbelievable for me to picture the magazine going bi-monthly." The "idea man" suggested raising the price of each issue, cutting the number of pages, dispensing with pictorial inserts and extra color, offering readers cut-rate subscriptions, and marketing copies at health food stores. Finally, he congratulated Bob for hiring such a good managing editor as Tom Holbrook who "knows and understands weightlifting and weight training and has the ability to put together a magazine that my friends and neighbors take delight in reading."[86] Despite these expressions of optimism, the magazine became bi-monthly with the June/July 1974 issue without Holbrook as editor or any more "ABC's of Weightlifting."

Kono, however, remained a valuable and well-respected member of the national and international lifting scene. According to Hal Wood, a Honolulu sports editor, he had turned down coaching positions in Oklahoma City and Minneapolis and an offer to coach Canadian weightlifters for the 1976 Olympics. Though not a native islander, Tommy believed Hawaii was "the only place to live. I've checked out just about every other place. My oldest boy, now 11, spent four years with us in Germany and speaks German fluently. But I'd rather all three kids spoke English fluently."[87] Eventually Miller accepted the position Tommy turned down, but it was reduced from coach to coordinator and provided just $3,000 for expenses to supplement his teaching salary in Albuquerque. Meanwhile, Kono conducted national championship clinics for the next two years. At Williamsburg in 1973 he "showed slides, and discussed lifting and pulling techniques," according to Crist. "He did an excellent job, and is a master of detail."[88] In October 1973 Kono had reason to be glad he was not national coach from a letter Hoffman sent him after the world championships in Cuba where the American team won no medals and finished 12th.[89]

> The U.S. team stunk. How fortunate that you're in no way connected with the team. Tommy, I've never seen an American that was regarded with such contempt as was this squad. Lowe, Capsouras, and Stefan were constantly referred to as "the queer brigade" with Lowe having been nicknamed "far-out-fredie." They really were rather sickening. The U.S. delegation, numbering about 22 individuals, and with only 7 lifters, was a laughing stock.... No fooling Tommy, I'm sure you would have been as ashamed of the team as I was. Often I heard comments such as "Where are the American *men*? Who are these queers? You used to have real lifters, like Kono, Berger, Davis. Where are your weightlifters?"

Hoffman was so upset that he had no wish "to go to any meet that will have Americans present."[90] He pronounced in *Strength & Health* that "U.S. WEIGHTLIFTING IS AT ITS LOWEST EBB."[91] The lifters responded by submitting two reports that blamed their administrators for the team's poor showing. They complained about the incompetence of coaches and assistants and "lack of knowledge and awareness" of the numerous "tourists" who accompanied the team. Their second report, recognizing that "the gap separating the U.S. from the other major lifting powers has been growing wider," focused on constructive proposals to restore America to a "respected," if not dominant, position in the world. But "implementation would cost money."[92]

This internecine strife, along with the bizarre conduct of the lifters he witnessed at the 1973 senior nationals, should have served as a red flag for Tommy to disengage himself from any further attempts to improve American lifting.[93] Yet in the comparative isolation of Hawaii, he continued to give exhibitions, conduct competitions, and coach fledgling lifters such as Pat Omori and John Yamauchi, all of which coincided with his new Parks and Recreation duties.[94] Prior to the 1974 nationals he was invited to give a clinic in Japan with all expenses paid, he reported to Hoffman. Otherwise he could not afford to make such trips, especially with a recently purchased house for his growing family.[95] Again through Crist's resourcefulness, funding was found for Tommy to come to York as "National Coaching Advisor." Drawing on his vast international experience, he compared training programs in the USSR, West Germany, and Japan to the United States, observed Crist. Kono pointed out that "the US has stood still since the late 1950's while the other countries have kept on improving. He stressed the importance of respect for coaches. Americans tend to question

When plans to work at York Barbell and become America's first national coach failed to materialize, Kono accepted a position with the Honolulu Parks and Recreation Department. However, he continued to coach weightlifters free of charge wherever his services were requested. Here, an unidentified lifter gets tips on his form as others, including such Olympic lifting champions as Phil Grippaldi (seated at left, in white), Joe Puleo (standing beside Grippaldi), and Russell Knipp (directly behind the lifter in a white shirt) look on.

authority and take an anti-establishment attitude. This interferes with the work of the coach."⁹⁶ At the 1975 nationals in Culver City, California, Tommy reported on a three-week coaching tour he had taken with Oscar State and English National Coach John Lear to China, Japan, and New Zealand. From Kono's ancestral homeland, Kenji Onuma, who had won the 1958 U.S. Senior Nationals and was president of Waseda University, extended his gratitude. "The Clinic was certainly a great success. I have never seen such an enthusiastic response from an audience comprising mainly middle-aged, non-weightlifter people. Certainly it was an epoch-making occasion for weightlifting in Japan."⁹⁷ Tommy was impressed with the potential of China which was struggling to escape the throes of the Cultural Revolution.⁹⁸ He confided to Hoffman that this trip enabled him to meditate on the problems plaguing USA weightlifting. "Bob, we have really slipped backwards and there seems to be no stopping unless something is done. Happily I believe I have seen the 'light' while on this trip."⁹⁹

American Olympic Coach

Although he was never able to shed this light, either through his clinics or pages of *Strength & Health* on others, he acquired an opportunity to reshape the destiny of American weightlifting on December 1, 1975, when the U.S. Weightlifting Committee appointed him team coach for the upcoming Montreal Olympics.¹⁰⁰ It was "something that I have aspired for since 1965," he told protégé Russ Ogata, which would enable him to follow the footsteps of Bob Hoffman and perhaps return to the glory days of the 1950s.¹⁰¹ Whatever doubts he may have had about his potential lifters were dispelled by their performance at a tri-country pre–Olympic competition on February 28, 1976, in Toronto when an American team consisting of Dane Hussey, Dan Cantore, Dan Caldwell, Al Stark, Jim Napier, Lee James, Phil Grippaldi, Mark Cameron, and Bruce Wilhelm defeated teams from Puerto Rico and Canada, scoring 98, 80, and 62 points, respectively, and setting several national records. Anxious to remove any ill-feelings stemming from the athletes' reports following the Cuba world championships and to promote "cooperation and communication between officials and athletes," Cameron composed a report on the Toronto meet based on a polling of team members. "Tommy Kono performed his duties as coach well and was a pleasure to work with" was the consensus. "After the competition Tommy answered many questions and gave much advice to the lifters." They deemed him "an excellent choice for coach of this team as well as the upcoming Olympic team." Likewise, Cameron extended kudos to officials Rudy Sablo, Karl Faeth, John Terpak, and Frank Bates for their supporting roles.¹⁰²

Tommy was equally pleased by this initial interaction. Whereas he formerly had a dim view of America's chances at the 1976 Olympics, he now saw some "bright spots." At the 1973 world championships "we had a bunch of long-haired hippies who complained about the officials and everything but themselves when they failed. Today's crop of lifters is made up of clean-cut young men who have been working hard at achieving success."¹⁰³ He admitted to being apprehensive about possible communication problems, but his doubts were quickly dispelled after their first pre-competition meeting. He expected some disagreement over starting attempts, he told USOC Chairman David Matlin, but "not one lifter raised any objection when some adjustments were made," thereby illustrating to Kono the prevailing spirit of cooperation and teamwork. "I was impressed with the concerted effort shown by all the lifters and officials of our team for good representation of themselves and the U.S. off as well as on the platform." Tommy reiterated these sentiments to heavyweight Bruce Wilhelm. "I anticipated some problem but it was unfounded after I met all of you. I feel the only problem would arise from Grippaldi … but even this can be worked out." Good open communication was vital. To Oscar State, Tommy was still buoyant a month later. "I am very excited about working with the U.S. team. The exposure with them in Toronto was the stimulus I needed."[104]

As opening day for the Olympics approached, Kono corresponded continuously with his charges, advising them to "follow a Spartan way of living" and make the Olympic lifts "a way of life." Most important, however, was psychological preparation. He viewed "team spirit" as "an essential ingredient" for maximal performance in international competition. In June, at a USOC meeting in Philadelphia, Tommy talked about his role as a team builder, the mental and physical preparation of lifters,

The 1976 American Olympic weightlifting team included (front, from left) Tommy (coach), Sam Bigler, Fred Lowe, Dan Cantore, Phil Grippaldi, and Rudy Sablo (assistant coach) and (back, from left) Mark Cameron, Sam Walker, Bruce Wilhelm, Gary Drinnon, and Lee James.

and the need to "pull together."[105] At training camps at York and SUNY Plattsburgh as well as the Olympics, Tommy and team manager Rudy Sablo worked well as a team, but recapturing the same camaraderie that worked so well in the 1950s proved challenging with current athletes. "It's hard to have a guy come in and coach you," recalled Wilhelm. "If he's coaching you and doesn't really know you, he can't spend quality time with you. After a while we got to know Tommy a little bit, but when a man doesn't train with you and then he's critiquing your lift that doesn't mean anything."[106]

Despite these imbedded individualistic tendencies, Kono moved on. "One of the main reasons for establishing a training camp prior to a big competition of international caliber is to establish team spirit," he later reported. "Though the team officials held several meetings stressing this point, personality clashes among several team members made this virtually impossible." The "most difficult lifter to work with backstage" was Grippaldi, who finished fourth as a mid-heavyweight. "His desire to win a medal clouded his judgment so much that he could have jeopardized his chance of totaling had we not kept his starting poundages down." Tommy felt that "Grippaldi's uncooperative attitude prevents him from attaining his true potential." Heavyweight Mark Cameron, who finished fifth, was also a problem. "The Steroid Test which Cameron was required to submit to six days earlier had greatly affected him psychologically." Only mid-heavyweight Lee James lifted up to Kono's expectations, setting three personal records and winning a silver medal. Tommy's other charges finished 12th, 11th, 11th, 14th, 10th, and fifth to place the United States eighth overall, far behind Russia and Bulgaria. Only three Americans exceeded their Senior National totals. Tommy concluded his lifters "could have performed much better had there existed a strong team spirit. Just about every lifter on the team appeared to be 'totally independent' as one lifter expressed himself to me." It was hardly the outcome Kono had anticipated. The United States remained an also-ran.[107]

Far more disappointing was news that emerged nine days later; Grippaldi and Cameron failed the drug tests. The rationalization that "they didn't intend to 'cheat'" and that their "prescribed" medication allowed them to compete at maximum bodyweight hardly mattered. They were disqualified and barred from international competition for a year.[108] Probably what Tommy did not know was that the remarkable feat of his brightest star was drug-aided. As veteran coach Ben Green points out, it was the first year of testing and there was a lapse of protocol. Green asked, "'how in the hell did you get out of it, Lee?' He said, 'by the time I lifted we knew about it, and as soon as I lifted Smitty [Trainer Dick Smith] grabbed me and said let's go. And I left.' So they didn't test him."[109] But enough damage was done to American credibility. As Kono noted, Sablo "had repeatedly announced in our team meeting in York, Plattsburgh and in Montreal that anabolic steroid testing will be conducted in Montreal. It was evident that some of the lifters did not take heed to this information."[110] Contrary to Tommy's old-fashioned focus on mental preparation and teamwork, the lifters adopted more expedient approaches that proved counter-productive.

Another unintended consequence of the Montreal Olympics was the loss of Carl Miller as national coordinator. For the past several years he had provided yeoman service to American weightlifting by staging weekend clinics nationwide. It was not so much that he was deprived of the Olympic coaches' position by a vote of seven to six at the 1975 AAU convention in New Orleans or that Tommy was ever disrespectful or made Carl feel unvalued.[111] Rather, it stemmed from the decision of Philip St. Cyr, weightlifting chairman for the 1976 games, to limit the United States to one coach and a manager. Crist appealed to lawyer Dave Matlin to seek additional credentials for Miller, but funding would apply to the "meet site and training quarter only," with nothing for the position or for housing and meals in the Olympic Village.[112] For Miller, it was an insult, after putting in so many hours and days of instruction to American lifters at great personal sacrifice and meager compensation. Nevertheless, it came as a surprise that he should tender his resignation at the AAU national meeting at Phoenix in October. Miller expressed no ill-will towards Tommy; rather, he was disenchanted with the bloated bureaucracy where so much emphasis was being placed on weightlifting administration and "less and less on delivering a coaching and strength training system. That's why I left."[113] Although he was succeeded by Denis Reno and other competent coaches, the program lacked Miller's consistency and drive, and his plans for a national residential training center did not materialize.

6

Public Servant

"Don't aim at success—the more you aim at it and make it a target, the more you are going to miss it. For success, like happiness, cannot be pursued; it must ensue ... as the unintended side-effect of one's personal dedication to a cause greater than oneself."[1]—Viktor Frankl, *Man's Search for Meaning*

The "Idea Man" Again

Although Tommy is best known for his weightlifting exploits, he spent most of his working years after 1972 employed as head of the physical education department at the Honolulu Department of Parks and Recreation. His responsibilities were far-ranging. As Recreation Specialist III, he was expected to supervise subordinates in developing and sustaining city-wide recreation and fitness programs. Initially, his monthly salary was $1,104 ($13,248 pa) which was increased to $1,278 ($15,336 pa) in May 1973 and then to $1,348 ($16,176 pa) in November 1973. These speedy promotions after only a year reflected the probationary appraisal report mandated by the Department of Civil Service. Kono's supervisor commended him for his work in physical fitness, especially in setting up jogging sites, encouraging their use, and conducting a fitness workshop for summer recreation aides. "You get along well with fellow workers and community groups. Your attitude and cooperation have been great." Three years later, Tommy's performance review was even better. "You have done excellent work relative to Physical Fitness Program for the City," wrote his supervisor. "Congratulations on being picked as weightlifting coach for the U.S. Olympic team." In July 1977, Kono's salary was boosted to $1,797 ($21,564 pa).[2] Again, Dr. You's wise counsel proved conducive to Tommy's career advancement and well-being.

It was also fortuitous that he was hired at a time of expansion and placed under the deputy superintendent who gave him a virtual free hand. "All of a sudden we exploded with all these different ideas," recalls Mike Mizuno, Tommy's long-time assistant.

> He'd think something up and say "okay, let's go to the city council and ask for funding, and we'll start a different section, and we'll start this program, and we'll start doing this and that," and after a while our budget started going out the window. And his ideas worked pretty much of the time because he was one of the few who were in tune with all these sports people.

> So anytime anybody had an idea, they knew if they could run it past Tommy it would probably get enough recognition that they could do it.

Initiating competition for boys and girls in surfing, usually considered an adult male sport, was one he proposed. "All it takes is a few," Mizuno noted, "and you can get some real aggressive little girls who want to learn and compete. And the schools started pushing it because they can get the rest of the student body involved in a sport. ... So now it gave an opportunity." Gender equity was another Kono innovation. "As long as I've known him, he's always had the idea that we're all equal, and he didn't have any biases." Mizuno and other males were skeptical when Tommy started to teach women bodybuilding at the Nuuanu YMCA. But he could hardly argue with the results.³

Owing to his renown in strength and conditioning, many physical educators, especially football coaches, sought Kono's advice on how to incorporate weight training into their programs. He was always generous with his time and low key in his approach to problem-solving, according to Mizuno. "He didn't want to interfere too much to the point where people would say, 'don't tell me what to do.' So, he would sit on the side, and if you wanted his opinion, he would give it to you." Most of the time during weekdays, however, Tommy was at his desk doing paperwork, writing proposals, answering questions, or writing reports for the city council or mayor. Whether he also used office time to tend to his voluminous weightlifting correspondence is uncertain, but Mizuno recalls that Tommy often worked until 9 p.m. "And I know on weekends, if he's not in the Nuuanu Y, he's in the office. If I call him

When Tommy retired from the active life of an athlete and coach, he effectively transitioned into the more sedentary existence of an office administrator.

at home, you could hear him using his typewriter or recorder, so he put in a lot of extra time. Any time he asked for time off, nobody would challenge it." By working so many extra hours, Tommy could get time off for his overseas trips. As a supervisor, he was no less accommodating to others in his office. Every Tuesday morning he held a staff meeting "to find out what work we are doing, and what kinds of ideas he needed to help. We just tossed things around until we were satisfied." He supervised by consensus-building, according to Mizuno. His strongest attribute as an administrator was that "he was always encouraging us to keep going, to do our best, and to share our ideas with each other. ... One of our administrators told us that we click like a machine, and we always seemed to be thinking alike and working alike. ... We always looked forward to going to work." Another positive feature of Tommy's service to the city was the way he dealt with difficult situations. "He didn't outwardly criticize people," observed Mizuno. "And if people got nasty, he would just sit there and listen, and the first thing to come out of his mouth was 'I'm sorry you feel that way. I was hoping we could work things out.' And then, of course, people would shrink in front of him and apologize and they would become good friends."[4]

Weightlifting Activist

It was a stroke of good fortune that Tommy was not only the first physical fitness director hired by Parks and Recreation but also that his supervisors seemed eager to take advantage of his fame and expertise. Although Hawaii had been a hotbed for weightlifting and bodybuilding since the 1940s, and there had been many competitions, there had never been an attempt to promote them, along with powerlifting, under an official umbrella. To encourage grassroots participation, Kono prepared a handout titled "Developing Muscle Size and Strength" to explain the number of exercises, sets, repetitions, and training periods novices should pursue. "All exercises should be performed slowly and smoothly with proper posture or technique always foremost," he advised.[5] Especially in such a relatively disjointed region with limited population and resources, recruitment was critical to developing future champions. On December 13, 1972, a committee of 16 approved eight weightlifting/bodybuilding tournaments and two in volleyball, to be held in the department's gym under Kono's direction. The competitions would begin with an Oahu Olympic Lifts and Mr. Oahu Physique contest in February 1973, and end with the Region V AAU Powerlifting Championships and Mr. Teenage Physique Contest in December.[6] So engaged was Tommy with his departmental work and extramural responsibilities that he had to turn down an opportunity to serve on the USOC Weightlifting Committee and to travel abroad on behalf of American weightlifting. "It is too early in the year for making a trip," he told Bob Crist on January 7, "leaving my position vacant for two weeks. I have to establish myself here first before I start running off on any trips." But he did intend to "comb the field here for new talents in lifting. Eventually, my hope is to have weightlifting accepted in all the high schools here in Hawaii."[7]

How busy Kono became with his new responsibilities became clear during the coming months. "Last week-end," he reported to Crist on Presidents Day, "the group from the President's Council on Physical Fitness came over which included three Olympian friends, Sammy Lee, Pat McCormick, and Bill Toomey. Of course all my spare time was taken up with them. I'm lucky if I can squeeze in 20 minutes workout three times a week."[8] To 1973 Bantamweight Champion Dwight Tamanaha he conveyed similar sentiments, noting he was consumed not only by regular meet responsibilities but also by extramural events related to his position and reputation. On April 28 he conducted a state-wide Olympic Lifts Contest which included Mr. Hawaii and Mr. Teenage Hawaii physique shows. Two weeks earlier "we had Arnold Schwarzenegger and Franco Columbu here for the big physique show. The McKinley High Auditorium had a nice crowd of about 1000 for this show. Incidentally, lifting is picking up here for we had about 200 persons in last night's show. I'm conducting a special weightlifting clinic in two weeks—Friday, Saturday affair. I also want to get into the schools."[9] Then on June 9 he took part in a weekend program sponsored by his department which attracted thousands of visitors. As he explained to Crist, it included "a Pacific Islands Power Lift Championships along with a physique contest on Saturday and then on Sunday an Olympic Lift Training Session at the Park with a chin up contest and tug-of-war competition." Coverage of these events in newspapers and television provided "terrific exposure of weight training."[10] Although it was not the lifestyle he had envisioned as a weightlifting champion, Tommy adapted well to his public service responsibilities. He was "really busy" and "getting involved in all kinds of things," he told Ike Berger. "Working for the City and County isn't as easy as punching in and punching out. I'm higher up in the ladder so I don't have to punch cards at all but I have to do a lot of P.R. work and keep on top of things all the time."[11]

No less notable were Tommy's efforts to build a formidable weightlifting team through his volunteer coaching at the Nuuanu YMCA. While USA weightlifting was floundering at the 1973 world championships in Cuba, it was flourishing on the islands where Kono continued coaching flyweight John Yamauchi, who placed third at the 1974 Senior Nationals in York in June, and bantamweight Patrick Omori who placed second.[12] In congratulating the former for making the team that would compete in England and Spain, Kono stressed decorum and teamwork and other qualities derivative of Buddhist Dharma.[13]

> Represent your team and your country well, whether on or off the platform. All those you come in contact with will judge you, the team, and the U.S. by the way you dress, act, and speak. You represent many things besides being a member of the U.S. team. Take pride in the fact that you also represent Hawaii, the Japanese ancestry your looks bear, and you also represent the Yamauchi family. John is the least important person you represent.
>
> If you should lose, take defeat with grace. But, always fight down to the wire. Some of my best remembered competitions were not when I won but when I gave everything I had and ended up in second place. I thrived on competition. Any contest won without a hard fight is shallow victory.
>
> And last but not the least important thing—take team spirit seriously. Remember the old saying, "In Unity there is Strength." ... Do things together and be considerate of your team members. Help them and they, in turn, will help you.

Reminiscent of Japanese American soldiers who fought in World War II, he advised Yamauchi to "'Go for Broke' on the last Clean and Jerk and not from the first

When a young Arnold Schwarzenegger visited Hawaii, he was welcomed by its leading weightlifters. Included in the foreground are, front, from left, Richard Tomita and Richard Tom, and back, from left, Arnold, Harold (Oddjob) Sakata, Paul Graham, Tommy, and Emerick Ishikawa.

Snatch." A final point critical to Tommy's own rise to fame was not to "forget your P.R. work. Drop a card to Hall Woods [sic] of the Advertiser and Bill Gee of the Star Bulletin when you are in Europe."[14] Neither Yamauchi nor Omori attained international stature, but powerlifter Gary Kawamura was inspired by them and Kono to take up Olympic lifting. "If someone as famous as Tommy Kono telling me I might be good, it took me about two seconds to quit powerlifting."[15] Kawamura eventually placed sixth as a featherweight in the 1976 Olympic trials and set records in masters lifting.

By 1976, Kono was promoting and directing all weightlifting contests in Hawaii. He was also heavily involved, owing to his reputation and nature of his employment, in many other extramural fitness activities. He coordinated Oahu's jogging program, offered clinics at Kapiolani and Pearl Harbor parks, and served on the Nuuanu YMCA Health and Physical Education Committee, the Community Fitness Committee, the City Bicentennial Committee, the Hawaiian AAU and Olympic fund raising committees, and during the summer coordinated the President's Council on Physical Fitness and Sports award program. Less formally, he promoted physical fitness and sports for numerous civic organizations, schools, and public functions. Most notable was a powerlifting contest Tommy organized for Oahu Prison inmates in 1975. The prisoners expressed their gratitude in a letter stating that "the contest would not have been possible without your help and interest."[16]

In 1976 he won the Scotty Shumann Award for his achievements and contributions to sports from the Honolulu Quarterback Club. In April 1977 at the annual Freedom Banquet of the Honolulu Sertoma Club he won the sports award, and in July he received presidential sports awards for jogging and weight training from Jimmy Carter.[17] Tommy, of course, had been equally active in public affairs a decade earlier in Maui, but the intensity of his involvement in the public sector on the capital island along with his reputation as Olympic champion and three-time international coach brought enhanced recognition.

Marathon Man

What might have seemed to some a lowly bureaucratic desk job for a great champion did not occur to Kono. While Tommy profited from his reputation, he sought opportunities to help other people pro bono. "I'm not interested in making millions," he once told Mizuno. Said Mizuno, "He kept volunteering and teaching at the YMCA, and I said, 'that's crazy.' Then he got pulled more and more into the marathon ... and me and a whole bunch of parks people and friends got recruited to help."[18] According to Steven Todd, an information specialist in mayor's office, the marathon resulted not from a single source but from "the convergence of individuals, organizations, ideas, talents and resources."[19] Long-distance running, in fact, was a decades-old tradition capped by the annual Hawaiian AAU Marathon. As one of his many athletic interests, Dr. You served in the 1950s as a member and chairman of the Hawaiian AAU Long Distance Running Committee whose objective was to send runners to the national championships, the Boston Marathon, and the Olympic Games.[20] It is likely that Kono's involvement with the Honolulu Marathon was influenced by his close association with You.

Indeed, Tommy was not unfamiliar with distance running, having made the acquaintance of famed Hawaiian distance runner Norman Tamanaha in San Francisco in the early fifties through Dr. You, and at the Melbourne Olympics he met the legendary Emil Zatopek who had won gold medals in the 5,000 and 10,000 meters and marathon in Helsinki.[21] Kono was not a runner because of flat arches, according to journalist Paul Drewes, but he gave a boost to the idea by responding to a mayoral appeal. "There was a letter written to the mayor, from the long distance running club, asking for assistance with a run and the mayor said, 'why don't you stage the Honolulu Marathon? I'm familiar with the Boston Marathon back east and we could have it here,' said Kono." Called the Rim of the Pacific Marathon in 1973, the December event attracted about 200 runners, but "less than 165 finished," Tommy estimated. "The following year, there was double that. Then the next year double that. It just kept getting bigger and bigger."[22] According to journalist Michael S.K.N. Tsai, the Parks and Recreation Department

> provided funding and whatever ancillary support was needed. Tommy Kono drew on his network of personal and professional contacts to gather supplies and giveaways. He arranged for a donation of 200 blank T-shirts from local sporting goods store Honsport; then the executive board members, volunteers, and Kono himself hand-stenciled them, producing the first

race finisher shirts. Parks and Recreation was most obvious on race day, when hundreds of city and county workers set up and took down course markers, staff registration tables and aid stations, and the start and finish areas. As Kono explained, the department's greatest value lay in the number of ready personnel it could provide.[23]

In 1977, Tommy reported to John Grimek that 3,500 runners started the race and about 3,000 finished with 619 women entrants. "I'm quite involved with this, having been with it since its inception and I'm quite proud that we have per capita the most runningest state."[24]

Marathon administrator Jeanette Chun observes that Tommy performed several critical functions. Since its inception, he was on the board of directors, served as the marathon's liaison with the city and county of Honolulu, obtained permits for passage through city streets and parks, supervised the bus loading of thousands of runners, and handled security for parking in Kapiolani Park. "Tommy was a very detailed person," Chun recalls, "drawing maps so there was no question of where to park the vehicles or how to get somewhere. Tommy always followed through on whatever he did" and was "well-liked by everyone. Tommy was such a humble person, we would forget he was an Olympic champion. He never talked about his Olympic experiences."[25]

Home Life

While Tommy enjoyed widespread celebrity status, he increasingly had to reckon with the reality that his emotional well-being stemmed from his family. After a decade of instability, first in Maui and then on various coaching assignments, he and Flo decided to purchase a home closer to his workplace. The family assets, despite years of peripatetic existence, were considerable. Their major holdings in February 1973 included $5,000 cash at the Hawaii National Bank, $9,395 in Savings & Loan Associations, $2,500 in life insurance, $18,000 in real estate, and $3,500 in personal property for an estimated $40,645 total. These figures did not include 1,620 shares of stock in three corporate funds which fluctuated daily and $4,200 held by Dr. You in their application for a mortgage loan.[26] With monthly expenses of $720 ($8,641 pa), including rent of $335 for lodgings on Kula Street in Honolulu, it appeared that his annual income of $14,645 would be ample.[27] Upon approval of their loan request for $47,878 (with $354 monthly payments), the Konos moved into their new home at 94–934 Lumimoe Street in Waipahu, a community west of Honolulu.[28] To ensure financial security, they liquidated the property in Maui where they once intended to build a home, and Flo sought employment with the army, then the navy, and eventually at Hickam Air Force Base as a clerk-stenographer for $7,976 per annum.[29] Also, the University of Hawaii hired Tommy in the fall of 1973 to teach a physical education course for $280.[30] By the end of 1974, the Konos' adjusted gross income was $20,788, and for 1977, it was $28,334, quite an advance from the miserly amount Tommy earned as an Olympic coach.[31] Still, it was the abstemious lifestyle he practiced as a bachelor and the many sacrifices of Flo and the children that enabled his family to enjoy the fruits of middle-class America.

His daughter joAnn recalls that he was endowed with a combination of talents. "He was able to write and accompany it with very good illustrations. He always had his triangle or a ruler for everything he did around the house." Reminiscent of his days as a draftsman with the California highway department, he had a mechanical drawing board, used mainly for the marathon. joAnn remembers him "doing his drawings, making signs and stuff." Flo recalls that "he had a very analytical mind" which he applied to carpentry and gardening projects at home. But he never seemed to mind menial tasks. "No, he took delight in doing them," says joAnn. Her husband Gary Sumida concurs that household chores gave him "a sense of accomplishment. Then he'd move on to the next thing."[32] As was the case throughout his lifting career, Tommy was very goal oriented.

It would be a misconception, however, to assume that because the Konos were finally settled in their own comfortable home that they did not experience the many trials and tribulations of normal family life. In 1975 they were subjected to a series of trying circumstances. One of the worst occurred in September when joAnn fell off her bicycle and the handle struck the side of her head and cut her ear so badly, Tommy told his twin brothers, that "a piece of her ear was hanging … but luckily Dr. You was available to sew it up. He must have thrown in about 45 stitches."[33] An even more serious misfortune occurred in late 1974 with a recurrence of Kono's asthma when his bodyweight dropped to 144 pounds. "No matter what medication my doctor prescribed it didn't seem to improve my condition," he explained in October 1975 to Kenji Onuma.

> Anyway, after carefully thinking things over I had a very deep discussion with my doctor and we both agreed that it might be psychological but more so brought on because of my low resistance from lack of almost my lifelong habit of weight training. This was three weeks ago and I have started to train with the barbells at home and consequently I have started to gain back my bodyweight. Slow but I don't want to pack on fat. My asthmatic condition has improved so I am not taking any medication. Boy, but my condition was so bad a couple of months ago and early September I didn't do anything at home and it was a great effort to do things at work.[34]

It was much the same story he shared with his brothers in Sacramento at the end of 1975. "I let myself get run down too much last year and the result was a bad beginning and had relapse. I'm still down in Bodyweight (154) but starting tomorrow I am going to be on a rebuilding plan and get in top physical shape (weighing about 170) by middle of June when the Sr. Nationals will take place. … I want to look good and be really fit to impress people."[35] If Tommy's condition was the result of stress from family life, work, and efforts to sustain his reputation, the addition of his rigorous two-week, three-nation clinic in Asia in April 1975 and upcoming coaching duties for America's 1976 Olympic team could only have exacerbated it. No mention was made that, at age 45, he was possibly enduring a mid-life crisis. But an awareness that he now belonged to the older generation of his family could hardly have been overlooked when, on January 27, 1976, shortly after the death of Flo's father, Tommy's father, Kanichi Kono, passed away at age 89. Although Tommy took no direct part in the funeral service at the Buddhist Church of Sacramento, his hand was evident in an incense offering by the AAU of the United States.[36]

Home Alone

Life for the Konos at home often existed without the presence or attention of Tommy. "We knew him in a different way than the public," commented joAnn. "Yeah, he wasn't endearing," said Flo. "It was understood. The hugging and all that." joAnn's husband, Gary Sumida, observed that his father, also Japanese American, was the same way. "You don't want people to see, especially when you're hurting or in need. It's a sign of weakness and really frowned on." Tommy tended to be a private person who kept his emotions intact. joAnn observes that "of course my mom coming from Hawaii, the culture is not like that. You know hugging and being sensitive and all that stuff. She was that way with us." Differences in their cultural backgrounds, Portuguese/Christian vs. Japanese/Buddhist, led to some incongruities in children's upbringing. Meaningful contacts with joAnn's father were limited, even when he was at home. As joAnn notes:

> When I was young the place to talk to him would be when he was with me in the car. My mom was the one who taught me how to drive the stick shift. It wasn't my dad. And my dad's the one who taught us the Lord's Prayer and not her, but she's a Christian, and he's not, so that's odd. ... When you'd go to bed and after you'd say your prayers he would give you one of those protein tablets. Well we thought they were yuck, and that was our reward. We were deprived of candy, and that's probably why I overdosed on baby aspirin thinking it was candy. So he tried sticking his big fingers in my mouth when I was only four or five years old. ... That's the one time he was involved in a crisis. Most of the time he wasn't around. My mom ended up having to deal with emergencies. When I broke my leg he wasn't there.

Flo remembers when she was in the hospital giving birth to her younger son, Mark, Tommy "would go to work and leave you guys [joAnn and brother Jamie] in the car. ... I didn't think it was right." joAnn concurs. "You just gave birth, and I'm waiting in the car." Flo admits that "sometimes" he could be cruel or insensitive. "I guess he was concerned because he was working for the Germans and he didn't want to take time off for family."[37] Despite his heroic feats, success in the workplace, and caring for others, Tommy never seemed to have time for his family.

Tommy and Flo's younger son Mark was born in 1970 in Mannheim, Germany. In lieu of relating much with his parents, who were busy earning a living as he was growing up, he associated mainly with his sister. "We were not necessarily fending for ourselves but she definitely looked out for me, and I recall spending our summers with her and other kids in the neighborhood." Relations with his older brother Jamie, however, were somewhat distant. "He wasn't really around very much. He hung out with his friends. It was kind of like a disconnect. It's sort of ironic because I shared a bedroom with him." Mark remembers his father as the disciplinarian while his mother was a comforter. "Do what you should before you do what you want is the big thing he would say. Live by the sword, die by the sword." joAnn was the most rebellious of the Kono kids, and she "clashed quite a bit" with her father. But she was "never so rebellious that it got to be a problem," according to Mark. In the end it made her "stronger as a person, because as she got older she started working and making her own money and being more independent. She was strong—strong willed. And very smart, not only proving herself time and again to him but to herself. There was a mutual respect between them." His brother, on the other hand, "had his own ideas of what he wanted to do." He just wanted to "get out of the house early on." Mark, as the youngest, "had things a little easier" and "was probably the least troublesome." Their father "wanted us to be self-sufficient and take care of ourselves, and I've only called on my parents a couple times for help. I think my brother and sister took the brunt of everything growing up."[38]

It was not until Mark was six, when Tommy returned from the Montreal Olympics, that he realized his father played a significant role in sports. "That's where I made the connection that he was an Olympic athlete … and I was putting the pieces of the puzzle together. That's a huge event, and he was part of it. And he brought back some memorabilia." As for participation, Tommy never pushed weightlifting on his children.

> For my brother it was more of a showy thing, so he didn't take it very seriously. It was more like playing off the fact that my dad was who he was than internalizing it and building his own character. As opposed to my sister who wasn't necessarily into weightlifting or any other sports, but through the years she has trained and seriously likes lifting weights and does it at home. … And my dad never really pushed it on me. His philosophy always was if you are interested, come and ask me. He wanted us to follow our own interests. I think I can speak for my sister as well that we enjoy physical activity, and that's definitely a byproduct of my dad. I always had to be in motion or doing something in that realm. So for a long time I was skateboarding. When I stopped skateboarding I still had a lot of energy, so I started looking at martial arts and went to a kick boxing gym that was close to my house, watched them for a while and later went to a Brazilian jui jitsu gym, and I decided that I was going to do that.

What Mark remembers most about his father was the public service commitment entailed by his employment and volunteer efforts on behalf of the islands community.

> My dad did a lot of stuff through his work, and yes, he did help out with the marathon every year. That was a huge chunk of time throughout the year, and especially leading up to it. I remember the Department of Parks and Recreation putting on a kite festival at one of the larger parks along Waikiki Beach. … So he was very active in different things regarding physical fitness. I know he was very interested in getting out to the senior community and imploring them to lift weights as part of their limited exercise, and they could do it from a seated position.
>
> In terms of my father's popularity, I never brought it up in terms of oh, you know who my dad is. Someone would always bring it up, and I would smile and nod and agree. … It was definitely the recognition that yes, that is my father, and he accomplished a lot of things, but I never said, hey, you'd better watch out. You know who my dad is.[39]

Although Mark believes his father was not religious, there were elements of his Buddhist upbringing that occasionally surfaced. One of them was the Japanese New Year tradition of mochitsuki. "It's a dessert made of rice and sugar," Mark explained. "Then on top of two pieces of mochi you put a tangerine, and it's to welcome the New Year. So there were small things like that my father kept doing year after year."[40] What remained was a residue rather than a robust association to his kin and culture.

A spiritual practice, contrary to the Buddhist Dharma of being in the present, and to which Tommy did not prescribe, was divining the future. On March 30, 1976, he and Flo attended a presentation by renowned psychic Dr. Richard Ireland at the

The Kono family at home in the 1970s. Back row, from left, Jamieson (Jamie), Florence (Flo), and Tommy; front row, from left, Mark and joAnn.

Sheraton Waikiki Hotel. In response to Tommy's question about whether KIO Co., a business he was starting, would be a success in two years, Ireland told him, "'yes' but in less than 2 years … more like 9 months!"[41] In the fall of 1977 Flo "dragged" him to a Chinese soothsayer, he told his brothers. After praying, this elderly woman read their future and answered questions. Flo wanted to know whether they should buy a new house and inquired about Tommy's health. "Eventually, she asked about Mama and Papa and where they were buried. She said that the two of them were not pleased with the ashes split between Japan and US. And that it would be better for them if it was all in one place … in Japan." Conceding that there was wisdom in the soothsayer's remarks, they made Tommy think about the burdens of family life and the simple life he had forsaken as just a weightlifting hero. "There is always things to do around the house. Sometimes I wonder if it is worth being a house owner."[42]

Man on the Move

Travel, typically long-distance travel, provided a relief from the mundane responsibilities of homeowning and family life, as long as it was affordable. Hence Tommy was able to officiate, along with John Terpak, Bob Hise, and Russ Knipp, the first World's Strongest Man Competition at Universal Studios in Hollywood in September 1977. Most memorable of the 10 unique events was the 410-pound refrigerator carry where Franco Columbu suffered a knee dislocation that required surgery.⁴³ Nor did Kono need to pay his own way to Kansas City to conduct a Junior Olympic Weightlifting Training Camp supported by York Barbell.⁴⁴ On November 25 he attended a testimonial dinner honoring Ed Yarick in Modesto, California, with about 80 guests, including many leading lights in the iron game.⁴⁵ That he was able to afford this event owed much to his celebrity status and the influence of the national weightlifting committee led by current and past chairs Murray Levin and Bob Crist. Provision of airfare, room, and board also allowed him to officiate at the Record Breakers Invitational at the Aladdin Hotel in Las Vegas and to "piggy-back" a business trip to San Diego and a visit to his family in Sacramento. No records were broken, but Tommy shared the limelight with eleven lifters from six nations before an enthusiastic audience of 2,500 and millions more on *CBS Sports Spectacular*.⁴⁶

Back home, Kono's level of activity was equally intense. As the Honolulu Marathon attracted thousands more runners, his workload increased proportionately. It drew additional national attention when it was featured in a 1978 issue of *Sports Illustrated*. The article focused on the clinic devised by Dr. Jack Scaff, a Honolulu cardiologist who wanted to "educate people in the benefits of recreational long-distance running," Scaff claimed that 95 percent of the 2,000 participants in his 1977 clinic finished, The article also pointed out that "from a population of 350,000, the Honolulu Marathon attracted 3,050 entrants last December—one out of every 115 citizens" and that "the number of runners per capita in Honolulu is three times that of any other city on earth."⁴⁷ As representative of the sponsoring department, Tommy was immersed in this additional dimension of public service. The clinic, as he explained to Lothar Spitz in 1978, started on the first Sunday of March and continued every Sunday morning with "an average attendance of over 2,000 'joggers' and we have

Notable West Coast physical culturists at the prime of Tommy's life. From left: Walt Marcyan, Clancy Ross, Bill Pearl, Joan DeMillo, Betty Stern, and Tommy. The photograph was likely taken by noted bodybuilder and San Diego gym owner Leo Stern, Betty's husband.

about 125 to 150 new persons signing up each weekend."⁴⁸ Each Sunday morning, reported Carol Hogan, Kono would open the bandstand at Kapiolani Park.

> Then Scaff and [Dr. John] Wagner would lecture. When everybody started running longer runs, Kono would close the bandstand, put jugs and paper cups in his car and drive to Hawaii Kai. There he'd make punch to hand out to runners, then move to Aina Haina and set up another aid station. The clinic had no budget. ... "In 1978 we hit the peak," Kono said. "We had 1200 people turn out to hear Dr. Scaff give his talk. That same year we rented 10 MTL buses to run people to Hawaii Kai."⁴⁹

Eventually Tommy had five clinics running in Oahu. "I was never home on Sunday because I had to be at one of them. ... Hawai'i (had) the most runners because every Sunday morning, everybody is running. That was a fad." Although Scaff called it the Honolulu Marathon Clinic, Tommy preferred the term "jogging clinic," thinking "the word marathon would scare people away."⁵⁰

For this reason he eventually launched a free eight-week walking clinic program in 1986 to coincide with the seven marathon clinics he supervised. "Walking is an ideal form of exercise, especially for those wanting to get into shape," he argued. "Compared to jogging, walking—with its gentler rolling motion—puts much less stress on the knees, ankles, and spine." Kono's clinic was designed for sedentary citizens who wanted to start exercising. "We tell them to swing their arms vigorously so that their legs will keep pace (with the movement)." He advocated doing it three times weekly for an hour. "The walk should be vigorous enough so that you breathe hard and perspire." Tommy hoped this form of aerobic exercise would "create a lifetime habit."⁵¹ Despite his anaerobic athletic and coaching background, he approached the clinics with gusto. "We have more people into aerobics, more runners, more people into physical fitness than ever before," he observed. Clinics entailed more work and time, but it was his job to "meet the needs of the community."⁵² However stressful these activities were to his already complicated life, he was always prone to take on more, not less.

His supervision of clinics continued until he retired, but it was only part of his commitment to the marathon and one aspect of his overloaded schedule. As he told Lothar Spitz in 1978, he was taking on a part-time business, planning to sell his house and build a new one, attending work-related training classes, and conducting a weight training class for teachers. "All this plus my work which involves long distance running and track and field ... have really got me busy."⁵³ He elaborated on his busy schedule to Otto Ziegler, a Houston promoter who asked him to conduct a lifting clinic. On the rare occasion he declined such an invite, Kono explained he was in charge of

> a Summer Fun program for kids 6–13. I'm in charge of physical fitness programs and this hasn't been difficult because I have another person to help me. But, this I have "inherited" Track and Field and also Biking (Rodeo). I've also initiated writing a booklet for the Dept. for Physical Fitness for Senior Citizens and have accepted a teaching assignment at one of the universities here on weight training. The whole thing has become a little nightmare.

Nightmare or not, Tommy reveled in the attention he received as a weightlifting authority and coach. He revealed to Ziegler that he had recently conducted a "Basics of Barbell Training" seminar where he arranged for 80 seats but "over 130 turned out, half of them high school kids and the rest parents and coaches. It went over extremely well and there has been request for another such 2-hour session." Only his myriad of local commitments prevented him from coming to Houston, but he was very willing to assist Ziegler in finding an able substitute. "Please let me know and I will follow through by writing them."[54] Tommy probably did not realize that it was not so much the knowledge he might impart but his weightlifting celebrity status that prompted Ziegler's invitation.

That Tommy was able to devote so much time and energy to so many interests beyond his regular employment meant that sacrifices had to be made in other sectors of his life. Prior to his assumption of family responsibilities in the early 1960s, he was consumed by his training and aspirations for weightlifting championships. Now, he admitted to Spitz that his weight training, "minimal for conditioning only," was limited to two or three sessions and that jogging was out of the question. He had torn the lateral meniscus on his left knee while conducting a fitness class and would soon have an operation. Although family responsibilities had once supplanted his total devotion to weightlifting, they, too, assumed a lesser priority. "Everyone is fine and I am enjoying Mark growing up," he reported to Spitz. "Jamie is trying to be very independent and his interest is not that of the family. JoAnn is beginning to copy Jamie although she acts more matured."[55] Further light is shed on their growing-up years in a conversation Sarah Fair had with joAnn seven months after her father's death.

> joAnn got teary while talking about Tommy and said he really wasn't home very much or involved with the family. He did, however, try to discipline from afar and would ask them if they'd exercised that day, helped their mother or other things he wanted them to do. He encouraged good principles. joAnn also said it was sad because their Dad meant so much to other people and they (the family) would have appreciated some of his attention that he gave out so freely to everyone else. joAnn said THEY never had him.[56]

Mark conveys much the same sentiment, though in more muted fashion. "My sister still looks back that he was gone so much, and like when someone passes away you wish you had more time with them."[57] Even to his brothers in Sacramento, to whom he had always been close, he increasingly limited contacts to long distance phone calls rather than letters for the sake of time. Seemingly unconcerned about the sacrifices he was making at home or his physical well-being, Tommy intensified his activities. Upon learning his family would need to occupy temporary quarters pending completion of their new home, he expressed hope to Spitz that "in this transit time I can do many things," possibly even assisting him with a new magazine on fitness training.[58]

Amidst this swirl of activity, the Konos assumed the financial burden of constructing their home in an upscale neighborhood overlooking Pearl Harbor and Honolulu. Rising inflation in the late 1970s affected their transaction in two ways. The cost of housing was increasing dramatically, and they needed $85,000 to finance the cost of $115,353 for their new property which was nearly double what they had borrowed in 1973, but the $20,298 realized in escrow from their Waipahu home enabled them to make a down payment of $29,228 towards the construction of their new home at 98–2025 Hapaki Street, Aiea.[59] Monthly payments of $662 ($7,944 pa) were easily accommodated by the Konos' combined 1978 income of $37,602 which included $606 from extraneous sources. By this time, Flo was contributing substantially to the family's income. In addition to the $10,999 she earned at Hickam, she received $3,254 from her part-time job at Honolulu Sporting Goods (Honsport).[60] And jobs for both Konos seemed secure. Flo received frequent commendations for her performance from the Air Force, and Tommy's 1979 evaluation indicated that he "exceeded requirements" in all job categories and was complimented for his "congenial personality" and being "dependable and conscientious."[61]

Aspiring Entrepreneur

Financial security, however, did not lessen Kono's desire to earn more money or need to curb his public service activities. In May he reported to Murray Levin that he had just conducted the state AAU track meet, masters track meet, and high school powerlifting competition, all on the same day. "That was hectic." As a result of Hawaii's jogging boom, Tommy had to hire a jogging specialist. "Can you imagine attending 4 meetings in one day ... pertaining to jogging?" Additionally, the annual Summer Fun program he had been directing for kids included two more projects in 1978. Still, he regarded weightlifting as "my first love but would you believe it that I haven't been able to train with weights for the past 2 months! I've lost my calluses on my hands. Yet, I am booked to give a weight-training workshop Wednesday for all the volunteer instructors of the 4 YMCA's here in Honolulu. I'm also scheduled to teach at a College in late June and my subject will be weight training."[62] For July, he told his German friends, he would be "extremely busy" because of two large undertakings. "Run America Run," a 10,000-meter race, would attract 3,000 runners, and the World Age Group Games would feature trampoline and acrobatic competitions for teenagers for several days. Then for the second year he would serve as an official for the World's Strongest Man Contest in Hollywood and in August for the second Record Breakers competition in Las Vegas. For the latter, he would receive travel and per diem, whereas the former, funded by CBS, would include a gratuity of $400.[63]

To increase the family income further, Tommy sought other opportunities in the wider realm of business. He had already sampled this field in the 1960s with his Maui health studio and creation of the knee and waist bands marketed by York Barbell. In the 1970s, as York's business declined, Kono reassumed his copyholder rights but lacked an outlet. While TK Knee and Waist Bands remained on sale for weightlifters and other athletes, he took on a more serious enterprise in 1977 by selling Total Image products for weight reduction, vitamin supplementation, and face lifting. It was a proposition Tommy embraced from Gary Watanabe, a major distributor. By November, however, Tommy was struggling to promote these products. From May to December, Kono's income was only $2,169; expenses for 153 items, 26 trips for business luncheons, and 15 long-distance phone calls that totaled $1,829 left him with only a $340 profit.[64]

Nevertheless, he shared this money-making scheme with Kenji Onuma, a former Japanese weightlifter whom he had met at the 1956 Olympics. Onuma, who discovered weightlifting as a member of his college rowing team, became one of the top lightweight lifters in the world and a two-time Mr. Japan. Tommy called him "The Tokyo Titan." At Melbourne, Onuma "astonished veteran lifters at the training hall with an easy 402 pounds front squat and left even the Soviet coaches and trainers dazed by successfully cleaning 330, 342 and finally an unbelievable 352 pounds at a bodyweight of 146½ pounds." With Kono as a role model, Onuma aspired to become an Olympic champion. Now the president of Waseda University, he became Tommy's business associate.[65] Their friendship warmed as a result of several visits of Onuma to Hawaii and Kono to Japan. After visiting Tokyo in June 1974, Kono expressed gratitude to Owao "Ban-san" Omokawa, Kenji's business associate, for "showing me the rich cultural background of my ancestors. I appreciate even more the fact that Japanese blood flows through my veins."[66] Ban-san represented Japan Deep Hole Boring, a company created in 1964 to manufacture drilling components for scientific and industrial use.[67]

Tommy, with nostalgic ties to his ancestral homeland and friendship with

In addition to being the best weightlifter in the world and a leading bodybuilder, Tommy wanted to be a successful businessman, much in the manner of Bob Hoffman. He teamed up with Japanese weightlifting champion Kenji Onuma to form the KIO Company to market Japanese-made industrial goods in the United States. Onuma is pictured here training in Honolulu with Kono for the 1958 Senior National Championships in Los Angeles. Tommy's article on "The Tokyo Titan" appeared in the March 1959 issue of *Strength & Health*.

Kenji, deemed it a possible fertile ground for investment and to that end created the KIO Company after his visit to Japan in November 1974. With Tommy as president and headquarters at his home in Aiea, it included Omokawa; Kenji; and two other businessmen, Richard Fukuda (Hawaii) and Masayuki Ito (California) on its board. The KIO Company was to facilitate the sale of industrial products imported from Japan in Hawaii and the mainland.[68] joAnn recalls that "Omokawa spoke no English. He had a sister over on the big island, and whenever he was in town they'd go to dinner at the nicest Japanese place, of course. They were in business—the three of them, and they just wanted to use my father's name. He wasn't actively involved." Flo concurs, adding that "they had a lawyer, and he worked with the lawyer. They made him president." They had "an accountant and a realtor," notes joAnn, but "I think all of the money was in Japan." Flo observes that Tommy was "always coming up with ideas for things." There was Barley Green and Shakley and Melaleuca, ideas fostered by Dr. You. "And then he got into a pyramid or something."[69] But none of these business ventures ever took off.

Meanwhile, despite his own limited success with Total Image, Kono tried to interest Kenji in it and described Watanabe as "a hustler and doing very well in selling and promoting his 'chain' of distributors." Tommy even sampled some of the products himself. Prospects for mutual profits, however, seemed uncertain. "I didn't think that Ultra II Diet would go over too well for it meant restricting your intake of rice and other carbohydrates; something which I am sure would be extremely difficult for the average Japanese. ... But, result-wise and for lasting affect this Total Image can't be beat." Tommy suggested that Onuma might also consider "a liquid vitamin-mineral-protein concentrate that the average businessman in Japan can take a 'shot' of before they begin their work or during an informal business get-together. ... Formulate it in individual personal bottle (like the whiskey comes in during your airplane flight) and sell it that way by the cases to business offices. With a touch of alcohol in it (like Schnapps) it might go over real big."[70] What concerned Onuma was the "incredible" increase in yen value which made it more expensive to export goods from Japan. Nevertheless, Tommy, through the KIO Company, was already marketing boring and fittings products manufactured by Nippon High Speed Boring. What Onuma wanted him to consider was a new health food produced by a friend, "a vegetable protein vitamin/mineral concoction reinforced with various enzymes." Such drinks were "very popular" in Japan, and Onuma wanted to know if Kono thought they would sell in Hawaii.[71]

The health drink of Onuma's friend was just what Tommy "had in mind. One 'shot' of it will fortify the businessmen and then he can drink, eat and make merry, knowing that he has taken the necessary nutrient for his health and well-being." But nothing materialized in real sales or profits for either Tommy or Kenji. Likewise, uncertainty prevailed about an idea that germinated from a dinner the Konos had with Mits and Dot Kawashima of marketing weights manufactured in Japan, much as Hoffman and Weider were doing in Taiwan and India. Possible outlets in Honolulu would be Mits' health food store and Honsport, Flo's place of employment where there was a "constant demand for barbell sets and weights." Tommy asked Kenji whether he thought "a 'KIO' or 'KONO' brand plates can sell here? It all depends on how much it would cost to produce it there and ship it in, or I can investigate here and have the molding made in Japan and castings of weights here." Tommy ascertained that spas and gyms were "sprouting up all over the place and training with weights and Nautilas [sic] Machines plus jogging is the 'in' thing in Hawaii and U.S." Seeking to exploit this enthusiasm, Tommy's latest idea was a Collapsible Abdominal-Slant Board which he felt "could be a terrific product to market if it can be made." Impressed with Tommy's ideas, Ike Berger, also an aspiring entrepreneur, expressed interest in buying them for $2,000 and providing royalties.[72]

What hampered fulfillment of such plans was Kono's continued involvement in physical culture activities in Hawaii and the mainland. On June 17, 1979, he served not only as head judge for "a big physique show" staged by Mits Kawashima at the Honolulu concert hall but also coordinated the judging and pre-judging. Then on June 24

> my work of 6 weeks culminated in a 10 km. run which had 3,200 entries. Handing out race numbers and tee-shirts, and coordinating the over-all run was a task. It was the second biggest run staged in Hawaii. That night, after the run, I flew to California for 5 days to serve as a judge for the "World's Strongest Man" TV competition. I returned Saturday, June 30 to put on the annual Independence Day Physical Fitness Festival at Kapiolani Park Bandstand, the following day. ... End of this month July 25 to August 1, I will be in Colorado Springs, Colorado, for the U.S. Olympic Committee Sports Festival which will attract 40 weightlifters and 4 coaches plus administrators. July 20 and 21 I will be in Maui for their County Fair to MC the Power Lift and Olympic Lift competitions.
>
> It seems I have been going like this for the past 3 months and I guess I am at fault to try to be involved so much when I am asked, I should concentrate on BUSINESS.

He came to this realization after Tommy's bookkeeper informed him that he needed to start moving his products in the islands and mainland. "My head isn't screwed on right for business," he admitted to Onuma, "but I promise it will be better. It has to be for I do not want to have the KIO company only by name." Even more neglected by Tommy's busy schedule was his physical well-being, leading him to confess he had not trained for three weeks but "took a short workout" on July 7. "I reached my 49th year during my trip to California and I had voweled [sic] that I will be in great shape by my 50th birthday ... so, I have to start training regularly and hard."[73] Having to juggle so many balls—job, family, coaching, business, and public service—was taking a toll on Tommy's ability to focus and prioritize the most important aspects of life.

Onuma shared many of Tommy's interests and responsibilities. He, too, vowed to get in "great shape" by his next birthday the following March, but his immediate concern was Kono's fledgling company. He believed it was

> necessary for KIO to start doing substantial business if it were to avoid tax disadvantages, let alone to benefit the officers concerned. We feel that we at NHSB are to blame for the lack in the past of business through KIO, and we are determined to really get "the wheels turning" now. Fittings, both carbon & stainless steel, are one candidate, barbell weights are another, for KIO's business take-off. As I mentioned in our telephone conversation, we are sure that a KONO Brand will sell much better there, if there's demand at all, than will say, a KIO brand. As I said, we can supply you with weights of your design at prices that can compete with any other manufacturer.

With regard to other business arrangements, Onuma planned to send samples of his friend's health drink for Tommy to test for marketing in Hawaii, and he was impressed by Berger's offer to buy his ideas. "You have the special gift of producing unique ideas out of nowhere. This is one thing that one can't learn; one must be born with it."[74] Tommy was still "the idea man."

Iron Game Icon

By the end of the 1970s Kono's accomplishments were being recognized in Hawaii and abroad. In June 1979 he was invited by Trans World International to officiate at the third World's Strongest Man Contest at Universal Studios and again in August 1980 at the Playboy Resort at Great Gorge, New Jersey. There he shared the spotlight with other iron game celebrities, including Olympic hammer thrower Harold Connolly, shot putter Parry O'Brien, powerlifters Fred Hatfield and Terry Todd, and John Terpak, who were also invited to officiate.[75] At the 1982 version in June at Six Flags Magic Mountain in Valencia, California, Tommy organized a Japanese-style sumo wrestling event where competitors wore ceremonial garb and performed ritualistic gestures.[76] In October 1979 his weightlifting accomplishments were recognized by a reunion organized by the USOC and hosted by Frank Sinatra for 160 gold medalists in Atlantic City. Kono was one of nine Olympians from Hawaii, which boasted the highest per capita titlists of any state. Tommy and Flo had a "grand time," he told Lothar Spitz, and they were able to visit his brothers in Sacramento on the way back.[77] Although the U.S. entry, Mark Cameron, placed just fourth at the IWF Invitational Superheavyweight Championship on December 1 in Tokyo, Kono was honored by his selection to serve as head referee.[78] Other accolades ensued from his organization (with Pete George) of the America Cup competition in Honolulu on October 25, 1980, after the boycott of the Moscow Olympics. On behalf of the city of Honolulu, he was asked by the State Department and the AAU to stage this international event within three months. It attracted "106 competitors from 19 countries and was held over a 3-day period," Kono recalled. Years of marathon experience enabled him to handle intricate details of transporting athletes and officials, security, interpreters and entertainment.[79] Murray Levin congratulated Kono and George who "knocked themselves out to ensure the best of facilities."[80] As the 1984 Los Angeles Olympics approached, Tommy, in consideration of $1,000, agreed to prepare a colorful brochure and poster on weightlifting history, rules, and records for Mobium Corporation of Chicago.[81] Then on November 16, 1982, he was one of two dozen athletes of Asian descent, including Ford Konno, Sammy Lee, and Harold Sakata (posthumously), honored at a banquet sponsored by the Asian American Voluntary Action Center in Los Angeles.[82]

The greatest tribute, however, was bestowed on him by the International Weightlifting Federation. In a 1982 statistical analysis conducted by Hungarian Ferenc Fejer based on medals won, Tommy was rated first among the 30 "most successful lifters of all times" with 70 points, followed by Arkadi Vorobiev with 67, Pete

As a leading authority on strength, Kono was invited along with other iron game luminaries to serve as an official for several of the earliest World's Strongest Man contests. In 1980, it was held at the Playboy resort in the Great Gorge of the Pocono Mountains of upstate New Jersey. To Kono's left is Bruce Wilhelm, winner of the 1977 and 1978 versions of the event, and to the far right of the photograph is Harold Connolly, 1956 Olympic gold medalist in the hammer throw who served as director of the 1980 event.

George (62), John Davis (61), and Waldemar Baszanowski (60).[83] Back home this high honor was celebrated by the headline "He's the Greatest, That's All" in the *Honolulu Star-Bulletin*. "Gee, that's nice" was Tommy's reaction. That he attributed his selection to having "just outlived everybody else" was a characteristic gesture of humility that no doubt enhanced his status as an iron game icon.[84]

7

Retro Coach

"Nothing is more rewarding than to know you've influenced people in a positive way and they have picked up the habit of improving themselves morally as well as physically."[1]—Tommy Kono

Back to Basics

As Tommy entered his fifties, the intensity of his activities increased along with a need to redouble his commitment to those ideals, institutions, and people who were critical to forming his identity. Weightlifting remained his foremost loyalty, and although he could no longer compete, he enjoyed a vicarious commitment as a coach, referee, and promoter. "Though lifting future here doesn't seem bright we haven't given up," he vowed to Murray Levin in the fall of 1981. "We are out to produce new, young lifters. It will take time but Olympic lifting will never die here in Hawaii." Tommy considered Levin's newsletter vital to "bringing the message out to everyone," encouraging lifters to "aim higher" than national recognition. To facilitate this process, he volunteered for any trip to Japan or Asia, arguing that his flights would cost less than trips for mainland officials, and his ability to speak Japanese would assist the lifters. With his international referee's card he could "work in any capacity."[2]

Although no such opportunities were immediately available, Tommy funneled his enthusiasm into building local talent. Flyweight Brian Okada of Maui welcomed his revelation in December 1981 that he wanted to get back into coaching for the 1988 Olympics. "Being coached under you and watching other coaches coach lifters made me realize how lucky I was. … You made me think, think, and keep thinking of how to lift and improve myself. You use to always ask me 'why?' Right now I know all the basics you taught me and I still can improve because I know the right way to lift." But having the right attitude was the most important thing Tommy taught Okada. "So much of weightlifting lies in the mind," observed journalist Lee Imada as he observed Tommy's protégé. "Only 'positive' thoughts cross his mind as he prepares for the lift."[3] Further to encourage Okada's progress and state of mind, Kono sent him a copy of *Secrets of the Squat Snatch* and shared his plans for revitalizing weightlifting by showing motivational tapes before workouts. He also established recruitment programs for high school lifters through a series of clinics with such incentives as tee-shirts, badges, and certificates, much in the manner of Hoffman's

Strength & Health League of the 1930s.[4] Okada believed Tommy planned his program well, but it was going to be a tough sell, "especially when there are many sports in the islands & almost all are more popular than weightlifting"[5] Okada eventually won his class at the national championships in Northbrook, Illinois, with a 72.5 kilo snatch and a 97.5 clean and jerk.[6]

Featherweight Brian Miyamoto was runner-up at Northbrook with a 92.5 snatch and 112.5 clean and jerk. He met Tommy after winning a chin-up contest in Kapiolani Park and wanted to go to the Olympics in gymnastics, boxing or weightlifting, but "gymnastics wouldn't work because I couldn't split," he concluded. "I was strong ... so I started powerlifting then went into weightlifting, and Tommy had such high expectations of me. Although I won four nationals ['83, '85, '86, '87] I never made it to the Olympics which I thought disappointed Tommy." Russell Ogata finished 11th as a middleweight at the 1982 nationals with lifts of 122.5 and 150 kilos. He encountered Kono when he went to the Nuuanu YMCA after three months of training elsewhere.

> Tommy came down and he looked at my weightlifting shoes which had built up heels, really really high, and he said, "you lift with this?" and I said, "yeah, why?" And that's how our relationship started, but we got along, especially after I retired, so he didn't have to scold me anymore. But he and I would talk about the lifters and different things and what made a good lifter and things that he respected. That's why he respected Pete a heck of a lot because he and Pete had the same background, and they worked the same way, and they never looked for excuses, always opportunities, and he filled me in about Pete's lore and about the people he respected in the game. And it was not so much their lifting prowess, although Pete was Olympic and world champion. It was about who they were and what they did, and toward the end about the goodness of each person.

Darren DeMello was never a national contender but a keen observer of Kono's methods and contributor to the spirit Tommy deemed so vital to team success.

> So I entered a contest in 1983, and Tommy was on this table and Pete was the emcee. I remember I was so nervous. I had just learned the snatch lift, cause I used to only do power cleans and clean and jerk. So I went up for my opening snatch and I was so nervous and missed the lift. I was so upset because I was so fired up to beat Russell, and I missed it again. ... I got one more chance, and I could hear on the side Tommy's voice as I was setting up on what I was trying to focus doing, and he said, come on Darren, you can do this. Concentrate. ... And that's what I did, and I made the lift. I'll never forget that. So every time I would hear Kono when I lift, and I would focus on his voice. It was always calm. He was not like Russell, all fired up. Russell had his own way, and it worked for him, but Tommy had this inward, like nothing would disturb him. I imagine him lifting like that. Even in his presence, I see him every Saturday at the gym he was always calm. And I would do a perfect attempt, and he goes, "aw you cut your pull." Never a good lift that I thought I did. "Not so good. What did you think of that one? That was a good one." Okay. But he could see things. He was my inspiration.[7]

Mike Harada remembers "the coffee candy he gave us when we did good lifts, and him saying 'it was a fluke! Try it again!'" Then on the night before a major meet, "he'd send an encouragement. It would always end with the Japanese word 'ganbatte' which in English means 'do your best.'"[8]

But it was Ogata, from the training center in Colorado Springs, who best appreciated Kono's busy schedule and sacrifices he was making for his lifters. While congratulating Tommy in March 1982 for "charming" the Business and Professional Women of Honolulu, he hoped "you have more time to prepare the Hawaii guys for the nationals." Ogata felt guilty for taking up Tommy's time "because your phone is probably ringing or you have got to head off to a meeting."[9]

In a broader context, Ogata's presence in Colorado Springs indicated a shift of emphasis from local to national training protocols. It coincided with the passage of the Amateur Sports Act in 1978 which replaced the AAU, formerly in Indianapolis, with the United States Weightlifting Federation which was housed with other national governing bodies at the Olympic Training Center. The weightlifting hall enabled 15 elite Americans to train year round.[10] Heading this operation was Harvey Newton, a veteran coach/administrator from Florida, who instituted a registration system for prospective center trainees. Although Tommy developed a respect for Newton, he was reluctant to encourage Hawaiian participation. "Way out here in the middle of the ocean we do not have that many active lifters, and those who are into it I want to keep." Regardless of the merits of the registration system, "people born and raised in Hawaii are uniquely different and you can't force them otherwise you would lose them to other activities such as surfing." But he desired to become more involved in national and international affairs. He was "very much interested in serving either as a coach or assistant coach for the 1983 world championships" in Moscow. Although he did not speak Russian, he had visited the Soviet Union numerous times and would feel "comfortable and qualified for such an assignment."[11]

Although no such arrangement ever materialized, Kono became eligible for an even greater opportunity when Dr. Donn Moomaw, weightlifting commissioner for the 1984 Olympic Games, visited the islands and conferred with him and Dr. You. "I believe Tommy could be a tremendous asset to you in your administration of the weightlifting event," You assured him. "Kono is a name respected by the head of every national weightlifting delegation to be represented in the L.A. Games."[12] You's endorsement was reinforced not only by Kono's lifting and coaching record but his recent selection as greatest weightlifter of all time and a plethora of other honors bestowed on him every year. Moomaw became a strong proponent for Tommy to become director of weightlifting competition which would require permission for a leave of absence by the city of Honolulu from January 15 to August 15, 1984. In his appeal to Mayor Eileen Anderson, Moomaw argued that "there is no one in our nation who is as respected in weightlifting as Mr. Kono" and that he "would return to Hawaii with a whole new enthusiasm for his work with you."[13] Unfortunately, the term of his prospective service coincided with his busiest time of employment and public service in Hawaii. Even with his salary and expenses covered, it was unreasonable to expect Parks and Recreation to operate without his services for seven months.

Therefore, he became an assistant competition manager, with Don Wilson of Houston, reporting to Director Jim Schmitz of San Francisco. He would receive $427 per week along with round-trip airfare, lodging, and per diem from July 9 to August 10. Tommy was not unhappy with this lesser role. The 10 days of competition, held at Loyola Marymount University's Gersten Pavilion, he deemed "the best weightlifting competition to date!" Foremost of his responsibilities, which entailed working sometimes 14 hours a day, was an obligation to "maintain high morale of all the workers, particularly the loaders and those who worked ringing the stage." He had to "keep individual personalities from either dominating or clashing." In tending to myriads of daily details, Tommy worked "hand-in-glove" with Wilson to conduct "the smoothest competition possible."[14] Their efforts, added to the organizing genius of Peter Ueberroth, helped make the 1984 Olympics extraordinarily successful financially, earning a surplus of nearly $250 million of which the USWF received $656,000.[15]

Business Ventures

It seems remarkable that Tommy continued to pursue his own means of capitalizing in the business world, especially in light of other more primary interests and responsibilities. Since his coaching days in Germany, he remained in touch with equipment manufacturer Josef Schnell who wanted him to distribute an exercise machine in the USA, presumably through his KIO Company, and possibly interest Kenji Onuma in securing a patent for it during his forthcoming trip to Japan. Isaac Berger also expressed interest in marketing any exercise equipment available. Tommy told Onuma that Berger, after examining a prototype, would pay royalties upon marketing it. "He also said that he will take out a patent under my name and refine it so it will be more marketable. He is selling a rope gadget and evidently making well on mail order business."[16] To promote his new exerciser, Isaac formed Ike Berger Enterprises and sought to utilize Tommy's name and fame. He asked Kono to send an old photograph wearing his Olympic suit and gold medal, provide a testimonial of the exerciser's effectiveness, and secure a photo of a trainee using it under his supervision. For these services, Ike was willing to pay 50 cents for each unit sold stemming from the advertisement.[17]

Berger's pitch, however, far exceeded Tommy's expectations or ethics. Ike intended to publicize his Miniversal as a "$29.95 Miracle!" which offered over 100 exercises "to melt away every ounce of excess fat." Ike contended that it "does As Much for Your Body as a $6,000.00 Universal Gym (or your money back)." In returning the advertisement copy on February 12, 1981, Tommy cautioned Isaac that he and Dr. You believed that "the claims you make are not justifiable and you may end up with a law suit if you publish it as it is. Lavish claims by YOU is okay but if we are backing up everything you say, then we have to protect ourselves." Tommy wanted to "settle this as soon as possible so we can go on with making money." Dr. You, after conducting a series of case studies from a cross section of different age groups and ethnic backgrounds, provided Berger with a general assessment of his product's efficacy. "I have endorsed your exercise and exercise routine as one of the methods to greatly improve a person's health and physical well-being."[18] But You's cautionary advice hardly tempered Berger's proclivity for hyperbolic claims. A decade later, using his own fame as an Olympic and world champion, Berger refined his device into a SPEED SHAPER which he claimed could "Turn Belly Flab into a Rock-Hard Lean Stomach in just 7 Short Minutes a Day" for only $9.95. In developing it, Ike "accidentally discovered" a new science he dubbed Synometrics based on both isometric and isotonic principles.[19] It was almost a too-good-to-be-true scenario.

Tommy, however, was never so flamboyant or worldly wise to marketing gimmicks, despite decades of experience with Hoffman. On August 21, 1980, Kono, as KIO Company president, signed a three-year agreement with Iwao Omokawa, president of Nippon High Speed Boring Company of Kawasaki, Japan, to conduct sales in the United States of deep hole drilling machines, tools, accessories, elbows, structural materials, and other products manufactured by the Japanese firm. It required a deposit of $46,000 by KIO to cover initial expenses. In return, KIO would receive a 7 percent commission from gross sale proceeds. On April 1, 1982, this agreement was extended to carbon steel built-welding elbows.[20] The treasurer's report from December 1981 to December 1982, however, showed the company earned $117,413, of which $14,000 came from Hawaii, while expenses, including $80,461 to Nippon High Speed Boring, amounted to $127,813, showing a deficit of $10,400.[21] It was not the kind of losses the company could long sustain, so in February 1985, Kono recommended to Onuma the dissolution of KIO Corporation. Onuma's foremost concern, however, was "the possibility of your spending, at least temporarily, your own money to pay KIO's corporate expenses including attorney and CPA fees, and we feel prompted to take necessary steps for dissolution at an early date." Tommy reassured Onuma that $618 remained in the firm's account at the Bank of Hawaii which would cover the $286 owed to attorney Richard Fukuda and partially pay for the $572 owed to the Ernst & Whinney book-keeping firm. The remainder Kono would pay himself.[22] It was much the same story with Barley Green, a company that produced a dietary supplement developed by Yoshihide Hagiwara, a nutrition scientist and health food entrepreneur. Hagiwara claimed barley grass was an excellent source of nutrients to prevent disease and cure common ailments.[23] From March 10 to September 20, 1983, Tommy's Barley Green franchise earned $1.811 while incurring a $1,910 loss.[24]

These business setbacks, however, appear to have had little impact on the Kono family's financial health. From 1981 to 1983, Tommy's gross pay progressed from $27,466 to $29,942 (9.01 percent) to $31,463 (5.08 percent), while Flo's income from Hickam increased from $13,260 to $14,089 (6.24 percent) to $17,857 (26.74 percent), both of which exceeded respective inflation rates of 8.9 percent (1981), 3.8 percent (1982), and 3.8 percent (1983). The Konos also benefited from numerous interest-bearing accounts.[25] Although Tommy was frequently away, the family seemed "fine," he reported to Lothar Spitz. Jamie was married and living in Honolulu where he was working at the Ala Moana Shopping Center. joAnn was nearly finished high school and "trying to show her independence," and Mark was into surfing and skate-boarding.[26] Though not unaware of Tommy's status, they seemed to be enjoying a comfortable lifestyle without much guidance or support from their famous father whose name and talents were in demand elsewhere.

Noblesse Oblige

Ample personal assets not only provided a sound financial footing for his family but enabled Kono to expand his activities even further. As a former physique champion, he readily agreed to conduct the Mr. Waikiki Contest on July 4, 1981, at the Kapiolani Park bandstand. When the heat of the concrete floor under the hot sun caused contestants to start hopping from one foot to another, Kono encouraged them to "keep moving to keep cool. You gotta have kanaka [native laborer] feet, you know."[27] Then at the invitation of promoter Gus Rethwisch, he conducted the NPC Mr. Hawaii Contest in 1982 at Honolulu's Pacific Beach Hotel and served as head judge for the Maui Women's Bodybuilding Championships.[28] A year later, he was tapped by meet director Herbert Ishibashi to oversee the Physiques Bodybuilding Classic at the McKinley High School which featured two-time Mr. Olympia Larry Scott as guest poser. For the women's event, where he was not a judge, there was a scoring miscalculation rectified by head judge Cathy Chang who consulted Tommy for verification. "Honestly, I can always count on your expert advice in many situations, and even after making the decision, until I spoke with you, I was actually relieved."[29] Despite new rules by the American Federation of Women Bodybuilders (AFWB) specifying that judges must score 80 percent or higher on tests at several contests and that the majority on any women's judging panel must be women, Tommy was one of five who qualified.[30]

His workplace provided even greater opportunities, under official guise, for Tommy to exercise his volunteer spirit, especially for Olympic lifting. On official letterhead, he beseeched high school athletic directors and coaches in February 1983 to encourage their athletes to take part in the annual Oahu High School Clean and Jerk Contest, sponsored by Parks and Recreation and the Nuuanu YMCA. He argued that unlike powerlifting movements which were popular because of their ease of execution, "the Clean & Jerk lift requires explosive quality which is so vital to sports." It would have a significant impact on a player's athletic ability. "The more dynamic and explosive his muscles react, the better he will perform as an athlete." This contest on March 5 would be followed by a Hawaii State version and a Mr. High School-Hawaii contest on April 23 to enable contestants to measure improvement.[31] The annual Independence Day Physical Fitness Festival he conducted provided for public participation, featuring a Miss Fourth of July contest, fitness competitions, and demonstrations.[32] Tommy's election as president of the Hawaii Association of the AAU seemed a natural consequence of the many leading roles he played on behalf of fitness.[33]

By this time other forms of recognition were pouring in, especially after the widely publicized IWF ranking of greatest all-time weightlifter. On February 21, 1983, the Honolulu Quarterback named him Sportsman of the Year at its annual Banquet of Champions at the Queen Kapiolani Hotel. The award included a round-the-world trip for two on Pan American Airways.[34] It was followed by a resolution from the Hawaiian House of Representatives which, among other things, recognized Kono's "giving nature, always ready to offer assistance and coaching to anyone who asks" as well as "his unassuming manner" and "dedication and clean living" by which "he has popularized weightlifting as a serious sport."[35] At the 1983 Record Maker's Tournament sponsored by the United States Weightlifting Federation and Mack Trucks in Allentown in March he shared the spotlight with John Davis and absentee Vasili Alexeev for achieving eight world and Olympic titles.[36] "I

On March 26, 1983, Mack Trucks, then a sponsor of the United States Weightlifting Federation, joined with the school district of Allentown, Pennsylvania, to bring together many of world's best weightlifters in a meet called Record Makers IV. Lending prestige to the affair were (from left) Norbert Schemansky, Tamas Ajan (secretary general of the International Weightlifting Federation), Isaac Berger, and Tommy (courtesy Bruce Klemens).

am really basking in the glory of the past," he reflected to long-time friend and former lifting colleague Walter Imahara.[37]

It is not surprising that this renown led to myriad requests to tap his expertise. One of them came from distant American Samoa which shared a cultural kinship with Hawaii. Al Lolotai, who attended high school in Honolulu and played briefly for the NFL Washington Redskins, was training weightlifters. Four of them competed in the Hawaii Open at Farrington High School in October 1986, but they lacked the expertise of their Hawaiian hosts. Tommy concluded they needed more practice, especially if their travel was being independently funded. "If you can study the big jumps made by the American Samoan lifters between their 1st attempt and their second attempt lifts, as compared to seasoned lifters such as [Vernon] Patao (15 years old) and Brian Miyamoto, it becomes apparent that they either need better coaching or are not sure of their ability." Kono recommended a plan for Samoans to learn lifting basics and for young lifters to "correct movements and habits before they are influenced by wrong technique." To facilitate this program, Tommy was willing to provide a clinic, without honorarium, if arrangements could be made for travel, room, and board for himself and Flo. The Samoans responded enthusiastically, and for six days Kono promoted weight training and weightlifting at Samoan high schools and bodybuilding gyms. "The Lt. Governor and the National Olympic Committee there asked if I would return in 7–8 weeks," he told Russ Ogata. "I must have gone over pretty well. (Ahem) Maybe they're just being kind."[38] In retrospect, he pondered his ongoing commitments with no obvious personal gain. "Some of us keep plugging away because we don't know any better," he told Ogata. "I got a lot out of lifting so I guess I am trying to put back what I can."[39] He could easily have added that it had become his raison d'être.

An opportunity to indulge in his favorite form of volunteer activity occurred in March 1987 when he became head coach for American lifters at the Moomba Weightlifting Tournament in Hawthorn, Australia. It featured a young American team that won two gold, one silver, and four bronze medals against relatively weak contingents from Egypt, Hungary, New Zealand, Taiwan, and Australia. Nevertheless, Tommy was delighted to see the American flag raised seven times and the national anthem played twice. It was "a moving experience for a veteran lifter like me coming from the 1950s and early '60s when it used to be played a lot more often." He was Ajan (secretary general of the International Weightlifting Federation), for his achievements. What most impressed him, however, was the demeanor of American athletes. "I feel that the U.S. has some good young lifters who can perform well internationally." Unlike those he had coached a decade earlier in Montreal, Kono was proud of these lifters for their "good conduct and manners" on and off the platform. "The lifters cooperated and worked well together and in the short time an esprit de corps was developed to pull the team together."[40] Team manager Marty Cypher of Cabot, Pennsylvania, was equally pleased. "It is a long trip to Australia, but well worth it."[41]

Melbourne served as a wake-up call for Tommy to reenter the deep water of international coaching. "I got my appetite wet when I went down under with the team to Melbourne (Hawthorn) for the Moomba Tournament," he observed to Levin. "I learned how much even some of our more 'experienced' lifters *didn't know* about warming up for a contest or the last week of preparation."[42] Although

Also attending the Record Makers event was iron game icon John Davis, who passed away the following year, shown here with Tommy (courtesy Bruce Klemens).

he could not be available to officiate at all international competitions, he reiterated his desire to become more active to Harvey Newton and to IWF General Secretary Tamas Ajan. Though unfamiliar with the selection process, "should my name ever become mentioned for the possibility of officiating in the Seoul Games, I wish you could use your influence to sway them to accept me." He regarded himself especially qualified "because I am an oriental that many in Asia could identify with."[43] Notwithstanding Kono's outstanding qualifications, the board of directors selected current USWF president Jim Schmitz, whose lifters at the Sports Palace in San Francisco had won six national championships, to coach the American team in Seoul.

Nuuanu Coaching

A lower profile of voluntary service occurred each Saturday morning when Kono coached weightlifters of all ability levels at the Nuuanu YMCA. Although Tommy was always on call for advice and troubleshooting, his work consisted mainly of training lifters, observed Mike Mizuno, a regular swimmer at Nuuanu. "He was always in the gym."[44] The impact of these sessions was most evident from correspondence with expatriate islanders. Tommy advised Kenny Nishihara that "you must increase your leg power." This could best be done by low repetition squats with heavy weights. "Anytime you perform 8 to 10 reps in training you are 'pumping up' your muscles ... and that is bodybuilding." To maximize meet performances, he needed to do full squat snatches, not power snatches. "Isn't it easier to power snatch 60 kg. for 3 reps than to perform full squat snatch with 60 for 1? So, don't get lazy and do power snatch when you are warming up." Tommy also recommended that Nishihara perform front squats three workouts weekly. At least by following Kono's advice in part, Nishihara won the flyweight class at the 1987 national championships in Livonia, Michigan, in May with lifts of 80 and 107½ kilos.[45] He thanked Tommy for his "help on the squats. I have improved my front squat from 95 kg (a single as of Jan 1987) to 110 (two weeks before the Nationals)." He was also "breaking my bad habit of power snatching and power cleaning."[46] Another happy outcome of the Livonia championships was the third-place finish of Team Hawaii, owing to performances of Brian Miyamoto (to claim his third national title) and others who benefited from the coaching of Yoshi Yogi of Maui, and Tommy's mentoring. It also helped that Team Hawaii, headed by Kono, offered to fly athletes from neighboring islands to compete in state contests and pay part of the way to compete at national championships.[47]

Ogata, though living in Colorado Springs, was another beneficiary of Kono's coaching wisdom. "There isn't much new under the sun," Tommy wrote on January 11, 1987, "but most U.S. lifters and coaches think that 'they' have better steroids, ideal conditions, better coaches, better programs ... and the grass looks greener across the ocean." He proposed a "revolutionary" solution to America's ills.

> Go back to the ole American training system that created Charlie Vinci, Isaac Berger, Peter George, Schemanski, Sheppard and some others. Can many of our current top three lifters

come near or exceed the lifts that these former lifters of 20–30 years ago made (B.S.) before steroids? They must have done something right otherwise how could Berger's Jerk still remain on the American books? Lifters now days want something for nothing. They have better equipment, more knowledge (?), more opportunity to train and travel, and more incentive, BUT, something is lacking. Maybe, Russ, you can find the answer since you are living in the "heart" of American lifting [Colorado Springs].

Again, he encouraged leg work three times a week, emphasizing front squats. Tommy also recommended inspirational readings, including his old-time favorites, Napoleon Hill's *Think and Grow Rich* (1937) and psychologist Charles Garfield's *Peak Performers* (1987).[48]

Natalie Mew was Kono's first female pupil. She started as a powerlifter at the Nuuanu gym which was shared with the Olympic lifters. "One of them was Gary Kawamura, a long-time lifter," she recalled. "He approached me and said you ought to try Olympic lifting. Come over here and meet Tommy." As a teacher, Natalie warmed at once to Kono's coaching manner. "He was like a father figure to me, and I could tell him anything." "Everything that came out of his mouth was positive and encouraging and genuine." He was also generous with his time. "He didn't just coach me. He coached everybody. He was there every single Saturday for two to three hours. If I would come beforehand, he would come at nine and leave at noon. He would go to the Y on Wednesday and work out too, but he was always there. I didn't know he had a family. We were his weightlifting family."[49] These sessions would culminate in a local or regional meet in the main gym. But the board of directors expressed concern that the floor was being weakened by the dropping of heavy weights. Tommy argued that adequate protection was provided by a double-layered wooden platform, large rubber bumper plates to cushion impact, and rules requiring lifters to control the barbell. "The demise of weightlifting in Hawaii will come about if the Nuuanu YMCA no longer permits Olympic weightlifting to take place in the main gym." To conduct meets in the basement weight room would be regressing, and to hold them elsewhere would entail greater expense, labor, and paperwork. "Olympic weightlifting and the Nuuanu Y are synonymous." Nevertheless, reconstruction was necessary to reattach and reinforce the wooden floor to its concrete base.[50]

To encourage and improve the quality of Hawaiian lifting leading up to the Seoul Olympics, Kono wanted to establish a training center for Olympians passing through the state. "This would give our community an opportunity to see not only American but all the great athletes from other countries in training," he told Dr. You in 1985, "and in turn help our local athletes reach for higher goals." He also suggested holding periodic coaching and training seminars to prepare Hawaiians for national and international competitions, including the 1988 Games. Finally, he believed there should be an "Olympic Hall of Fame to honor our many Olympians who have brought so much glory and fame to Hawaii. This will help perpetuate the idealism of athletic excellence for the future generations of local athletes."[51] The idea man never stopped promoting ways to improve the sport on all levels and in all locales.

The Women's World Championships

With the passage of Title IX in 1973 and increasing women's participation in virtually all sports, there was a gradual movement to admit women to weightlifting competitions. It began when National President Levin appointed Mabel Rader to chair a Women's Committee which led to the first women's national championship in Waterloo, Iowa, in 1981.[52] Encouraged by a simultaneous surge of international interest, Levin launched his "brainchild" in 1987, after a three-way phone conversation with USAW Executive Director Newton and IWF Secretary General Ajan. The first Women's World Championship would be held in Daytona Beach, Florida, and the American team would be coached by Kono, for whom Levin had high regard. It was preceded by a team trials at the San Francisco Sports Palace on August 1 and a training camp at Daytona from September 27 to October 2. Tommy took a keen interest in preparing the women after the trials with lots of training tips: that they should concentrate on muscles specific to the quick lifts, avoid recreational activities that could cause injuries, and allow time to restore nervous energy. "Muscles recover faster than nerves," he told them on August 14. Above all, they should rely on mental preparation rather than drugs. "Napoleon Hill wrote, 'Anything the mind can conceive and believe, you can achieve.' And I sincerely believe that."[53] Four of the six goals of the camp (mental training, team spirit, pride in self, and a positive personality), superseded technical and strength aspects, coinciding with Kono's philosophy that weightlifting was 50 percent mental, 30 percent technical, and 20 percent strength. He advised his charges to "train as a team with definite purpose and you are bound to improve faster."[54]

Virtually all the women expressed satisfaction with the coaching and camaraderie at the camp. It was beneficial to one of them that "I got to really know the other team members and train with them rather than compete against them." Another believed that "being able to get to know each team member is vital" and "what I learned contributed a lot to my lifts." For another, the camp "intensified my incentive to train. ... It was fun." Team manager Marty Cypher concurred that Kono and former Olympian Mike Huszka "did a fine job of coaching" and that "the team worked well together as a unit."[55] "Kono was a perfect coach," Levin recalls. He "communicated with them by mail, and everyone received a hands-on answer. I use to go to Daytona Beach to watch him coach the women and to teach them their faults."[56] What Sibby Flowers, who placed third in Daytona, remembers about Tommy's coaching was his calming influence. "He was very kind and generous with his time, and he was very calm and wanted you to think and visualize what you're doing." He taught Sibby to believe "there's nothing around you, you're right there in the moment, you see yourself doing it."[57] Silver medalist Robin Byrd was no less grateful for Tommy's "time and support" and pleased he was returning in 1988.[58] Tommy reciprocated similar sentiments with the women, that "working with all of you was a great and enjoyable experience." He was "very proud of the way you conducted yourselves. We did things together as a team and it came across to the public that way. You did an exemplary job of promoting women's weightlifting."[59] In succeeding weeks Tommy provided follow-up advice to each team member, often with diagrams. "You've got problems, write it down and give me a phone call," he advised Suzanne Kim of Katonah, New York. "I can answer your question in less than 3 minutes which is only about $1.00 for the phone charge. My number is (808) 488–2998."[60] Tommy was determined to leave no stone unturned to ensure success for American women in their world debut.

The Daytona Beach competition from October 30 to November 1 attracted 100 lifters from 22 countries. "This was our finest hour," proclaimed Levin. The United States placed second to China, and Karyn Marshall won the heavyweight class, the first gold medal since Joe Dube and Bob Bednarski won their classes at Warsaw in 1969.[61] The achievements of the nine women included over 68 percent successful attempts, eight American records, and many personal records.[62] USAW board member Arthur Drechsler was no less enthusiastic. "The women did themselves proud, demonstrating not only high qualities of athleticism, but the very highest levels of sportsmanship."[63] Kudos for Kono came from many quarters, including Newton who attributed the team's performance to the confidence instilled by his involvement.

> Tommy enjoyed being part of this new wave of weightlifting, and he fully supported the members' efforts to achieve success. Expectations for each athlete were expressed positively. He kept strategies realistic and achievable. Most of the team had international experience and were not overly concerned about the pressures of a world championships. However, there was another pressure on Team USA, the pioneers in women's lifting. Although not openly discussed, they knew they needed to put on a good show and set the stage for eventual Olympic Games involvement. And, this team was very successful. ... Tommy's ways of coaching were such as to bring out the best in any lifter, male or female. He worked tirelessly to remove any psychological barriers the athletes may have placed on themselves.[64]

Newton believed "women's weightlifting is off to a very good start."[65] For Tommy, this experience validated his coaching credentials. "I thoroughly enjoyed my role as head coach for it brought back a lot of memories," he reported to Levin. The "girls" were "really a breed apart."[66] The success of this inaugural event insured the perpetuation of women's world championships and eventually admission to the Olympics in 2000.

Meanwhile, Tommy coached the next two competitions in Jakarta, Indonesia, and Manchester, England, with equal success. Although there was no formal training camp in 1988 and the Olympics intervened, Kono continued to correspondence-coach the nine women chosen to compete in Jakarta. He advised Robin Byrd to perform only front squats, practice "dead hang cleaning," and develop rhythm for squat cleans. For team members he underscored the importance of "peaking" and "sacrifices, making weightlifting first in your life."[67] Tommy arranged for the team's journey to include a three night stop-over in Honolulu to assemble everyone, lessen jet lag, and "develop camaraderie and team spirit." He also scheduled an impromptu training session followed by an inspirational talk by Pete George on "How Records Are Broken." It was arranged "so the lifters would be better prepared psychologically," Tommy explained.[68]

The women did well at the championships in early December where 103 lifters represented 23 countries. The United States again placed second to China. In accumulating 11 medals, no American "bombed out," seven national records were set, and there were 29 of 54 completions. Tommy was "proud of the way the team pulled together and performed. I was especially happy to see the U.S. team of 12 always trying to sit together at the dining room table which was for ten persons."[69] A favorite memory for Assistant Coach John Coffee, who had trained Robin Byrd and Colleene Colley, occurred outside the competition.

> The team had been shopping and was just getting back on the bus, when this little guy with an armload of paintings came onto the bus. Eventually, he approached me as a potential customer for his art. I'm no art connoisseur and I really didn't have room for a framed painting in my luggage, so I politely waved him away.
>
> Tommy evidently saw all this and he comes over and tells me I should buy one of the little guy's paintings, "it could mean he'd be able to feed his family that night." I gave the man a $20 bill and learned a great lesson about humanity. I still have the painting hanging on the wall at my condo. It's really beautiful, and it was probably the best $20 I ever spent.[70]

Although the women had not performed as well as in 1987 and room remained for improvement, Tommy deemed the Jakarta trip a "success and a great start of international competition."[71]

Preparations for the 1989 women's world championships in England featured another training camp headed by Kono in Colorado Springs. Again he focused on fostering team spirit. "Training and performing things together will set up a good 'family' feeling; a team working together." His emphasis in pre-camp conditioning was on cardiovascular fitness and flexibility exercises such as jogging, swimming, yoga, and bodybuilding movements related to lifting.[72] At the camp from September

Under Tommy's supervision, the American women's weightlifting team took second place at the 1988 World Championships in Jakarta, Indonesia. From left: Kono (head coach), John Coffee (assistant coach), Giselle Shepatin, Lynne Stoessel, Glenda Ford, Melanie Getz, Karyn Marshall, Robin Byrd, Arlys Johnson, Colleen Colley, Diana Fuhrman, and Denis Reno (manager).

25 to 30 there were two sessions a day where Tommy was assisted by Ben Green of Georgia, and manager Denis Reno of Massachusetts. Coffee was not part of the official coaching staff, but several of his lifters were on the team, and Tommy allowed him to share his room. Coffee recalls an incident redolent of Tommy's cultural background.

> There was a karate, judo, or martial arts group that we ran into in the hall. And one of the guys was making some off-color remarks to some of the lifters. They told Kono who told their coach, and the boys had to apologize and all that shit. When we got back to the room Kono says, "you know, they don't know real karate. Real karate commits suicide." And he wasn't smiling when he said it.[73]

Overall response by the lifters was positive with six of the 12 athletes making personal records. "Just being here has improved my lifts by 2.5 kg already," Colley reported.[74]

Despite excellent training facilities, veteran coaches, and nutritious food, positivity did not prevail for all team members. Diana Fuhrman complained that "the staff" lacked any "scientific (educated) background. Just because a person was a great athlete at the time, shouldn't automatically qualify them to coach. ... I feel most of the women at the camp wanted to know whether we should be physiologically 'peaking' at times or 'overtraining.' The staff could not answer questions like that." Fuhrman recommended Mike Stone and John Garhammer, "both of whom had Ph.D's and have concentrated all their efforts on Olympic weightlifting. Why haven't they been approached?"[75] Karyn Marshall did not attend the camp but was nursing a grudge from the previous year.

> Last year I was troubled by your comments regarding my bodyweight. I hope you will accept the fact that I have chosen to be a SHW and that it is working. Even though I don't look like Flo Jo, I still think that I represent the sport well.
>
> In addition, I was troubled by your last minute surprise in changing my opening attempts. While I realize you have the final say, I would appreciate it if you let me know your intentions well in advance so that I can prepare properly.
>
> I expect to open with 100–102.5 and 130 in Manchester. I also expect [husband] Peter [Marshall] to work with us again this year as he knows me best [on the] day of the meet and knows what I need to focus on.
>
> Please consider this in making your decisions. I respect your opinion and hope that as 8 time National Champion and 1 time World Champion that you will respect mine.[76]

Despite these rebukes, Tommy seemed pleased with the camp results. He reported that several lifters "were following more or less the 'Bulgarian' system of training and it was beginning to take its toll as the days went by. I believe they understand now that the 'tonnage' is not conducive to improvement in Total so they profited by the experience in Colorado Springs." Denis Reno concurred that it was "a very successful camp."[77]

The euphoria and camaraderie that characterized the two previous camps and competitions were not as evident in the 1989 world championships at the Royal Northern College of Music in Manchester from November 24 to 26. With 133 lifters representing 25 countries, the Chinese defended their team title. Bulgaria and the United States finished a distant second and third. The American women earned one gold, three silver, and five bronze medals and set four national records. Marshall set a world record snatch of 110 kilos in placing second to China's Han Changmei.[78] For Reno, the championships were an awakening that the rest of the world was catching up with America's early lead in women's lifting. "Now is the time for those interested in women's weightlifting to take some action!"[79] At least the women could take satisfaction that their third place far exceeded that of their male counterparts earlier in Athens who finished 15th, over 300 team points behind the Bulgarians and Russians.[80]

Coaching Afterglow

"I really enjoyed the women," Tommy told Walter Imahara in the aftermath of his experience. "They're very good athletes, and they listen. They miss a lift, and they cry, and I don't know what to do. But otherwise they are good athletes."[81] Veteran official Pete Miller observed Tommy coach many lifters, including some at one of the women's world championships. "I asked him how did he, as the greatest weightlifter ever, enjoy coaching women. And he said he really enjoyed it because they would listen to him, and his coaching was serious."[82] "It was a real pleasure working with the girls," Tommy reported to Levin. "Their cooperation and willingness to cheerfully accept appearances at various schools and functions even during our limited period of training camp made me all the more appreciate being a part of the team and scene."[83] What seemed remarkable about Tommy's coaching is that he transcended any vestiges of his patriarchal Asian culture and, as Mike Mizuno previously observed, treat his charges as equals and without bias.

One suspects, however, that there was more than what meets the eye regarding Tommy's affinity for the women. Stemming from his early days in Tule Lake, he was always somewhat shy and awkward around women. Mike Harada recalls an occasion in Los Angeles when all the lifters wanted to go to the burlesque show. "Burlesque," Tommy asked. "What is that?" "So you go in, and you have like a movie," explains Harada.

> Then they turn on the lights and have the girls come out, and all the weightlifters are in the crowd, including Tommy. Yeah, it was like, "come on, Tommy," because I was like a friend with him too. "You were Mr. America. You have a good body. You compete in these big meets. You can get women." There was this lady that worked in American Express, and she had blond hair and I don't know if he had sex or anything, but he really liked her. And the Russians wanted to beat him with Russian women. Get a girl pregnant or something. They wanted his genetics. There were all kinds of stories.

One would never know from reading his training logs that Tommy ever experienced a love life or had sexual thoughts, but Harada remembers times at meets when seeing a good-looking girl he would say, "she's got a nice derriere. Mike, talk to her, get her attention. He didn't say 'ass,' but he looked." "I'd rather help the guys," Harada explains, "but Tommy liked helping the girls. He wouldn't say it was because he finds them physically attractive but because they listened to him. When the local girls came to train, he would pay more attention to them than to us."[84]

Tommy was inclined to believe females possessed more natural performance advantages than males. While "women take to suggestions more readily and conscientiously try to perform their lifts correctly," men allowed their egos to "get in the way" and were more likely to "use power for making the lifts." Also, given that "women are the weaker sex," they "tend to rely more on technique, or good leverage" and "pay attention to details," whereas men "want to progress to heavy weights as soon as possible and many times forget the technique part and use only strength." He realized that "female lifters can be very emotional, so it is important to keep your instructions positive." Channeling emotions properly could be critical to winning. "Success will breed success," Tommy believed, "so when female lifters are able to attain their goals, they become more convinced of their capability." He believed females had an "extra plus" in relying on "emotional power rather than only physical power. When they tap into this source, they can perform extraordinary lifts at crucial times."[85] Kono protégé Beth Terry recalls winning Hawaiian championships "because Tommy believed in me more than I did" and "followed that old maxim, 'Where the attention goes, the energy flows.'"[86] This kind of gender awareness provided a basis for coaching future women. The confidence Kono instilled in these first international teams was a factor leading to acceptance of women's weightlifting. It was a far more positive experience than he had with American men he coached two decades earlier in Montreal.

Kono sustained these exuberant feelings in the afterglow of his three successive years as America's first world weightlifting coach for women. Although he was increasingly playing a peripheral role in national weightlifting, Kono continued to offer his assistance and advice for improving the sport, even after surgery on his left hand severely limited his ability to type.[87] Firsthand experience at the Olympic Training Center led the idea man to propose rearrangements with diagrams in building 23 where the lifters trained. "The gym should be run similar to a 'dojo' of judo and martial arts. They stress discipline and putting things away in their proper places would be a very good start. It will eventually be a habit." He also designed an Olympic bar rack, a chalk box, and a "TK Loading Master" to facilitate changing weights for different weight classes.[88] To the board of directors, he suggested early production of proper fitting lifting suits, distribution of banners, pins, and posters for public relations, early flight reservations, mandatory code of conduct signatures, traveling as a team, and discouraging interaction of family and friends with lifters during competition. "All lifters must train, eat, relax, have fun as a team and his/her foremost and only thought must be on the best performance of themselves and their team members."[89] Perhaps more than any other quality, Kono's stress on teamwork and team spirit reflected his Eastern collectivist heritage and upbringing which was being sustained directly by frequent visitations along with his personal and business associations with Japan.

"An old fire horse"

When the women's championships in Sarajevo, Yugoslavia, was moved to May 1990, he had to relinquish his coaching role to Bob Takano of Los Angeles because it conflicted with his work schedule. Tommy again likened himself to "an old fire horse" to team manager Reno. "Knowing the Championships is going on and not being there where the action is, I will have itchy feet and experience restlessness." Nevertheless, he felt obliged to share his thoughts on concentration from his lifting days with his replacements. "I let the coaching staff select my starting weights, jumps and making decisions. In that way I could blame them if things go wrong other than my lifting technique. I just concentrated on making each attempt with perfect technique." Takano later thanked Tommy "for his previous work with the team and his spiritual presence."[90] Kono exercised a more direct influence at a post-championships training camp staged in Colorado Springs by John Garhammer. The best part of the camp, Tommy estimated, was that the lifters were not seriously training for competition and thus more amenable to suggestions. He was also pleased that a camaraderie had developed during off hours from a "common bond of nursing their aching and sore muscles from training hard."[91]

For years afterward, Kono continued to encourage proteges to perform front squats and bridge stick high pulls. To Jackie Mah of Sacramento he recommended "correct leverage" for her to lift efficiently. "If you perform your Snatches and Pulls correctly you should tire in your legs when you perform 3 repetition Snatches or High Pulls. If your legs don't get tired by the third rep then you are performing the pulling part with your back ... which is incorrect."[92] He reminded Lauren Kenneally of Reno's club to "always use your LEGS to START THE PULLS. This means you wait until the bar is almost by your hips before you explode on your pulls. Also, keep the bar close to your chest in the pull for the Snatch."[93] On October 7, 1990, Tommy told Stephanie Zurek of Emeryville, California, to "work on your legs. Use wider stance in squatting and learn to love to squat. To avoid them is not facing facts." Zurek responded on the 14th that she was "squatting now three times a week and don't dread it."[94] Of all the women and men Tommy coached over the years, Melanie Getz of Brentwood, Missouri, was probably the most appreciative. "I have much respect and admiration for you Tommy," she wrote on September 7. "I want to be a World Champion too!! Sometimes I read over and over your letters and information and I think to myself (only sometimes) 'Whoa I can be a world champion.' Your positive encouraging style of communicating information works well and I'll take it *as often* as I can."[95] Buoyed by the unstinting confidence placed in him by his female charges, Kono volunteered to serve as head weightlifting coach for the 1992 Barcelona Olympics.[96]

What bolstered Tommy's chances was the outstanding performances of flyweight Chad Ikei who won five national titles, and between 1989 and 1991 set 21 national records. Ikei was initially an adept powerlifter until, after graduating from Kaiser High School in Honolulu, he began training with Tommy at his Nuuanu Saturday sessions. "He spends his time just training us," Ikei noted of his mentor. "He gives us a real positive attitude. He teaches us to think attempt by attempt, lift by lift." In 1991 Ikei became a resident at the Olympic Training Center and continued to set records.[97] Two-time Olympian (1992 and 1996) Vernon Patao also names Tommy as one of the biggest influences in his lifting life, but it was Dr. Masayoshi Nelson Yogi of Maui who inspired him to abandon football for weightlifting.[98] Tommy continued to work tirelessly to promote local lifting and physique contests and to protect gyms, such as those operated by Timmy Leong and Mits Kawashima, from burdensome government regulations.[99] For Olympic coach in 1992, however, the board of directors selected Roger Nielsen of Deerfield, Illinois, who had led the 1991 world championship team.

Retro Hero

Consolation was soon forthcoming for any self-doubts Kono harbored. Shikata-Ga-Nai, of course, was a powerful sustaining force through disappointments, and the certainty of his Parks and Recreation position was a solid base on which to build hopes for the future. Joint income tax returns show an increase from $54,062 in 1986 to $55,064 in 1987, reflecting a twice-monthly increase in 1987 from $1,499 to $1,568. It was justified in the high marks Tommy received from his April 1988 evaluation where supervisor Euphemia Nagashima recognized his "organization, implementation, and assistance of various physical fitness programs," but she recommended delegation of more responsibilities to subordinates.[100] No less important than his financial well-being and competence at work was his physical fitness. In August 1987 a film crew from NBC came from New York to film a promotional program for 1988 on what past Olympians were doing. He told his brothers that "I train 2–3 times a week in the garage so they wanted to interview me at home and show me working out."[101] "It is nice to be remembered," he told Bill Toomey of the USOC.[102] Tommy also needed to look fit for local physique contests he was asked to judge and for the opening of a large Gold's Gym in February 1990 where he was being honored along with Pete, Timmy Leong, and the late Duke Kahanamoku. "Being involved in all these things forces me to train regularly," he told Onuma. "Though I don't look like I train I feel better knowing that at least I am trying to keep some semblance of condition."[103]

In the wake of the 1988 Olympics, Tommy experienced an unusual number of recognitions. Following his induction into the Sacramento Sports Hall of Fame, the Sacramento History Center organized an exhibit displayed at the City/County History Museum featuring memorabilia of local sports activities. Tommy's achievements were portrayed as unique not only as a Japanese American but as Sacramento's first gold medalist.[104] In August 1990 the Japanese American National Museum in Los Angeles immortalized his life in its Heritage Film Series. "I'd love to produce a film on your life for children," commented producer Karen Ishizuka. "Our kids need role models to help them better understand that they can go into anything and be anything."[105] Another significant honor was bestowed on Tommy by the Downtown Athletic Club in New York City when he was invited to accept the Steve Reeves Award at the 10th annual Fitness Awards Dinner on September 21, 1990. "The name of Reeves is legendary from my high school days and to be listed with the past nine fitness and sports recipients such as Buster Crabbe, Jack LaLanne and Rafer Johnson is honor plus," he responded. On this occasion, he requested permission to include Flo who "has always stayed at home or in the background" when he received such honors.[106] No less eager to recognize Kono's heroic status was his home state of Hawaii which sought his presence to give dignity to major sporting events. On June 11, 1991, he and the widow of famed swimmer Duke Kahanamoku lit the torch to open the Aloha State Games. And on December 25, 1993, Tommy received the Mackey Yanagisawa Lifetime Achievement Award at the Jeep Eagle Aloha Bowl.[107]

Serving as a catalyst for these recognitions was Kono's induction into the U.S. Olympic Hall of Fame on July 6 in Minneapolis along with pugilist George Foreman, diver Sammy Lee, swimmer Tracy Caulkins, figure skater Scott Hamilton, and oarsman John Kelly, Sr. It was recognized in Honolulu with a testimonial dinner sponsored by the Japanese Chamber of Commerce and coincided with a plethora of congratulatory messages from public and iron game notables, including Senator Daniel Inouye, Congresswoman Patricia Saiki, Governor John Waihee, Tamas Ajan, John Grimek, Reg Park, Alyce Yarick, and Peary and Mabel Rader, and a resolution from the City and Council of Honolulu.[108] Well wishes from Arnold Schwarzenegger seemed special. Tommy was "a big inspiration to me when I started to train," Arnold recalled. "I remember seeing you for the first time in the early 60's in Vienna when you won the world championships both in weightlifting and in bodybuilding—all in the same week. ... When I first arrived in the United States in the late 60's one of my trips took me to Hawaii where you showed me the greatest hospitality, introducing me to many great athletes and giving me lots of moral support."[109] Meaningful, too, was a letter from President George Bush in October 1990 "offering a sincere apology" for injustices done to Japanese Americans during World War II.[110] But neither it nor $20,000 provided by the Civil Liberties Act of 1988 signed by President Ronald Reagan for surviving detainees in internment camps were likely viewed as recognition for losses so much as gains by Kono whose athletic and financial success and love for America could be attributed to the deprivations he experienced as a child at Tule Lake.

8

Political Quagmire

"I don't like politics but if you want to see the right things happen, you have to get involved."[1]—Tommy Kono

The irony of Kono's heroic elevation in the 1980s, stemming from his unprecedented achievements in the 1950s, contrasted with the existing state of American weightlifting where demoralization had set in after decades of decline. Coincident with the many accolades showered upon Tommy in the wake of his Hall of Fame induction, there emerged a growing disenchantment with how the sport was administered. Organizational issues with political ramifications increasingly confronted the board of directors and its attendant bureaucracy. By the late 1980s, the weightlifting hierarchy was transformed by the replacement of Harvey Newton as executive director of the Colorado Springs training center by George Greenway, and Murray Levin's replacement as federation president by Gene Baker. In talking with lifters and officials nationwide, Baker quickly perceived the negative impact of the "we" and "they" atmosphere that existed under his predecessor between old guard administrators and rookie coaches and their athletes. "What has happened is that we have lost our ability to work together and trust one another." By professing openness to new ideas and complaints, Baker hoped to "get American lifting moving again" by replacing the adversarial "*they*" with a "*we*"-can-do-it attitude. His democratic approach might reduce dissension, but it hardly coincided with former national coordinator Carl Miller's diagnosis of what made Eastern European weightlifters so successful. It was "lack of discipline," Baker vaguely believed, "that prevents good talent from achieving its potential."[2] The most serious blow to American hopes for improvement through its existing free enterprise system, however, was the loss of two publicity mediums in 1986—*Strength & Health,* soon after Bob Hoffman's death, and *Iron Man,* which became a bodybuilding magazine after its sale to John Balik. Both publications for a half century had been critical sources of inspiration and recruitment, two qualities most lacking in American weightlifting.

Lessons from Eastern Europe

Soon after the 1988 Olympics, Naim Suleymanoglu, who had clean and jerked 419 pounds at 130 bodyweight to set a world record and win a gold medal at Seoul, visited Colorado Springs. He was treated like a celebrity. "If we could just develop someone of his caliber, weightlifting in the U.S. would skyrocket," USWF Coach Bob Morris observed. Suleymanoglu explained how it could be done. His secret to success was not so much superior technique but discipline and his love for the sport. "I train six days a week, six hours a day," he revealed. Although he lifted for Turkey, he credited his former Bulgarian coach for instilling in him this regimen. It never seemed possible, however, for American lifters to replicate the kinds of physical endurance of the Bulgarians. In July 1990 at Gettysburg College, Leo Totten organized a training camp called "hammer time" where athletes experienced high intensity workouts. His assistant, Chris Polakowski, noted that "the highlight of the week was Wednesday's Bulgarianized workout, which consisted of six half-hour sessions of very high intensity. ... The feeling from the group was that Americans can incorporate this method of lifting in the right dose."[3] Exactly what was meant by "right dose" is uncertain, but the intense program Totten administered was still a far cry from the regimen of Suleymanoglu. A more sustained effort to imitate the Bulgarian system was put in place in 1991 by Dragomir Cioroslan, coach of the new national resident training program at Colorado Springs. Here America's elite lifters would train five or six hours a day with high quality coaching, excellent nutrition, access to the latest in sports science, and no worries about rent or transportation. Significantly two-thirds of training time in Cioroslan's high intensity plan was devoted to strength-building.[4] Former Bulgarian coach Angel Spassov, who had moved to Texas, was skeptical whether it would work on Americans, and it was "shocking," he told a reporter, "that in a country such as ours, with our heritage in WL, we have set fairly modest goals."[5]

After so many decades of relative decline, there seemed to be no stone unturned to achieve higher goals. Still, the stagnation continued. In the 1989, 1990, and 1991 world championships the United States finished 15th, ninth, and 11th, respectively, while the women ranked second (1988), third (1989), fourth (1990), third (1991), and sixth (1992) in their world rankings. While most emphasis was always placed on recruiting, the number of registered weightlifters grew slowly from 1,687 in 1985 to 2,389 in 1991, likely the result of more women. "One of the greatest mysteries" to Jim Schmitz was why Olympic lifting was not popular in the United States. While the number of weightlifters over 30 years had increased only 50 percent (1,000–2,500), the proportionate growth of powerlifters at 2,900 percent (1,000–30,000), bodybuilders at 199,900 percent (1,000–2,000,000), and weight trainers at 749,900 percent (10,000–75,000,000) was vastly greater. Untoward trends notwithstanding, Schmitz was upbeat about prospects for the 1992 Olympics, speculating that 20 or more lifters would equal or exceed IWF qualifying totals. At Barcelona, however, against 247 weightlifters from 69 countries, the team did just "all right." No American placed higher than eighth, and the United States finished 13th.[6]

For the previous two decades, the sole intent was to raise American lifting to world standards, but in the early 1990s an unexpected windfall occurred when it appeared, with the collapse of totalitarian regimes in the Soviet Union and Eastern Europe, the world might be moving closer to the United States. In a perceptive article, "Weightlifting After the Cold War," Jim DeCoste pointed out that superiority in the Eastern bloc was made possible by massive government support enabling athletes to train full time. "Not even moderately subsidized programs in free world countries could train lifters in this manner. ... Now things are on the verge of major change," DeCoste predicted. With economic deterioration, environmental crises, housing shortages, industrial decline, and emerging capitalist democracies in former Communist countries, newly enfranchised masses would no longer tolerate the charade of expensive sports programs designed to showcase socialism's superiority. He believed "Russia and all of its former satellites will be dealt a weaker hand" while "the western democracies and their allies will ... clearly be gainers."[7] The iron curtain had fallen, the Soviet Union had self-destructed, and millions of liberated people could practice free-market capitalism, but would these seismic changes result in a dismantling of the authoritarian structure that had always given the formerly Communist programs such an edge?

What happened over the next several years was the development of a new balance of power where the Soviets (now the Russians) and the Bulgarians, deprived of their stranglehold in the lifting elite, were forced to relinquish some of their medal harvest to former USSR republics. At the 1993 world championships in Melbourne, Ukraine, once a fertile recruiting ground for Soviet lifting talent, ranked first with three medalists and several world records. While Bulgaria and Russia still placed second and sixth in the standings, it is notable that newly-liberated Belarus and Armenia ranked eighth and ninth, respectively, and the recently reunited Germany was fifth. Of the non-former Eastern bloc nations, Turkey, benefiting from Bulgarian defector Suleymonoglu, placed third, while newly naturalized Stefan Botev, trained in Bulgaria by Ivan Abadjiev, enabled Australia to claim seventh. Within this new mix of weightlifting celebrity nations, there seemed to be no room for the United States which dropped from 13th of 50 nations in 1993 to 22nd of 52 in 1994 to 31st of 63 in 1995. What was galling in the latter instance was that the 30th position was held by Nauru, a tiny island in the middle of the Pacific Ocean with barely 8,000 people.[8] Nor did matters improve during the next decade when American men, at the 2002 Warsaw world championships, descended to 32nd, just behind Ecuador and Croatia. Even the women could fare no better than 10th.[9]

What DeCoste failed to reckon in his optimistic rendering was not only the greater impact of former Soviet republics and satellites but also the increased number of other nations seeking recognition through weightlifting. The number of athletes increased from 160 from 55 nations at the 1968 Olympics to 247 from 69 nations at Barcelona in 1992. But the real squeeze started with a 1994 IWF ruling that allowed only those nations that placed in the top eight in the 1995 world championships to send a full 10-man team to the 1996 Olympics.[10] With even more restrictive quotas in succeeding years, an increasing number of the 155 eligible nations wanting to be represented in weightlifting, and finally a reduction of weight classes in 1998 to five, the United States was relegated to standing room only for some of its best lifters.

A Slough of Despond

Kono's disenchantment with the weightlifting establishment accompanied the general malaise related to America's less than world class performances. His revelation went back to July 1979 when he witnessed "the 'new' crop of lifters in action" at the National Sports Festival in Colorado Springs. "The feeling I experienced," he observed to Murray Levin,

> was like the time I was coaching the Mexican team and the West German team, meeting the officials and lifters from the U.S. I felt an "outsider" looking "in" on the U.S. lifting scene. And, I couldn't help but feel that the U.S. lifters were just doing their own thing. By that I mean they were competing only in their own "league" and with no real ambition to get into the international level ("big league").... We have better and more equipment, more money and programs to help aspiring lifters than ever before; but, where are the good results?

Tommy fondly recalled the postwar years when "everyone looked up to the American team as THE team" with the likes of Stanczyk, the George brothers and other stars. Though scattered from Hawaii to New York, they were highly motivated and pursued a common goal. "The American lifter today," he concluded, "is too much of an individual and when thrown together cannot function as a team."[11] This pronouncement for Tommy was a sound of alarm, but he remained reticent for a decade while America's performance showed little improvement. Finally, on July 25, 1988, in response to the urging of board chairman Artie Drechsler that he serve on an IWF committee to promote American weightlifting internationally, Tommy sent Artie a copy of his 1979 letter. Despite his disappointment with American efforts, he agreed to represent the USWF by serving on either the technical or scientific committee. But he was "stuck right in the middle of the Pacific," and the cost of attending meetings was beyond his means.[12]

Tommy's disillusionment was complemented by rumblings from athletes Tom Hirtz of Springfield, Oregon, and Bud Charniga of Livonia, Michigan, who laid the blame largely on present and past USWF presidents. John Garhammer, physical education professor at California State University, Long Beach, took the athletes to task for also criticizing the new president, Gene Baker. "Well he's only been in office a few months, an attempt has been made to throw him out." As for the executive director, Garhammer believed Harvey Newton "has been very good" and reports of his doing "a terrible job" should not be taken seriously.[13] Levin, on the other hand, resented Garhammer's criticism of the women's program. "In knocking a name of the 50s coach of the women's team ... you are no doubt knocking the greatest lifter this country has ever produced. ... TOMMY KONO." While admitting some mistakes, Levin was proud of his 12-year presidency and suggested Garhammer take his complaints elsewhere, namely the rival American Weightlifting Association under Bob Hise, Jr. "The USWF doesn't want radicals ... who only know how to criticize and throw stones but who haven't done a damn thing themselves to improve United States weightlifting."[14]

Tommy remained on the sidelines of the in-fighting, but he came closer to involvement by joining a chorus of Newton sympathizers who were encouraging the board of directors to rescind its decision to oust him as executive director. Newton attributed his ouster to the machinations of "several highly motivated individuals" and a conflict between well-intentioned volunteer leaders and professional managers that seemed endemic to Olympic sports. "Perhaps this conflict will go on forever. While I have seen a great number of strange happenings behind the scenes during the past eight years, as an employee of the USWF, the political bickering and failure to focus on the 'big picture' demonstrated by many of the USWF's 'leaders' has been extremely disappointing." In thanking Tommy for his support, Newton admitted that "I have never considered myself a politician, and this case proves that!"[15] Undaunted by these experiences, Kono continued to pursue high-profile positions with George Greenway, Newton's replacement.[16] This enabled him to capitalize on his special relationship with IWF Secretary General Ajan to become a referee at the 1991 world championships in Donaueschingen. Germany. It was an "enjoyable" experience, he told Ajan, "because my background in coaching all the time have kept me alert of all lifting faults." He also complimented Ajan on his well-run organization and its first class magazine. "Keep up the wonderful work." Not surprisingly, Kono's support was rewarded by his selection as a referee for the 1992 Olympics and election to the IWF technical committee.[17] Though overlooked for any major role or voice in USA Weightlifting, he was accumulating political capital on the larger international stage where his celebrity status resonated.

Disenchantment persisted, however, as a result of the poor finish of Americans at the Junior World Championships in Cheb, Czech Republic, in May 1993. No lifter of the six-man team finished higher than 10th, and the team placed 22nd among 40 nations.[18] According to Tommy, it prompted some officials to pressure Greenway into asking board members to consider lowering qualifying totals to allow a 10-man team. "It made me angry because we were being asked to compromise." He reacted to a June 23 letter from Coach Dennis Snethen of the Wesley Weightlifters, one of the country's leading teams, urging the federation to send a full team to the next Junior World Championships. Kono argued it would require additional expenditure for lifters who had no prospect of meeting international standards. "If anything, Dennis, standards should be raised so lifters will think of performing at higher level. You get what you expect of the lifters and our lifters need goals to shoot for," he reasoned. "By lowering the standards you cut their incentive to improve. Pump your lifters with positive ideas and poundages." Unlike Snethen and other coaches of the new era, Tommy's

Harvey Newton was the first executive director of the Olympic Training Center in Colorado Springs. Along with Tommy, he had to endure the vicissitudes of USA Weightlifting during the 1980s (courtesy Harvey Newton).

thinking harked back to the days of Davis, George, and Stanczyk when "lifters set their standards high and trained for it. No excuses!"[19] He repeated these sentiments on July 8 to John Thrush. "As coaches we have to set high goals for our lifters. We have to have them feel they can catch up to those who win medals. Anything less is just for fun or a free trip."[20] It was the "world standard and not national standard" that mattered he argued at the October board meeting.[21] Ten men and nine women qualified for the 1993 world championships in Melbourne, but the United States ranked only 13th and fifth, respectively, amidst 297 total competitors.[22] Although Tommy attended the championships as an American referee and delegate, he recalled "not once was I invited or called to a meeting organized by the U.S. group during the 15 days I was in Melbourne. It made me wonder if I was considered an outsider."[23]

Kono posing with Vasily Alexeyev, Soviet Olympic and world champion and holder of 80 world records during the 1970s. They were most likely photographed at the 1996 Atlanta Olympic Games where Tommy was recognized as one of the one hundred greatest Olympians.

A Coach for All Seasons

To the younger generation of lifters, however, Tommy elicited much support for his gentle manner of coaching and personalized concern, especially for women's participation. Assured of his sympathetic ear, athlete's representative Lynne Stoessel-Ross shared with him a comment brought to her attention by a federation member, that National Coaching Director Lyn Jones "'don't give a rat's ass about women's weightlifting.' Allegedly, this comment was made in the training hall when a majority of the resident athletes were present."[24] Kono's main concern about Jones heretofore had been his organization of a coaching conference at Colorado Springs in early 1991 which featured a surfeit of presentations on biomechanics. "I wonder if the technical 'jargon' or the scientific approach to explain things might have made it more difficult for the attendees to thoroughly understand the 'findings'" He would have liked to have the information summarized in "kitchen English." Confident in his own message and delivery, he volunteered as "a possible speaker" at a subsequent conference.[25] But he was impressed by the muscularity and protocol of the lifters at the training center who, unlike those in Oahu, lifted at set hours rather than staggered times. He "firmly believed in the concept of training together, at the same time, so everyone can help each other out. The enthusiasm of one rubs off on the others and everyone gets a better workout. ... Enthusiasm begets enthusiasm and enthusiasm is what you need to make progress!" Again he was reminded of the days of yore during America's golden age when lifters from surrounding areas would gather at the old York gym every Saturday to perform their best. Mutual reinforcement, he believed, was "the only way to make FAST improvement."[26]

While collective training was the desired end, Tommy worked assiduously with each lifter in his reach. It was especially evident in the lead-up to the 1991 national championships in Blaine, Minnesota, with the attention he devoted to Chad Ikei, Phyllis Nishimoto, and Rae Nakasone, each of whom was obliged to submit a pre-competition information sheet. Ikei's best training lifts at a bodyweight of 55 kilos were an 82.5 kilo snatch and 100 clean and jerk. Expecting to do 85 and 105 in the meet, he psyched up by telling himself: "The weights are light, hold your technique, be strong, and saying 'Come on Chad, let's *do it!*'" At Blaine he placed first in the 52 kg. class with an 85 snatch for a junior world record and a 100 clean and jerk. Nishimoto's best training lifts were 47.5 and 62.5 kilos at 53.2 bodyweight, and she was expecting to perform a 50/52 snatch and 65/67 clean and jerk. Her mental preparations included intense concentration and visualization before each lift. At the nationals Nishimoto placed third in the 52 kg. class with lifts of 47.5 and 62.5, same as her best training efforts. Nakasone's best training lifts were 37.5 and 45 while weighing 44.5 kilos, but she was hoping to make 40 and 50 in Blaine. "Technique, technique, technique" were her bywords. "Pick a focal point; concentration to point of blocking everyone out. Relax, don't panic, don't rush," all respected Konoisms. Nakasone could manage just 35 and 47.5 in placing fifth in the 44 kg. class. Among other Team Hawaii lifters, Kawamura placed third in the 56 kg. class.[27] Although American lifting appeared to be at an all-time low, Hawaiian lifters, thanks to the coaching of Tommy in Oahu and Dr. Yogi in Maui, were earning a disproportionate share of national honors.

Tommy took special pride in the performances of Ikei who, at the American Open on December 6, 1991, broke two national records and tied the national total record of 451 pounds. The secret to coaching success, he believed, was restraint. It was important to "not force them to perform what you want. I found I got better results communicating with the lifters and having them want the instructions. ... Only on vitally important competitions do I work real closely with them."[28] His competent coaching, and that of Yogi, enabled Ikei and Vernon Pateo to earn berths at the Olympic Training Center and qualify for the Olympic team trials in Peoria, Illinois, in May 1992. Assisting in this process was a Honolulu dentist, Dr. Lawrence Tseu. Initially a supporter of local bodybuilding, he told Tommy that he wanted to know more about weightlifting and "get more involved to help you, at least financially. ... To me this is a true sport and not like Bodybuilding." Tseu's cash contributions enabled Kono's club to purchase a Fairbanks scale and a VCR with slow motion capacity for technique analysis.[29] Encouraged by Tseu's support and performances by Ikei, Pateo, and teenager LeGrand Sakamaki, Kono appealed to area athletic directors and coaches to employ weight training for all sports and use weightlifting to include guys too small to play football and basketball. "This is an area we can excel in here in Hawaii for we have a lot of short and light persons. Groom them for weightlifting contests" he advised.[30]

His advice extended well beyond the rarefied atmosphere of the islands. Most meaningful to Kono was how size differential played out on the national scene where the little guys were lifting more proportionately than Mark Henry, the heaviest man in competition. In August 1993 Tommy reminded Mark that Norbert Schemansky had split-snatched 363 pounds 30 years earlier. "The fact that you weigh 100 pounds more than him should make you lift more! So, Mark Henry, why aren't you lifting far more in the snatch?" Tommy noted that in two and a half years at Colorado Springs, Henry's improvement had been "painfully slow" and not on pace to do well at the Atlanta Games which would be "a great let-down for everyone who have high hopes in you—your fans, your family, USWF, U.S. Olympic Committee and the black community." Data compiled by Kono indicated Henry's snatch was 30 kg. (66 lbs.) less than the best at the 1992 Olympics and 37.5 kg. (82.5 lbs.) behind in the clean and jerk. "The fact that you are physically big, lifters look up to you but if you don't push yourself, how can they, your team-mates, have respect for the Big Man?" Tommy encouraged him to raise his goals. "You have to THINK BIG AND LIFT BIG!"[31]

Kono's strictures for heavyweight Wesley Barnett were equally harsh. Although he complimented Barnett's progress, Tommy reminded him in February 1994 that as one of the original training center residents, he had a "powerful influence on the thinking and development of the younger and/or new lifters. ... One thing is certain, nothing is more rewarding than to know you've influenced people in a positive way and they have picked up the habit of improving themselves morally as well as physically." He deplored the letter resident athletes signed to boycott the recent world championships in Australia. To emphasize positivity, Kono provided an article entitled "Mind Game" he had written for *Milo* and a sheet on "Attitude" distributed at a recent board of directors meeting. Tommy encouraged Barnett to "do something extraordinary" and to "think BIG." Not unlike the scenario he created for Henry, Barnett needed to remember that "if you expect someone like Chad Ikei to improve 2½ kilo on the Snatch, you have got to improve 5 kilos at the same time because you weigh almost twice as much as him!"[32] Later, however, Tommy focused on Barnett's lack of progress, citing the Eastern European training methods employed at the training center which emphasized heavy loads and subjected lifters to injuries. "When Chad Ikei left Hawaii over two years ago he was making steady progress. After he started training there he had surgery performed on his knee. Subsequently he had back problems. More recently he had a bad wrist that required an injection. During my last visit to C.S. I was told he had back problems again." The root of Ikei's problems, Tommy concluded, was that his pulling technique had changed since his days in Hawaii. "He was a great technician when he was lifting here but now he is strong but certainly not the technician he once was."[33] Clearly Barnett and others at Colorado Springs were following a training protocol injurious to the progress of USA Weightlifting.

On his own turf Tommy could espouse his traditional training without restraint. To Nuuanu newcomers David Isaacs and Mel Miyamoto, he advised the basic movements conveyed at the Saturday sessions be practiced daily. "Learning

Olympic lifting is a step-by-step process" whereby during the introductory phase "you have to be exposed to the right way of performing the movements otherwise you fall into bad habits that becomes extremely difficult to correct later on." In what became a familiar coaching mantra for him: "Practice does not make perfect. **Practice makes permanent** so if you learn incorrectly, every movement thereafter reinforces the inefficient technique."[34] To his female charges, Tommy emphasized technique and secondarily squats. For Arlys Johnson, he prescribed a routine of striving only once a week for record squats.

> It is the old fashion[ed] way but really the American way which developed lifters like Schemansky, Sheppard, George brothers, Berger and all those who carried the U.S. banner onto the international platform. These handful of guys kept the U.S. right up there with the thousands of lifters whom the Soviets drew upon to make their team. Just think, we didn't have any incentive program, training camps, coaches and other things that the elite lifters have now.[35]

What Tommy recommended for Lea Rentmeester whose progress was stifled from overtraining was moderation. "The lifters now days train too hard and too long and the majority of them end up icing their knees and the muscles become hard and the joints stiff."[36] At fault was the East European system which included the double knee bend pull espoused by Carl Miller in the 1970s. "The weightlifters in U.S. need to be groomed differently," Kono confided to Coach Dick Smith. "We've gotten away from good old American system that groomed **results** and kept the lifters in par with lifters of other nations. Additional tonnage just seem to create more bad knees, bad backs and injuries that delay progress." After observing the hard training of so many American lifters with the "wrong technique," he intended to "take a more active role in coaching."[37]

Playing the Political Card

By the mid–1990s, the tide of USA Weightlifting governance was turning against Tommy's coaching principles and influence. It surfaced at the board of directors meeting in Colorado Springs in October 1995 where Kono abstained along with Artie Drechsler regarding the renewal of the four-year contract of USWF president Lyn Jones; eight others voted for his continuation.[38] Also, his ally Dick Smith was demoted from Manager IV to Manager III and replaced as team manager by Leo Totten for the upcoming Atlanta Olympics. Afterwards, Tommy congratulated Drechsler for speaking out against Jones. "You had him trembling, Artie, and we need that kind of 'clout' over him otherwise he will do all kinds of shady things and not be accountable." He believed "too many guys are on an ego trip and/or vote whichever way the wind blows. ... We have to orchestrate our action so we overwhelm them when the time comes."[39] Tommy told Wayne Oyafuso, Hawaii's athlete representative, that despite his presentations at the recent meeting, it seemed "the other Board members cannot think independently. ... I don't like to dabble in politics but I am afraid I am forced to if I want to see U.S. lifting come back up again."[40] He rationalized to Robin Byrd Goad that owing to "the presence of Jones in the room and because it was voting by roll call, I believe a few more could not vote the way their conscience wanted them to."[41] Kono commiserated to Christian Polakowski that "we are spending more money on our athletes than ever before, have a full time paid national coach and coaching coordinator but our lifters always perform better at the Nationals or Sports Festival." It was evident to Kono on returning from the 1995 world championships in Guangzhou, China, where the American team placed 31st, "the worst placing we have ever had."[42]

Although his immersion into the thick of weightlifting politics weighed heavily on him, Tommy regained his sense of equilibrium by involvement in the 23rd Honolulu Marathon on December 10 which he deemed a "grand success." With nearly 27,000 runners crossing the finish line, it became the year's largest in the world, surpassing even the New York Marathon.[43] In months ahead, however, Kono realized how much at odds he was with the weightlifting establishment. At the February 1996 board meeting in Albuquerque, a proposal was considered to raise the salary of Dragomir Ciroslan to the level of Jones and Greenway. Kono vigorously resisted. The discussion "got a little heated," he told Drechsler, who missed the meeting, "but I stood firm so nothing came about regarding raising of the salary for Dragomir." He also disputed the notion that progress was being made in the sport.

> Lyn said something about everything is going along fine but I said that things don't have to remain the same for 5–7 years. What was okay 4 years ago doesn't have to continue on for the next 3–4 years. I was the maverick in the room but I decided to speak my piece. I think I came across as a non-team player. Incidentally, that was the first National Juniors Championships I attended and I was extremely disappointed in the technique used by majority of the teen lifters!

To remedy this situation, Tommy decided to offer a one-hour lifting clinic at the Senior Nationals in Shreveport, Louisiana, in early March titled "ABCs of Weightlifting Reviewed." It would coincide with the election of USA Weightlifting officers. "The course of American lifting will be the result of the outcome of this election," he predicted.[44]

It proved disastrous for Kono's hopes for the sport and his voice in its conduct. Not only did his friend and ally, Murray Levin, lose the presidency to Brian Derwin of Minnesota but also another long-time friend, Rudy Sablo, was no longer on the committee, and Tommy was replaced on the board by John Thrush of Washington. Tommy rationalized to Denis Reno that Murray's wife would likely see more of him now, and "I will have more time to pursue things locally and maybe even start on my weightlifting book." He also expressed hope that "Derwin can turn things around for US lifting. My personal feeling is that with Thrush, Snethen and Cohen [sic] on the Board they will use up all the funds to *send complete teams all the time whether the lifters qualified or not*. Unless they make the lifters really earn their spot on the teams, U.S. lifting will not start coming up." Again Tommy expressed dismay at the technique employed by the some of the nation's best lifters at Albuquerque and why neither Jones nor Ciroslan could "see the terrible form that almost 90% of the lifters used? ... Ever view the video tape made by Lyn with Wesley on the correct pulling technique? ... Even the correct technique is performed incorrectly." It was one reason he had not approved extending Jones' contract and resisted raising Ciroslan's salary.[45] But in doing so, he contributed to his own political demise by identifying himself as a troublemaker to the powers that be. It was the nadir of his influence.

Outgoing President Jim Schmitz, who sided with the majority, agreed that the board meeting was not pleasant. "I wish we all agreed more on what's best for U.S. Weightlifting, but we don't. I guess that's the American way." What most concerned Schmitz was that he had aggravated Tamas Ajan, perhaps by his "constant pushing for enforcing anti-drug programs and asking for accountability." At stake was the number of slots for American lifters at the 1996 Olympics. Tommy agreed that Ajan's recent communications with Schmitz and board members showed "great distrust" and "indignation," and he hoped U.S. representation would not be limited to just three lifters in Atlanta.[46] To reclaim some face in the eyes of the board, Kono prepared an "Incentive Plan for 2000" which he distributed after the Olympic Trials in St. Joseph, Missouri, where numerous lifters rose to the occasion by exceeding national records and making personal records. They validated his point that "we must raise the standards for making any team or trips." Because of the high standard, "every lifter started with heavier weights than usual for their first attempt." Money was not the answer, he argued, but it was critical to "raise the Standards each year for all the national championships." Further to justify his point, he estimated that none of the late additions to the junior world team in 1995 (men and women) at a cost of $12,435 came close to the qualifying totals, and that subsequent performances at the junior, national, and world levels were uniformly sub-par.[47]

Although no Americans medaled in Atlanta, *Weightlifting USA* gleefully reported that this year's squad showed "great improvement" over the previous year's world team by tying for 14th place out of 81 countries. At sixth in the 108 kg. class, Barnett placed the highest but his 395 kg. total was still less than the winning totals of the next two lower classes.[48] For Tommy, who was recently consigned to the political wilderness and had a painful hip requiring surgery, it was a bittersweet experience. But his significance was enhanced by Ajan's asking him to serve on the jury overseeing referee performances. Tommy had previously served on juries at world championships in Istanbul (1994) and China (1995) but never at an Olympics.[49] He was accorded a far greater honor by being recognized as one of "100 Golden Olympians" at the 1996 Centennial Olympics.[50] He and Pete George were the only weightlifters included in this list of America's greatest gold medalists. Like the honor he received in 1982 as the "Greatest Weightlifter of All Time," it had the hand of Ajan in it. Despite his lack of influence and respect in the political arena of his homeland, Kono was trumping everyone else by the continued enhancement of his international reputation.

Meanwhile, setbacks in his domestic political agenda only made Tommy more determined to pursue his goals, albeit independently. For that reason he declined the position of competition secretary for the national championships in Blaine, Minnesota, where two lifting platforms were to be used. To meet director Larry Hanneman he expressed concern about having "two different scoreboards in back and front, two sets of loaders, referees, timers, marshals, etc. Probably the most damaging of all will be to the lifters and coaches with twice as many lifters warming up backstage." But Tommy expressed to California official Jack Hughes and

Rudy Sablo the real reason for not accepting the position. He believed "it is too precarious of a job because I just don't trust Lyn Jones and Larry Hanneman. Anything goes wrong at the Seniors would be blamed on the Competition Secretary. There is too much at stake for the athletes who want to qualify for the World Team ... and I don't want to be the scapegoat."[51] Now regarded as a deep-seated dissident, Kono continued to pour fat on the fire, even with athlete board members. He expressed pride to Artie Drechsler that Robin Byrd Goad had told Decia Stenzil that she was a disgrace as an athlete's rep and that Wes Barnett and Jeff Macy were not voting in the best interests of the lifters. Tommy remembered telling Robin a year earlier that "she has to get involved and be vocal otherwise guys like Lyn Jones will take over. Maybe I struck home." Tommy recognized that maybe "stimulation from irritants like Derwin and Jones" was needed "to make us cohesive. It could be that everyone was all too complacent and just letting things happen by a few. Anyway, maybe it awoke the sleeping giant in us and we are now ready to 'attack.'"[52] More fundamental to Tommy's disagreement with the establishment was its efforts to professionalize the sport. Sadly, so much money was devoted "to groom good lifters yet we are missing some fundamentally important aspect of training," he told Bruce Wilhelm. "It has nothing to do with the capacity of a lifter to train long, hard and lift great tonnage. ... These lifters now days are true professionals and they make their living lifting while those of the old time did it really for the love of the sport and a chance to represent the U.S."[53]

A Voice Crying in the Wilderness

Tommy continued this "back in the good old days" theme in Reno's newsletter. After perusing old issues of *Strength & Health*, he noted at his final competition in 1965 as an 82.5 kg. lifter he, along with Joe Puleo and Gary Cleveland, performed "much better" than lifters at the 1997 senior nationals in Minnesota. "We've had professional people at the helm since 1990 but we have not made progress to show we are catching up to the world in our sport. Six-seven years later are we still laying the foundation for good lifting?" It seemed the only alternative to USAW incompetence and being a voice crying in the wilderness was to go outside official channels. Thus, after witnessing the flawed technique of lifters at the 1996 junior nationals, he conducted "a short lifting technique seminar at the '96 Nationals, much to the chagrin of those who should have seized the opportunity to do something positive." Another source of his displeasure was the lack of an instructional medium for rank and file lifters. "The lifeline to the common lifters who train in the garage or at the local YMCA weight room with no coach or instructor needs information from the magazine, yet, to save money or funnel the money 'more usefully,' the USAW has reduced their publication to four times a year." In the following issue, Reno reported receiving "a large number of positive and affirmative letters" responding to Kono's complaints. "One line from one letter sums it up. 'Tommy's letter says it like it is.'" Though stopping short of an outright condemnation of current USAW leaders, Reno vaguely endorsed Tommy's protest. "Let's get rid of the bad apples, and open up a clean fruit stand for our future."[54] Tommy followed up his displeasure with the current state of affairs in an e-mail letter with a list of leading questions to the four new board members. Kono also believed the federation was in deep trouble financially and would hit "rock bottom" by the end of the year.[55]

Indeed, it was money matters that brought the deepening crisis in USA Weightlifting to a head in the fall of 1997. President Derwin's unexpected request that Executive Director Greenway resign prompted a firestorm of controversy. The rationale for this sudden move stemmed from the latter's estimate that Derwin's extravagant expenditures were resulting in a budget deficit. USWF finances appeared to be flush with over $2,400,000 of which about $225,000 in interest was available yearly to facilitate its programs. These funds were supplemented by about $800,000 from the USOC for a total income of $1,025,000. Unfortunately, 1998 expenditures were estimated to be about $1,250,000. "This is why George Greenway could not accept this coming year's budget. He is a realist," contended Levin who spent his career in the business world. "George was not disloyal to our President—he simply knew that two and two makes four—*not seven*. He could not accept a budget that was not realistic, and in coming years, could bankrupt the Federation."[56] These sentiments underscored those of Jim Schmitz who had a high regard for Greenway. "Ever since George has worked for us [1988–97] he has been the glue that has kept us together, keeping us in line and on track, both financially and administratively. He has been completely fair, honest, and extremely hard working." A secondary issue was the USOC Development Center set to open in Minneapolis in January 1998 for which Derwin designated himself full-time coach. "This seems like a conflict of interest and unethical," argued Schmitz. "No announcement of this job opportunity was made, so that others might apply." It was imperative to Schmitz that the USWF keep Greenway, return to prudent financial management, and be open and above board with all further job opportunities.[57] Former board member Don Wilson was more blunt and to the point—"Derwin SHOULD SUBMIT HIS RESIGNATION AT THE SOONEST POSSIBLE TIME."[58]

In his spirited retort to Wilson's concerns, Wes Barnett questioned whether the federation was on the verge of bankruptcy and that funds were being misused. "The reason we are experiencing financial strain now is because of all of the great performances that we've had so far. Over $50,000 has been paid to athletes for World placements and records. If this is always the cause of our financial strain, I welcome it any time." Barnett also denied the BOD was devoid of "independent thinkers. That is why there is so much turmoil. We are not doing things the same way we have for the past thirty years and people are often reluctant to and fear change." A positive step, however, was the board's decision to raise qualifying totals to 90 percent of world gold medalist totals, the goal being to send the best athletes to the world championships. "When Tommy Kono was a board member, this was one thing he really pushed hard for." Lifters making these qualifying totals, based on a three-year average, would become members of Super Squad 2000. "The USAW would pay a stipend to help alleviate some of the costs of living, so athletes can devote more of their time to training" and "become a professional weightlifter."[59] In a follow up, Derwin justified Greenway's dismissal on grounds that he "did not seem to be in favor of most of our major initiatives" and opposed his reducing office staff to cut costs. As for his new Minneapolis position, Derwin "asked the Board if they had any objections to my heading up the Weightlifting part of the program. No one had an objection." He had no intention to resign.[60] To athlete representative Jeff Sunzeri it was clear that "US Weightlifting is experiencing a very serious upheaval."[61]

What transpired over the next several weeks was a hardening position by the dissidents. First Vice President John Thrush believed Greenwood would be "a critical part of getting us through the current fiscal crisis." He opposed scrapping Derwin's Game Plan 2000 but believed it should be "drastically scaled down and re-vamped."[62] Larry Hanneman concluded that Derwin "knows sentiment has turned against him. ... Sometimes an organization has to hit bottom before it begins to turn."[63] The most intransigent of Derwin's opponents was Bob Crist who took a hard line over Greenway's firing, excessive spending, misappropriation of funds, and conflict of interest in an appeal to William Hybl, president of the USOC. *"I hope and pray that he is removed, for unethical behavior."* Tommy also informed Hybl of the "grave situation" that existed in the federation, citing his concurrence with the views of both vice presidents, treasurer Howard Cohen, and former president Levin. It was necessary "to check the course of action taking place by the current President and the Board of Directors of USAW before it is too late."[64] On October 9, Karl Faeth, athletic trainer for 22 years, pointed out to Hybl the irony that Derwin served on the USOC ethics committee although "he obviously does not comprehend the definition

Pictured with Tommy are Bob Crist (left), Murray Levin (beside Tommy), and Jim Schmitz (right), who were stalwart allies as he struggled through weightlifting's political quagmire (courtesy Bruce Klemens).

of the word Ethics." Faeth suggested his removal from that committee and resignation as USAW president.[65]

By the end of October, three additional issues intensified the crisis. On the 10th, Levin was informed that his grievance to a Board of Review that the 1996 board of directors election be disallowed, alleging irregularities, was rejected. The board concluded that there was no conspiracy to declare him ineligible to run for president.[66] A decision otherwise could have dramatically altered the power structure. Then Hybl's office informed Kono that "the USOC does not become involved in an individual organization's problem(s) unless there is a breach of USOC policy." Obviously the USOC did not want to get involved in weightlifting's internal conflict. But to Tommy the use of USOC money for the Minneapolis sport center entailed a double conflict of interest and violation of USOC code.[67] What most incensed him, however, was that nine athletes at the Olympic Training Center—Corey Wilkes, Greg Schouten, Charles Paiva, LeGrand Sakamaki, Jose Santiago, Walter Sisto, Travis Grimm, Chris DeMartini, and Robin Ruiz, violated IOC policy on use of banned substances. He could not restrain himself in placing blame for the "USOTC Weightlifting Plight" on his political adversaries:

> As many know we've had problems with the President and majority of the Board members (because they are like puppets) who have been pursuing the idea of "performance at any cost." President Derwin even went on record to say he wants to 'professionalize' the lifters. Well, their idea of bringing in the cream of the crop, young lifters based on the evaluation of Lyn Jones, Dragomir Cioroslan and Bob Morris was okay but these young lifters were evidently not given correct guidance and outside the training hall, unsupervised. My feeling is that these three in charge, who see the lifters (boys and girls) nearly every day, must *take some or all the responsibility. A thing like this doesn't happen over night.*

For doing such a "great injustice to the sport," he believed the athletes should be barred from competing for two years and possibly life. Kono found it ironic upon looking through the U.S. Olympic Collection catalog on the same day he learned of the drug violations that two of the lifters served as models for Olympic apparel. "What message are we sending to everyone if USAW cannot take a firm stance on the drug issue?"[68]

On November 15, after months of entreaties to the USOC, Tommy finally received Hybl's response, but it dealt solely with the drug problem with nothing about more fundamental issues pertaining to Derwin. Hybl duly appointed an eight-person Weightlifting Oversight Task Force, headed by a former executive director of U.S. Swimming. "I can assure everyone involved that the United States Olympic Committee will move swiftly, in coordination with USA Weightlifting, to resolve the situation with equity and a guarantee of fair process." But when the task force's initial report was not completed by the specified date of December 15, Tommy asked Hybl the following April why he had received no word of its progress. Meanwhile, he contended that the president and the board of directors "have embraced a philosophy that has regressed the sport. If this trend continues for another year weightlifting in the U.S. will become just a past-time activity and conducted purely for recreational purpose." As an example, he cited Wes Barnett whose bronze medal at the 1997 world championships, though commendable, was five kilos less than his total at the Atlanta Olympics where he placed sixth. Tommy accounted for his high 1997 placement to the great distance to Chiang Mai, Thailand, for many European athletes. In the forthcoming 1998 championships in Lahti, Finland, Tommy predicted, "he will have a very tough time to come in 10th place even with a new personal record in the Total."[69]

These predictions did not materialize because Barnett did not compete in Lahti. But data compiled by Don Wilson indicate that America's three best males—Tim McRae, Tom Gough, and Barnett—decreased their combined total from the 1996 Olympic Games to the 1998 national championships by 10 kilos while their combined bodyweight increased by nearly 30 kilos. It was obvious to Tommy that "our top athletes are not performing as professionals should. Payments to these lifters have been on-going since the policy was adopted under the Derwin regime (after the 1996 Olympic Games). Proportionately, these athletes performed better when they didn't receive funds for training." Their performance, Kono concluded, "reflected the quality of coaching they received in Colorado Springs."[70] Jim Schmitz concurred with the dissidents. "USA Weightlifting is being grossly mismanaged since September 1996" for which he blamed Derwin and Jones in an open letter to USAW members. "Since Brian has been our president ... our high level organization and administration have deteriorated to the lowest level since I've been associated with U.S. weightlifting, beginning in 1960."[71] For Tommy, the philosophy at Colorado Springs was "totally wrong and since they are the leaders everyone else has followed the system." Their harsh training led to bad knees, bad backs, and strained wrists, but no world championships.[72]

These observations contrasted sharply with validations of the Derwin regime in USAW's official organ. Editor Mike Cady reported the Board of Governors meeting where Derwin faced his accusers for over eight hours. "Although the discussion was at times emotionally charged, our members always conducted themselves in a respectable and respectful manner. By acclamation of the Board of Governors, the secret ballot vote was not announced, just the results. Brian Derwin is our President." A further motion to remove Derwin as representative to the USOC also failed to pass.[73] Yet Cady was critical of the decision of Derwin and the board to undermine the financing of *Weightlifting U.S.A.* "and censorship of varying view points and information printed in the publication." This unpleasant reality, along with the decline in membership as a result of large sums of money being poured into the development of elite athletes rather than grassroots programs, prompted his resignation.[74] With Cady gone, a new executive director (James Fox) in place, and the president's position secure, the magazine took on a hyperbolic tone with such cover come-ons as "Reaching New Heights" (June 1999), "Taking on the World" (Winter 1999/2000), and "Unstoppable" (Spring 2000). An article by Oliver Caitlin entitled "USAW's Super Lifters" focused on American records broken at the 1999 national championships in Flagstaff.[75] In the September 1999 issue Derwin confidently reported that results from the recent Junior World Championships in Savannah and the Pan Am Games in Winnipeg indicated "our programs are working and our athletes medaled when it counted."[76] But at the 1999 world championships in Athens, Greece, featuring 626 athletes from 84 countries, no American lifter medaled and the placement for men and women was 25th and sixth, respectively, entitling them to only two male and four female slots at the forthcoming Olympics.[77] Nevertheless, as the conclusion of his four-year term as president approached, Derwin was satisfied that he and his board had "succeeded in all areas" of his high-performance plan.[78]

Ultimate Frustration

These disparities of vision culminated at the 2000 Board of Governors at the national championships in Frederick, Maryland, where Tommy, one of 12 nominees for five at-large seats on the board of directors, was defeated. Secretary Les Simonton had "a hard time understanding how one doesn't vote for Tommy Kono, but there obviously were a bunch who didn't. Sigh." Even more exasperating to Simonton was Kono's failure to attain one of eight positions on the Coaching Committee. Given his unrivalled coaching record, "Tommy Kono's lack of support among the delegates was even more unbelievable to me in this contest than the other."[79] Stella Herrick concludes "it was a cognizant decision they made. They didn't want him there. It hurt him. It hurt him deeply. It was a very political atmosphere with people who were jealous and felt threatened by Tommy. They had their own vision for the sport, and he was not part of it."[80] As former executive director, Newton had warned Tommy of the pitfalls of politics in amateur sports, and suggested he read *In Spite of Us* by David Prouty who once directed the U.S. Cycling Federation. "He, like many of us, became a victim of the politics."[81] Prouty regretted that "the most important game for too many people is not producing results on the playing field but accumulating and maintaining power in the boardrooms." Until he entered the world of amateur sports, Prouty had "never seen so many people so casually vicious and destructive over so little, and within something that the rest of society perceives as being so positive: the Olympic movement."[82] That individuals so passionate about weightlifting could not cooperate for the good of the sport was beyond comprehension to Kono whose Asian values stressed consensus and teamwork.

Nor could he understand his exclusion from any role in the decision-making process. It would be "an understatement," observes Lou DeMarco, to say that Tommy was frustrated with American lifting. "Tommy and I would talk often times about these home-made experts that would crawl out of the woodwork who thought they knew so much. And here you have this man who's the master of thought, a Newton. ... They're giving the impression that it was that way back then, but what does he know now? The old man routine. Yea, Tommy was very hurt by all that. He would go on coaching assignments sometimes, and these people would not listen to him. A terrible waste."[83] Rejection by the people who needed him most, however, did not daunt the indomitable spirit of America's greatest weightlifter. He took his coaching expertise directly to lifters at large during the next decade through his two inspirational books: *Weightlifting, Olympic Style* and *Championship Weightlifting*.

III

ATHLETIC IMMORTALITY

9

Rising Above the Din

"He who has a why to live for can bear almost any how."[1]
—Friedrich Nietzsche

Coaching Elder

From his island home in the mid–Pacific, Tommy could seek refuge from weightlifting politics and indulge in activities where he could have a greater and more immediate impact. To do so, he focused on the Nuuanu YMCA and Team Hawaii which inherited the proud tradition of weightlifters who excelled at the 1948 Olympics and won the 1952 national championships. "To increase public appreciation of the sport," according to a 1995 promotional brochure, "Team Hawaii now conducts competitions and championships at large public areas such as Ward Warehouse, Aloha Tower Marketplace, and the Royal Hawaiian Shopping Center." Along with team president Russ Ogata and secretary Phyllis Nishimoto, Kono requested coupons from Hawaiian Airlines "for the athletes that live on the neighboring islands so they may be able to participate in our events and provide Hawaii with maximized potential."[2] A further fillip to Team Hawaii was the visit of Denis Reno and his wife, Karen Christiansen, for a vacation in the spring of 1995. Tommy felt "we should recognize him in some way while he is here in the islands. He has always published the result of our meets and he's always included some blurb regarding Hawaii lifters when he hears something interesting about us." To cap the event, the Renos were treated to a dinner at the Outrigger Canoe Club where Pete George had a membership.[3] That Tommy derived joy from these associations is revealed in his remark to a lifting colleague from Tule Lake days that "the socializing side really makes it a great sport to be involved in."[4]

On March 18, 1995, Kono was gratified that Phyllis Nishimoto staged an exhibition at the Ward Warehouse, thereby relieving him of some responsibilities. "I've known Phyllis as a lifter and coached her," he told John Thrush, "but, I never knew the promoter she is. She is a real go-getter." She was also planning another exhibition for May 20 and had persuaded the airlines to donate a few tickets to fly Catherine and LeGrand Sakamaki from the Big Island and Vernon Patao from Maui.[5] Although only 12 lifters participated in the state championships in March 1996, Tommy seemed pleased that he, his donors, and volunteers had raised $3,038 and "able to promote lifting with new brochures, additional bumper plates, new shopping center sites for competition and support for our top lifters for the Sr. National Championships."[6] In all these events, Kono played an active role as promoter, director, master of ceremonies, referee, or scorekeeper. Most notable, however, was his coaching with local lifters at the Nuuanu YMCA. For this purpose, Tommy formulated a program of "Weightlifting Notes" for participants in his coaching sessions from July 1997 to July 1999. On Thursday, July 19, 1998, he focused on form.

> Before you start any lift, take a huge breath so your lungs become full and it helps tighten up the back arch. ... This will do two things. 1) drive you straight down so you would bounce, and 2) the bar impact on the chest will bow the bar downward on the ends so you can wait for the springing action of the bar to help you stand up. This is where good timing comes in so you use the rhythm of the bar to "spring" out of the deep squat.[7]

To Melanie Getz, Tommy revealed a level of consciousness that went beyond technique and delved deeply into his Japanese American heritage. In February 1997 he recounted how he told Gary Kawamura, much in the manner of "Go for Broke," that in order to "reach great heights ... you don't know unless you 'go for it.'" He advised Kawamura to turn

> his thoughts "inward." Don't think of technique but rather concentrate in going by the "feel" of the movement. I told him that he has to think like a blind person so nothing external distracts him and he focuses his "eye balls inward," meaning the weight on the bar or movement of people in the gym doesn't contaminate his inward thoughts. ... I told him that this is like practicing "Zen"; you reach a plateau where the weight on the bar makes no difference. The practice of this releases the anxiety of the bar getting heavier because you are not focused on the weight but the total movement ... by "feel."

"Remember," he told Melanie, "Practice 'Zen,'" and he identified himself as "Your 'Zen' coach."[8] Perhaps more than anything else he ever wrote, these passages capture the essence of his approach to competitive weightlifting.

For the Love of Lifting

What inspired Tommy was an article that appeared in the *Honolulu Advertiser* on February 16, 1997, about the Three Year Swim Club of Maui which overcame all obstacles to win national championships and Olympic gold medals. "Imagine swimming in a sugar cane/pineapple field irrigation ditch with a vow and commitment to make the U.S. Olympic Team in three years," he explained to Denis Reno. With the war eliminating two Olympic Games possibilities, it was not until the 1948 London Games that one member, at age 24, could compete. "Bill Smith, whom I worked with in the same office for Parks and Recreation before he retired, won two gold medals." Tommy suggested to Levin that the article illustrated "a very critical thing that Colorado Springs and everyone else have failed to recognize all these years. ... Had I been in a better position I would have brought these things to the attention of the Board of Directors and to the Board of Governors." He regretted that so much money was spent "trying to groom good lifters yet we are missing some fundamentally important aspect of training. It has nothing to do with the capacity of a lifter to train long, hard and lift great tonnage. It is a matter of commitment, character building; and, as Smitty would say, 'Integrity!'" Again he looked back fondly to lifters of yesteryear like Norbert Schemansky who, unlike the current lot of "professionals," had no coach or subsidies. The old-timers "did it really for the love of the sport and a chance to represent the U.S. You can't compare amateurs of then with professionals of today." That some virtue in sports remained, however, was evident in the recognition of John Sakamaki by the Honolulu Quarterback Club at its annual Banquet of Champions on February 17. By grooming his son LeGrand and daughter Catherine, he served as a "good example of advancing Hawaii's sports nationally." And Tommy's selection as main speaker for the annual John Hancock banquet on the 21st recognized his own services rendered for the good of local sports. "It is a formal thing so I have to be at my best," he explained to Levin.[9]

In January 1998 Tommy seized the opportunity to train athletes and reinforce links with his ancestral homeland by accepting a USOC invitation to help condition the American team at the Nagano Winter Olympics. Concurrently he was coaching Kris Kamura, a Hawaiian weightlifter, budding coach, and student at Whittier College. To overcome Kamura's time constraints, Tommy advised him that getting "squats in three times a week" was "the key exercise that will keep most of your lifting muscles in shape." Kamura should take advantage of disadvantage as Kono once did in his early days as a GI in Germany.

> How well I remember when I used to dash up three flights of stairs to get to the attic of a building that had weights when I was in the army. I'd roll my pants leg up and ride the pants high so it won't rip when I go into a full squat and I would perform 3 to 4 sets of squats and then report back to duty. This was done when I was in Germany putting guard duty and done during my coffee break.

Arigatai (be thankful for what you have) would provide Kimura with strength to face adversity. Kono counseled him to "make do the best you can and be thankful you can find even a little time to train."[10] These qualities are evident in Kimura's eventual role as coach for the Southern California Youth Weightlifting Association, Its website credits Kono for teaching him the Olympic lifts and how to coach them. "More importantly, Mr. Kono was a mentor, and a model of uncompromising character. Each training session was not only a lesson in improving in the sport of weightlifting, but how to live life: seeing things as opportunities and not obstacles, being grateful regardless of the circumstance, to believe in oneself, and to always strive to be better."[11]

A more prosaic example of Kono's commitment to grassroots development occurred in July 2000 when he conducted an "Olympic-Style Weightlifting Clinic" for the East Alabama Weightlifting Club at Auburn University. It was organized by Stella Herrick, whose husband, Richard, was team physician for many American overseas trips. Tommy arranged to visit Auburn on his way to New Orleans for the Olympic Trials and "paid his own way," Stella remembers. "He said, I have some airline points ... and we covered the rest."[12] It was a bargain. Attendees paid $10 for two eight-hour days of hands-on instruction from the master on the fine points of lifting from pulling technique to contest preparation.[13] On Friday evening Tommy presented a video on lifting and coaching technique. Next morning, he opened the clinic with a picture of the backs of several elite lifters, asking which one was best.

I will always remember it was David Rigert. "Yes, Tommy was always big on lats," Stella responded. Much of the clinic was devoted to working with individual lifters, all of which was taped. "Tommy was such a phenomenal coach," Stella recalls. He had such a good eye and innate understanding of what was happening that he knew what would be the result. But he was also

> a phenomenal reader of personalities, and he could tell when someone was receptive or not receptive. And if someone was open, Tommy felt that he could not do enough. When we were in New Orleans for the nationals, there were a couple of guys that didn't have coaches. I went to Tommy and said these two guys don't have anybody to help. Would you be kind enough to help them? He said "of course." He was not intrusive by telling them what to do or how to do it; it was "if I can help you in any way just ask me." He was such a gentleman.

It was an "act of love" reflecting Tommy's approach to lifting, "that if anybody needed him, he would be there." For Simonton, the clinic was "a perfect example of Tommy's personality. He was instructive, humble, and even-keeled the whole time. In addition to the lectures, he worked with everyone one-on-one. He corrected our flaws in a polite, even kind, way."[14]

Tommy's generosity extended also to the practicalities of staging competitions. As meet director for local contests, he faced the problem of how to change weights efficiently with lifters ranging from 105-pound female lifters who might negotiate no more than a 100-pound clean and jerk to a 290-pound male lifting 400 pounds. While the "Round System" proved successful with successive increases on the bar, the problem confronted loaders who would have to break the bar down after completion of all first and second attempts. "At best I have a hard time finding a pair of loaders!" The idea man was inspired by a loading rack devised by German entrepreneur Josef Schnell, a bent pipe that could elevate the heaviest barbell an inch off the platform for easy loading. Tommy came up with the idea of a wooden wedge the thickness of a 1½ kg. plate with a notch to cradle a large barbell plate. Called "Tommy Kono's Loading Master," drawings for its construction were distributed to meet directors for use in training and contests. "Necessity is the Mother of Invention," he believed.[15]

The People's Race

From its origin in 1973 with only 162 entrants, the Honolulu Marathon grew into a major international event, attracting tens of thousands each year. In 1997, there were 33,682 entrants from 46 countries, including 17,952 (53.3 percent) runners from Japan and 14,460 (42.9 percent) from the United States, including 10,910 (32.4 percent) from Hawaii.[16] The race was adding over $135,000,000 to the island's economy at an otherwise slow period. Organizer Jeanette Chun attributed the large number of Japanese entrants to the sponsorship of Japan Airlines and Honolulu's desirability for first-time marathoners. "They've heard through the Bamboo Pipeline that the Honolulu Marathon is primarily a 'People's Race' and that we care for each runner. The climate and beauty of our Islands and almost immediate access to Waikiki hotels from the Finish Line is another major factor."[17] President Jim Barahal expressed pride that the Honolulu Marathon, though soon surpassed by London, New York, and Chicago, was the world's largest. "It's the combination of it being a world class race at the front, but still a people's race for the recreational runners and even the walkers. It combines the look, feel and experience of a mega marathon and yet offers the relaxed feeling of a smaller race." To provide less inconvenience for the local populace and save runners from the heat, Barahal pushed the starting time back to 5 a.m. "The roads are closed earlier and so the race ends earlier."[18] A 1995 survey indicated nearly 90 percent of East Oahu residents indicated satisfaction with advance notification, noise level, lack of hazardous conditions, rubbish cleanup, and traffic control.[19] Included in a list compiled by Chun of the hundreds of organizations and agencies that unselfishly volunteered their "time, goods, and services" were the U.S. Army which constructed a massive photo bridge at the finish line and members of the Navy, Air Force, Seabees, and Marines who helped with the set-up and dismantling of park construction. A hundred licensed Shiatsu therapists donated their services to relieve runners of aches and pains, Young Laundry and Dry Cleaning provided towels for Shiatsu and medical personnel, and Menehune Water Company furnished pure water. Along with support from city-county governments, Chun cited the Parks and Recreation Department for sponsoring "year-round marathon clinics for the novice runners."[20]

This aspect of preparation was largely Kono's creation and responsibility. Although he continued to be recognized as an Olympic gold medalist and member of the board of directors with a private office, he never avoided mundane assignments, including coordination of "No Parking-Tow Away" sign placements, tree trimming, dumpster arrangements, and finish area sweeping.[21] Unlike most organizers, Tommy received a monthly stipend and reimbursement for expenses, which included promoting the Honolulu Marathon at expositions staged at other marathons.[22] In February 1992 he and Flo manned a booth, with 250 other exhibitors, at the Los Angeles convention center. They brought 10,000 entry forms and 8,000 stickers, but their booth was blocked from sight by a double Gatorade booth.

> On the third day my wife stood in the incoming traffic handing out the entry forms and stickers. From 8:30 a.m. to closing time 6:00 p.m. on the final day (Saturday) not once did she sit down or go to the bathroom. ... I stuffed the entry forms with the stickers and manned our booth and answered questions regarding our marathon.[23]

Tommy's daughter joAnn estimates that after retirement he was eventually making as much as $27,000 or $30,000 yearly as vice president of the Marathon Association, but he was more than worth it because "he created the map of the run and he put the signs together and lined up a lot of the buses. He'd drive down to the park and get up to the workers. He was often upset because he would just find them lounging around all the garbage cans." Furthermore, he was always trying to save the organization's money. "He wanted to save them money all the time. ... He believed in them." Later, however, "things sort of fell in the wind." There was "not a falling out, but he didn't like the way Barahal was running it. He was bringing people from the mainland to replace the locals. Special runners and all that." It was becoming too commercialized.[24]

Tommy traveled throughout the nation and world to promote the Honolulu Marathon. This picture shows him dispensing information at the 1993 Denver Marathon.

Tommy recognized the problems inherent with Barahal's reliance on outsiders. "When he brings those guys in, you've got to pay for their flight, room and board, and transportation, maybe they need a car or something. ... Whereas we have all these people that live here. They're all volunteers." A hotel room for one night before the race, lunch, and a t-shirt was all they would get, and "the very next day, they got to clean up the whole place." Unlike his experiences with the weightlifting

Preparation for each year's marathon required many months of planning. For Tommy, it also required a lot of practical responsibilities on the day of the race. He is pictured here with a co-worker in the early hours of December 11 for the 1999 marathon.

hierarchy in which he had a larger stake, Kono chose not to get involved in marathon politics. "When they start bringing in well-known runners and give them money that to me wasn't good. I thought it's money being wasted. But it was their money."25 joAnn's husband Gary concurs that "the sport aspect of it was being lost. I remember having a conversation with Tommy about how money was destroying all sports, not just the marathon." The weightlifters at Colorado Springs were "lazy. All they're wanting to do is train, and the guys are there with their ipods on." Tommy, according to joAnn, "didn't believe in any of that stuff. No distractions when you're working out." She believes he was all about focus—a Japanese trait. "Things were changing, and it was unfortunate that he was one of the last great ones of his era because of all the changes. He couldn't accept it." And it was that attitude and outlook that put him at odds with the powers-that-be in the marathon and weightlifting.26 Tommy stated that he supported the marathon over the decades to encourage people to improve their health, but he admitted "you got to be crazy to run 26 miles."27 In 1999, he was inducted into the Honolulu Marathon's Hall of Fame.

This 2008 photograph shows Tommy receiving a surprise birthday greeting from fellow race official Ronald Chun. Prior to Kono stopping by Chun's house to pick up a blueprint of Kapiolani Park (site of the marathon's finish line), Chun's wife Jeanette quickly made a birthday cake for him. Tommy loved sweet things (courtesy Jeanette Chun).

Serving the People

Kono's contribution to the health and well-being of participants in the Honolulu Marathon was merely the most visible aspect of his public service. On November 17, 1992, he; Pete George; Emerick Ishikawa, Sr.; Emerick Ishikawa, Jr.; Richard Tom; and a high school weight room supervisor—along with their protégés—were invited to present a "show and tell" program at the Pearl City Regional Library. Its librarian, a Miss Chun, explained that Tommy and his group would "take the place of books and be human being subject experts who can demonstrate briefly Pumping Iron, staying in school, and about how to excel." Their involvement was designed for "neighborhood kids," an age group between 12 and 28.28 In June 1996 Kono conducted a three-day summer fitness workshop for several hundred new student university hires.29 On the other end of the age spectrum, and despite his own health concerns, he lectured to senior citizens in May 1997 and February 1998 on the benefits of regular exercise as a means to delay or reverse aging. It would prevent osteoporosis, arthritis, and hardening of the arteries; improve sleep, digestion, circulation, and mental alertness; and enable one to feel more energetic and self-confident. He advised listeners to eat fresh, wholesome foods; get lots of sleep; be active socially; and exercise at least three times a week. "Use it or lose it" was his persistent theme.[30]

Some of Kono's service activities verged on honorific. In support of its "Keeping the Memories Alive" series in 1993, Tommy signed 200 milk covers and donated $500 to Hawaii Nostalgia, of which 25 percent of projected $20,000 proceeds would be donated to his favorite charity.[31] In July 2000 he participated in Patriot Night, an annual fund raiser for the Hawaii Food Bank which honored local Olympians. "There were 14 of us and it was a real bang-up affair" with the governor and his wife attending, he told Drechsler. At $125 per seat and with 10 persons to a table, there were "81 tables sold!" Tommy lamented it was "too bad the USAW can't do something similar to that. It would get everyone motivated instead of the usual money waiving bit."[32] Even closer to his charitable soul was the Straub Foundation, a non-profit organization which sponsored the annual Keiki Asthma Fair at Waimanalo District Park. His all-day participation on September 30, 2000, and donation of $100 marked

Support of the annual Keiki Asthma Fair was one of Kono's most important public service activities. He is pictured here in 1998 decorating the winner of one of the event's athletic competitions.

his third year of involvement. Medical Director Bo Eklof reported that "we had more than 700 participants, including 120 families (comprised of 180 Wheezers, 110 sibs and more than 200 parents). Our 200+ community volunteers staffed the modified Olympics, children's and parents' modules, registration, workshops, food booths, first aid stations, Keiki Asthma Fair Store, etc." Tommy was "pleased that so much good is spread to those afflicted with asthma and especially, to the parents."[33] Such an organization might have alleviated some of his own childhood suffering, but it might have also denied him the deprivation that led to his success as a weightlifter and public figure.

Family Milestones

In 1990, Tommy Kono turned 60 and was anticipating retirement. His performance reviews were uniformly outstanding. On May 8, his supervisor, Euphemia Nagashima, recognized that, with his "positive and quiet manner, resourcefulness and excellent public relations with corporate businesses and organizations," he had secured their assistance for many of the department's sports and fitness events. "You are well respected and received in the community as evidenced by the many invitations to speak on your experiences and motivation." In January 1997, Christine Sablecky complimented him on his "positive and mature attitude." She described him as "dependable, trustworthy, efficient, sincere," and always willing, as the department's leader in fitness and sports, to share his knowledge and resources. In both evaluations, "attitude to work" was his strongest quality.[34] As his final days of employment approached, Tommy confided to Melanie Getz that he was "excited and anxious, like I am preparing for a contest. Haven't had this feeling since 1965 from my last contest."[35]

By this time, his family was growing. All three of his children had married, the last being Mark, whose marriage to Sherri Lynn of Las Vegas he and Flo only learned about later. His well wishes included a check for $2,000 and some paternal advice on how to use it. "It is easy to earn $2,000," he reckoned, "but to save that amount in cash takes time." His son would be well advised to "think things through before you use it." Before buying a car, he should think about costs for repair, maintenance, and auto insurance, and that for most jobs, the paycheck comes two weeks after employment. On New Year's Eve of 1993, joAnn and then husband Melchor Miles Kanoa went to a Kabuki restaurant. "After that they came up to the house to usher in the New Year with fireworks right in front of the house. Mel brought along his friend's $2,000 karaoke machine so they sang in the house until almost 2:30 a.m." Son Jamie, living near Seattle, worked that night, and his wife Miriam went to bed early because she had to get up at 4:30 to go to work.[36] Coincidently, Tommy and Flo also became grandparents when joAnn gave birth to a daughter, Harley. joAnn later married Gary Sumida who adopted Harley.[37] At age four, Harley was already showing signs of responsibility and decorum so characteristic of her grandfather. While Tommy was attending the Nagano Olympics, she told him that she was "being a good girl and listening to grandma and mommy. I miss your cooking for me," she said. "I am watering the plants—just like you told me to and am marking my calendar everyday."[38] Significantly, or perhaps a sign of the times, all three Kono offspring were married and divorced by the turn of the century.

The Wounded Warrior

With old age, the aches and pains Tommy had been suffering since his lifting days in the 1950s became more accentuated. Shortly after the Atlanta Olympics, he underwent a three-hour total hip replacement operation. Knowing that John Grimek, age 86, was undergoing a similar operation, Tommy shared a detailed account of his physical complaints. "My knees are very bad but eventually it took its toll on my left hip." An X-ray in May 1996 revealed that his "left hip had *no space* between the thigh bone and hip socket. No wonder I was feeling pain because there was no lining for the bones. It was bone grinding (not gliding) on bone." The operation was successful which enabled Tommy to leave the hospital on the 8th and resume normal activities at home by early October.[39] It was much the same story he shared with Tamas Ajan. After getting 26 staples removed, he could "shower without the bandages getting wet. I am walking around the house using one crutch. I have started my rehabilitation program and my goal is to be able to go to work in two weeks." But he was also looking forward to retirement and "more time to devote to weightlifting" and offering "my services to IWF." Indicating he was on the mend, he observed to Ajan that "for the past 4–5 years the U.S. has been on a wrong path," owing mainly to the hiring of outsiders with little understanding of American lifters. "Wish us luck, Tamas."[40]

By January 1997, he was hoping for full physical recovery. "My recovery from the hip operation is coming along," he told Grimek, "but I guess I am impatient." "The therapy exercise I perform three times a week is helping a lot. Since I started two weeks ago I have improved my walking gait. I don't rock from side to side or lean on one side." He was also encouraged that former Mr. America George Eiferman, who had suffered a heart attack, was out of the hospital and "recovering nicely"; that Hawaiian bodybuilder and gym owner Timmy Leong, age 70, was "doing fine"; and that

> Pete George is busy writing two books. One book, which should be a best seller, is regarding staying in shape by exercising 58 seconds a day. Pete's got better imagination than Hoffman ever had!
>
> Richard Tomita is into golfing so we never see him around. Richard Tom drops by the Nuuanu Y every now and then. Richard spends his time watching football on TV, going to movies and making model ships.
>
> Emerick Ishikawa is the one that is in great shape! He trains 4 to 5 times a week that includes jogging and weight training. Since he retired from work several years ago he started exercising in earnest. I've never seen the guy in better shape.[41]

A final physical failing for Tommy occurred when he had to have surgery for carpal tunnel syndrome on his left hand after helping with the 1999 Honolulu Marathon. After recovering, he called it a "simple operation and very common."[42]

Hawaii's Greatest Living Olympian

Despite his many physical ailments during the nineties, Kono's spirits were buoyed by continuous recognition of his weightlifting achievements. Readers of *Weightlifting USA* were already reminded by Deb Nelson in its "Heroes of Weightlifting" series of Tommy's greatness, calling him "the most legendary of U.S. weightlifting heroes.... Never before or since has a U.S. weightlifter accomplished so much and commanded such world-wide respect." Then on September 22, 1990, the Association of Oldtime Barbell & Strongmen honored him, along with bodybuilder Reg Park, golfer Frank Stranahan, and Rudy Sablo at the Downtown Athletic Club in New York.[43] In 1993, Kono received the Mackey Yanagazawa Award at Aloha Stadium in Honolulu during the Aloha Bowl football game for his many years of promoting sports. Also at Aloha Stadium, Tommy was tapped to do the "Rocky thing" by lighting the torch for the opening ceremonies of the 1994 Aloha State Games. It was the state's largest amateur sporting event, attracting over 7,000 local athletes competing in 47 sports. According to reporter Pat Bigold,

> it was with humility and reluctance that Hawaii's greatest living Olympian agreed to step briefly into the limelight before 8,000 spectators.... "I didn't want to do it," said Kono, whose litany of accomplishments was read during the televised torch-lighting ceremony. But he said he did it because it was for every average athlete who fantasizes about competing for gold, silver and bronze. It was for the Aloha State Games motto, "There's a Hero in Each of Us."[44]

Complementing his recognition at the Centenary Atlanta Olympics, Kono received an appreciation certificate from the Nutrition branch of the Hawaii State Health Department and the 5-A-Day-Coalition.[45] The year culminated with Tommy's induction into the inaugural International Weightlifting Hall of Fame at IOC headquarters in Lausanne, Switzerland, and being one of seven Asian Americans receiving an Excellence 2000 Award from the United States Pan Asian American Chamber of Commerce in Washington, D.C.[46]

In 1997, the Japanese American *Hawaii Herald* heralded Tommy as "The Greatest Weightlifter of All Time," stressing his positive attitude towards life. "For example, if you're short or speak with an accent, people can remember you easier." That is what he meant by turning what many believed to be a negative into a positive.[47] In February 1998, Tommy became one of the inaugural class of 35 sports legends enshrined in the new Hawaii Sports Hall of Fame in Aloha Stadium. Most notable were baseball founder Alexander Joy Cartwright, Olympic swimmers Duke Paoa Kahanamoku and Buster Crabbe, and Francis Hyde L'i Brown, so-called "Mr. Golf of Hawaii." Governor Ben Cayetano praised the honorees for representing "140 years of athletic accomplishment" and being "inspirational models for our youth." Tommy also received accolades from both Hawaii senators. Daniel Inouye praised him for encouraging "a countless number of children to work hard and play hard," and Daniel Akaka believed his selection "ensured that you will forever be recognized for the national and international prominence of your achievements."[48] He became so busy from his increasing celebrity status that he had to resign from the board of directors of the Honolulu Quarterback Club as well as its Sports Person of the Month meeting.[49]

So great was media attention that he was hard put to meet the many requests for his presence and even unable to attend the 50th reunion of his class at Sacramento High School. "I have been busier now than when I was working," he explained to former classmate Gloria DePrato Tomei. "An average of 3 or 4 letters a week is forwarded to me from the U.S. Olympic Committee" requesting an autograph and photo. "These are usually autograph collectors." Normally he would respond with his autograph and a biographical sketch to provide meaning to the signature.[50] Although he found the attention lavished on him satisfying and signed all of the cards and photos sent to him, Tommy eventually learned that some of the extra cards and pictures were being sold. Not wanting to be exploited, he decided to sign only one card or picture and address it to whoever sent it. For the approximate six requests per week he received from fans or collectors, he reasoned it would cost a "small fortune to supply every requestor for a photo. I am pleased to be remembered and flattered by the request," he responded in a general notice, "but unless you are willing to pay $10 for an 8x10 glossy print, I cannot accommodate you."[51] Kono was learning that fame, though it availed him of many opportunities, was also a burden to bear.

10

Weightlifting Sage

"If thou wouldest win Immortality of Name, either do Things worth the Writing or write Things worth the Reading."[1]—Thomas Fuller

Take Advantage from Disadvantage

Despite the many physical ailments he endured and setbacks suffered at the hands of the American weightlifting establishment, Tommy showed no signs of slowing down. He relentlessly advocated positivity in the coaching sessions and clinics he held in his years as a weightlifting elder. Denied a role in formulating national policy, he avidly promoted his ideas for improvement during weekly training sessions at the Nuuanu YMCA where he not only provided hands-on instruction but also "stories about inspiration and success," according to Darren DeMellow, much of it in handouts. "Every Saturday we train, and he gave me this, 'The Best of Everything.' Here's Alexeev, his story. He gave me this to get inspired. He would just stand there and say, 'I want you to read this,' often in the locker room." Brenda Salgado concurs that "he always had something to hand out."[2] What made Tommy's coaching unique was his emphasis on the mind as critical to physical performance. "The mind must be groomed for success," Kono believed. "The mind must be set in a positive mode all the time." He attributed this outlook to "the health problems I experienced when I was growing up, plus the frustrations I encountered in my early career in the sport. ... My background made me look to the positive side of most everything."[3] There were so many facets to Tommy's positive pursuits—weightlifter, bodybuilder, coach, inventor, entrepreneur, public servant, administrator, photographer, and artist—that it is often difficult to discern where his priorities lay at any particular time. With only limited formal education and more inclined towards technology than the literary arts, it seemed unlikely that his legacy would be sustained through his writings. But Kono was an avid and prolific writer.

Much like multiple Mr. Universe Bill Pearl, who was besieged with requests for training advice, Tommy found a way to satisfy this demand and the urge to extend his coaching career. For Pearl, it took the form of a series of training books he started writing after he and his wife Judy moved to Oregon in the late 1970s to escape the Southern California smog. They envisioned "a manual where Bill could do personal training by mail with anybody anywhere who had a post office." Reasoning that anyone who spoke English could use it, he advertised "that if you wanted me to train you, you have to buy this book. And I swear to God, we were getting our mail back in sacks, not just in handfuls." Pearl's large training book, *Keys to the Inner Universe*, appeared in 1978, and his most successful publication, *Getting Stronger* (1986), "sold more than one million copies." It seemed incredible that he could make more money as a writer than he did from decades of bodybuilding and gym owning.[4] That Tommy could promulgate his lifting philosophy by similar means must have occurred to him for years. He had already laid a basis for it with his 19 "ABC's of Weightlifting" articles in *Strength & Health* in the 1960s and the constant coaching tips he dispensed by regular and electronic mail to anyone seeking advice. His remoteness in Hawaii and cost of long-distance phone calls left few other options.

Telling His Story

At the outset of his first volume, *Weightlifting, Olympic Style*, Tommy recognized several veteran lifter/coaches—Louis DeMarco, Walter Imahara, and Pete George—for providing input. No one, however, furnished more material assistance than Artie Drechsler, who had just published his massive *Weightlifting Encyclopedia* which served as a template for Tommy's enterprise.[5] Kono's primer focused first on such fundamental principles as maintaining a strong back arch, acquiring knee and hips flexibility, pulling properly, and utilizing training aids to enhance the body's natural movements. Counterintuitively, to create a sense of distance between the bar and platform, he encouraged trainees to "think of pushing the floor down and away from the bar" instead of "thinking of lifting the bar away from the floor." To explain the Olympic lifts, broken down into segments, Tommy made lavish use of photos of world-renowned lifters as well as stick-figure drawings to illustrate perfect performance. Although the snatch is seemingly one simple movement, he explained its execution as a series of nuanced motions through sequence picture analysis. Kono argued against "trying to execute the lift quickly. Don't try to 'explode' at any time in the pull; but, rather, start slow and gradually speed up the pulling movement so you have a continuous, lengthy extended pull that will automatically accelerate because of added leverage coming into play as the body straightens out." Likewise for the clean, though balance was less a factor, a smooth and deliberate pull was critical to positioning the weight for shoulder-racking and recovery. He encouraged trainees to think of using the bar "to pull your body down" once full extension is reached. The perfect jerk, he argued, results from proper leverage to propel the bar overhead to support the weight with locked arms. Contrary to popular belief, jerking depends far more on leg than arm strength. "Study some lifters who are holding world record weights overhead in the Jerk, and you'll find that in almost all instances they do not have large arms." Similarly, female lifters often exhibit "relatively thin arms supporting enormous weights." Arms serve chiefly as "pillars" to provide "bone on bone" alignment with the torso.[6]

The training plan Kono developed, Quality Training (QT), was based on the principle that muscles must be taxed, but time must be allowed for rest and recovery. His system contradicted the "European System" which swept the weightlifting world in recent decades whereby lifters trained obsessively with heavy loads five to six days a week, sometimes twice a day. Tommy was highly critical of these routines. While some seemed to benefit initially from these brutal methods, "they soon found themselves 'icing their knees' after their workouts because their knees were not fully recovered from workout to workout; many altered their technique as a result of fatigue and began to use more of their back for lifting. In some instances, even the back was affected from the extra load and from not enough recovery time, resulting in injury." Training hard and long would less likely yield results than performing the right amount of exercises correctly. "Performing too many sets and repetitions of any single exercise is counterproductive because … once fatigue sets in, the lifting movement can change." To avoid fatigue leading to incorrect movement, Tommy advised that technique work be done early in workouts. Training sessions of 90 to 120 minutes just three times per week would "create more enthusiasm, and because you enjoy the training, you put more heart and soul into it and reap the benefit of improving faster." There was less chance of going stale and more time to recover. "You should be looking forward to your workouts and not dreading them. Workouts should be challenging, enjoyable, and productive. … Better to be under-training than over-trained." Embedded in these remarks was a strong criticism of the East European "loaded" system perpetrated on American lifters which indirectly led to Kono's USAW rejection.[7]

An American Way

To ensure maximal results, Tommy prioritized flexibility over strength, particularly in the low position of the squat clean. He encouraged trainees to develop knee and ankle flexibility to help keep the body upright in the full squat and capable of bouncing out of the bottom. Shoes with slightly elevated heels will facilitate this process by providing some tilt to the pelvic area for descent into deep squat cleans. This flexibility is complemented by the natural flexibility of a heavily loaded bar which bends up and down. Using "the rhythm of the flexible weightlifting bar in bouncing out of your squat will add 5 kilos to your Front Squat ability and it will be a great asset for the Clean and Jerk." Although this flexing was most advantageous in the heavy squat clean, it was also obvious in the uplifting effect at the outset of the jerk. Its impact in competition was most obvious to Kono at the 1971 world championships in Lima, Peru, which featured superheavyweights Ken Patera (USA), Vasily Alexeev (Soviet Union), and Serge Redding (Belgium). He deemed Patera to be the strongest, but owing to his stiffness he was using power to make his lifts, while Redding and Alexeev were employing leverage and flexibility. In the comparative photos he displayed of their deep position in the snatch, Patera "was not going into the deep squat positions that both his opponents were able to hit when they cleaned or snatched. Because of his stiffness, he had to catch the barbell high, which means to lift the same weights as they were, he had to pull the barbell higher than they." Years earlier, Tommy learned a lesson in bar/body coordination when he attempted to jerk a springy eight-foot, 374-pound globe barbell at Cayeux's Paris gym just after the Helsinki Olympics. After taking a quick dip with his knees, the bar sprung quickly to arm's length. "The 374 pounds felt like 330, so easy was the 'kick.' However, I was not prepared for the 'kick back' of the bar coming down on my locked arms. The weight coming down felt like 402 pounds!" Although his arms were braced, his knees buckled under the shock. Kono had more success with a flexible bar a year later at the Stockholm world championships where he cleaned and jerked 371¼ pounds. On this occasion, he synchronized his bounce out of the bottom position with the upward lift of the bar.[8]

Repeatedly, Kono advised against overtraining, not only in the Olympic lifts but also in squats and heavy pulling exercises. "High pulls should be limited so your speed of movement will not be affected and you can pull it to the required height without working on your nervous energy." The final two weeks should be devoted less to assistance exercises and "more on the technique of the actual Olympic lifts." Additional caution was necessary to avoid three factors that could destroy months of hard training—injury, catching cold, and overtraining. These conditions often resulted from training too hard for too long. "When I taxed myself repeatedly, I ended up with an injury because of over-stressing my fatigued muscles or catching cold through lowered resistance."[9] He admitted, however, that "the trend now is to workout continuously leading up to the contest" with heavy weights, having been "toughened to lift as much in training" and even more "than in a contest." Contrary to the protocol of the earlier Olympians John Davis and Yoshinobu Miyake, who rested during the fortnight prior to a contest, he often heard of "Eastern European lifters missing a heavy attempt on the platform but making it backstage afterwards."[10] Yet it had been East Europeans, with their "loaded" system, who were winning the most Olympic and world championships for four decades. That this record of achievement was the result of covert drug-taking by foreign athletes was never addressed in Kono's book, despite the controversies that were swirling around performances in multiple sports. In 2004, President George W. Bush even brought the issue to national attention by condemning performance-enhancing drugs in his 2004 State of the Union message.[11] Tommy's message, however, continued to stress tried-and-true training methods that fostered his own rise to the top of the weightlifting world two generations earlier. To illustrate these successful strategies, he provided 10 detailed descriptions of his competitive prowess, ranging from his first contest in San Jose in 1948 to his heroic victory at the 1963 nationals in Harrisburg.

A challenge of a different kind confronted Tommy at a meet he describes in Northern California as he prepared to clean and jerk 350 pounds. "As I got set to begin my pull my eyes momentarily focused on the wife of one of the lifters who was sitting almost directly in front of me with her right leg crossed over her left leg and her right elbow resting on her knee. One of her hands was cupping her chin and she was looking straight at me. I ended up dead lifting the weight." The lesson he learned from this experience was "when you mount the platform for an attempt, let nothing distract you."[12] A somewhat different version of this story is related by Kono protégé Mike Harada who insists the incident occurred at the Nuuanu YMCA. "There was this girl sitting right in front," as Tommy told it, "and she had her legs kind of spread, and I went to clean, and I saw that, and I missed the lift. I lost my concentration."[13]

Data compiled by Osmo Kiiha suggests this incident occurred on December 5, 1953, at the San Jose YMCA, two years before Tommy moved to Hawaii.[14] Regardless of time and place, the message was clear to him of the importance of concentration. Among the 150 gems of wisdom he imparted in his book, perhaps none is more salient than the need to remain focused. "If anything can distract you backstage, or while you are on the platform, you are not truly focused. If noises, sight, smell or negative thoughts cross your mind, you are succumbing to the opponents of fear, failure and defeat. Concentration on the task at hand, with positive outcome in mind must be nurtured." Tommy considered concentration to be the "'Zen' part of Olympic lifting ... that of being totally lost in thought of what you have to do with the bar rather than the heaviness of the weight being attempted."[15] For all his talk about technique, this aphorism most succinctly conveyed the outlook he wished to provide in *Weightlifting, Olympic Style*.

Prestige, Publicity, and Profit

The extent to which altruistic motives dominated Tommy's thinking during many months of drafting cannot be determined, but pedagogic and commercial considerations weighed heavily on him. Most of all, he craved recognition and acceptance for his ideas on saving American weightlifting. He also realized that before any profits could be made, money had to be spent on production and publicity. Fortunately, owing to his celebrity status for over a half century, there was a large pool of admirers and aficionados to whom he could appeal. To that end he distributed complimentary copies to 83 family, friends, iron game associates, and promoters. The latter included Tamas Ajan (*World Weightlifting*), Denis Reno (*Weightlifter's Newsletter*), Randy Strossen (*Milo*), Roy Edwards (*Health and Strength*), Gary Cleveland (*Avian Movement Advocate*), Vic Boff (*Oldetime Barbell and Strongman*), Bill Clark (*USAWA Newsletter*), and York Barbell Company. But the recipients did not include his nemesis *USA Weightlifting* or Clarence Bass, whose Ripped Enterprises website offered the most intelligent rendering of iron game developments.[16] It was Bass who succinctly describes and lavishes praise on the book.

> To my delight and the great good fortune of his readers, Kono's ability to communicate what he learned over the years comes close to matching his lifting prowess. Like the bar coming off the floor in a well-executed snatch or clean, Tommy's book starts slowly and builds momentum chapter by chapter.
>
> If you're expecting hard-to-follow explanations of complicated lifting techniques, and training plans full of confusing percentages and complex cycles, you're in for a surprise. If you're looking for all day, every day European-style workouts, look elsewhere. However, if you want straightforward explanations and training plans born of long experience and common sense, Tommy's book is just your cup of tea.

Bass assured readers that, although his records have long been eclipsed, "few lifters, if any, cast a longer shadow over international lifting than Kono."[17]

These uplifting remarks were complemented by endorsements he received from the weightlifting community. To market his book, Tommy replaced his nearly defunct KIO Company with a Kono Company LLC which he registered with the state of Hawaii in November 1999.[18] Book orders were brisk. From March 30 to April 14, 2001, he sold 46 copies, including 20 to Walter Imahara and 6 to Jeanette Chun, for $1,467. By the end of June, sales reached 138 for which Tommy earned $4,606, and by the end of the year Kono's earnings reached $19,724 for 591 books for which he paid $799 in state income tax and $2,478 in postage. Lest it be assumed that Tommy was getting rich, a further outlay of $6,950 was required for printing 2,046 copies to Data Repro. Co., $983 for graphic design, $275 for ISBN registration, and $450 for miscellaneous expenses. Thus the gross earnings of $19,725 Kono received from the sale of *Weightlifting* was offset by $11,94 in expenses, leaving a profit of $7,781; not a bad bottom line, considering that probably 90 percent of the expenses, mostly for printing, were incurred for just one year. And earnings for the first two months of 2002 of $1,814 suggested that sales would only increase, especially with greater awareness through the "iron grapevine."[19] What is not so evident is the immense amount of labor, sacrifice to his physical and mental well-being, and time not devoted to his family that was required to bring it to fruition.

Kono's success may be attributed to the staying-power of the image he projected as one of the greatest weightlifters of all time, a world-class coach, and a revered icon of sport. Publishing on such a large scale admittedly was risky. But any concerns about failure were allayed by his growing financial portfolio which showed an income (excluding investments) for 2002 of $53,851, including social security ($17,292), city/county pension ($21,936), and Marathon Association ($14,623). The Konos' expenses totaled only $12,096, the largest being $3,425 they wisely invested in long-term health care. By now, they were no longer burdened with a home mortgage and had a yearly property tax of only $1,071. For 2003, Tommy's income appreciated to $54,965. The family's assets also included $175,745 in insurance and annuities, $7,400 in checking at American Savings & Loan, $67,167 at the city/county federal credit union, and an estimated $9,000 in Kono Company. Excluding home and car, the Konos' total wealth exceeded $314,000.[20]

An opportunity to expand his financial opportunities emerged in January 2005 when he went into business with Leo Falasco, Jr., who operated the Country Power health food store in Waianae. Leo had designed a product called "Powerhooks" that enabled lifters to do dumbbell presses on a bench without having to maneuver the weights into place. To promote Powerhooks, he rented a booth at a trade show for strength coaches in Las Vegas and invited Tommy to join him to market his "fantastic" book.

> There was a line at my booth once they found out who Tommy Kono is. But Tommy spent so much time on people who were nobodies. He had two kids, and he was teaching them how to coordinate their grip better while all these other people wanted pictures with him and everything else. ... He was such a humble man. In 24/7 I never saw him get angry. That's the way relations should be. I was so glad to be exposed to someone like him. If it was Arnold Schwarzenegger versus Tommy Kono, I would take Tommy Kono any day.

Afterwards Tommy explained that he was trying to get his knee and waist bands back on the market but could not find the right material. Falasco informed him that he had a possible source in Taiwan. After testing several samples

Tommy said, "this is it." From there I said, "okay Tommy, we're partners." It was handshakes all the time. ... We didn't make millions, and it's probably because I'm not that great of a marketer, and I even told Tommy that. And he said he didn't care. He picked the right man because we got it out on the market at least. And we did really well one year. I gave Tommy a check for $16,000.[21]

After an initial outlay of $3,540 each to Taiwan, their venture included promotional trips to weightlifting events and health and fitness shows in Denver; Las Vegas; Columbus, Ohio; Saddle Brook, New Jersey; and Edmonton, Canada, in 2005. But sales came mainly from word-of-mouth endorsements. At the 2006 Arnold Expo, Tommy noted the knee bands were purchased by large men for their elbows as well as knees.[22] Kono estimated that the inventory on his books was 2,415 at the end of 2005.[23] Altogether his business expenses, including promotional costs ($1,037), office supplies ($668), subscriptions ($524), dining ($298), donations ($260), and miscellaneous items ($1,758), totaled $4,545. Tommy's direct income (exclusive of Flo's) for 2005 totaled $80,424 while his interest earnings amounted to $2,830. Significantly, the former included $3,857 from book sales and $5,300 profit from sale of his knee and waist bands by Country Power.[24] These figures show that even with increased expenses, Tommy's ventures into American capitalism were paying off and helping his family live a good life.

Tommy's "Thoughts"

Much uncertainty prevailed, however, about Kono's standing in the weightlifting world. The issue emerged when he applied for 2004 USAW registration. Despite his distinguished experience as an athlete, referee, and coach, he did not fit any of these categories under the organization's certification program. "I am considered 'out of the loop' with the USAW," he complained to administrator Laurie Lopez. She responded that he could simply register as "coach" which "will not preclude you from refereeing." That his status as "senior international coach" would be recorded in his file, though not his membership card, no doubt satisfied Tommy's desire for recognition.[25] Another matter that aroused his indignation was an editorial that appeared in the September 2003 issue of *Milo* magazine. Randall Strossen's views stemmed from having observed Bulgaria's remarkable rise as a world weightlifting power under Ivan Abadjiev who

> cuts the team no slack, forcefully stating that their stipends depend upon their performance, reminding individual lifters that another lifter is on their heels, and at the root of things, demanding that they lift more today than they did yesterday. ... It used to be almost at the level of a truth recorded in stone and presented by Moses that you lifted weights three times a week—no more, no less. For those of us who were raised for years, if not decades, on this truth, it has been hard to learn that there are other ways to play this game.

Strossen's conversion to the Eastern European "loaded" system as the answer to America's weightlifting woes occurred when he attended presentations in 1990 in San Francisco and San Anselmo, California, by Dragomir Cioroslan who was interviewing to be national coach.

Dragomir's account marked a turning point in what I believed we could do and what I expected was necessary for maximum progress, and from that day on, I adjusted my sights upward from the rigid formula of three workouts per week, and think we need to be ever mindful of Bill Starr's comment that 'comfort does not lead to a higher strength level.'[26]

These professions of apostasy to the American way contradicted the gospel propagated in Tommy's book.

Kono duly drafted a strongly-worded rebuttal motivated by his recollection of similar sentiments expressed in Peary Rader's *Iron Man* magazine. Those articles led him to start his ABC series in *Strength & Health* to counter all the "incorrect" training ideas being circulated. What Strossen did not reveal was the results of Dragomir's tutelage. Tommy believed "the proof of the pudding is what has Dragomir produced at USOTC using this 'train harder' formula?"[27] What most concerned Kono was the influence Strossen "has with his magazine to those who follow Olympic lifting." He expressed his views in an e-mail letter to Strossen.

> Your recollection of what Dragomir said in 1990 leaves readers with the impression that the lifters have to be constantly tired because they put in many hours of training per day otherwise they will not make the grade. … If training harder and more often is what is required, what kind of improvement have the lifters quartered at USOTC shown since moving over there? They have the most ideal conditions and with Dragomir there to really build up their "volume," where are the results? … When you reflect back to the collection of records prior to 1993 (some dating back to early 1980s) and the current records now, there isn't much difference. So we have really been in a stand-still for almost two decades.[28]

Whether Strossen ever received or read Tommy's missive cannot be determined, but it never appeared in *Milo's* letters to the editor section.

As the Athens Olympics approached, Kono intensified his criticisms in a private log titled "My Thoughts." "Weightlifting in the U.S. has become a joke," he declared on July 21, 2004. "It is a hobby, a past time and not a sport. The gym is a social club. Getting into the elite status here means you have made it so now you can coast. USOTC has become a retirement home for elite lifters." He believed that if American lifters "went back to the basics of Snatch, C&J and Squats and train 3 times a week with a light medium, heavy session and train no more than 2 hours at any one session, they would enjoy it and show improvement." Seemingly gone were the halcyon days of yesteryear when Americans mentored by Hoffman developed into "real LIFTERS to represent the USA." Tommy concluded that the USAW coaching program was motivated mainly by desire to make money. A not unforeseen consequence of the certified coaching scheme created by Lyn Jones was that it contributed to his own demise by helping to

> eliminate the older, more experienced, self-taught "coaches" and bring up-to-date accepted coaching practice. This helped reduce seasoned, veteran "coaches" and eventually eliminate them from the USAW organization by politics. This was well orchestrated by Lyn Jones from the national office. … The coaching program became a means of raising funds and it brought about a false sense of know-how of lifting to those who took the course. This in turn was spread far and wide and so rather than make lifting better, lifting became worse.

Tommy concluded that the "USAW has actually lost sight of what they are there for." Although his contacts with those in power were severed, he was determined to show "the other side of the coin. This is the reason for my second book. It is revolutionary ... but it will be result producing. Everyone has forgotten the basics and made weightlifting complicated as hell." In this respect it would likely be more reactionary than revolutionary.[29]

Further fuel for Kono's private thoughts came from Harvey Newton, also recently excluded from the corridors of power and wishing perhaps to rationalize or vindicate himself. He acted on a hunch that although male junior weightlifters had increased in quantity, there was no increase in quality. "This is not a 'half-empty' observation," he contended. Like Tommy, he was "concerned with maximizing results." To test his progression/regression theory, he analyzed the National Junior Championship results at 10-year intervals (1984, 1994, and 2004).

> In terms of entries, 1984 had 48 competitors; in 1994, 97; and in 2004, 100 lifters. This suggests our junior ranks are growing, a fact confirmed by USAW registration statistics. However, in nearly all categories, the lowest Total in 1984 is greater than the lowest Total in 2004.... We know which direction qualifying totals have gone over 20 years. A greater number of lower qualified lifters have provided an economic impact for the organizers. However this does not address the primary focus of the organization's mission statement, namely winning international gold medals. Quantity is important, but quality moves the program forward more decisively.

These calculations confirmed what Tommy had been saying for decades. Newton regretted that "those at the highest level are not interested in gathering such data annually."[30]

Successive calculations confirmed Newton's conclusions. Leo Temosheko's compilation of the performances of eight American men at the 2006 world championships in Dominican Republic indicated only two increased their totals, averaging three kilos over their previous best, while the remaining six decreased by an average of 7.2. The women's results were only slightly better, with two showing a four-kilo average improvement and the other five registering a 5.6-kilo average decrease. These data validated Tommy's contention that, unlike his own lifting record, American weightlifters were performing worse, not better, on the international stage. Further statistics compiled by the IWF showed that placement of American men in senior world championships declined from eighth in 1990 to 33rd in 2007, reaching a low point of 39th in 1998. Decline for American women was less steep, from second in 1987 to 11th in 2007, reaching a nadir of 22nd in 2001.[31] Obviously, after decades of East European influence something was wrong and not being fixed. Against these inconvenient truths, Tommy was still a voice crying in the wilderness.

"Divine" Interventions

Such was Kono's stature in the sports-minded public and international weightlifting world that his exclusion from USAW's decision-making process hardly mattered. His brilliant career in the 1950s and subsequent coaching exploits were fondly recalled, and he continued to receive requests for advice from lifters with Olympic aspirations. Kudos continued unabated. He was "a marvel of power in a small package," proclaimed an "Olympic Flashback" in 2000 by Pat Bigold in the *Honolulu Star-Bulletin*. It recognized how "restrictions on lifters have eased and how Kono, who turned down a well-paying role in Mae West's Las Vegas revue in 1954 and some Japanese movie offers because of the strict amateur rule of his day, often had to hitchhike to training and competitions." Tommy recalled that "anything that had to do with your title or using your body was banned."[32] On February 13, 2003, he was recognized by the USOC at a special awards ceremony at San Diego State University as an "Olympic Titan."[33]

Other nostalgia-based honors included a Certificate of Honor from San Francisco mayor Gavin Newsom for creating "bridges of friendship" with the city's Asian American community, and at a gala dinner on October 29, 2004, he received, along with Sammy Lee, the Asian Pacific American Leadership Award on the occasion of *AsianWeek*'s 25th anniversary. A week later Kono, Kristi Yamaguchi (figure skating), Wat Misaka (basketball), Wally Yonomine (football), and Ann Kiyumura Hayashi (tennis) were inducted into the Japanese American Sports Hall of Fame at San Francisco's Pacific Bell Park.[34] Although he never attended Sacramento City College or played any of its sports, he was inducted into its Athletic Hall of Fame, presumably as a son of the city, in October 2005.[35] Probably the most heartwarming recognition for Tommy, however, came from York, Pennsylvania. While he was never a member of the York Barbell Club, he had made his greatest gains and fame while associating with Bob Hoffman. In August 2004 this link with past greatness was perpetuated in a mural painted by Max Mason on a building in downtown York titled "York, PA, Muscletown USA" depicting Hoffman as "Father of World Weightlifting," John Grimek as "Mr. America, 1940–41," and Kono as "America's Greatest Weightlifter."[36]

Kono's finest hours as an athletic celebrity, however, were vested on the national and international levels. At the 2004 annual Arnold Sports Festival, Randy Strossen reported that Schwarzenegger, after entering the Olympic lifting venue, stated,

> "This is the highlight for me ... for many years I wanted to bring Olympic lifting here," and then he would point out to Tommy Kono and say, "This is my inspiration, right here."

By now, Arnold's

The masterly artwork on a downtown wall by Max Mason depicting three seminal physical culture figures—Bob Hoffman, Tommy Kono, and John Grimek—with roots in York, Pennsylvania.

Tommy and Arnold Schwarzenegger at the 2012 National Weightlifting Championships and Olympic Team Trials in Columbus, Ohio. It was one of numerous occasions where the Governator recognized him as "my inspiration" (courtesy Bruce Klemens).

Flanked by Iranian heavyweight Hossein Rezazadeh (left) and International Weightlifting Federation secretary Tamas Ajan (right), Tommy accepts an award as "IWF Best Weightlifter of 100 Years" in Istanbul, Turkey, in 2005.

overflowing, refreshingly boyish enthusiasm had taken over as he described how much he had looked up to Tommy, how he had seen him in person in Vienna at the 1961 World Championships and the FIHC Mr. Universe contest. Arnold left no doubt that the governor of the Golden State had iron in his veins when he wrapped up his tribute by saying, "I wanted to be study like Tommy, so strong and so muscular," and at that point the room gave him enough support that gravity was probably suspended at least momentarily.

Ironically, Arnold's presence overshadowed Strossen's earlier disparaging remarks about Kono's training methods and included a picture with a smiling Cioroslan in the entourage.[37] No less significant was Kono's selection at the IWF Centenary in Istanbul on March 1, 2005, as "Best Weightlifter of 100 Years."[38]

Clinical Alternatives

As memories of Tommy's bygone lifting heroics and sage advice in *Weightlifting, Olympic Style* permeated the weightlifting community, he also provided a visible alternative through clinics to the failure of America's current protocol. His presence was eagerly sought by budding lifters and coaches throughout the nation. Artie Drechsler told him that plans for a clinic in February 2002 at the Lost Battalion Hall in New York were uncertain, but when he informed his panel members that Kono was coming, their hesitation ceased. As soon as the clinic was announced on the USAW web site, "I had a number of people call to say they were coming just to see Tommy Kono." Tommy called Drechsler's undertaking "a real plus for all lifters and coaches. It is the kind of thing that Lyn Jones should have done with Dragomir heading it ... but they rather work only with the Colorado Springs resident lifters."[39] In January 2002, Kono attended a forum in Charleston, Illinois, where he worked with young lifters. Then, prior to another clinic in New York City, his plans called for a symposium in April in Mexico City, including three one-hour classroom sessions on technique, programs, and coaching, and one hour of practical training where he would correct lifters' form. Typically, as he explained to organizer Martha Elizondo, his lectures consisted of one-hour segments with other speakers in-between "so the class is not hearing the same lecturer for 2–3 hours in one sitting."[40] Although these presentations followed the chapters in his book, Tommy was prepared to lecture on such details as jerking, jumping, thigh banging, and auxiliary movements.[41]

Arguably the most consequential of Kono's clinical engagements were ones he conducted while visiting his family in Sacramento. They were facilitated by Bill Kutzer, a kinesiology professor at Sacramento State University who, after coaching football, formed Team Sacramento. It was around 1985, Kutzer explains, that Tommy "found out that we had a club. So whenever he came over for a visit he would swing by the university or I would see him at a local meet. So I got to know him pretty well." To Kutzer, Tommy was "a special guy. He always had a smile and was always encouraging and had something to say that was positive." Kono conducted several clinics at the university. "It was like E.F. Hutton," Kutzer recalls. "When Tommy spoke, everybody listened." Typically, 40 or 50 people showed up. "It was almost a word of mouth thing." It was also a big boon for Kutzer's club that Tommy's clinics were free, since he was already in town and paying for his own flight.

Kono's coaching was mostly not hands-on but observation and response to questions. "I think he was conscious of the fact that I had a team I was coaching," Kutzer believed, and did not want to infringe on his authority. "Here's this guy who is the greatest and has competed all around the world, but he's taking the time to come over and say 'hi' and watch us and offer suggestions." For Kutzer, winning the national collegiate title four times was "a big deal," and "Tommy was a great help." Kutzer observes that in all of his endeavors, Kono was totally dedicated. "In everything he put out his best, and weightlifting was, of course, his passion."[42] Most memorable was Tommy's willingness to help people in the sport and treat everyone equally.

A major aspect of Kutzer's contributions was his creation of an annual contest called "No Guts, No Glory." In 2006 he relinquished it to Paul Doherty, football coach at Sacramento High School, who renamed it the Tommy Kono Open.[43] Doherty was a veteran lifter who met Kono through his Hawaiian wife who was coached by Mel Miyamoto, one of Tommy's protégés. Doherty explains that

> I knew who Tommy was, and my wife didn't, so we went to the Nuuanu YMCA, and we saw this old obscure Japanese man in the corner of the weight room. "This is Tommy Kono. Do you know who Tommy Kono is?" My wife said, "no idea." Of course, I was star struck. I had to meet him. There was a weightlifting meet that weekend. I competed and I had a chance to meet and talk to him, and it was the funniest of coincidences. He asked me where I was from, and I said from the bay area of California, but I had just started working in Sacramento. He said, "I'm from Sacramento." I said, "you know I'm into the weightlifting thing as the football coach. I'm gonna have a weightlifting meet in August to kick off our football season. I'd love to call it the Tommy Kono." "I'll tell you what, I'll be there," Tommy said. … And sure enough, three months later we have the meet at Sacramento High School, and he shows up. And we had an assembly on campus, a school rally, and we exposed the kids to this history of Sacramento High School and the history of Sacramento, and the history of the internment camps and America, and we just developed a relationship for the Tommy Kono meet, and every year he kept coming.

As Doherty's kids kept improving, the team received an invitation to the Arnold Sports Festival where Tommy had been conducting annual lifting seminars.[44] In 2010 Werksan Barbell was offering a $3,500 competition set to the best high school team. Doherty's Hassle Free Barbell Club won every weight class in every male and female age group.

> Arnold Schwarzenegger comes by and says, "I got to meet these kids from Sacramento High School." He said his background was in weightlifting. … I said, "yeah, I know, I heard about you through Tommy Kono." He said, "Tommy Kono," and he stopped dead in his tracks. Tommy Kono was Arnold's biggest idol. "Each year we host an event called the Tommy Kono Classic, you ought to come out." He made it a point, "I will be there this year." I thought he wouldn't be there, but Arnold followed through and came to the event with Tommy.

Taking advantage of this propitious encounter, Doherty mentioned that his team held a fund-raiser every year to send lifters to international competitions.

> I was taken aback again, and he wanted to know more about our program and how much money we needed, and I said our annual budget is about $50,000. We send kids all over the

world, and some of our kids are funded by USA Weightlifting and some are not. He thought that was incredible and came back with a response of "why don't I host the fund raiser for you?" So we jumped on that train, and he did it and held a little cocktail party with appetizers and drinks at a little restaurant by the capital where he spends much of his time.

Doherty contends that the $85,000 from Arnold's fund-raiser helped USA Weightlifting "bridge the gap" leading to full support for international travel. For his own program, "it kept weightlifting alive," enabling his teams to win national championships for 10 years and for his women to compete in world championships. "Tommy was there every step of the way."[45]

Meanwhile, Kono continued to conduct clinics whenever his services were requested. On March 8, 2008, he held a Jerk Workshop at the Nuuanu YMCA. It was designed for the "thinking lifter" where he stressed self-control, that "you control the barbell—not the barbell control you, and that the bar should travel within the area of balance." He encouraged listeners to visualize all movements in slow motion. Upon completing the jerk, the barbell should be "supported in 'plumb-line (bone on bone) over the base of your feet."[46] At a self-improvement clinic in Sacramento on August 9, 2008, Kono's emphasis was on weightlifting as a numbers game. "What is lifted in Training isn't important. What is IMPORTANT is what is done in a CONTEST. ULTIMATELY IMPORTANT IS THE BIG CONTEST LIFTS."[47] It was a mantra he had been repeating for decades. At a "Back to Basics" seminar at the USOTC on September 27, 2009, a greater emphasis was placed on technique and technology, including a computer program that detailed each lifting phase. Virtually all of the 17 lifters and coaches expressed satisfaction in a participant survey. "I attend between 4 and 12 seminars annually," responded Stewart Venable of Lansing, Kansas, "and this is the best seminar I have ever been to." Participants also benefited from a technique analysis from a DVD recording of the recent nationals.[48] It seemed ironic that the USOTC should host an event so antithetical to the training approach of its leaders and that Tommy Kono should be granted a lifetime membership in 2008 by USA Weightlifting and recognized by the USOC in 2010 for his "commitment to Team USA."[49]

Nor was Tommy's coaching limited to the young, healthy, and strong. Clinics of a different kind were the many occasions when Tommy conveyed health and fitness advice to elderly citizens. On May 17, 2010, he spoke to the Oahu chapter of senior citizens about exercise, walking, jogging, and swimming at least 20 minutes, and recognized *koshi no chikara*, the power of the hips, whether swinging a golf club, throwing a ball, throwing a punch, or chopping lumber. He likened this "seat of power" to the "sign of youth."[50] These gatherings were also pertinent to Tommy's current life as he was experiencing the impact of old age and the need to stay relevant.

Championship Lifting

In 2010 Kono published his second major book, *Championship Weightlifting*, designed to focus on mental conditioning and complement his earlier work which he likened to "a very good instructional manual." It owed much to iron game veterans DeMarco, George, Drechsler, and Imahara, and University of Delaware professor Douglas Stalker who recalls that Tommy

> would go back and forth about one thing or another for the book, month in and month out, year in and year out. How much criticism of the USAW should there be? What was wrong with today's Masters lifting? How could you break the notion of the mental side of lifting into specific things a lifter could do? When he was wondering what to title this book, I suggested "Championship Weightlifting." I am honored that he took my suggestion. That was, after all, what he wanted for American lifters.[51]

Inspiration for *Championship Weightlifting* stemmed in part from a "revelation" Tommy received while asleep on November 5, 2005. "I woke up this morning and felt like the monk who came down from the mountain. I had this revelation that Olympic weightlifting is not a sport but an art. It is not power or speed but using good leverage that creates power and speed." "The Zen of lifting as it were," responded Stalker. "Reducing lifting to power or speed only makes drones. ... They don't do whole lifts but pieces of lifts. The Nautilus machine approach."[52] Tommy's "revelation" was confirmed by a conversation he had with Nautilus founder Arthur Jones. When asked how his invention could help Olympic lifters, Jones stunned Kono with his wisdom. "He said that for developing muscles and strength it is no challenge to him but weightlifting technique is something that has to be worked on because of the timing, balance, and applying the power correctly." Smooth, exact movements using "efficient leverage," Kono concluded, provided the pathway to championship performance.[53]

This training principle served as a conceptual basis for *Championship Weightlifting* and validation for his political stance in the sport. The book was as much a criticism of current training approaches as it was a justification of the protocol fostered by Hoffman and practiced by Tommy and his gold-medal winning colleagues in the 1950s. Echoing sentiments he had been expressing for decades, he believed that **"over training is worse than under training"** and it was **"quality of training** that was important." The key component to success, he believed, was mind power. "It all starts in the brain because the muscles respond only when thoughts are generated in the mind and transmitted to the muscles to contract. When we can control that thought process, train that, direct that to our athletic end, we have a handle on the major component involved in Olympic weightlifting." To train the mind, it was necessary to "focus on the positive side of all things that come your way." So important was the mind that 50 percent of training should be devoted to fostering mental force, 30 percent to technique, and only 20 percent to physical power. Olympic lifting, Kono contended, "is a blend of Applied Power to Efficient Technique coupled with a great State of Mind Control."[54] Training systems based on load production serve only to brutalize and fatigue muscles whereas mental conditioning produces the opposite result of unleashing the body's potential.

In a sense, it was easier for weightlifters to stay focused than other athletes. Unlike boxing and wrestling, where opponents continuously counter each other's moves, in weightlifting the opponent is the barbell and only indirectly an adversary. "The barbell has no brains," Kono argues, "for it is nothing more than dead weight and the challenge is to lift it overhead to beat your opponent's lift."

A great teacher of martial arts in Hawaii once told me in a private meeting that he had studied the action of different sports and he found that Olympic weightlifting was the closest sport that came to put to practice "Zen." Unlike the yelling and cheering that takes place in Power Lifting or in most other sports, Olympic lifters need to fix their attention on what has to be done and have dead silence before the attempt is made so they can concentrate solely on the task of harnessing their power to apply it correctly for the ultimate lift.

It was critical to focus on correct leverage, Tommy maintained, not brute strength. "Once good technique is mastered ... then it is a matter of increasing your 'leverage' power." To facilitate his knowledge of the critical moments of good technique, he perfected his skills as an amateur photographer. "With a relatively basic background in the science of physics, some knowledge of anatomy and a smattering of kinesiology, I was able to analyze the Olympic lifting movements so it became a logical sequence of applied leverage." It enabled Kono to "visualize the exact moments required for a successful lift." To illustrate the importance of the video-camera to coaching, he included sequence photos in his book of the 170 kg. clean and jerk he missed and then made at the Prize of Moscow tournament in 1961.[55]

Most evident in these photographs and throughout *Championship Weightlifting* is the testimony of a great champion. Permeating the book also is a tone of regret over the course of American weightlifting since his departure. Contrary to the Greek ideal of "*mens sana in corpore sano*," American lifters "put the Body training first and neglect the Mind part of training." The key to championship performance lay in having enough power and good technique, and focusing on "the task at hand." The significance of "harnessing the power of the mind dates back for centuries from the teaching of the Zen masters," he contended. "I have always believed that if you can focus your thoughts like using the magnifying glass to focus the sun's ray to a pin point to start paper or wood burning, you have gained the mental focus intensity required of achieving a new personal record." It was a question of mind over matter. Only when an athlete is "in the zone" is he capable of peak performance. Biographical sketches from the 1950s illustrate a time when American champions were in the zone. On a more personal note, however, it was disappointing to Tommy that though he was an eight-time finalist and four-time runner up, he never won the James E. Sullivan award honoring the nation's most outstanding amateur athlete.[56]

Again, the most immediate of many favorable responses Kono received for his book came from Bass who reminded website subscribers that Tommy's "mind made him a champion." It was "filled with wonderful stories and observations that made Tommy Kono, well, Tommy Kono." Included also are "stirring photos of Tommy and many others, of which world record high jumper Valeri Brummel kicking a basketball is the most dynamic, and a marvelous series showing the physique that earned Tommy one Mr. World and three Mr. Universe titles."[57] That he did not use more photos in his first book likely owes much to Kono's well-known humility, but Imahara strongly urged him to "add more photos, as it makes reading interesting. You can't use enough."[58]

The Steroid Predicament

The most glaring omission in *Championship Weightlifting* is any meaningful discussion of how or whether performance-enhancing drugs were responsible not only for the superior lifting of Eastern Europeans but also their ability to endure such brutal training routines and consequent failure of American efforts. It was a subject that was on the minds and in the conversations of all athletes, coaches, and sports commentators, especially in the wake of Jose Canseco's 2005 expose of Major League Baseball in *Juiced*, subsequent congressional hearings, and widespread drug-testing mandates.[59] Tommy seems unduly dismissive of the influence of steroids. Only once, on page 77, is it even mentioned. Yet Lou DeMarco and most other lifting leaders believe steroids produce a minimum 10-percent increase in performance, enough to win medals and set world records. Although he privately concurred with Tommy who told him that Americans' lack of progress "has nothing to do with the fact that their taking drugs," DeMarco believes "that has a lot to do with their winning." USAW coaching director Mike Conroy had

> a lot of sports scientists tell me that anything that can be achieved with drugs, 90% of that can be achieved without drugs. But it takes longer because you've got to be more patient. You realize we go to the Olympic Games, and the country that's using drugs snatches 200 kilos, and we snatch 90% of that, 180, we're in the B session. So you're not on the podium and in the end being on the podium is still what drives what goes on.

Conroy was told that cheating was "all part of the program," and when American weightlifters get caught, it is "because they're not getting assistance from the NGB to control what's going on with the tests." And the USA could not afford failures because they would show up in the press.[60]

Arguably the best example of the impact of drugs was the meteoric rise of Bulgaria in the 1970s under Abadjiev, known for his brutal coaching style—intensity, volume, maximum weights virtually all the time. Jim Schmitz argues, however, that "his training methods were probably no stricter than Bear Bryant's, the University of Alabama's famous football coach. You know what they do, they're philosophy is train the dickens out of them, and if they don't break we got a champion. They play the numbers game." Wes Barnett recalls being told by some friends

> "look, if you want to be clean and never win a medal, that's your problem." These are world and Olympic champions telling me this. I had another one tell me, "if you even want to dream of stepping up on the podium you have to take something. Otherwise you have no chance." ... When you are taking drugs and you're going six or seven days a week and two or three times a day in training sessions, obviously you're going to see the effect you're going to have. Really it's recovery more than it is the strength because you're able to do more because you can recover. So when you aren't doing it under the guise of medical scientists and professionals in a systematic way, you're just kind of on your own ... and you really don't know what you're doing or what dosage or any of this kind of stuff. You're at a huge disadvantage.

Exercise scientist Mike Stone credits the Eastern Europeans and the old Soviet Union for having "really good sports science programs" in the 1970s. "They got a big head start on everybody. There's no doubt that our lifters took drugs at that time, but ours was more of a hit and miss proposition." It was not that other countries had a genetic advantage or some secret knowledge about training as it was a "program of concerted effort on ergogenic aids.... When they started taking drugs they were able to do things they couldn't do before—not only lift more but train harder, I mean much harder."[61]

It seems obvious to strength coach Mark Rippetoe that a change in America's steroid policy would do much to level the playing field. "Everybody has the same drugs and availability. What we have different is a national organization that is determined to be clean at the expense of winning. They don't care if we place 35th as long as no one tests positive." John Coffee observes that the Colorado Springs training center "may be the only place in the world where Olympic weightlifters train and are kept, but they're not taking drugs. Who would have a damn training facility and spend all that money to produce weightlifting champions without using drugs? The rest of the world has enough sense not to do that. Until there is a fool-proof way of testing to see if people are chemically enhanced, and as long as we're as stringent about it in this country, we won't win any more medals."[62]

These views, extracted from interviews conducted several years after Tommy's book appeared, flew in the face of his portrayal of the weightlifting world, yet he had no misgivings that he could pour old wine into new bottles. Ignoring the transformation that had taken place over a half century, he pressed ahead with a reprinting of *Weightlifting, Olympic Style*.[63] It was designed to set the stage for *Championship Weightlifting*, which, by the end of June 2009, sold 59 copies for $2,347.[64] "My effort to see what can be done for U.S. lifting is seriously in this latest book," he told Drechsler. "I hope the readers take to heart what is within the covers and help rebuild U.S. lifting."[65] Stalker complimented Kono for how his criticism of the current lifting scene "comes scattered throughout the book," allowing it to sink in. "And they learn by example about your inspiring career."[66]

Political Déjà Vu

It is unlikely that the views expressed in Kono's books had any impact in reshaping American weightlifting. Nor did this less direct form of involvement remove him from political wrangling. On January 20, 2009, he informed the USAW board of directors that he was filing a grievance against USA Weightlifting for being "unfairly denied the right to compete for a position on the IWF Executive Board." Although he had been informed several weeks earlier of its availability, he was unaware that it had been posted on the USAW website on December 19, 2008. When he learned on the 29th that the deadline was the following day, he hastily applied for the position. Tommy's application was late, but assumptions based on a call from USAW/USOC liaison Tim Willis on January 6 led him to believe all was well. To his surprise, he received the next day an e-mail from President Ajan with an attached letter from Executive Director Dennis Snethen, dated January 5, declaring incumbent Cioroslan the USAW nominee for the IWF position. Tommy protested to the USAW board.

I have now learned that there was a Board meeting on January 6, during which Mr. Cioroslan, who happens to be an employee of the USOC, was permitted to appear/be on the phone, and explain his qualifications and performance over the past 4 years in the capacity of IWF Executive Board member (many members of the USAW are completely dissatisfied with his performance, which included supporting a relaxation of IWF anti-drug penalties that directly and adversely affected the number of athletes we had competing at the 2008 Olympic Games). The Board then voted 3 to 2 to make Mr. Cioroslan the sole nominee of the USAW for the IWF Executive Board.[67]

Tommy had valid reasons to suspect the cards were stacked against him. The 3–2 telephone vote was improper, according to elector Nicholas Curry who revealed to Leo Temoshenko that his colleague Bob Giordano "was not on the call and did not vote but his vote did go for Drago. Regardless of what YOU think, we had only one choice and that was for Dragomir to be elected because that is who the USOC wanted, if not they threatened to pull our charter."[68] Schmitz, who voted against Cioroslan, concurred that "the USOC really does exert great pressure on us. ... I would just love to say the hell with the USOC, Dennis, and Dragomir, dump Dennis and Dragomir and tell the USOC to let us run our own sport, but I'm not prepared for the consequences. They have really stacked the deck against us."[69]

Arguably the most damning evidence of chicanery in high places for Tommy was the fact that Snethen sent his letter to the IWF president on January 5, a day before the Nominating and Governance Committee vote. On the 6th, USOC executive Kelly Skinner testified to the Board that he had ordered Snethen's letter. Kono believed he had been "terribly wronged" by these improper procedures. "I have been grievously harmed by the USAW's treatment of me, embarrassed with the IWF and denied an opportunity to represent the sport and country I love." He requested that his nomination be brought before the IWF, that Snethen and Skinner be reprimanded, that the USAW Board issue him an apology, and that an explanation be provided for the irregularities relating to its decision to revoke his nomination.[70]

No doubt to Tommy's surprise and satisfaction, redress came quickly as a result of a new board of directors brought into being on February 13. After a lengthy discussion at an executive session on March 8, the new members unanimously passed a motion to offer Tommy a formal letter of apology, agreed that "better reporting and more communication" was needed between the IWF representative for the United States and the Board, thanked Kono for his involvement, and encouraged his continued commitment to USAW affairs.[71] Perhaps to make amends or improve relations with a revered athlete who symbolized much of America's glorious past, Tommy was invited to conduct a seminar in Colorado Springs in the fall of 2009. Further reconciliation followed with his appointment to the Board in 2011.[72] Curiously, citing family responsibilities, he resigned at the end of July. "Having been a part of the new Board for the past year, I can see from the exchanges of many emails amongst this group every member is sincere in identifying and correcting the mistakes made by the previous Boards." He felt he could "step down in full confidence on the future of USAW success." Although Tommy no doubt savored some semblance of victory, the underlying reason for abandoning his struggle was likely his declining health.[73]

11

A Heroic Ending

"The spirit is willing, but the flesh is weak."—Mathew 26:41

Remaining Relevant

Tommy spent virtually his entire life overcoming physical challenges by summoning the spiritual resources of his mind. His final years were no less dedicated to this aspiration, but he was hampered by persistent injuries incurred during his lengthy competitive career and the debilitating impact of old age. Without abandoning his positive outlook, Kono was increasingly drawn to nostalgic representations of the past to contextualize his achievements relative to current strength athletes. After watching a training DVD of Mr. Olympia Jay Cutler in 2008, he pronounced "the guy is unbelievable! How can so much muscles be packed on the body?" he speculated with an old training partner. "It must be steroids," he concluded. "When I see what [Ronnie] Coleman and Cutler has to go through to retain their position in the bodybuilding field, I am glad I was into Olympic weightlifting." Now Tommy's shoulders were so bad he could not rest the bar behind his neck for squatting, even if his bad knees would allow it.

> In 1971 the German doctors were taking X-rays of the knees and shoulders of the leading lifters there. I had gathered the lifters together but then I got caught in it too since the Doctor said as an X-lifter they would like to take X-rays of mine. The result was that I "needed new set of knees." I knew that but then they added, "you need new shoulders too." Until then I never had any problems with my shoulders. ... I guess all the heavy, taxing weights I used in the presses and squatting wore my joints out. Eventually something has to give and it isn't going to be the weights. I just stayed in competition too long.[1]

To relieve his stiff shoulders, Kono turned to Indian club swinging. It was not so much the weight of the clubs, merely a couple of pounds, but the "smoothness of the swing and the rhythm that increases the flexibility of the shoulders, elbows and wrists," he concluded.[2] Following the termination of his 2009 grievance with the USAW and replacement of his right knee in 2011, Tommy spent his remaining years trying to survive and remain relevant.

An important facet of his attempt to stay positive and contribute to the sport was his continuing conduct of clinics, especially to service clubs and senior citizen groups whose members sought better health and appearance. One with special meaning was a gathering of two dozen Japanese Americans with origins in

Hiroshima ken on April 23, 2011, at the home of Fannie Kono in Honolulu's Manoa district. Tommy's talk, titled "Use It or Lose It," emphasized exercise. And on January 11, 2012, he spoke to the Newtown Estates Community Association in Aiea which attracted many residents whose comments, the general manager told Kono, were "very positive." They were "thrilled to see you in person." As a test for life, Tommy told them to repeat the "clinch fist action—morning, noon, & night every day.... When it stops, you are dead."[3] Most consequential of Kono's public appearances were his presentations to the annual University of Hawaii Strength and Conditioning Coaches Clinic. In December 1910 he expressed concern to its director, Tommy Heffernan, that it was held so close to the projected surgery for his right knee in early January. He wanted to be "in top shape for the surgery and also to work hard on the rehab part so I can fulfill my obligation for your clinic." In 2012, Kono spoke on the value of core development to over 230 attendees. He explained that "power comes from the hips or the center of the body" and "the best core power development exercise is the deep knee bend." A commentator likened Tommy's core emphasis to the karate concept of combining core power with Ki or center. "In Zen thought, they are two and they are one. While the hip or core power is physical, the Ki is the inner strength or force that comes into existence as one with the physical strength. This combination, when applied correctly, exerts tremendous power in karate movements and techniques."[4] It was hardly coincidental that these Asian aphorisms, focusing on body, mind, and technique, was Kono's formula for weightlifting success.

No less gratifying was a voice from Tommy's past, Michael Whitson, a protégé who became a gymnastics trainer in Santa Barbara. Whitson fondly recalled Kono's Saturday morning coaching sessions at the Nuuanu YMCA in the early 1970s.

> I used to listen to YOU during those Sat session and you even sent me to Dr. You and I indeed followed XDR as to this day.... Exercise (frequency, intensity, type, time) to target specific muscle fiber types! Nutritional supplementation to enhance recuperative powers, anabolic vs catabolic states, and the speed of these movements ... then rest ... i.e., PERIODIZATION ... are still relevant. But NO ONE will duplicate the wide range of body weight you were able to attain/sustain was truly AMAZING. There ought to be a MOVIE about your life.

Most meaningful to Whitson, aside from the records set and championships won by Kono, was "the fine example YOU set in spite of damn racist government" and "the many people YOU inspire[d] to never give up."[5] Equally appreciative of Tommy's coaching was Kat Ricker who attended his clinic at Bodytribe Fitness in Sacramento when she competed in the 2013 Tommy Kono Classic. Calling him a "gifted teacher," Ricker valued "the moments that I got to sit at your feet and listen to your wisdom before your official talk.... You talked to me about two topics which are very pertinent to me right now—the concept of competing only against yourself and the need to continue to compete often to ensure true progress." Ricker was also pleased that the pictures taken by commercial photographer Laszlo Regos at the Classic (including ones of her and Tommy) would "become archived at the Stark Center for Strength. I am honored that our connection, however brief, will become part of the greater history of our beloved sport."[6] Kono could reflect that "lifters and coaches have changed but certain basic principles should never be compromised" and that "communication is an essential part of coaching."[7] In this way, Tommy was, as Artie Drechsler concludes in his posthumous tribute to him, "a gift that never stopped giving."[8]

Fiscal Conservatism

What enabled Tommy to continue coaching, often at far-away places, was time gained after his retirement in 1997. He had always been a prolific correspondent and willing, to share his advice to other weightlifters since the 1950s, a process eventually facilitated by e-mail. He became a master of distance learning. Nor was travel to clinics or contests from his remote corner of the world a significant barrier. Yearly trips to the Kono Classic in Sacramento and other mainland locales were assisted by his increasing financial portfolio. Despite assurances to protégés each new year after 2012 that meaning in life could not be measured in dollars and cents, he was gradually getting rich. Although it is impossible to assess his total wealth at any particular time, successive statements reveal an impressive array of investments.

E*Trade Securities (7/31/11)	$15,885.93
United Development Funding (6/30/12)	$30,000.00
American Savings Bank (6/30/2012)	$47,834.79
Aloha Pacific Federal Credit Union (6/30/12)	$60,442.33
Community Banks of Colorado (7/19/13)	$304,890.48
	$459,053.53

On July 6, 2013, Mike Kono, Tommy's older brother, died and left his savings to Tommy. It included presumably the assets of John who had died in 2007 but nothing from Frank who became estranged from Mike and Tommy years earlier over investments. When Frank died, his estate was likely inherited by his wife and two daughters. But Mike had no heirs and deposited assets of $562,750 at various financial institutions with Tommy as sole trustee. Although these figures do not include proceeds from the sale of the family home in Sacramento or life insurance annuities, they show that Tommy's personal wealth was approximately $1,021,803 in 2013. It must also be reckoned that this figure likely increased each year owing to the fact that there was no longer a home mortgage and only two people living at 98–2025 Hapaki Street. In 2013, Kono calculated his income (including $58,500 from the Hawaii Marathon Association and $9,500 from Power Pit) at $115,548.[9] Aside from Bob Hoffman, Tommy was possibly the only athlete who became wealthy based on his weightlifting accomplishments. All the more remarkable is that it stemmed from such an unpromising beginning. But it was just the "American Way."

A primary reason for Kono's financial success was his lack of materialism and lifelong dedication to frugality and mental gratification. "It is not a material thing that you can place dollars and cents value on but a 'thought' when taken serious and carried through, can have a tremendous impact on your life." He encouraged his adherents to value time, "a precious commodity of life and we all have the same amount of time no matter who you are, how wealthy or poor you are." Not unlike Olympic lifting, he argued that "the whole purpose in life is to keep forging ahead, accomplishing things and being positive in action."[10] Mental resourcefulness and positivity, of course, had always been the core of his training philosophy. Whether the same disciplined way of life could also be applied to his family life was another matter. "My dad was definitely the disciplinarian," recalls Mark Kono, while his mother provided comfort. "We all thought he was a bit strict in our upbringing, but it was just to instill discipline." Its impact, however, was lessened from Tommy being gone so much. Moreover, the family was never in need. "My parents provided for us very well, not to excess. We were never in dire straits monetarily. My dad was very much a frugal person so he would not spend frivolously, and he tried to instill that in us as well." Jamieson responded to Tommy's discipline by escape. "My brother had his own ideas of what he wanted to do and wasn't around very much." Consequently, a strong bond developed between Mark and his sister joAnn.[11]

Flo also tried to escape Tommy's controlling grip by working outside the home. Although she did so to contribute to the family income, joAnn insists that her mother "wanted her own money. My dad was very controlling. He would control every nickel and dime." Flo agrees that he was "very methodical," accounting for every cent she spent. By going to work, joAnn explains, her mother "would not have to depend on him or ask for spending money because he always wanted the receipts, and he wanted the change. It just got ridiculous." Flo's extra income also enabled Tommy to pay his own way as a volunteer to overseas events, but it also served to publicize his fame and generosity. Flo, according to joAnn, even started paying the family's medical and dental bills "so that he could go places."[12] Tommy told Mike Harada that he was "worried about Flo going through all the money. 'What should I do, get a trust?' I guess he and Flo had some arguments about what to do with it." He feared she might "blow it. Tommy was very frugal." He was worried about what Flo wanted to do about the house. "Twenty, thirty, forty grand here and there, but Tommy was a saver. She wanted to give the money away now."[13] Whether their differences over financial matters was rooted in their disparate cultural backgrounds is uncertain, but the distinctions between Flo's dysfunctional Western upbringing and Tommy's highly practical Asian origins is striking.

Conservatism also prevailed in his political outlook. It was a natural outgrowth of his distinctive form of patriotism. "Tommy had the values of a Republican," notes Russell Ogata, but he was "a little more conservative. Tommy believed in patriotism in spite of the injustices he was dealt." Ogata jests that in Hawaii "a Republican is about as rare as an honest politician in Washington."[14] Pete George concurs that "Tommy's views were definitely conservative. I don't believe he voted regularly, but if he did, it more likely would have been Republican." He also had a "low opinion" of Barack Obama and was "fully in accord" with the opinions of African American journalist Thomas Sowell, whose syndicated column appeared for decades in local newspapers. Two such articles titled "People self-sort; government unsorts" and "Just standing out vs. being outstanding" show up in his papers. In the former, Sowell argues that "government programs to unsort people who have sorted themselves out have produced one social disaster after another. The decades-long attempts to mix black and white schoolchildren through school busing produced no real educational benefits but much racial polarization and ill will." Likewise in colleges it persisted "in the name of 'diversity'—and with the same bad results." In the latter article Sowell speculates that Americans are "preoccupied with standing out—without doing anything that merits our standing out. Maybe we want distinction on the cheap." He observed that "blacks and whites used to give their children pretty much the same names. No more. Since the 1970s, racial segregation has returned, this time in names." Asian Americans, whose achievement levels were already high, seemed oblivious to this trend of self-inflation. Parents of other races, however, seeking to be "clever or cute," found "making a statement" irresistible, Sowell argued.[15] What made these articles compelling for Tommy and Pete, notes Ogata, is that both had immigrant parents. Pete recalls that they "often talked about our good fortune that our fathers came to America, the land of opportunity through free enterprise."[16]

Arnold Knows Me

Tommy's political and social views, however, were not widely known. His celebrity status was based almost solely on his reputation as the world's greatest weightlifter, generosity, and humble demeanor. As he entered his eighties, his heroic status was being publicly recognized more than ever. At the 2012 Arnold Sports Festival, Burkhard Bilger interviewed him for a *New Yorker* article titled "The Strongest Man in the World." Emphasizing his humble physical and cultural background, Bilger cites Kono as "a prime example of the miraculous change that weight lifting can effect."[17] Then Panini America solicited him in a lead-up to the 2012 London Olympiad to autograph 500 trading cards for $5 each. As business manager Zachary Rosenberg explained, the trading card set would "feature Olympians across various sports and decades who were 'extremely decorated,' including such notables as Mark Spitz, Bruce Baumgartner, Dan Gable, and Gary Hall. Two months later Tommy received a $2,500 check for participating."[18] His special status in weightlifting was recognized in March of 2013 when Tamas Ajan invited him to address the IWF Congress elections in Moscow in May, believing Kono's presence "would elevate the prominence of the event."[19] Whether Tommy could withstand the rigors of international travel, given his declining health, seems doubtful. On December 24, 2012, he told Osmo Kiiha that "I still go to the 'Y' 3 times a week but more for socializing and coaching than working out. I'm 82 now and my joints are feeling the effect of all the heavy taxing I did on my shoulders and knees. It is not a 'maintenance' program I am following but a 'rehab' program."[20]

The most consequential honor accorded to Kono was the documentary film *Arnold Knows Me: The Tommy Kono Story,* that appeared posthumously in 2016. According to Paul Doherty, it originated when Arnold visited the Kono Classic in 2010 and met Sacramento journalist Ryan Yamamoto who filmed the event. He was "blown away. He knew none of this history and background, so I started talking to Ryan about it, what Tommy Kono had done, and what he meant to Sacramento High School and the city of Sacramento."[21] Yamamoto admits that he "never met Arnold" and had "no idea who Tommy was at the time. I'm thinking, I'm an idiot for not knowing who this person is. Why isn't he a household name?"[22] Yamamoto's subsequent interview in 2014 led to a 27-minute film that incorporates numerous historical clippings, site visitations, comments from contemporaries, and personal insights. Kono observes that he was "a bodybuilder turned weightlifter, not the reverse" and that competing at the 1956 Olympics "was like nothing because I had gone through it four years before." In 1960 at Rome, however, he was "very disappointed because it was the first time I got defeated." Tommy also explains how his relationship developed with Schwarzenegger who, at age 13, watched him compete at Vienna in 1961. Yamamoto adds that Schwarzenegger idolized him so much that Kono's photo hung on his bedroom wall. And when Arnold was governor and found out Tommy was in town, he made a special visit to see him. Though somewhat embellished, Schwarzenegger recollected:

> After he won the world championships, after he was the greatest weightlifter, the next day he competed in the Mr. Universe Contest and he goes on and wins the bodybuilding championship. So he inspired me, and after this competition I started working out two hours a day, three hours a day, and became the youngest Mr. Universe at age 20 because I saw people like this. So he gave great inspiration to me, and if I had not won these championships, I would never have come to America.

Tommy made Arnold's memory more memorable: "Lots of times people would say, 'Do you know Arnold?' You mean Arnold Schwarzenegger? What do you mean? **Arnold knows me**."[23]

Arnold Knows Me was broadcast on KVIE, the Sacramento PBS station. Its executive producer was David Hosley, a former general manager, Yamamoto explains, who "got me into the pipeline of PBS. It never ran on the national network but was picked up by local affiliates. When it ran in 55 markets, I was blown away. I think a lot of that had to do with people were looking for Olympic type stories because it was 2016." Yamamoto and co-producer Suzanne Phan never planned it that way, nor did they intend to appeal to any sector of the country or time frame. But requests for the DVD came from such unlikely places as North Carolina and Indiana, and there was a spike in sales each May, Asian American History Month. Nationwide interest in Tommy's story exceeded expectations.[24] What made Kono so appealing and noteworthy was his manner. Former Olympic champion Zygmunt Smalcerz, who witnessed him at an exhibition in Poland, "understood why people loved Tommy Kono. 'It was something easy, and he smiled. He's enjoying touching the bar and he was enjoying everybody who was watching him. It was something fantastic.'" To Doherty, it was this kind of "draw that Tommy Kono has to anyone in the world, and that's where a guy of Arnold's stature first fell in love with the sport." Yamamoto recognizes that even in his eighties, "it is a new generation of weightlifters that now know Tommy Kono." For 10 straight years, he paid his own airfare and booked his own hotel to attend "every competition" of his Sacramento Classic. Olympian Cindy Stinger acknowledges his immortality. "His legacy is his ability to share what he's learned with others."[25]

Physical Breakdown

In a 2014 interview with Edward Pierini, Tommy confirms Stinger's insight, saying, "I'd like to share my life experiences and words of wisdom because I know that once you're gone, that's it! Sadly, many people may look at me as a 'relic' because times have changed." Lifters, he admitted, want to be led, not pushed, and "it's better to give than to receive so whatever I have to share, I know someone will appreciate it." That was the point of his books. But at this stage of life, he was "worn out." When asked whether he was still working out hard in the gym, Tommy replied, "No—you know in the old days when I was young, I worked hard trying to improve my strength and fitness. Later in life, my focus changed to trying to maintain. Now my focus is trying to survive." Yet he remained optimistic. "Everything is going my way," he assured Pierini. "I'm very comfortable with the way things are going."[26] A year later he told Kiiha there was "something about aging that is good. You learn to accept it [as] inevitable. ... You get senior discounts and people are always trying to help you." Admittedly, his appearance had changed. "I've shrunk in size and it shows when I strip down to take a shower. I have loose skin hanging all over ... but that is life. The only thing I advise you to maintain is flexibility in your joints. If you[r] mind is 'sharp' that is the most important thing." He also advised Kiiha to maintain social contacts, especially with young people. "Aging is a state of mind. Accept it and you will be better off."[27]

Tommy was now aware of his approaching death. The passing of his brother Mike served as a grim reminder of what was in store. Between February and July 2013, he told Pete George, he had flown five times to Sacramento to care for Mike and assist with his affairs. "In the end I even had my daughter JoAnn come help me and she took a tremendous burden off my shoulders."[28] But even putting his own affairs in order proved daunting. "My father was very meticulous in his record keeping," joAnn recalls after Tommy's death in 2016. "He spent most of the last four years trying to get organized but it was just overwhelming."[29] "If it's not one thing it is another that keeps me busy," he confided to Pete, but "I am moving slower."[30] Finally, he saw the need to divest himself of many outside responsibilities. In 2014 he finally relinquished his marathon duties after 41 years and resigned from his leadership of the Hawaii AAU chapter after 21 years. "These departures taught me that eventually you need to drop out of things at some time. In hindsight, it really wasn't that hard to do. I'm actually enjoying being more relaxed," he told Pierini. "You have problems as you get older. I'm fortunate that I've survived this long."[31] What few in the weightlifting world knew, however, was that Kono was experiencing more than the normal aches and pains that comes with age. To Kiiha, he explained that he had liver disease. "I've had this problem for years and finally it is taking its toll." He also stated this would be his last letter and that Osmo should not correspond with him because he would "not have time to respond." Yet their friendship would remain uppermost in his mind.[32]

Soon Kono drafted a similar letter to his many friends about his condition. Extant medical records indicate he was diagnosed in August 2011 by Drs. Elaine Doi and Kenneth Hong of the Moanolua Clinic and Medical Center with abdominal pain, and upper gastrointestinal bleeding which was symptomatic of an interruption of blood flow to the liver. Treatment included placing a lighted tube into his upper intestinal tract to remove growths and stop bleeding as well as medications for other ailments, including ventral hernia, hemochromatosis, biliary cirrhosis, high cholesterol, elevated blood fats, hypertension, diabetes type 2, swelling, rash, stomach acid, and gout.[33] These conditions were confirmed by diagnoses performed on November 15, 2012, as well as a determination by optometrist Ronald Ling that Tommy's vision was impaired by cataracts. Most seriously, Dr. Doi discovered that Tommy suffered from hepatic encephalopathy, a form of brain dysfunction often associated with liver disease.[34] It was an affliction with a high mortality rate normally prevalent among alcoholics and in recent years with football players which the 2015 film *Concussion* brought to public awareness.

Hemochromatosis

How Tommy may have contracted this deadly condition mystified his friends and followers because he rarely consumed alcohol and never played contact sports. But he did consume lots of vitamins and minerals, especially iron, at Dr. You's direction, which was believed to oxygenate and energize red blood cells to enhance athletic performance. But overconsumption of this mineral, according to the Cleveland Clinic, can lead to hemochromatosis,

> a disorder in which the body stores too much iron. Iron is an important nutrient that helps the hemoglobin in blood cells carry oxygen to your body's organs and tissues. Your intestines absorb the iron your body needs from the food you eat. The amount it absorbs is finely calibrated to replace the small amount of iron lost each day. If you have hemochromatosis, your body absorbs more iron than it uses. The body has no way to remove the extra iron, so it stores it in the joints and organs—especially the liver, heart, and pancreas. The organs cannot manage the overload of iron, and so they can be damaged and may eventually fail.[35]

As the Iron Disorders Institute explains, "the liver is the principal organ responsible for the storage and detoxification of iron," but it is "the first and foremost organ damaged by heavy iron overload."[36] According to E.D. Weinberg in *Exposing the Hidden Dangers of Iron*, "the greater amount of supplements, the higher were the body iron burdens" in cases he examined, but patients "can be safely de-ironed by a series of phlebotomies. Removal of 200–250 mg iron by each blood-letting is quickly replaced by mobilization of iron from tissue deposits." Therefore "because iron loading is not stopped by depletion, periodic phlebotomies, often 3–6 per year, must be continued for life."[37] R.L. Nelson, in an iron risk article in *Nutrition Review*, argues, "it is likely that as many people are being injured by iron supplementation as are receiving medical benefit." Particularly at risk were the top 5 percent of vitamin users. "Iron doping of healthy individuals to improve performance may well have dire health consequences not less severe than anabolic steroids."[38]

Iron supplementation, chiefly for persons suffering from anemia or women who were pregnant or had heavy menstrual periods, extends back to tonics that proliferated in the 1930s. A broader public awareness emerged from the development of Geritol by Pharmaceuticals Inc. in 1950 which contained an active ingredient of ferric ammonium citrate with 12 percent alcohol, inverted sugar, and B-vitamins. It appealed to the geriatric set through 1950s television with such shows as *What's My Line, The Ted Mack Amateur Hour,* and *Twenty-One.* Having "twice the iron in a pound of calf's liver," Geritol was alleged to cure "iron-poor tired blood."[39]

Newspaper records indicate that Dr. You, who had supported and treated Hawaiian athletes in numerous sports since his discharge after the war, showed an interest in nutritional aids in the early fifties. "I have been treating athletes for speed and stamina," he stated on April 27, 1951, "and I know the value of vitamins, minerals, and other foods in building up boys and girls and men and women for athletic competition."[40] An example of the efficacy of You's vitamin supplementation treatment was provided by Norman Tamanaha who finished a surprising fifth in the Boston Marathon in April 1952 with a time of 2:51.55. For six months prior to the race, according to the *Honolulu Star-Bulletin*, Dr. You "fed him gobs of vitamins and other food concentrates orally and intravenously. 'They helped me plenty' says the 45 year old. 'I was never in better shape for a race in all my years of running.'"[41] The extent to which iron was critical to Tamanaha's success or that of the Hawaiians' upset victory over the York Barbell Club in the 1952 senior nationals is unknown, but it is significant that his vitamins were administered "intravenously" as well as orally. So quickly did You's idea that diet as much as skill catch on that a promising protégé, boxer Willie Caesar, was dubbed the "Vitamin Kid" and You was the "Vitamin King."[42] Tommy possibly adopted Dr. You's nutritional protocol as early as 1952 when they met at the national championships, followed by subsequent encounters at the Helsinki Olympics, and during his visit to Hawaii in March of 1953. But Kono did not become intimately involved with its utilization until he entered a partnership with You in August 1955, barely a month after moving to Honolulu. Their business, the York Company of Hawaii, was dedicated to "maintaining and carrying on a massage studio & wholesale & retail of athletic supplies & health foods." It would thus provide easy access to supplements Tommy needed, likely for free or nominal cost as well as expert advice on their use.[43] Over the next nine years he followed a strict dietary regimen prescribed by Dr. You which allegedly improved his performance. It also enabled You to use Kono's growing reputation as the world's greatest weightlifter to enhance his own reputation as a "trainer of champions" and establish a platform to treat other athletes.

Flo believes Tommy was receiving iron shots from Dr. You "since the beginning of his association with him, and I think that that led to the overdose. That's what I always thought." But it was mainly in the fifties and not so much later. He was not taking them, Flo says, when they were married in 1963, "but I think they had a residual effect on his system," possibly from taking them so long and in stronger doses. Ultimately, she believes, "it did him in."[44] Testimonials from other athletes reveal the extent and the efficacy of Dr. You's vitamin treatments. Swimmer Ford Konno, Olympic gold medalist in 1952 and 1956, attributes his success to You's advice to "get the liver shots or iron" and vitamins to improve his strength and stamina. "Dr. You did not administer any drugs or steroids ... or anything like that. His idea was to build up the blood count ... build up our endurance and gain more strength from that treatment." Likewise Dick Cleveland, freestyle world-record holder in the early fifties, confirms that You "would give us liver intravenously to build up our red blood count," trusting in his knowledge that "your red blood count enables you to carry more oxygen in your body. ... Dr. You would build us up until we felt we could do virtually anything." Two-time Olympic medalist Evelyn Konno recalls:

> I would go into his office to get these shots to build up my blood count in order to sustain the strenuous kind of training that we had to go through. He also gave us vitamin shots. We were not always eating properly, being on the go and training so hard, and so he provided for that. And you know, he never asked us for anything. We didn't have to pay a cent. This was the way he works with people.

University of Hawaii basketball star Dwight Holiday was anemic at age 22 when he visited Dr. You to revitalize his body. "Dr. You said, 'You build the body from the inside out.' He explained to me about building the blood. The red blood cells are the major blood cells that he wanted to build first of all ... which brings oxygen to the areas of the muscles which enables you to run and jump and do your thing." As a result of the weekly vitamin shots Dr. You advised, Junior Light Weight Boxing Champion Ben Villaflor's stamina "got stronger and stronger" and made him "feel better." According to You's long-time secretary, Mildred Nomura, even drug addicts whom he also treated free of charge were administered "vitamins by mouth" as well as "vitamin shots ... liver shots ... about 3 times a week." After several months of treatments, she could see "they had detoxified themselves." Exactly what Tommy took, how much of it, and how long remains an uncertainty. But he did divulge in 1996, shortly after You's death, that he "had a lot to do with my success in the '52 and '56 Olympic Games. His treatments were way ahead of his time as he helped me perform at my peak and win championships."[45]

The impact of You's treatments shows up not only in Kono's coaching protocol in Mexico but also in the testimonies of Hawaiian lifters about their experiences in the 1970s. Gary Kawamura, whom Tommy coached upon his return from Germany in 1972, recalls that

> Tommy asked me to see Richard You, and I used to go once a week or once every two weeks, and he used to give me iron shots. He would also give B12 shots. I just trusted Tommy, but when I think back, I'm in insurance, I sell insurance. Tommy was one of my first life insurance accounts, and so we would underwrite. He was rated, in other words, his health was rated. ... Underwriting determines whether you're a good risk. I was kind of surprised when it came back and he was rated a higher risk because of the iron in his blood.

Tommy could hardly have realized that he had hemochromatosis, since he was still relatively young and likely unaware of the disease. Also, Kawamura, who became a national contender, experienced no ill effects during his experience. "I just did it because Tommy asked me."[46] Russ Ogata was another protégé of Tommy who received iron injections in the seventies. "I think it was iron and desiccated liver or something," but it was a pink or brown liquid, and he knows Dr. You "wasn't giving steroids to me. If it was steroids I would have seen a big jump. After while I didn't want to get shots. I don't like needles. But Doc would treat me for free. I did that because he said this will be great for your exercise."[47] What Bruce Wilhelm, whom

Tommy coached at the 1976 Olympics, remembers is that "he was big on B12 injections under Dr. You" and that "Kono and Dr. You were like peas in a pod."[48] Tommy's adherence to Dr. You, however, was not without misgivings. During the years he worked in You's office, it was "open 7 days a week. Where else can you find a doctor that dedicated? He would see as many as 80 patients just in the morning, one after another. I don't know how he did it. ... And more than half of them were NC. He would always say, 'NC,' meaning No Charge."[49]

Medical Malpractice

By the late 1970s, it became evident that something was awry with Dr. You's medical practice. On July 2, 1977, Honolulu newspapers revealed that the state attorney general's office was charging You with issuing excessive prescriptions which "may be a significant source of drugs illicitly trafficked" in the city. Based on investigations by federal and state narcotics agents, it requested that his license be revoked for "prescribing an unusual, inordinate and excessive amount of dangerous drugs." During a nine-month period, "You had prescribed 21,193 doses of a controlled substance—more than Amfac Inc. a wholesaler of the substance, sold during the entire year." It was "four times as many prescriptions for 'dangerous drugs' than all of the physicians on Kauai issued during the entire year, and twice as many as the physicians at Kaiser Hospital issued." According to the petition,

> On 12 occasions during the past two years, three undercover federal agents bought prescriptions signed by Dr. You from his employees. They said they weren't examined for any medical condition and did not state any medical need or purpose for the "dangerous drugs." Prescriptions were allegedly made out to persons who did not know You and did not live at addresses checked by the investigators.
> The petition says medical records for the three federal undercover agents "contained descriptions of purported medical conditions which they did not have and did not represent what they had. ... Medical records of other patients contained little or no information" on results of medical tests, response to treatment or referral to any specialist although the drugs had been prescribed over an extended period.[50]

Dr. You vigorously defended his conduct, calling himself a "drug use pioneer" in treating anxiety. His treatments consisted of not only pills but also "health programs" resembling the X-D-R system he devised decades earlier. "These involve a controlled diet regime, rest, 'rehabilitation,' with emphasis on sports and other physical activities" designed to relieve depression and alienation. You insisted that "when you are a pioneer, you are bound to meet criticism."[51] Despite repeated appeals and legal wrangling over two years and support from Tommy and Harold Sakata in a final hearing, Circuit Judge James Burns revoked You's license to practice medicine on August 21, 1979, citing "gross carelessness" and "professional misconduct."[52]

No longer could Dr. You prescribe vitamins, iron, or anything else to athletes or so-called "dangerous drugs" to other clients. It had been a slippery slope from helping young athletes perform on the highest level to helping indigent and unhealthy street people enjoy a normal lifestyle. Dr. You never committed a criminal act, but ironically the Schedule II drugs he prescribed, chiefly barbiturates and amphetamines, had unpredictable outcomes and often led from one form of dependency to another. "If Dr. You has a real weakness," testified retired University of Hawaii professor Donald Gustuson in 1977, "it is his great sympathy for and understanding of those who border between cases acceptable to the general medical profession and those who are now overcrowding our welfare and penal institutions."[53] Tommy, though disheartened by Dr. You's conviction, never lost his respect for Dr. You or unfriended him. But for other weightlifters at the Nuuanu YMCA, who did not appreciate his relevance, he became a subject of ridicule. As a young lifter in the 1980s, Darren DeMello remembers him showing up at meets during intermissions

> while we were warming up. I knew who he was because he was always there to make a speech and the same speech about that team that went to York Barbell and beat them. It was a great story, but it seemed more about him than anything. And then later on we had a show at a high school and he came and started handing out these little pamphlets. You want to be a world champion? Here, call me. You want to make a million dollars? Here, call me. Oh this guy! ... Every single conversation between the snatch and the clean and jerk he would be out there. He would just show up and dressed in a nice suit too.[54]

What Tommy's protégés did not understand was that following the revocation of his license, Dr. You lost his chief purpose in life, promoting his ideas and himself. Although he did regain his license and established a "World Sports Medicine and Health Clinic" in 1986, his health steadily declined, and he died on November 24, 1995.[55] Dr. You will be remembered for his many contributions. His legacy should include the vitamin and iron treatments he administered to athletes over many years, but few would realize their impact, both beneficial and life threatening, on Hawaii's most illustrious champion.

Final Days

Exactly when Kono became aware of the deleterious effects of Dr. You's iron treatments cannot be determined. Mike Harada recalls his initial diagnosis of liver cirrhosis when he visited Tommy in the hospital some years before his death. "I knew what it was, but Tommy didn't, and the doctor kept going on that his iron content is so high. So he told me, he should always go to the doctor to drain blood." For many years, they drained blood from him and added new blood. But it could never cleanse his system of the excess iron, and eventually "he was losing a lot of weight and getting skinny."[56] joAnn recalls that her father "was looking to cure himself by reading articles on line and advertisements from the computer, and he was doing the blood-letting, but that wasn't working." He also tried melaleuca, an herbal medicine, and glucosamine for joint relief, but nothing seemed to work.[57]

Increasingly, Tommy's weakened condition and changes in manner became obvious. "He would get towards the later years forgetful," according to DeMello. "When Dr. Yogi passed away, Vernon Pateo and his ex-wife had separated, and at the service he said, 'that's Vernon over there, but they're not together.'"[58] Kawamura recalls that Tommy frequented the YMCA three times a week to watch the lifters train. "But it was sad because he couldn't get down to the gym because physically he could not get down the steps."[59] Wilhelm observed that Kono's speech was impaired. "A few weeks before he died when I talked to him on the phone, I swear to God it was only four to five minutes, and I couldn't understand Tommy. This is going nowhere." It was a noticeable decline from when Bruce had seen him in 2012 at the Nuuanu YMCA when he had "a little bit of a speech impediment and was not quick with his answers."[60] According to Schmitz, Kono "seemed pretty darned healthy till the last time I saw him alive which I think was 2015 at a seminar he did. He was frail, but he had energy and walked around and just needed a little help getting in and out of the car."[61] Ryan Yamamoto interviewed Tommy twice for the *Arnold Knows Me* documentary. In October 2015, he and Suzanne Phan went to his house. "He was pretty sound of mind and physically slowing down. But he was in pretty good shape." In December, they found him declining quickly. Yamamoto remembers calling him in 2016 to verify certain facts. Once, about February, "his wife picks up the phone and says, 'he's not doing very well today, Ryan, he kind of goes in and out,' and I said 'okay,' just let me say 'hello,' and he would start out slow, and for whatever reason I would ask him something about his career, and his mind would snap right back into it and he would tell me this long story again."[62]

Despite his many ailments and certainty of death, Tommy remained positive. In

A final informal gathering of Tommy with his long-time weightlifting friends took place on October 31, 2015. Front row, from left: Gary Kawamura, Darren DeMello, Mike Harada, and Brian Miyamoto; back row, from left: Russell Ogata, Tommy, Pete George, and Melvin Miyamoto.

December 2015, an article in *NikkeiWest* retold his heroic story of rising from ruins in American society. "Kono does not show any bitterness while recalled the hardships faced by his family because of the internment. 'It's a case of *shikata ga nai*,' he said, using a Japanese phrase meaning 'it can't be helped.'"[63] Despite or because of hardships, he exemplified the American way. Finally, no longer able to respond to queries about his well-being, he sent out a general statement.

> Sorry I'm not able to respond to any written communication from my friends. You may have already heard that I have "end stage" cirrhosis, which is really taking a toll on my body. This is unusual because I have never consumed alcohol but due to previous medical treatments I have developed an overabundance of iron in my blood and my liver can no longer regulate the toxins in my body. We all develop health problems in the end. After all, life is for the living so enjoy the journey while you can![64]

It was the ultimate triumph of matter over mind, but Tommy, reconciled to his fate, remained upbeat to the end. In 2015, in response to a professor who wanted to publish a Japanese version of *Weightlifting, Olympic Style*, he admitted that "aging takes its toll. All the heavy stress I placed my body to break records shows up as we age."[65] Wilhelm put it more succinctly: "There's only so much pain the human body can take."[66]

When the Kono family was no longer able to care for him at home, Tommy spent his last days at St. Francis Hospice in Honolulu where he passed away on April 24, 2016. His funeral took place on May 23, 2016, at the Mililani Memorial Park and Mortuary and was officiated by the Reverend Sasaki.[67] Internment followed at the National Memorial Cemetery of the Pacific where the inscription, headed by the Buddhist Wheel of Dharma, read "Kono, Tommy Tamio Kono, PFC US Army Korea 1930 2016 Olympian," and a personal message from Flo.[68] Tommy Kono's stature beyond the weightlifting world was evident from the many condolences and memorials from public figures during coming months, including members of the Hawaiian Assembly and Senate, the City/County of Honolulu, and the United States House of Representatives. Nor was he forgotten by his hometown of Sacramento which recognized July 26, 2016, as "Tommy Kono Day," the same day *Arnold Knows Me*

Tommy's final resting place in the National Memorial Cemetery of the Pacific in Honolulu, signified by the Wheel of Dharma.

first aired.⁶⁹ Perhaps the most meaningful remembrance occurred at the 7th Sacramento Sports Hall of Fame Induction Celebration on January 26, 2019, where Tommy's son Mark recounted his father's life and paid final tribute to his greatness. "To the weightlifting community and beyond he was a tremendous and inspirational athlete. But all in all, to us as a family, he was dad."⁷⁰

Epilogue and Conclusion

> "Spiritual peace is not the opposite of physical force. Spiritual peace, in extremis, is a massive multiplier of physical force."[1]—J.C. Herz, *Learning to Breathe Fire*

On our return from visiting Tommy Kono's burial site in the National Memorial Cemetery in November 2016, Pete George remarked that Tommy spent the last 10 years of his life establishing his legacy. This comment made sense in light of the immense collection of materials we were shipping to the University of Texas. Unlike most weightlifters I've encountered over the years who have discarded records relating to their lives or participation in the sport, Tommy seems to have kept everything and even wrote about his experiences, something which others, even with persistent urging, nearly never did. This tendency some would say was evidence of hoarding, but hoarders are normally not organized and meticulous. Most likely it was the understated nature of his personality and a non-vocal way to express himself and be remembered for posterity. "I've always been an introvert and being a champion forced me to come out of my shell just to go to interviews," he told *Star-Bulletin* reporter John Christensen in 1986. "But in the U.S. it seems you have to be a self-promoter and I would have had to change my personality completely."[2] Letter-writing, record-keeping and publishing became almost an obsession for Kono.

Assertive Humility

This tendency for self-publicity by a different means was reinforced by two important role models Tommy encountered early in his career. Bob Hoffman, the so-called Father of American Weightlifting, was at the height of his influence when Kono encountered him at his first national meet in 1949. Until his death in 1986, Hoffman was heralded as architect for America's Golden Age of Weightlifting and Tommy as its greatest exemplar. "If it hadn't been for the generosity and patriotic pride of Bob Hoffman," Tommy declared in *Championship Weightlifting*, the

> USA would have never been represented at the various World Championships and I would have never had the opportunity to represent the U.S. at these meets. He was like a father image to many of us on the team because he took care of us when we were selected on the

team. ... He instilled pride in all of us and we did our best lifting on foreign soil because we took our role as ambassadors of the USA seriously.[3]

Though never a member of Hoffman's famed club, Tommy was Hoffman's greatest medal winner. Hoffman's influence was reinforced at the mid-point of Kono's career by his intimate relationship with Dr. Richard You. Tommy's gratitude to You was most evident in the late 1970s when You was under siege for malpractice and on the verge of losing his license. "In all the years I have taken part in world and Olympic competitions," he wrote on September 13, 1977,

> Dr. You, as my trainer and personal physician, has always advocated a sound medical and nutritional regimen. Based on his famous "X.D.R." principle of correct and the proper amount of Exercise, Diet and Rest, I was able to remain in world competition and show continued improvement for a longer length of time than other world class weightlifters.[4]

Two years later, he nominated You for the Hawaii Sports Hall of Fame to President Jann Yuen: "My own weightlifting career was given a tremendous boost by Dr. You's continued interest and support, which extended beyond 1956 after my second Olympics win, to 1965.... There isn't a champion weightlifter in the Islands in the last 30 years who was not helped by Dr. You."[5]

What Hoffman and You had in common was a dedication to Kono and promoting him as the world's greatest lifter. Beyond that, they were shameless self-promoters who sought to use Tommy to extend their influence in their respective spheres. Hoffman used the fortune he made through the manufacture and sale of oil burners, barbells, and health foods to publicize his philosophy of fitness and himself. His world-champion weightlifters were showcased through his widely-read magazine. To mix metaphors, York was Mecca and *Strength & Health* was the Bible for budding weightlifters while Tommy was winning world titles. Dr. You became a fervent admirer of Hoffman and likewise craved recognition through weightlifters and other athletes, whose achievements he attributed to nutritional supplements he prescribed.[6] This high regard is reflected in the names of the enterprises You created in Honolulu, including a York Health Center, York Athletic Club, York XDR Club, York Invitational Weightlifting Meet, and a high-rise York International building, all bordering on fawning. He was also a purveyor of Hoffman's products and ideas. But Bob's promotion of vitamin-mineral food supplements as early as 1951 likely owes its inspiration partly to nutritional notions popularized by You.[7] The importance of Hoffman's patronage and You's promotional efforts to Kono's widely heralded greatness cannot be overstated. Not unlike Hoffman and You, Kono sought to propagate an ideology of success.

What Tommy derived from both of these egotistical self-promoters was a sense of how to get along in a capitalist society, complemented by elements from his entrepreneurial native culture. His manner of making himself a cultural icon was thus deliberate and consistent with his origins. Kono's status as a social outsider stemming from his Japanese ancestry, Tule Lake internment, and weak physical condition predestined him to a humble disposition. But he used his outlier status to "take advantage of disadvantage." Even after winning four Olympic and world championships, he appeared to the public as "a wholesome, unassuming young man."[8] In 1956, journalist Sanford Zalburg observed how remarkable it was for Kono to possess so many world records along with "the finest physique in the universe. It's quite a feat for the man who was skinny and sickly when he was a kid." Yet he "takes it all with a grain of ajinomoto [salt]."[9] "Mild-mannered" and "soft-spoken" is how journalist Monte Ito portrayed him when he became Mexican Olympic coach in 1968.[10] Ann Miller, in a 1992 article, contends that "even at his brawny best, Kono's demeanor dismisses thoughts of intimidation. 'He is,' [Pete] George says simply and accurately, 'humbly assertive.'" Tommy was, according to Pete, "the most humble great champion I have ever known."[11] Of course, fame vanishes, but Tommy, unlike most champion athletes, managed to keep his legend alive his entire life. Nowhere is this more evident than in *Arnold Knows Me*. Producer Yamamoto concurs that although Tommy had an understated manner and comes across as a humble person, and people loved him for that, he promoted himself a lot. "Oh yeah, I got that from him. He was a marketing whiz."[12] As novelist Victor Hugo, an astute observer of human nature, assures us, "The very best of us are not altogether exempt from some tinge of egotism."[13]

The Silent Treatment

Throughout his life, Kono took every opportunity to project himself to the public, almost always in way to benefit the health and well-being of others, whether assisting with the marathon, teaching women's bodybuilding, coaching, administering clinics, giving exhibitions, lecturing to civic groups or something so simple as staging a novice powerlift contest, organizing a hula hoop or Frisbee contest, or training police women.[14] Virtually every newspaper report of his volunteering reminds readers of his illustrious athletic career and that he did not regard himself as better than anyone else. This sense of altruism and humility he conveyed, despite his greatness, proved to be a powerful stimulus to public acclaim. He was universally liked, respected, and even revered. Hoffman and You served as father figures for Kono. Like them, he was a self-made man who promoted himself, but unlike them, it was never blatant and always low key and under a veil of self-effacement. His deeds spoke for themselves.

Kono's humility and stoic manner, however, belies a determination to overcome the stigma of his Japanese American ethnicity by deeds rather than words or confrontation. He could have been bitter towards the adversity his people had suffered and become an advocate for social justice and redress for past wrongs. Instead, he took the seemingly illogical course of overcoming any animosity by supporting his country in a most tangible way. "The U.S had made a mistake," notes Artie Drechsler, but "Kono would not let that stop him." He turned the negative of his detention at Tule Lake, according to Pete George, into a positive experience. "He never dwelled on the injustice of it but accepted it philosophically, saying 'Hey, that's where I met Tad Fujioka. He introduced me to barbells.'" Even periodic encounters with racial discrimination did not deter him from his pursuit of physical excellence and good will to all. Lou DeMarco recalls Tommy relating an instance when he was staying at the York YMCA and having to walk to York Barbell past an elementary school where children were in a fenced playground during recess. As he walked past, "the children would rush up to the fence and stare at him as he went by because he was an Oriental which was foreign to them. He said to me in his softest tones, 'You know, Lou, that bothered me a lot.'" Many years later, Tommy had the opportunity to view the large mural of himself, Grimek, and Hoffman in downtown York. After he viewed the painting in silence, Walter Imahara asked him "what was he thinking. Tommy said that when he first arrived to train for a championship … folks would call him names of his nationality. Tommy said he endured in silence, and now his picture was on a building in York, Pennsylvania."[15]

Perhaps the best example of Tommy's racial consciousness and how he dealt with prejudice through the silent treatment stems from the recollection of Imahara of a 1968 meet at the Chicago YMCA where he increased his bodyweight to lift in the 148-pound class. Walter was targeted for being Asian by a group of Los Angeles lifters who did not like his becoming a lightweight

> because it seemed pretty certain that their lifter could not win the 148-pound class. During my warmup for the press, the team from California started with negative racial remarks about the Japanese and Pearl Harbor. This strategy was supposed to unnerve me or get me distracted so my lifting would suffer. I did not react. As I was warming up for the snatch, one of the lifters hit the bar. I just fixed the bar and did not lose my concentration. After I snatched 250 pounds, the group moved to another warmup location. I won this competition. The war with Japan was over for 23 years and they knew I was an American and had served in the military. Many months later, I spoke to Tommy Kono about the incident and he replied that he had been in the same situation. His reply was that I responded correctly: stay calm and beat them on the platform.[16]

This poignant example served to show not only how Tommy coped with Japanese American discrimination but also the confidential nature of his feelings about his native culture. Neither Pete George nor his family were privy to these understandings. Only Imhara, a fellow Japanese American weightlifter of his own ethnic ilk who shared his internment camp experiences and had overcome the adversity of racial prejudice, could be trusted with his innermost thoughts.

Strength and Mind

What made this scenario possible was his athletic achievements in the 1950s, which twice brought him acclaim by the IWF as the world's greatest weightlifter. Remarkably, he does not appear in the 2018 compilation by Seb Ostrowicz of *The Greatest Weightlifters of All Time*. This omission stems from his use of the Sinclair coefficient system, which equates athletes of different bodyweights and time periods with their respective totals to establish an overall qualitative ranking. But it only covers lifts and lifters after 1978, many years after Tommy retired, so how could Ostrowicz's rankings be considered "all time"? Most importantly, although he discounts "any total that has been linked to a positive drugs test," many weightlifters included in his analysis used them to enhance performance.

In fact, number 10, Anatoly Pisarenko, Soviet star in the early 1980s, admitted that "you could win a competition without being on drugs at the time of the competition, but 'to go through the preparation it is impossible.' He also said, 'In my times, in current times, and in the future, they used, do use, and will use. It is inseparable from the sport.'"[17] Such has been the sad state of affairs since the early sixties. But this was hardly the case during the fifties when Tommy made his greatest mark. By this standard, Ostrowicz's use of the term "greatest" has no more validity than "all time" as a meaningful measure of excellence.

Steroids, in all their manifestations, have their greatest impact on an athlete's strength and recovery time. Although Tommy later maintained that strength was the least important criterion (only 10 percent) to achieving excellence, evidence from his training logs, especially from the early 1950s, reveals that he trained with very heavy weights, especially for squats and front squats. What made Kono unique, according to Harada, was that "he was exceptionally stronger than all the other lifters. He was strong, but he didn't coach strength."[18] According to Kawamura, Tommy focused "mostly on technique. I know he was really strong, but he never really pushed the strength part. Looking back, I think if there was anything lacking in his coaching it was not more emphasis on getting stronger" because "the strongest athlete has it over the weak, that they are so strong that they overpower the weaker athlete and win."[19] Although it appears from his coaching and instructional books that Tommy focused mostly on technique, Harada, concluded the reasons for his success were more complex. "He would bring in his logs, and he says this is when I used to squat 400 for 12 reps. ... He did a lot of reps. He said to us, don't do reps, like high rep squats. But he did a lot of high rep squats. And he did curls too. I told Tommy, 'I know your secret, bodybuilding.' He smiled at me. He wouldn't deny it. 'You're stronger than me. You are strong. He just smiled at me." But much of Kono's success Harada attributed to his mental powers. "He had a strong mind. Strength and mind. If I were to put it in order I would say strength and his mind were high, technique was lower. It was his mind that got him through a lot of stuff."[20]

Family Factors

A hidden source of Tommy's strength, often overlooked, was his family. Initially it stemmed from his Japanese-rooted relationships with his parents and brothers in Sacramento and Tule Lake from whom he gained emotional stability and sustenance. It helped him gain advantage in an alien culture despite the disadvantages he endured. This impact persisted long after the death of his mother in 1956 and father in 1974 and was reinforced by periodic visits to Japan (where he was very popular) and friendship with Kenji Onuma with whom he shared a common bond in nationality, business, and sport. Indeed, whatever associations he had with the Japanese American community evolved into indigenous Japanese connections. But Tommy's most consequential personal relationship transpired with his wife and children. Prior to his marriage in 1963, Kono's life was almost totally focused on weightlifting and the fame and satisfaction he derived from it. All of that changed with his debilitating injuries, family responsibilities, and full-time employment with Honolulu Parks and Recreation. But he retained his commitment to the sport through his national and international coaching assignments and less formally through endless clinics, coaching, and business ventures. Kono became such a celebrity that USA Weightlifting, locked on the horns of a dilemma, found it difficult to resist his well-meaning advice on curing the sport's ills. His conservative outlook was linked inextricably to the days of yore when the United States, through the achievements of Schemansky, Berger, the George brothers, and others ruled the sport. Kono contended that "hardships endured by these athletes was the very factor that later bred the character, strength, and drive" that propelled them to world-class level.[21] While USAW powers-that-be followed a foreign model of recent successes, Tommy embraced an American model based on what had worked during its golden age.

It was this same tradition-laden approach that he carried into his home life. The extent to which differences between Tommy's Japanese cultural background and Flo's European heritage led to their frequent clashes cannot be determined. Although they were married for over a half century and lived in the same house, their lives in a spiritual and emotional sense became distinct, owing mainly to Tommy's absences and abdicating child-rearing responsibilities to Flo. Even when he was not traveling, his many public service activities left little time for quality home life. Not unlike the way he once focused so intently on weightlifting during the fifties, he applied the same intensity to his coaching and other activities outside the family for the rest of his life, all of which enhanced his reputation and popularity. However much his self-centered and thoughtless behavior reflected Japanese cultural norms, it elicited a negative response from Flo. According to joAnn, she acted "pretty terribly" to Tommy. They fought all the time for years. She always questioned him; she would not cook him anything and would not anticipate his needs when he was sick. Part of their problem was poor communication. According to Flo, Tommy was "a very private person" and did not share a lot of things with her. Consequently, she did not realize how serious his illness was when something was really wrong.[22]

A continuous source of contention was Tommy's extramural business ventures as "the idea man." The KIO Company may have fit his entrepreneurial spirit and satisfied his Japanese cultural instincts, but it did little to promote marital harmony.[23] "We never knew anything about it. That was another thing of tension," observes Flo. "He was quite protective." It seemed like an odd kind of business involving metallurgy, iron pipes and connections, and industrial products, far different from Tommy's physical culture pursuits. And "he was always gone so much, we never knew where he was."[24] Yet Tommy needed a wife and family for emotional stability and to promote and perpetuate his celebrity image. And Flo, who was sometimes included in award ceremonies, never ceased to project the impression of a loving and supportive spouse. Tommy was never apt to display his inner feelings openly, but in 1996 he sent a brief note to Pamela You Cox, Dr. You's elder daughter, thanking her for inviting him to a testimonial birthday celebration for her mother.

> Your dad was a great person with so much warmth and understanding. We all enjoyed working with him for he brought so much enthusiasm and positive vibes with him. Your mother was equally great for she took care of the family while Doc pursued his sporting interest. She

made it possible for him to do all the things he did, keeping the home fire burning all the time. I believe my wife, Flo, has a kinship with your mother because she had to go through much the same things while I concentrated on my sport. When I reflect back, I realize the patience she exercised and the load she carried.²⁵

It was a rare realization for Tommy of the sacrifices Flo and the children had made over the years which enabled him to indulge his passion for weightlifting. To a great extent, without their deprivations, it would have been less likely that Tommy would have become, as Artie Drechsler memorably put it, "A Gift That Never Stopped Giving."²⁶

But these shortcomings, virtually all of which occurred after age 40, should not detract from his illustrious earlier achievements. Kono's weightlifting record in the 1950s was the solid foundation upon which all subsequent aspects of his life were constructed. His mindset, according to Harada, was one of unrelenting achievement. "Whatever Tommy did, he did big time. Whether it was pressing 135 lbs (barbells, not dumbbells) one in each hand, ripping a phone book in half, squatting 365 lbs for 20 reps at a bodyweight of 157 lbs. or blowing up a hot water bottle until it exploded. He always did things in an impressive fashion."²⁷ Ann Miller, calling him "the greatest weight lifter on the planet," states that concentration was the ultimate weapon for his success. "The key," Kono says, "is knowing you can go beyond. ... Maybe that's where Zen comes in. You have all this power in you and yet you have to control the output of that power. ... You just have to know you can do it."²⁸ This "can do" attitude helped him become the "elevator man" and establish world records in four weight classes. "While I'm in one class," he explained, "records would be broken in heavier class. So it was a challenge for me to break that record made by another person, so I would go up in body weight and try breaking that record." Coincident with America's Cold War agenda, he was "always trying to break a

A final photograph of the Kono family. Top, from left, Jamieson and Mark; middle, Florence and Tommy; and bottom, JoAnn.

The Path to Positivity

Weightlifting Olympic Style and *Championship Weightlifting* are chock-full of wisdom accumulated over six decades of experience in virtually all aspects of the sport and reveal the essential ingredients to his greatness. The crux of his message lay in tapping one's mental strength to produce desirable results in competition. "Too much emphasis is placed on the physical side of lifting when in reality it should be 'mind' training,"[30] This principle encapsulated both Tommy's own success and a prescription for his country's weightlifting woes. What came to be known as his positive mental attitude goes back to his early days in Sacramento. These sentiments were refined later in a series of articles in *Strength & Health* on "The Mental Attitude of the Champion" by Pete George who invoked the familiar example of how Roger Bannister used his mental powers to break the physical barrier of the four-minute mile. "There is nothing physiological about exactly four minutes, but there was something very psychological about it." It was a powerful barrier built up in the minds of all runners who had been in the sport long enough to be in physical condition to run that fast. But Bannister "convinced himself that it was physiologically possible to run a mile in less than four minutes" and "as soon as he had accomplished this mental feat, there was nothing to prevent dozens of other physically well-trained milers from following him." What was important for applying this approach to weightlifting was physical conditioning and a conviction that it should be "an essential part of your training program. You will have to Work at it!"[31]

And work at it George did. In addition to training religiously at the rustic ACMWL garage/gym in Akron to improve his body, strength, and self-confidence, Pete would repeat, at Larry Barnholth's behest, the phrase: "Every day in every way I am getting better and stronger." This mantra, Tommy notes, was derived from Émile Coué, a French psychologist/pharmacist who developed a self-improvement technique based on optimistic autosuggestion. In his popular 1922 book, *Self Mastery Through Conscious Autosuggestion*, Coué attributes to the unconscious state of mind a profound influence on human behavior. "The *Unconscious* not only presides over the functions of our organism but also over the performance of *all our actions*." It is possible to tap this hidden power, Coué argues, through the conscious method of autosuggestion. "If you induce in yourself a belief that you can do a certain thing (provided it conforms to the laws of nature) you are going to do it, no matter how difficult it may be." Even for young children, his formula of "Every day, in every way, I am getting better and better," repeated 20 times, twice a day, would "produce excellent health—physical, mental and moral."[32] These revelations of the power of positive thinking, adapted to weightlifting by Barnholth, had no less an impact on Tommy than Pete, with whom he admits to sharing a "meeting of the minds."[33]

Embracing these precepts proved efficacious in helping him overcome his initial nervousness and prepared him for the international stage.[34] Tommy's mental conditioning was also reinforced by several motivational books he encountered in the fifties. Norman Vincent Peale's *Power of Positive Thinking* (1952) re-awakened the general public to the concept of self-mastery in much the same way Barnholth advocated. To "build up feelings of self-confidence," Peale recommended "repetitive suggestion of confidence ideas" as a "dominating habit." Like Coué, he believed "our physical condition is determined very largely by our emotional condition, and our emotional life is profoundly regulated by our thought life." In much the same way that Tommy later coached his lifters to visualize, Peale used the term "picturize." to induce positivism. "Optimistic visualization combined with prayer and faith will inevitably actualize achievement."[35] Pete confirms that the Barnholths "strongly espoused his philosophy."[36] That Peale's words had special meaning to Kono is evident in a clipping in his papers where he highlights the phrase that "anyone can do with himself just about what he has a mind to do."[37] It is also evident in a 1954 *Sports Illustrated* article titled "Think and Grow." For Tommy, concentration was the key.

> While you're walking up there to the bar, you try to think of what you have to do. You try to concentrate to eliminate any noise going on. When I get there, I try to have a positive attitude. I try to think of myself lifting it—whether my back breaks or not. If I concentrate hard enough, it's actually like being in a room all by myself. There's darkness all around, and all I have is the weight before me. If I'm nerved up for the effort, I feel the weight for the first three or four inches. After that, I don't feel the weight at all.[38]

No less impactful on Tommy's growing reliance on mental conditioning was Napoleon Hill's *Think and Grow Rich*.[39] Not unlike Coué, Hill recognized the power of the subconscious and autosuggestion. He believed that a mind dominated by "positive emotions" could "give the subconscious mind instructions, which it will accept and act upon immediately." Aware of the intangibles in human behavior, Hill was convinced this "other self" was more powerful than the "physical self" and through it, man could master himself and his environment.

> THE SUBCONSCIOUS MIND WORKS DAY AND NIGHT. Through a method of procedure, unknown to man, the subconscious draws upon the forces of Infinite Intelligence for the power with which it voluntarily transmutes one's desires into their physical equivalent, making use, always of the most practical media by which this end may be accomplished. You cannot entirely control your subconscious mind, but you can voluntarily hand over to it any plan, desire, or purpose which you wish transformed into concrete form.

This transmutation of desire into physical action, Hill contended, was accomplished through autosuggestion, "the agency of control" into the "rich garden of the mind." Concentration and persistence were critical to one's desire becoming a burning obsession.[40] "Whatever the mind can conceive and believe, it can achieve," Hill's most inspirational quote, was also inscribed on a sign in front of the lifting platform of the Barnholth gym, according to Pete George. "It was Hill's philosophy of the boundlessness of the human potential that attracted them."[41] Hill was no less appealing to Tommy, as reflected in his apothegm that "the mind wills the body" and "the mind must be groomed for success."[42]

Kono attributes much of his own success to his ability to overcome adversity. "The human body can adapt itself to the most adverse condition and make miraculous improvement," he believed. It was "because I made use and profited by the experience of disadvantage that I have been able to do so well wherever I appeared."[43] The cultural context for this sanguine frame of mind coincides with the Buddhist outlook of his upbringing—"shikata-ganai," meaning to accept things as they are, and "arigatai," meaning be thankful for what you have. Adversity, Kono believed, enhanced, not detracted, from athletic performance. "Obstacles and problems are nothing more than challenges thrown down and should be welcomed if you want to be toughened for big time competitions."[44] Pete confirms that "Tommy never wanted to go into competition where he'd win by default. … He'd go where the competition was toughest. He wanted to make sure when he won, he was the better man. He never held back."[45]

That this derivation stems from his Tule Lake experience is evident from Kono's continued association with "27" which was his birthday and the number of his camp barracks. As Drechsler recognizes, Tommy had the "special ability to take something positive from the experience." Many others would have "carried the number 27 as a symbol of hatred, injustice, emotional suffering for the rest of their lives." Kono believed "the only way to limit the negative power of what was done is to focus on the positive and move forward."[46] He embodied what James Michener calls a "majesty of character" which enabled Japanese Americans, "after their lives had been torn asunder and their property stolen from them," to display "freedom from malice."[47] Indeed, an essential ingredient to Kono's greatness, rooted in Tule Lake, was his love of America. "I've always been a flag-waver!" he admitted. His "greatest thrill" came just after the 1952 Olympics when the American team was competing against Belgian, British, and French teams in a little town in eastern France. "Suddenly a blond teammate stuck an American flag in my hand and said, 'Tommy, boy, you lead us!' A tinny brass band tried to play the Star-Spangled Banner as we marched in. It was just a small arena in a small town, but somehow I felt more honored than ever before or since!"[48]

A fuller comprehension of this unique adaptation, hardly characteristic of all racial and ethnic minorities, is the subject of a compelling study of the impact of the imprisonment of Japanese Americans that appeared in a 2019 article in the *American Psychologist* subtitled "Examining the Scope of Racial Trauma" where Donna Nagata, Jacqueline Kim, and Kaidi Wu focus on coping responses and healing strategies. Two manifestations relevant to Tommy and his generation was a desire not to talk about their incarceration, thereby creating "an acute Sansei awareness of an ominous gap in their family history" and also a significant Nisei desire to Americanize, "to blend into mainstream society by de-emphasizing Japanese culture and language."[49] Another macrosocietal theme applicable to every stage of Kono's life is a statement stemming from a 1980 study on "The Japanese American Family" by Harry H.L. Kitano and Akema Kikumura. Added to other unsettling conditions, there was a combination of factors that set Japanese Americans apart from other racial minorities. "First, they were nonwhite; second, they were soon to be identified as coming from an enemy nation and eventually an 'enemy race,' Third, they belonged to a 'strange and unassimilable culture.' Several groups have had one or two of these charges leveled at them, but never has an immigrant population been in the position of facing all three."[50] Often these challenges were less overt than covert but nonetheless real and fraught with social and psychological consequences. Tommy Kono, as an outlier, was probably confronted with more untoward circumstances than other Japanese Americans, but he overcame them with his extraordinary physical strength and an indomitable spirit.

The Power of Zen

A final, albeit subtle, influence on Kono's development comes from his Japanese cultural background and awareness of a link between Zen Buddhism and weightlifting. Tommy never overtly professed or practiced any religious belief, but his behavior betrayed a strong underlying Buddhist mindfulness. As historian Edwin Reischauer points out, "No people has been more concerned than the Japanese with self-discipline" and the development of will power. "Since medieval times Zen meditation has been popular but often less for the original reason of achieving transcendental enlightenment than for the cultivation of self-discipline." Although few modern Japanese practice Zen, their lives are "full of traces of Buddhism as a sort of background melody."[51] Such was the case with Tommy who exhibited a proclivity for Zen which he acquired more through osmosis than any purposeful absorption.[52] This connection was evident in my 1992 interview with him when, after explaining that "mental concentration comes from positive thinking," he cited a quote from Hawaii Zen master Tanouye Tenshin Rotaishi: "Among all the sports, weightlifting is closest to Zen."[53] The manner of its impact was evident to Walter Imahara who shared much of Tommy's cultural background, including internment experiences.

> In that way Tommy and I discussed these things that nobody else maybe talked about because we're of the same race. We used Zen power, Zen power. Zen, Zen, what's Zen. The Zen religion. It was the concentration. Just concentrate. Zen power. ... Not to the degree that he did, but in our later years we used to correspond, and I would see him at the meets. These were the things we discussed. The things he never talked about with other lifters. He never did. In fact, I never did that either. ... We were at a different level, one to one friendship. ... Meditation. We both were at camp and our parents were Buddhists. We went into the camp Buddhists. We got out of the camp, our parents were Buddhists. ... But always in our life coming up, there was that Buddhist background. ... They have a lot to do with his life. What he ended up as because he practiced it with me. Maybe he won't talk about it with no one else, like you've got to use a lot of Zen power. What I notice about Zen, I know they want you to believe that you can do something. They make you concentrate, meditate, what words you can use. When you see Tommy at a meet, like put a weight on the bar. Don't tell me what's on it, I'll do it.[54]

This thought process corresponds to the 1958 incident when Terpak tried to tell Kono what he needed to beat the Soviet lifter. "Don't tell me how much I need," Tommy retorted. "Just put it on the bar and I'll lift it." And he did.[55]

His association with Japanese culture was also observed by his son-in-law, Gary Sumida, who attributed it to Tommy's upbringing in an immigrant family and that "his adherence to Buddhist principles may have provided him with a mental edge during his competitive career." Children raised in a traditional Japanese family are taught that when they bring shame on themselves, they also bring shame on the whole family. Therefore, it was imperative to "conduct yourself with honor, AT ALL TIMES" and that one should "win with grace, but lose with equal or greater graciousness." Sumida, a Buddhist himself, believes Tommy's faith in these principles "contributed heavily to his stoic nature. One of the major tenets of Buddhism is the belief in living in harmony with everyone and every THING in the world. I feel that whenever he faced his toughest tests, he probably relied heavily on that belief."[56] On a more practical level Zen Buddhism, according to D.T. Suzuki, "always deals with facts, concrete and tangible."[57] And for Tommy, mental concentration was critical to tangible results.

Tommy contended that "the importance of harnessing the power of the mind dates back for centuries from the teaching of the Zen masters." He believed it was possible to "focus your thoughts like using the magnifying glass to focus the sun's ray to a pinpoint to start paper or wood burning." Peak performance is attained when an athlete is "in the zone," with his attention totally focused on the task at hand. He developed a "do or die" attitude and devoted total effort making the lift. "Your thoughts are on a few key things that are vital to your performance on the platform."[58] Nothing else matters. As the Rome Olympics approached, Tommy shared his method for building confidence with a *Time* magazine reporter.

> To Tommy Kono, the secret lies in the power of positive thinking. "Successful weight lifting is not in the body," says Kono. "It's in the mind. You have to strengthen your mind to shut out everything—the man with the camera, the laugh or the cough in the audience. You can lift as much as you believe you can. Your body can do what you will it to do."[59]

Drechsler adds that his powers of concentration were so great that "when a fire alarm went off during his last C&J at the 1964 Olympic Trials, he didn't ask for another attempt because he said he didn't hear it."[60] A further link to Tommy's Japanese heritage was revealed by Hawaiian protégé Mel Miyamoto, who was training his 11-year-old granddaughter for local competitions. "I give her all the sayings that Tommy had, like Shikata-Ga-Nai and Arigatai, be thankful for what you have." Drawing from the same Coué-Barnholth-George mindset, Miyamoto conveyed another Kono didacticism about achieving total effort. "One time he told me about injuries. If your arm doesn't fall off, you're okay. So that's what I tell my granddaughter all the time. I told her, no, it didn't fall off, you're okay."[61] Tommy articulated these sentiments as the key to championship performance. "Usually it is self-preservation that prevents us from achieving an all-out effort. The thought of being injured or having pain will prevent you from exerting yourself so failure becomes eminent [sic]." A do-or-die attitude free of all distractions, even pain, was imperative. "Your mind must take control of your physical side."[62] Tommy was, after explaining his methodical approach in 1997 to protégé Melanie Getz, "Your 'Zen,' coach."[63]

These values are hardly exclusive to Zen Buddhism. However much Tommy benefited from his Japanese cultural conditioning, it merely reinforced an attitude appropriated for weightlifting by Barnholth and practiced by George in distant Ohio. Revelation came at the 1950 national championships at Philadelphia. Hereafter their philosophies of weightlifting and life meshed. This approach is prevalent in his earliest training manual in 1954. "The mind governs all our movements, thoughts and action. It is 'Mind over Mind' that we must all strive to grasp to improve our total … or anything worth-while in our life." He believed "the most important thing at this moment is to fully realize the magnitude that the 'brain-power' has in direct relation to our muscle-power." He subscribed to the adage, a la Marcus Aurelius, that "as a man thinketh, so he is."[64] Sustained by the motivational writings of Peale and Hill, and the subliminal influence of Zen, Tommy retained this belief in the power of positive thinking throughout his competitive years and subsequent decades of coaching challenges, business vicissitudes, and administrative struggles. Even the onset of debilitating bodily afflictions and prospect of death could not quell his optimistic and indomitable spirit. In a final farewell to his friends, he remained stoic and upbeat, that "life is for the living to enjoy the journey while you can!" *Shikata-Ga-Nai* and *Arigatai*.[65]

Appendix I: Tommy Kono's Record of Achievement

Major Weightlifting Competitions

1 U.S. Junior National Championship (1952)
15 U.S. Senior National Championships (1950–1965), 11 firsts, 2 seconds, 1 third
12 years of international competition (1952–1963)
    3 Olympic Games (1952, 1956 and 1960), 2 gold and 1 silver
    9 World Championships (1953–1963) 6 gold, 1 silver and 1 bronze
    3 Pan American Games (1955, 1959 and 1963), 3 gold

Records

26 World (Official) in four weight classes (Press 13, Snatch 2, Clean & Jerk 4, Total 7)
37 American (Official)
7 Olympic
8 Pan Am

Physique Titles

Mr. Sacramento, 1953
Mr. Iron Man, 1954
Mr. World (Roubaix, France), 1954
Mr. World (Munich, West Germany), 1955
Mr. Universe (Tehran, Iran), 1957
Mr. Universe (Vienna, Austria) 1961

Awards and Honors

Most Outstanding Athlete of 1952 for the AAU Pacific Association
Greatest Lifter at the 1953 World Championships
Commendations from Hawaii House of Representatives, 1959
Honored in a *This Is Your Life* program staged at the Sacramento YMCA, 1960
Sullivan Award Nominee (1956–1963), 2nd four times—3rd, 4th, 5th, and 6th one time
Outstanding Senior Nationals Lifter for 1952, 1953, 1955, 1957, 1959, 1961, and 1963
IWF 25 Years Service Award, 1978
"Greatest Weightlifter of All Time" in worldwide IWF poll, 1982

Helms Hall of Fame
USWF Hall of Fame
U.S. Olympic Hall of Fame, 1990
One Hundred Golden Olympians, 1996
IWF Best Weightlifter of 100 Years Award, 2005

Referee

1 Pan American Games, 1967
1 Central American Games, 1966
2 Mexican National Championships, 1967 & 1968
4 U.S. Senior National Championships, 1972–1975
International Referee, Category II, 1966
International Referee, Category I, 1968

Manager

Mexican National Team, 1966–1968
West German National Team, 1969–1972

Coach

National and Olympic Coach for Mexico (1966–1968)
National and Olympic Coach for West Germany (1969–1972)
Olympic Coach for the United States (1976)
Women's World Championship Coach for the USA (1987–1989)
Attended the First International Coaching Clinic held by the IWF, Spa, Belgium, 1971
IWF International Coach Title, 1975 (one of only four worldwide)
Coaching Clinic Conducted:
    Mexico, 1966–1968
    France, 1970
    Scotland, 1970
    West Germany, 1968–1972
    Japan, 1974–1975*
    New Zealand, 1975*
    People's Republic of China, 1975*
        *IWF Sponsored
Only international professional coach from the USA (1966–1972)

Elected or Honorary Positions

U.S. Weightlifting Team Captain and/or Lifter–Official Liaison Person, 1958–1963
IWF 15-year Service Medal
IWF 25-year Service Medal
Competed and/or performed in Match/Exhibitions in over 20 different countries as official representative of the USA:
    Finland, Sweden, Denmark, W. Germany Poland, USSR, England, France, Austria, Switzerland, Iran, Iraq, Egypt, Afghanistan, India, Burma, Japan, Australia, Brazil, Hungary, and Brazil.

Appendix II: World Records

Date	Contest	Site	Bodywt.	Class	Record	
July 26, 1952	Olympics	Helsinki	148.75	148.75	Snatch	259.25
Aug. 29, 1953	World Champ.	Stockholm	163.25	165.25	C&J	371.25
Aug. 29, 1953	World Champ.	Stockholm	163.25	165.25	Total	898.50
Oct. 10, 1954	World Champ.	Vienna	173.50	181.75	C&J	380
Oct. 10, 1954	World Champ.	Vienna	173.50	181.75	Total	958.75
Oct. 17, 1954	Invitational	Lille	165	165.25	Press	288.75
Oct. 17, 1954	Invitational	Lille	165	165.25	Total	903.50
Mar. 15, 1955	Pan Amer.	Mexico City	169.50	181.75	Press	316.50
Mar. 15, 1955	Pan Amer.	Mexico City	169.50	181.75	Total	965
June 18, 1955	USSR vs USA	Moscow	164	165.25	Press	292
Jan. 20, 1956	Honolulu Champ.	Honolulu	163.75	165.25	Press	293.50
Feb. 17, 1956	Oahu Champ.	Honolulu	164	165.25	Press	295.50
Mar. 9, 1956	Hawaii Champ.	Honolulu	174	181.75	Press	317.50
Sept. 15, 1956	Honolulu Open	Honolulu	183	198.25	Press	322.50
Oct. 12, 1956	Honolulu Invit.	Honolulu	178.50	181.75	C&J	382.50
Nov. 26, 1956	Olympics	Melbourne	178	181.75	C&J	186
Nov. 26, 1956	Olympics	Melbourne	178	181.75	Total	986
Feb. 21, 1957	Oahu Champ.	Honolulu	179.50	181.75	Press	319
Mar. 9, 1957	Honolulu Champ.	Honolulu	179.50	181.75	Press	321
Sept. 19, 1958	World Champ.	Stockholm	163.50	165.25	Snatch	294.50
Sept. 19, 1958	World Champ.	Stockholm	163.50	165.25	Total	948
Sept. 8, 1960	Olympics	Rome	164	165.25	Press	308.50
Mar. 11, 1961	Moscow Cup	Moscow	176	181.75	Press	337.50
Mar. 11, 1961	Moscow Cup	Moscow	176	181.75	Total	1,014
May 26, 1961	Hawaii Champ.	Honolulu	183.50	198.25	Press	350.50
June 17, 1961	Japan Nationals	Tokyo	180	181.75	Press	338.50

Chapter Notes

Preface

1. For general accounts of Kono's career, see Osmo Kiiha, "Tommy Kono," *The Iron Master* 5 (December 1990) and Osmo Kiiha and Herb Glossbrenner, "The Amazing Tommy Kono," *The International Olympic Lifter* 10 (1991): 18–20. See also "Tommy Kono," in Bill Pearl, George and Tuesday Coates, and Richard Thornley, Jr., *Legends of the Iron Game: Reflections on the History of Strength Training*, vol. 2 (Phoenix, OR, 2010), 189–96; Bob Sigall, "Tommy Kono," *Health and Strength* (October 2015): 19; "Tommy Kono 70!" *IWF Magazine* (2001): 33–34; and Walter Imahara and David Meltzer, eds., *Book of Remembrance for Tommy Kono* (Mesa, AZ: 2017).

2. Tommy Kono, *Weightlifting, Olympic Style* (Honolulu, 2001), and Tommy Kono, *Championship Weightlifting, Beyond Muscle Power, The Mental Side of Lifting* (Honolulu, 2010).

3. Born on June 29, 1929, in Akron, Ohio, to immigrant parents of Macedonian/Bulgarian descent, Pete won a gold medal at the 1952 Helsinki Olympics, silver medals in London (1948) and Melbourne (1956) and five world championship titles from 1947 to 1955, and setting four world records. Dubbed a "boy wonder," he was the first 15-year-old to clean and jerk 300 pounds. I would rank George in the top five of all-time drug-free American weightlifters behind Kono, John Davis, and Norbert Schemansky, and ahead of Chuck Vinci. See Osmo Kiiha, "George Brothers," *The Iron Master* 6 (April 1991). A cultural context for his athletic career is provided in John D. Fair, "The Ethnicity of Ohio's Strength Culture," *Ohio History* 117 (2010).

4. P. George to the author, September 6, 2018.

5. Pete George, "Tommy Kono: Greatest Weightlifter of All Time," *Iron Game History* (hereafter *IGH*) 14 (July 2017): 45.

Introduction

1. Title of the 1951 MGM film about the World War II exploits of the 442nd Regimental Combat Team of Japanese American volunteers, written by Robert Pirosh and starring Van Johnson, Lane Nakano, and George Miki.

2. Tommy noted that the IWF paid all expenses for his Istanbul trip and that he had the honor of carrying the Olympic flag to the stage during the opening ceremony for the centennial celebration. Kono to the author, June 24, 2005.

3. Dorothy Swaine Thomas, *The Spoilage* (Berkeley, 1946); Roger Daniels, *Prisoners Without Trial: Japanese Americans in World War II* (New York, 1993); Michi Nishiura Weglyn, *Years of Infamy: The Untold Story of America's Concentration Camps* (Seattle, 1996); *Personal Justice Denied: Report of the Commission on Wartime Relocation and Internment of Civilians* (Seattle, 1997); Donna K. Nagata, *Legacy of Injustice: Exploring the Cross-Generational Impact of the Japanese American Internment* (New York, 1993); Richard Koichi Tanaka, *America on Trial!* (New York, 1987); Toru Matsumoto, *Beyond Prejudice* (New York, 1978); and John Howard, *Concentration Camps on the Home Front* (Chicago, 2008). For a bibliography on Japanese American scholarship prior to 1994 see Paul Spickard, *Japanese Americans: The Formation and Transformations of an Ethnic Group* (New Brunswick, 2009), 191–207. On page 195 Spickard recognizes that, after 1970, a new generation of scholars, "having come of age in the late 1960s and early 1970s in the context of the Asian American Movement and leftist politics generally, carried activist visions of the purposes of scholarship."

4. See Timothy J. Hollan, *The German-Americans and World War II: An Ethnic Experience* (New York, 1996) and Salvatore J. LaGumina, *The Humble and the Heroic: Wartime Italian Americans* (Youngstown, NY, 2006).

5. Disagreement persists over the nature and motivation of the camps. To Paul Spickard the term "'evacuation' conveys the impression that this was a rescue operation, that somehow the army was acting to save Japanese Americans and deliver them to higher ground, rather than to punish and imprison them for their race. The other euphemism, 'relocation,' is equally odious. It implies a moral neutrality—people were merely being moved from one place to another, with no adverse consequences. Hence, what were manifestly prison camps were referred to in WRA and JACL literature as 'relocation centers'—such a nice

term and so irresponsible!" Spickard, *Japanese Americans*, 118. Roger Lotchin, however, accepts "evacuation" and "relocation" centers as appropriate for Japanese American encampments and rejects the race paradigm endorsed by Roger Daniels and others. "It has so far escaped the notice of historians of Japanese American experience that the concentration camp solution was specifically considered and rejected. The principal actors in the drama understood very well the difference between a concentration camp and a relocation center." Roger W. Lotchin, *Japanese American Relocation in World War II: A Reconsideration* (Cambridge, 2018), 120.

6. Yamato Ichihashi, *Japanese in the United States: A Critical Study of the Problems of the Japanese Immigrants and Their Children* (Stanford, 1932), 90.

7. Takeyuki Tsuda, *Japanese American Ethnicity: In Search of Heritage and Homeland Across Generations* (New York, 2016), 15.

8. Spickard, *Japanese Americans*, 59.

9. David Mas Masumoto, *Country Voices: The Oral History of a Japanese Family Farm Community* (Del Rey, CA, 1987), 129. In his essay on Shin Buddhism, the largest and best organized sect in America, Alfred Bloom enumerates the cultural characteristics transferred from Japan. "These are *shikata-ga-nai*, which means to accept those things over which one has no control; *mottainai*, which generally suggests modesty, conveying a sense of unworthiness; *gaman*, which means to endure and persevere in the face of difficulty; *enryo*, which is a nonassertive restraint or reserve; and finally *okage-sama-de* and *arigatai*, which express gratitude and appreciation to all those factors supporting our lives, though unseen. ... They have been conducive to more introspective and less aggressive personality formation, but also a flexibility to adapting to the changing conditions of society, while lessening tension with traditional values." These are characteristics easily associated with Tommy Kono. Alfred Bloom, "Shin Buddhism in America," in Charles S. Prebish and Kenneth K. Tanaka, eds., *The Faces of Buddhism in America* (Berkeley, 1998), 38.

10. William Petersen, "Success Story, Japanese-American Style," *The New York Times Magazine*, January 9, 1966, 41.

11. Stephen S. Fugita and David J. O'Brien, *Japanese American Ethnicity: The Persistence of Community* (Seattle, 1991), 5 and 10.

12. Daisetz T. Suzuki, *Zen and Japanese Culture* (Princeton, 2010), 16–17.

13. Mitchell T. Maki, Harry H.L. Kitano, and S. Megan Berthold, *Achieving the Impossible Dream: How Japanese Americans Obtained Redress* (Urbana, 1999), 24.

14. Stephen S. Fugita and Marilyn Fernandez, *Altered Lives, Enduring Community: Japanese Americans Remember Their World War II Incarceration* (Seattle, 2004), 46.

15. Tsuda, *Japanese American Ethnicity*, 61–62.

16. Bill Hosokawa, *Nisei: The Quiet Americans* (Boulder, 2002), 367.

17. Tsuda, *Japanese American Ethnicity*, 65.

18. *Pacific Citizen*, April 10, 1944, and Masayo Duus, *Unlikely Liberators: The Men of the 100th and 442nd* (Honolulu, 1987), 231.

19. Tsuda, *Japanese American Ethnicity*, 66.

20. David Yoo, *Growing Up Nisei: Race, Generation, and Culture Among Japanese Americans of California, 1924–49* (Urbana, 2000), 107.

21. Maki, et al., *Achieving the Impossible*, 44.

22. Tsuda, *Japanese American Ethnicity*, 70.

23. Petersen, "Success Story," 21.

24. Kaoru Oguri Kendis, *A Matter of Comfort: Ethnic Maintenance and Ethnic Style Among Third Generation Japanese Americans* ((New York, 1989), 18–20; Kevin Wildie, *Sacramento's Historic Japantown, Legacy of a Lost Neighborhood* (Charleston, SC, 2013), 125–26.

25. Paul Spickard argues that "Japanese American abilities and virtues were spread across the bell curve in patterns similar to those of other ethnic groups. The model minority myth hid from public view those Japanese Americans who were poor or socially disadvantaged" and used as a "bludgeon to punish other people of color," especially African Americans. Spickard, *Japanese Americans*, 156–57. David Palumbo-Liu, however, puts a more constructive spin on the model minority stereotype in *Asian/American: Historical Crossings of a Racial Frontier* (Stanford, 1999), preferring to call it a "discourse" rather than a "myth" and positioning it with "self-affirmative" as an inclusive concept for all races. "Both self-affirmative action and model minority discourse are predicated upon subsuming or erasing the political under the force of an idealized individuality that transcends the specificities of material history and underwrites an ideology that is seen to be timelessly true, valid, and ethical—individual happiness is only limited by one's own inner resources." This more neutralist approach appears consistent with Ellen Wu's important study, *The Color of Success: Asian Americans and the Origins of the Model Minority* (Princeton, 2013) which shows that "the invention of the model minority took place in multiple arenas" and helped illuminate the process of how "the nation accepted Asians as legitimate citizens while continuing to perceive them as indelible outsiders." The highly critiqued model minority stereotype has had an ongoing relevance and even served as a "rallying point" for innovative discussions about Asian American racial identity.

26. Imahara and Meltzer, *Book of Remembrance*, 27–28.

27. Norman Vincent Peale, *The Power of Positive Thinking* (New York, 1952) and Napoleon Hill, *Think & Grow Rich* (Cleveland, OH, 1937). Hoffman's optimistic zeal is best captured in *Weight Lifting* (York, PA, 1939).

28. Maki, et al., *Achieving the Impossible*, 57.

29. Interview with Hirofumi Tanaka, April 25, 2018, University of Texas, Austin.

Chapter 1

1. Tommy Kono, "Weightlifting Paid Off," March 3, 1953, Tommy Kono Papers, University of Texas, Austin (hereafter KP).

2. Japanese immigrants (Issei) first appeared in Hawaii in 1868 when 149 contract laborers arrived in what was then a native monarchy. Although Hawaii would not achieve statehood until 1959, mainlanders were already in Hawaii administering sugar cane plantations. Eventually, many more Japanese arrived in Hawaii and the United States seeking work. By 1880, there were only 446 Japanese settlers in the latter, but by 1890 there were approximately 27,000 (mostly in Northern California). A disproportionate number of them relative to the native and white population lived in Hawaii, which was not annexed by the United States until 1898. The 1910 census revealed 185,502 ethnic Japanese living in Hawaii out of a population of 191,909. Wayne Maeda, *Continuing Traditions: Japanese Americans, Story of a People: 1869 to 1992* (Sacramento, 1992), 2, and Department of Commerce, Bureau of the Census, Hawaii, 1910 (Washington, 1913), 5.

3. Fugita and Fernandez, *Altered Lives*, 15–16.

4. Kanichi Kono, "Individual Record," May 16, 1943, KP.

5. Tommy Kono, "Untitled Typescript of Early Family History," September 29, 1996, KP. "Most of the early immigrants were young men from farms in southwestern Japan, who came to the United States to make money," concludes Yasuko I. Takezawa in *Breaking Silence: Redress and Japanese American Ethnicity* (Ithaca, 1995), 4.

6. Roger Daniels, *The Politics of Prejudice* (Berkeley, 1962), 24.

7. "Individual Record," May 16, 1943, and "Kanichi Kono," biographical sketch, KP.

8. Warranty deed from Louisa M. Cody and William F. Cody to K. Kono, February 7, 1916, Lincoln, Nebraska, and stock certificate no. 5372, The Skinner Company, January 2, 1920, KP. See also Jim Robbins, "Spirit of Wild West Lives in Buffalo Bill Historical Center," *The Sacramento Bee*, July 13, 1988.

9. Kanachi Kono, Income Tax Return for 1920, KP.

10. Ichimi Kono was born on November 28, 1898, in Oda Musa, Hiroshima, Japan, daughter of Ichiro and Ohata Oiji Kitamusa, who were farmers in Hiroshima ken. She had eleven years of formal education. "Registration, War Relocation Authority," March 24, 1943, KP.

11. Departure and return dates were May 8, 1929, and February 28, 1930. Income Tax Return for Departing Aliens, 1929 (61976), and the Imperial Japanese Government Passport for Ichimi Kono (182502), KP.

12. Kono, "Untitled Typescript," and Standard Certificate of Birth, Sacramento, 983, KP.

13. Prior to World War II, CPC had five plants in Sacramento. According to William Burg, "Sacramento's canning industry canned every imaginable farm product, but tomatoes were the best-known, earning Sacramento the nickname 'The Big Tomato.'" "The Big Tomato," *Midtown Monthly*, March 11, 2011, http://www.midtownmonthly.net/life/the-big-tomato/.

14. Kono, "Untitled Typescript." Tommy's worried parents also tried some traditional Japanese remedies to cure his condition, including "burnt birds, bears' livers and powdered snake," all to no avail. Don Bloom, "Kono: Runt to Record-Breaker," newspaper clipping, KP.

15. Philip R. Ward, "Verification of Detention Dates of Civilians during World War II," January 13, 1988, Civil Archives Division, National Archives, Washington, D.C.

16. Bruce Elleman, *Japanese-American Civilian Prisoner Exchanges and Detention Camps, 1941–45* (London, 2006), 65. While much disagreement has persisted over the nomenclature of the camps, ranging from "concentration" to "relocation centers," most scholars settle for less controversial terms, such as internment or imprisonment. Roger Daniels reassures us that they were not death or extermination camps and that "more persons were born in them than died in them," but they were "ringed with barbed wire" and had "guard towers manned by armed soldiers." Richard Drinnon's 1987 account, *Keeper of Concentration Camps*, provides the harshest and most sustained criticism of them (44): "The most that can be said is that incarceration had unintended consequences and by-products, not all of which were negative." Tommy Kono or Hollywood actor Pat Morita, both confined at Tule Lake as children, would have been good examples. Arguably the best scholarly account of this proposition is David Yoo's 2000 rationale of how the "Nisei negotiated the complexities of identity formation in the toss and tumble of their times." It was clear to Yoo that "no other second generation has had to face the questions of its place in America under the extraordinary conditions that the Nisei encountered." Negotiation entailed a comprehension of how assimilation to American culture encouraged by camp authorities could be reconciled with traditional Issei values fostered at home and in camp Japanese language schools. Tommy Kono would have been fully involved in this process.

17. James A. Michener, "Introduction" in Weglyn, *Years of Infamy*, 31.

18. H[arry] Inukai, *Tule Lake Directory and Camp News, May 1942 through September 1943* (Hood River, OR, 1988).

19. According to a 1942 report, each morning 22 army trucks transported 400 to 450 workers from the Tule Lake camp seven miles to a 2,500-acre farm where they utilized $80,000 of equipment to grow vegetables. "The rich, black soil of the farm has already received $125,000 worth of seeds and plants. The acreage is apportioned into 2500 acres of potatoes, peas, beets, squash, turnips, cabbage, cauliflower, lettuce, celery, onions, and 'nappa' [sic]." *The Tulean Dispatch*, August 17, 1942.

20. "Tule Lake," *Life* 16, March 20, 1944, 34.
21. *Second Kinenhi: Reflections on Tule Lake* (San Francisco, 2000), quoted in Fugita and Fernandez, *Altered Lives*, 61.
22. Response to a question asked by a *Sports Illustrated* interviewer about camp life, KP.
23. Kono, Untitled 1996 Typescript. Tommy recalls that his father coped with camp life by "keeping himself busy making or fixing things. ... I guess having been born in Japan and living through the depression years made him very resourceful and productive." Kono to Sheila O'Neill, June 18, 2007, KP.
24. *Tulare News*, May 9, June 17, and June 27, 1942.
25. *Tulean Dispatch*, July 15 and August 24, 1942.
26. Brian Niiya, "The Nuuanu YMCA and the Glory Days of Hawaii Weightlifting," *Hawaii Herald, Hawaii's Japanese American Journal* 20, no. 17, September 3, 1999, 7. See also the reprint of Niiya's article in *IGH* 14 (Summer 2020): 30–36.
27. *Tulean Dispatch*, April 22, 1943.
28. *Ibid.*, July 13, 1943. The Klamath Falls Naval Air Station, converted from a small municipal airport after the outbreak of war, eventually included as many as 103 aircraft, 390 officers, 2,603 enlisted men and 200 civilians. "Remembering WW II—Sites That Brought the War to the Klamath Basin," https://www.craterlaketrust.org/article?articleId=341.
29. This easing of restrictions developed in part because of the exemplary behavior of interned Japanese Americans and increased demand for domestic laborers resulting from wartime manpower shortages. By 1943, the *Tulean Dispatch* was publishing a column titled "Job Jobs" featuring opportunities for medical assistants as well as domestic, skilled, and semi-skilled workers nationwide. *Tulean Dispatch*, July 6, 1943.
30. That Ishikawa was a role model was evident two generations later to one of Tommy's protégés, Russell Ogata. "He was always very positive, very encouraging to the younger ones. ... Something I'll always remember about him is how, from the depths of his heart, he wanted us to succeed." *Honolulu Advertiser* (hereafter *HA*), November 30, 2008.
31. Kiiha, "Tommy Kono," 3. By this time it appears Tommy was no longer suffering from asthma. A 1942 health report states he had "no major defects," and, aside from his tonsillitis affliction, a July 1945 report states "he has always been perfectly well until then." "Individual Record," June 17, 1942, and "Dispensary Minor Ailment," July 28, 1945. Likewise, camp school records indicate Tommy's infrequent absences were from less serious ailments or tardiness. Attendance cards, Tri-State High School, September 21, 1942–October 12, 1945, KP.
32. Sasaki to the author, May 3, 2020.
33. "Judo GI," KP.
34. Remembrance Fragment, KP.
35. "Olympic Champion Tommy Kono, World Champion, Olympic Weight Lifter," KP. Kono remembers the first weights he lifted at Tule Lake were purchased by Block 27 of Ward II from proceeds of a carnival hamburger stand. "We ordered a York Ten-in-One exercise kit, along with basketballs and other sports equipment." Niiya, "Nuuanu YMCA," 7.
36. Kiiha, "Tommy Kono," 3, Tommy Kono, "Body Building Program," March 27, 1948, KP, and *Iron Man* (hereafter *IM*) 20 (July 1960): 24–25.
37. Tommy Kono, My Records, KP.
38. At a novice contest at Tule Lake in late 1942 judged by Ishikawa, one of the lifters, Tom T. Kono, placed fourth as a featherweight. *Strength & Health* made much of this event, reporting that "Japanese-Americans are building themselves up so that when and if they are called, they hope to have an above-average percentage of physically-able men to serve this nation." *Strength & Health* (hereafter *SH*) 11 (January 1943): 11.
39. Kono, *Championship Weightlifting*, 194.
40. Annotated physique charts for August 24, 1943, February 4, July 10, November 8, and December 16, 1944, KP.
41. Hosokawa, *Nisei*, 367.
42. Yoo, *Growing Up Nisei*, 174.
43. Chris Baker, "Tommy Kono," newspaper clipping, KP.
44. Kono, "Untitled Typescript," KP.
45. E. J. Morrissey to John Kono, July 20, 1948, KP.
46. Tommy's family lived on M Street (Capitol Avenue) in the Japantown district of Sacramento. Lincoln School, which was three blocks away on P Street, consisted of 33 percent Japanese American students by 1941. Wildie, *Historic Japantown*, 46.
47. *York Dispatch*, August 6, 1960.
48. Tommy Kono, Pupil Progress Report, 1941–42, Sacramento Unified School District; Tommy Kono, Student Achievement Record, 1946–1948; and Tommy Tamio Kono, Grade Card, Sacramento Junior College, January 27 and June 11, 1949, KP.
49. Kono to Lou DeMarco, June 28, 2007, KP.
50. Results of Open Weight Lifting Meet, San Jose YMCA, March 6, 1948, Kono to V. M. Kasyanov, August 20, 1956, and "Brief Background of Tommy Kono," KP.
51. Tommy Kono, "Weightlifting Paid Off," March 3, 1953, KP. According to a 1954 account, Tommy had to overcome his parents' opposition "who feared, because of his weak constitution, he would strain himself too much. Kono used to sneak away from home to practice lifting the weights. Soon, however, his health strengthened and his parents were won over." *Sacramento Bee* (1954), clipping in KP.
52. "I'm getting fed up with education," he told Chester Teegarden. "I'm thinking forward to a state job so I won't be bothered at nights with any home-work. Then I think my lifting will improve considerably." Kono to Teegarden, April 18, 1949, KP.
53. For context on Teegarden's influence, see

Kim Goss, "Chester Teegarden," *Weightlifting USA* VII, no. 6 (1989), 4.

54. *Ibid.*, and Teegarden to Kono, April 9, 1949, KP. Teegarden also told Tommy that he was "becoming one of the strongest men of your weight in the world. ... I am hoping your youthfulness will not also let you become a silly fool at the same time." Teegarden to Kono, August 5, 1949, KP.

55. See the contrast between the lifts he performed on October 19 and November 15, 1949, Training Logs, KP.

56. Kono to Warren J. Stewart, June 19, 1993, KP.

57. Kono to Teegarden, September 5, 1949, KP.

58. Teegarden to Kono, October 19, 1949, printed in *Bulletin, California Weight Lifters Association* (hereafter *BCWLA*) 4/2 (August 1955): 1.

59. *BCWLA* 1/4 (November 1949): 1. Tommy often alternated bodybuilding with his lifting routine, especially after meets or when he was feeling stale. In August 1950, feeling "shot" and lacking sleep, he was "thinking of bodybuilding for awhile." He wanted to "get big arms" and "massive pectoral" development. Training Notes, August 14 and 16, 1950, KP.

60. *BCWLA* 2/6 (March 1950). Osmo Kiiha notes that, in addition to winning the best lifter award, he snatched 235 pounds on an extra attempt, pressed a pair of 90-pound dumbbells six times, one arm snatched 160 pounds, and squatted four repetitions with 400 pounds at 146½ bodyweight. Kiiha, "Tommy Kono," 7. Ed Yarick records that Tommy at this time squatted 20 repetitions with 360 and 12 with 390 at 153 bodyweight. *IM* 12 (May 1953): 7.

61. Undated note to Teegarden, KP.

62. *BCWLA* 2/7 (April 15, 1950): 2, and 2/8 (April 29, 1950): 2.

63. Kono, "Untitled Typescript," KP, and *BCWLA* 2/8 (April 29, 1950), 2. In addition to a donation by the West Sacramento Athletic Club, the "bulk of the plane fare" was paid by Tommy's parents. Kono, *Weightlifting*, 130.

64. Kono to Teegarden, June 5, 1950, KP.

65. *SH* 18 (July 1950): 11 and 32.

66. *IM* 10 (May/June 1950): 9.

67. *BCWLA* 2/10 (May 1950): 2. Perhaps the most important lesson Tommy learned from this experience was: "The tougher the situation, the more determined you must become to do well." Kono, *Weightlifting Olympic Style*, 131.

68. Kono to Teegarden, June 5 and 26, 1950, KP.

69. Kono to Teegarden, April 18, 1949, and *IM* 9 (March 1949): 26–27 and 45–46.

70. George to Bob Hogue, August 11, 1990, KP.

71. Lawrence Barnholth, *Secrets of the Squat Snatch* (Akron, OH, 1950). Although Pete wrote it, he used Barnholth's name as author to preserve his amateur standing. Training Logs, December 16, 1950, KP.

72. Tommy Kono, "The 'Mind Game,'" KP. The impact of mental preparation on Pete George was later reinforced when he shared sleeping quarters with Teegarden after a meet in Indianapolis.

"Our cots were next to one another, and he gave me a lecture on muscle physiology. He explained how impulses from the brain can contact a few or many muscle fibers per contraction, and the ability to contact more fibers per contraction is the most important way to lift heavier weights. I subsequently, after physiology classes, determined that building strength is a neuromuscular learning process and can be largely influenced by mental attitude." George to the author, January 31, 2017.

73. *BCWLA* 3/4 (September 1950): 2, and *IM* 10 (December 1950): 59–60. By this time the pedagogy conveyed in Barnholth's book was evident in Tommy's training protocol. "Try to conform as closely to Pete George's picture in 'Sq. Snatch' book," he recorded in his training log for December 16, 1950, KP.

74. *Sacramento Union* (1950) and Hoffman to Kono, September 8, 1950, KP.

75. *Pacific Citizen*, September 23, 1950. The loan was secured mainly by a group of high school students who earned the $300 airfare by selling cakes and holding a benefit dance. *Sacramento Bee*, February 24, 2005.

76. Imahara and Meltzer, *Book of Remembrance*, 28, and Grimek to Kono, October 11, 1950, KP.

77. *BCWLA* 3/4 (September 1950): 2 and Kono, "Untitled Typescript," 3. Sarah Fair also relates the following conversation with Tommy's son and daughter when we were retrieving the Kono collection. "The three of us were sitting around looking at family pictures, JoAnn was talking and then hesitated, looked at Mark, and said 'Oh, should we maybe not tell family secrets?' and then decided it was okay to mention that Tommy's mother ended her life—that she was suffering from depression related to menopause and there didn't seem to be any medical help for her back then." Kono conversation notes, November 20, 2016, in author's possession.

78. *BCWLA* 3/9 (1950).

79. Kono, *Weightlifting*, 133–34, and *SH* 20 (January 1952): 22.

80. Kono, *Weightlifting*, 135. That Tommy's hearing was possibly impaired by compulsory practice shooting while a cook is indicated by his unsuccessful claim for a veteran's injury benefit. Kono to Joseph Underdahl, July 6, 1953, and undated response. KP.

81. Kiiha, "Tommy Kono," 7–8.

82. *SH* 20 (April 1952): 8 and 20 and *SH* 20 (May 1952): 8.

83. *SH* 20 (July 1952): 22.

84. *IM* 12/1 (June-July 1952): 7. As Tommy points out, however, his total did not count as a world record since "the rules stated that three or more countries had to be represented." Kono, *Weightlifting*, 136.

85. *SH* 20 (August 1952): 10.

86. *Sacramento Bee*, July 28, 1952.

87. Contrary to popular assumptions, Kono was not a member of the Hawaiian team, promoted by Dr. Richard You, that won the 1952 national

team championships, nor was 1948 Olympic silver medalist Harold Sakata. You's lifters upset Hoffman's York Barbell team that had taken team honors for 20 consecutive years. "I was not on the Hawaii team," Tommy confirms, "but I was able to dethrone a couple of the best lifters so Hawaii's team came up that much more." Tsai, "Tommy Kono Interview," KP. Also see Niiya, "The Nuuanu YMCA," 7.

88. *IM* 12/2 (August–September 1952): 8 and 42–43. A physical examination on June 4 showed that Kono's health was excellent with a blood pressure of 120/68 and 72 pulse at 5'5½" and 158 pounds. KP.

89. *SH* 20 (October 1952): 39.

90. *IM* 12 (May 1953): 46.

91. After his evening meal on July 24, Tommy complained of "a stomach ache which lasted throughout the night. I took all kinds of pills and precaution but was no good. I think it was food poisoning for it was in the stomach & passed on into the lower abdomen (intestine) later on." Training log, July 24, 1952, KP.

92. Kono, *Weightlifting Olympic Style*, 137, and Chris Baker, "Tommy Kono."

93. *Pacific Citizen*, August 23, 1952, and "Tommy Kono Is City's First Individual Winner," newspaper clipping, KP. See also *Pacific Citizen*, December 19, 1952.

94. *SH* 20 (November 1952): 5. Afterwards, Tommy, John Davis, Pete George, and alternate Richard Tomita celebrated by staging an exhibition at a local orphanage before a sizeable crowd. *Honolulu Star-Bulletin* (hereafter *HSB*), August 12, 1952.

95. *Sacramento Union*, December 25, 1952.

Chapter 2

1. *Health and Strength* 141 (October 2015): 19.

2. Tommy Kono, "Weightlifting Paid Off," March 3, 1953, KP.

3. Before departing for Helsinki, Major General William Bergin reminded Tommy that "your conduct, both in the competitions in Helsinki and on the streets of the Olympic Village, will be closely watched by young sportsmen of many nations. You are, in fact, an ambassador without portfolio. Your actions in promoting international good will and friendships among the youth of the world will do much to promote peace." Bergin to Kono, July 7, 1952, KP.

4. Tommy Kono, "My European Tour," KP.

5. Kono to Lou DeMarco, June 28, 2007, KP.

6. Interview with Clyde Emrich, June 2016, Chicago. Although he was not pleased with his lifts, Tommy was gratified by the audience response at an exhibition on September 27 in Zeigelhausen/Heidelberg where he received a small plaque. He also did some posing and muscle control which "really went over big" and drove a nail through a plank. Training Logs, September 27, 1952, KP.

7. Tommy Kono, "Advantage of Disadvantage," March 3, 1953, KP.

8. According to Tommy's written account and that of Osmo Kiiha, he did 248–253.5–330 for an 831.5-pound total which exceeded the world record press of Alexander Nikulin by a pound and Stanczyk's record total by 23 pounds. Data from two authoritative accounts recognize the press record but not the total which both authors recognize was broken by Pete George at the 1953 world championships by 5.5 pounds. See Gottfried Schodl, *The Lost Past* (Budapest, 1992), 217 and 221, and Vladan Mihajlovic, *80 Years of the Weightlifting in the World and Europe, 1896–1976* (Budapest, 1977), 274 and 278.

9. Tommy Kono, "Weightlifting at Copenhagen for Tommy Kono," KP.

10. "Tommy Kono's Middle Weight Career," July 1, 1953, and "My European Tour," KP. Although Tommy followed a rigorous training routine, there is no evidence that it was complemented by a strict dietary standard. On October 7, in transit for a Danish exhibition, he snacked on beefsteak and apple cider, a cheeseburger, coffee and banana split, and "two large weiners." On the train he ate "cookies galore, pear, Coke, etc." On November 21, a day before his competition in Heidelberg, he drank "a Coke & I ate candy bars." Despite his careless diet, his total of 847, while weighing 152 pounds, exceeded his 799 in Helsinki and unofficially broke three middleweight world records. He also engaged in other forms of dissipation the following month in France when he drank whiskey and wine on several occasions and attended a performance of the Folies Bergère. Training Logs, December 11, 13, 14, and 15, 1952, KP.

11. Training Logs, December 1, 8, and 14, 1952, KP.

12. *IM* 12 (May 1953): 9.

13. Random notes, KP.

14. "Kono's Middle Weight Career," 2–3. See also *SH* 22 (May 1953): 16.

15. Training Logs, December 14, 20, and 27, 1952, KP.

16. Tommy Kono, "Weightlifting Paid Off," March 3, 1953, KP; Kiiha, "Tommy Kono," 8–9; *SH* 21 (February 1953), 31; and *SH* 21 (December 1952), 15.

17. "Kono's Middle Weight Career," 3, KP.

18. Tommy Kono, "The Last Performance," KP.

19. Tommy Tamio Kono, "Honorable Discharge from the Armed Forces of the United States of America," March 20, 1953, KP.

20. Statement of Earnings and Deductions, February 1955, and "Notification of Results of Open Examination," June 1954, KP. See also "A Champion," *California Highways and Public Works* 33 (November 1954): 30 and 63.

21. "Report of Performance," Department of Public Works, Division of Highways, State of California, June 12, 1953, to February 15, 1955, KP.

22. Tommy T. Kono, "Separation Qualification Record," KP.

23. "Weightlifting News," *SH* 22 (August 1953): 41.

24. "Kono's Middle Weight Career," 4, KP.

25. *HSB*, May 16, 1953.

26. Training Logs, May 15 and 16, 1953.

27. *Ibid.*, May 17–21, 1953.

28. *HSB*, May 23, 1953.

29. *HA*, March 20, 1955. Initially, he had hoped to extend his visit to Japan for a series of exhibitions. *HSB*, February 18, 1953.

30. Training Logs, June 3, 1953.

31. "Kono's Middle Weight Career," 4.

32. *SH* 22 (September 1953): 9 and 11.

33. *SH* 23 (December 1953): 9, 11, and 39.

34. *Ibid.*, 58.

35. Kono, *Weightlifting*, 141.

36. *SH* 23 (June 1954): 49–50.

37. Untitled memorandum by Kono, February 28, 1954, KP.

38. *SH* 23 (April 1954): 23, and Kiiha, "Tommy Kono," 10.

39. *SH* 23 (June 1954): 17–18.

40. Training Logs, April 24, 1954. A further comeuppance for Tommy came when he trounced Spellman (930–870) at the 1954 Senior Nationals in Los Angeles in June. *SH* 23 (October 1954), 8–10.

41. Training Logs, April 6, 9, 14, and 30, 1954.

42. See *IM* 14 (July 1954): cover, and *IM* 14 (September 1954): 55.

43. *SH* 24 (December 1954): 24.

44. Results du Concours du Plus bel Athlete du Monde, KP. Also at Cayeux's Gym in Paris he put on an exhibition where he clean and jerked the famous 363-pound Apollon Wheels with a 1½" bar and jerked it three times. Training Logs, October 14, 1954, KP.

45. *SH* 24 (February 1955): 52, and *IM* 14 (March 1955): 38.

46. *HA*, November 7, 1954.

47. *HSB*, August 27, 1955. On another occasion, Tommy demonstrated his irregular strength to a United Press International reporter by holding in each hand "a hard rubber ball that I couldn't dent with a hatchet. Tommy constantly squeezed the balls flat as easily as if they were marshmallows." *Sacramento Bee*, December 13, 1957.

48. Kono to Brewer, October 28, 2002, KP.

49. Kiiha, "Tommy Kono," 10–11.

50. Tommy Kono, "General Principle for Improvement on the Press," II, March 18, 1954, 6–7 and 10, KP, and "Training Systems for Improvement on the Press," III, March 24, 1954, 11 and 14, KP.

51. Tommy Kono, "Little Details that Helps for Improvement on the Press," V, May 3, 1954, 24–26, KP.

52. Kono to Reg, April 12 and May 17, 1954, KP.

53. Kono, *Championship Weightlifting*, 185.

54. *Lifting News* 1 (July 1954): 1.

55. Hoffman to Kono, September 8, 1954, Hoffman Papers (hereafter HP). On January 2, 1955, he also attempted to advise his Olympic champion on lifting technique.

56. *IM* 14 (December-January 1954): 8.

57. *SH* 24 (January 1955): 10 and 24.

58. *SH* 24 (March 1955): 8 and 34–35 and *SH* 24 (February 1955): 14, 18, and 40.

59. *SH* 24 (May 1955): 23 and *SH* 24 (June 1955): 24 and 66.

60. *IM* 15 (August–September 1955): 27.

61. *SH* 24 (September 1955): 50 and *SH* 24 (July 1955): 47.

62. *SH* 24 (August 1955): 12–13 and 44.

63. See Dominic G. Morais and Jan Todd, "Lifting the Iron Curtain, Paul Anderson and the Cold War's First Sport Exchange," *IGH* 12 (February/March 2013).

64. *SH* 24 (October 1955): 44 and 47. Though he missed his last clean and jerk, Tommy recorded that he had "never received so much applause after my last clean." Training Logs, June 18, 1955.

65. Tommy never had an intimate friendship with Anderson, but their relationship was always cordial and somewhat jovial. Occasionally the lifters training at York teased Anderson of "being big and slow." One day Kono "goaded him too far, and Andy offered to race Tommy up the steps to the second floor at [their training hall in York] at 51 North Broad Street. So they lined up on the sidewalk outside and took off at the signal—they hit the stairs neck and neck, and it sounded from our office as if the roof was coming in. At the half-way mark there is a turn in the stairs and Paul hit this first, switched gears and roared up the final flight. Tommy couldn't pass him because nobody had room to pass." *SH* 25 (January 1956): 60.

66. See Walter L. Hixson, *Parting the Curtain: Propaganda, Culture, and the Cold War, 1945-1961* (New York, 1997); Arch Puddington, *Broadcasting Freedom: The Cold War Triumph of Radio Free Europe and Radio Liberty* (Lexington, KY, 2000); and Peter Grose, *Operation Rollback: America's Secret War Behind the Iron Curtain* (Boston, 2000).

67. *SH* 15 (August 1947): 4.

68. *SH* 25 (December 1955): 42.

69. "U.S. Weightlifters Stage Impressive Exhibition in Egypt," newspaper clipping in the Hoffman Papers in author's possession. Tommy's log entry perhaps best reveals the Japanese trait of perseverance (ganbaru): "Stomach ache from 3 A.M. So hardly eat & stay in bed. Lift at nite—Tho' weak—feel better." Training Logs, June 26, 1955.

70. *SH* 25 (December 1955): 46–7.

71. Atlee Horner, "Kono Is Moving to Hawaii," *Sacramento Union*, July 15, 1955.

72. Training Logs, July 1, 1955, KP.

73. *SH* 25 (December 1955): 49.

74. Kono to Kanichi Kono, July 3, 1955, KP. During the preceding year Kanichi Kono suffered a stroke which necessitated his retirement. He also became a naturalized citizen. Tommy recalled being shocked by his condition after returning from a trip. "He was always so robust and I never saw him sick in his life but in the time I was gone, he looked like he aged 10 years!" Kanichi died on January 27, 1978, and was buried in a Buddhist ceremony at the Sacramento Memorial Lawn

Cemetery. His death marked the loss of another link with Kono's Japanese American origins. Kanichi Kono, Certificate of Naturalization, No. 7064761, September 1, 1954, Kono, "Early Family History" and "In Remembrance," KP.

75. *SH* 25 (December 1955): 49.

76. Hoffman to Nixon, 20 August 1955, Nixon Papers, Series 320, Box 346, Richard Nixon Presidential Library and Museum, Yorba Linda, California.

77. *SH* 25 (January 1956): 49.

78. Tommy observed to John Grimek that what impressed him most was Anderson's "amazing squatting ability. In the training hall in Munich he took a bar loaded almost to the ends with 20 kilo plates and he did 5 reps of very fast squats; like a rubber ball bouncing up and down, then he would pause to take three breath of air and then squat another 5 reps before replacing the barbell on the rack. He would then sit on the window-ledge for about 15-20 minutes sipping milk, and proceed to perform another set in the same manner. ... Incidentally, he did not warm up to this weight." Kono to Grimek, June 7, 1992, KP.

79. Training Logs, October 31 and November 1, 1955, KP.

80. *SH* 25 (March 1956): 10–11 and 54.

81. Ibid., 56–7.

82. National Archives Records, Group I, box 24, folder 13-IES Digest, 1956, Special Collections, University of Arkansas.

83. *SH* 25 (April 1956): 11 and 52.

84. Clyde Emrich Interview, June 9, 2016, Lake Bluff, Illinois.

85. Interview with Jim George, June 17, 2016, Akron, Ohio.

86. Training Logs, November 12, 1955, KP.

87. *SH* 25 (April 1956), 54–5, and George Interview.

88. "They called me up a half-dozen times to see the muscles I had in my back," Vinci recalls. Chuck Vinci Interview, August 23, 2016, Elyria, Ohio.

89. *SH* 25 (April 1956): 55.

90. USIA Research Reports, 1954–56, National Archives, College Park, Maryland, RG 0306, Container 2.

91. *SH* 25 (July 1956): 42.

92. Training Logs, November 17, 1955, KP.

93. *SH* 25 (July 1956): 43–44.

94. *The Times of India,* November 27, 1955.

95. *SH* 25 (August 1956): 40–2.

96. Training Logs, November 20, 1955, KP.

97. *SH* 25 (October 1956): 9 and 43–4.

98. *SH* 26 (December 1956): 8–9 and 45–7.

99. Emrich and George Interviews.

100. Newspaper clipping in KP.

101. Johnson to Hoffman, n.d., letter in author's possession. See also Barton Horvath, "The Hoffman Expose," *Muscle Builder* 6 (October 1956): 22–7.

102. Three years after the weightlifters' tours, W.J. Lederer and Eugene Burdick published their classic Cold War commentary on American foreign policy. *The Ugly American,* notes sociologist Paul Hollander, conveyed the notion that "Americans abroad, and officials in particular, were both totally ignorant of local customs, social norms, and culture and cheerfully insensitive to the feelings and beliefs of the peoples they were seeking to patronize and defend from the communist threat." William J. Lederer and Eugene Burdick, *The Ugly American* (New York, 1958) and Paul Hollander, *Anti-Americanism: Irrational and Rational* (New Brunswick, NJ, 1995), 39.

103. *SH* 25 (January 1956): 49.

104. *SH* 25 (July 1956): 53.

105. *SH* 25 (August 1956): 44.

106. *HSB,* April 29, 1936, and March 24, 1939. See also *HSB,* May 11, 1935.

107. For a biographical sketch of how You became passionate about weightlifting see Andrew Mitsukado's column in *HA,* July 23, 1953.

108. "A Celebration of Service for Dr. Richard You," March 29, 1996, Nu'uanu Congregational Church, Honolulu, x–xii, KP.

109. "Dr. Richard W. You, Background, Qualifications, Experience, and Achievements," HP, and *SH* 20 (October 1952): 44.

110. Tommy Kono to John and Mike Kono, July 8, 1952, KP, and *HA,* May 12, 1953.

111. You's high regard for Kono was evident in an October 1954 observation in the *HA* that he "waxes poetic and lyrical whenever the name of Tommy Kono, the world champion from Sacramento, California, and a good friend of his is mentioned. 'He is positively the greatest athlete in the world,' Dr. You claims." *HA,* October 21, 1954.

112. *HA,* January 20, 1957, 13.

113. Tsai, "Tommy Kono Interview," KP.

114. *HA,* and "Tommy Kono Arrives," undated newspaper clipping, KP.

115. "In competitive athletics," You believed, diet was "the most important" ingredient to success. "The most common nutritional deficiencies were in proteins, vitamins, especially B-complex, and minerals, notably iron." Food supplements that should be included in an athlete's daily diet are "high protein tablets and powder, multiple vitamin and mineral concentrates, liver, Vitamin B-12, and iron tablets." Richard W. You, "76 Montreal Summer Olympics," KP.

116. Richard W. You, "The Olympic Champion-1976," HP. See also *IM* 15 (May 1956): 16–17. It seems incredulous that iron game patriarch David Willoughby ranked Tommy only 20th in his listing of all-time leading performers in Olympic lifts. David Willoughby, "The All-Time Great Performers in the Three Olympic lifts," *IM* 15 (November 1955): 26.

Chapter 3

1. Mihaly Csikszentmihalyi, *Flow: The Psychology of Optimal Experience* (New York, 1990), 3.

2. Joseph R. Svinth, "Harold Sakata: Olympic Weightlifter and Professional Wrestler," *InYo:*

Journal of Alternative Perspectives (April 2001), https://ejmas.com/jalt/jaltart_svinth_0401.htm.

3. *HA*, March 11, 1956.

4. Dr. Peter T. George, "Eulogy for Tad Fujii," February 12, 1989, KP.

5. Interview with Gary Kawamura, November 10, 2019, Aiea, Hawaii.

6. Ogata to the author, October 12, 2019.

7. Tommy rarely mentions Fujii in his logs, but on April 23, 1958, after complaining that he had "no pep" and "joints all seem sore," he received a "massage on shoulders by Tad Fujii." Training Logs, April 23, 1959, KP.

8. *HA*, October 23, 1955.

9. Kiiha, "Tommy Kono," 12, and *SH* 24 (June 1956): 52.

10. Training Logs, January 13, 16, and 30, and April 7 and 8, 1956, KP.

11. Training Logs, April 14 and May 9 and 19, 1956, KP.

12. Training Logs, April 21, 1956, KP.

13. *SH* 24 (September 1956): 47.

14. Kono to Kasyanov, August 20, 1956, KP. See also "My Training Methods," *Health and Strength* 85/12 (October 11, 1956): 12–13.

15. *SH* 25 (December 1956): 13.

16. Tommy Kono, "The value of proper nutrition in weight training," KP.

17. Training Logs, September 4 and 15, and October 12, 1956, KP.

18. *Sacramento Union*, July 2, 1961, and *HSB*, July 12, 1992.

19. *IM* 16 (January 1957): 12–13.

20. Again he fell far short of his expectations of 318½, 302, and 382½ for a 1003 total. Also, on October 9 his vastus muscles were "sore as hell," a sentiment he frequently repeated before and after the Olympics. On October 17 he couldn't jerk "cause scared of knee." Training Logs, October 5, 9, and 17, 1956, KP.

21. *SH* 16 (February 1957): 60 and *SH* 16 (March 1957): 40. Ironically, while Kono's victory was duly reported by the *Pacific Citizen*, November 30, 1956, more coverage was devoted to George's world record snatch.

22. *SH* 16 (February 1957): 25.

23. Kono, *Weightlifting*, 142.

24. *SH* 25 (June 1957): 23.

25. Kiiha, "Tommy Kono," 13.

26. Training Logs, January 25 and March 20 and 27, 1957, KP. On May 13, Tommy records being "rushed cause of 'date' with Marian."

27. *SH* 25 (October 1957): 13, and *Official Score Book-1957, AAU National Senior Weight-Lifting Championships and Mr. America Competition*, Daytona Beach, Florida, June 22–23, KP.

28. *SH* 25 (November 1957): 18.

29. *SH* 26 (March 1958): 60.

30. Kono to the author, June 10, 1999. An unexpected consequence of his heroic performance in Tehran was a subsequent meeting with the Shah during his visit to Hawaii for an hour and a half at the Royal Hawaiian Hotel to talk about weightlifting. "He knows practically everything there is to know about the game," Tommy observed. "He rattled off the records just like that. He is also familiar with the accomplishments and potential of every outstanding weightlifter in the world. ... I enjoyed every bit of the time I spent with him." *HA*, June 15, 1958.

31. *HA*, November 18, 1957.

32. *Hawaii Herald-Tribune*, November 22, 1957.

33. *Los Angeles Times*, July 25, 1984.

34. *HSB*, March 6, 1958.

35. Kono, *Weightlifting*, 146–50. Tommy recollected that "the only advantage was, with all that continuous flying you didn't get jet-lag. You couldn't ... there were no jet planes." *HSB*, July 23, 1992.

36. Newspaper clipping, KP.

37. *New York Times*, March 24, 1958, 32.

38. *HA*, March 17, 1958.

39. *HA*, February 18, 1958.

40. *SH* 26 (April 1958): 64.

41. *SH* 26 (October 1958): 58–59.

42. Imahara and Meltzer, *Book of Remembrance*, 55.

43. *SH* 26 (September 1958): 62.

44. *SH* 26 (October 1958): 17 and 60.

45. This time Tommy nearly met his goal of a 963-pound total which included lifts of 303, 256, and 374. Training Logs, September 19, 1958, KP.

46. *SH* 27 (February 1959): 18, 43, and 50.

47. Interview with Isaac Berger, October 26, 2016, New York City.

48. *SH* 27 (February 1959): 50.

49. *SH* 28 (March 1960): 13 and 53–54.

50. *IM* 19 (December-January 1959–60): 25.

51. "Resolution," The House of Representatives of the State of Hawaii, October 22, 1959, H.R. No. 101.

52. *HSB*, December 10, 1959.

53. *HA*, December 11, 1959.

54. *IM* 20 (July-August 1960), 24–25. Kinya Noguchi, vice president of the Japanese American Citizen League in Sacramento, expressed his gratitude to YMCA director Vernon Miller for the event, observing that Tommy was "more surprised and happy than anyone else there" and that his father was "humble, but very happy and proud." Noguchi to Miller, nd, KP.

55. "Dad," Presentation by Mark Kono at the induction of Tommy Kono to the Sacramento Sports Hall of Fame, January 26, 2019, transcript in author's possession.

56. *SH* 28 (October 1960): 7–8.

57. *SH* 28 (November 1960): 23.

58. *York Dispatch*, August 6, 1960.

59. "Master at the Weighting Game," *New York Times*, March 24, 1958.

60. *York Dispatch*, August 6, 1960.

61. Kono, *Championship Weightlifting*, 154. Also see *York Sunday News*, August 8, 2004, and Kiiha, "Tommy Kono," 15.

62. *SH* 28 (October 1960): 12.

63. *IM* 20 (July-August 1960): 16.

64. *SH* 29 (February 1961): 15.

65. *SH* 29 (April 1961): 11.

66. *Time*, June 27, 1960, 69–70.
67. *SH* 28 (November 1960): 23.
68. *IM* 20 (July-August 1960): 16.
69. *IM* 20 (September-December 1960): 40.
70. *Time*, September 19, 1960.
71. "Tommy Kono Advises," *Tizkultura i Sport* (May 1961), typescript in KP.
72. *SH* 29 (February 1961): 16. According to Ike Berger, Tommy was suffering from knee problems even before the Melbourne Olympics. "It was one knee, then the other knee gave out," Berger recalls. "I don't remember the year, but I know it was before Melbourne because in Melbourne his knee was bad. He didn't hurt his knee that bad, but even if it's slight it's still a lot." Interview with Berger.
73. Grimek to Ziegler, September 7 and 15, 1960, Ziegler Papers, Olney, Maryland.
74. Those who gained over the Senior Nationals/Olympic Tryouts at Cleveland in June include Chuck Vinci (+60.5), Tommy Kono (+77.25), Jim George (+32.5), Jim Bradford (+44.75), and Norbert Schemansky (+27.25). Those lifting less were Isaac Berger (-11) and John Pulskamp (-36.75). Interview with George. Journalist David Maraniss interviewed Berger and Bradford for his book on *Rome 1960: The Olympics That Changed the World* (New York, 2008), "both of whom made it sound like they had never heard of steroids back then." Maraniss to the author, December 4, 2006.
75. Interviews with John Pulskamp, August, 19, 2016, Santa Barbara, California, Vinci, and Berger.

Chapter 4

1. "Favorite line from Tommy Kono that I quote most often." Val Matsunaga to Kono, February 20, 2016, KP.
2. Interview with George, November 8, 2019, Honolulu.
3. *SH* 29 (April 1961): 24–25.
4. "Tommy Kono Advises," KP.
5. Kiiha, "Tommy Kono," 15, "Kono Invited to Moscow," clipping in KP, and Kono, *Weightlifting*, 154.
6. Kono, *Weightlifting*, 154, and Kono to Hoffman, February 5, 1961, HP.
7. Kono, *Weightlifting*, 154.
8. *HA*, May 21, 1961.
9. *Arizona Daily Star*, newspaper clipping, KP.
10. *Sacramento Union*, July 2, 1961.
11. Hoffman to Kono, April 26 and 27, 1961, HP.
12. Kono to Hoffman, November 14, 1962, KP, and Training Logs, July 16 and 18, 1963, KP.
13. *Amateur Athlete* (April 1962).
14. John D. Fair, *Muscletown USA, Bob Hoffman and the Manly Culture of York Barbell* (University Park, PA, 1999), 253–60.
15. Transcript of Exhibit 1–1, R4-75-0033, recorded on February 24, 1976, by Special Agent Keith D. Earnst, utilizing a Bell and Howell SK-9 Receiver/Recorder. The conversation recorded on Exhibit 1-1 transpired during the purchase of non-drug exhibit H-1 from Dr. Richard You by Special Agents Ululaulani Hu and William Fernandes, at Suite #106, 1270 Queen Emma Street, Honolulu, Hawaii, KP.
16. Interview with George.
17. Kono to Bob Hoffman, May 20, 1971, HP. Interestingly, Riecke's thinking at the outset of his experiments with Dr. Ziegler was similar to Kono's. He was "convinced that a great percentage of lifting is mental." Riecke to Ziegler, October 22, 1960, Ziegler Papers. Tommy later admitted that he was "so naïve I didn't know Riecke was on to something then. I thought he had the right idea about isometric and it worked well for him." Kono to Lou DeMarco, October 28, 1993, KP.
18. Interview with Kono, March 21, 1992, Baton Rouge, Louisiana. For contemporary assessments on the efficacy of these ergogenic aids, see Stuart Auerbach, "Steroids: Superdrugs That Create Supermen, or Havoc?" *Washington Post*, August 20, 1972; Dan Hardesty, "New Exercise Principle Is Now Being Applied to Competitive Sports," *State-Times*, October 4, 1961; "High-Frequency Stimulation Improves Skeletal Muscles," *Medical Tribune*, July 13, 1964; and Terry Todd, "The Jovial Genius of Dr. John Ziegler, *SH* 33 (October 1965): 44–45.
19. Data for this graph are derived from Kiiha, "Tommy Kono," 11–18, and supplementary data in Kiiha, "George Brothers," 31.
20. *HSB*, October 13, 1961.
21. *SH* 30 (February 1962),:14 and *HA*, October 13, 1961.
22. Kono likely lost the title when Veres' 341 press was initially ruled invalid by the judges 2–1 but reinstated by an international appeals jury, 3–2. Kono was unable to make up enough ground in the clean and jerk, usually his ace in the hole, when his adversary did 385, thus exceeding Tommy's total by five kilos. "Veres Beats Kono for Lifting Title," newspaper clipping, KP.
23. Gubner, known for his raw strength, insisted he "never took steroids," thinking his own natural level of testosterone was so high that he did not need drugs. In a follow-up telephone interview, Gubner confirms Kono, Schemansky, and March were taking steroids as often as several times weekly but admits that his "tennis ball welts" reference may have been exaggerated. Interview with Gary Gubner, June 15, 1992, Weston, Connecticut, and telephone interview, June 21, 2016, White Plains, New York. Joe Puleo, on the other hand, who trained with Kono at York in 1962–64, claims that neither he nor Berger were taking steroids during those years. Interview with Puleo, May 2, 1987, Livonia, Michigan.
24. Kono, *Weightlifting*, 154 and 212. See also A. Grove Day, "America's Mightiest *Little* Man," *Coronet* 48 (July 1960): 110.
25. Kono to Hoffman, November 14, 1962, Hoffman Papers. For an analysis of the impact of the new pressing style, see my article, "The Tragic History of the 'Military Press' in Olympic and World Championship Competition, 1928–1972," *Journal of Sport History* 28 (Fall 2001).

26. *HA,* May 12, 1963. Indeed, he continued to perform exercises in training he believed would maximize his strength without aggravating his knees. On December 17 he did two sets of squats for five repetitions with 135 pounds which he found "easy & no effect" on his knees. On the 19th he progressed to double sets with 135 and 185, and thereafter he would increase by 20 or 40 pounds each workout for the two sets: December 21 (185/205) "pumped feeling—good," December 24 (205/225) "easy," December 26 (205/245) "easy," December 28 (225/265) "easy," December 31 (225/285) "easy," January 2 (245/305) "305 was strong," January 4 (265/325) "knees feel swollen—especially the L one," January 7 (285/345) "control my squat so I don't do it too violently on my knees," January 9 (285/365 for 4) "I could have gotten 5 reps but didn't want to push self." Training Logs, December 17, 1962, to January 9, 1963, KP.

27. Tommy Kono to John Kono, nd, KP.

28. *HA,* May 12, 1963.

29. *Sacramento Union,* May 7, 1963.

30. *HA,* May 8, 1963.

31. Three Japanese lifters, Bantamweight Shiro Ichinoseki, Featherweight Yoshinobu Miyake, and Middleweight Hitoshi Ouchi, took first places, and Ichinoseki and Ouchi set junior world records in the clean and jerk and total, respectively. *SH* 31 (October 1963): 15–16.

32. A decade later, he quipped that his knowledge of Japanese was somewhat elementary and antiquated. "They tell me that I speak a Japanese that only grandfathers use now." *HA,* April 28, 1974.

33. Kono Training Logs, August 24, 1962–February 5, 1964, KP.

34. Riecke to Ziegler, March 22 and April 9, 1961, Ziegler Papers. Despite Riecke's "trash talk," his rivalry with Kono was always friendly and sportsmanlike. By contrast, Tommy harshly criticized "the poor display of sportsmanship by the second-place winner in the Mr. America contest," Harold Poole. "I believe one of the greatest lessons to be learned from taking part in sports is that you can lose as well as win." *SH* 31 (October 1963): 7.

35. Kono to the author, May 9, 2005. "A nut" is how Tommy also described Ziegler to Lou DeMarco. "I didn't think much of Ziegler when he made the trip to the World Championships in 1954 because he wanted the team members to tell the Russians he was our new heavyweight!" Kono to DeMarco, October 28, 1993. See also Tommy's "Testimony Against the Use of Steroids," February 22, 1988, KP.

36. *SH* 31 (October 1963): 16. For the context of the 1963 encounter see Fair, *Muscletown,* 224–27.

37. *Harrisburg Patriot-News,* June 30, 1963, 38. At the conclusion of the lift, John Terlazzo observed that Kono, who normally showed little emotion, released "one of the broadest smiles he ever gave." *Muscular Development* 1 (January 1964): 63.

38. Kono, *Weightlifting,* 159.

39. In a caption for a picture in one of his "ABC's of Weightlifting" articles in *Strength & Health,* Kono refers to his Harrisburg triumph as "one of the most dramatic moments in weightlifting history." He is shown at the bottom of a heavy squat clean with grit and determination written all over his face. "Somehow he found the strength and courage to struggle his way out of this low position and fight the jerk, all the way to victory." *SH* 37 (October 1969): 17.

40. Training Logs, July 3, 26, and 31, and August 2 and 5, 1963, KP.

41. *SH* 32 (May 1964): 16.

42. *SH* 32 (January 1964): 75.

43. *HSB,* April 19, 1958.

44. *HSB,* July 12, 1992.

45. Conversation with Florence Kono, November 9, 2016, Honolulu, Hawaii.

46. J.L. Fay to Kono, "Social Security Account Number 554–406672," KP.

47. Interview with Florence Kono, JoAnn and Gary Sumida, November 10, 2019, Honolulu, Hawaii.

48. *SH* 30 (November 1962): 28–29.

49. Interview with Florence Kono, et al. In an obvious attempt to redirect attention from Flo's year-old son, Jamieson, an article in the *HSB* on October 2, 1963, stated that they had been "secretly married for more than a year."

50. Kono to Hoffman, October 6, 1963, KP.

51. Letter to John and Mike Kono, February 14, 1964, KP.

52. The Young Men's Christian Association, Nuuanu Branch, Weight-Lifting Instructor Certificate, May 15, 1951, to May 15, 1962, KP.

53. Kono to Bulgo, July 20, 1963, KP.

54. Bulgo to Kono, August 25, 1963, KP.

55. Letter to John and Mike Kono, February 14, 1964, KP.

56. Letter to John and Mike Kono, March 3, 1964, KP.

57. "Grand Opening of Kono's Health Center on Friday," newspaper clipping, KP.

58. *Maui News,* May 2, 1964, and June 17, 1964.

59. Maui Health Center promotional flyers, KP.

60. Personal Interview Records, KP.

61. Maui Health Center promotional card, KP.

62. See "Keeping Mauians Fit," "Tommy Kono to Show on Maui Tonight," "Free Movies for Strength-Health Fans on Tuesday," newspaper clippings. "Kohala Community Fair" program, April 6 and 7, KP, and "Listen to the Tommy Kono Show Every Friday Morning," *Tommy Kono's Maui Health Center News* I (September 1965): 2.

63. *Maui News,* March 10, 1965.

64. *Maui News,* September 6, 1965.

65. *Maui News,* September 4, 1965. Kono's celebrity status was also recognized in a long-play record titled "Great Moments For Young Americans" that was broadcast on October 5, 1964. It was hosted by television news anchor Hugh Downs and featured Mike Ditka, Bobby Isaac, Stefanie Powers, and other public figures.

66. Tommy and Florence Kono and Russell

Elwell to Friends and Students, December 1964, KP.
67. Kono to Hoffman, June 11, 1964, KP.
68. *Lifting News* 11 (October 1964): 4–6.
69. *Lifting News* 11 (December 1964): 4.
70. *Maui News*, June 12, 1965.
71. Training Logs, May 30, 1963, KP.
72. *Lifting News* 11 (August 1965): 12 and 18, and *SH* 33 (September 1965): 18.
73. Kono, *Weightlifting*, 159.
74. *HA,* March 31, 1984.
75. *HSB*, July 12, 1992.

Chapter 5

1. *Newsweek*, July 22, 1996, 35.
2. Baker, "Tommy Kono."
3. Kono to de la Cerda, January 23, 1965, KP.
4. "Kono Studio Up for Sale," undated newspaper clipping, "Contract Offered by the Mexican Olympic Committee to Mr. Tommy T. Kono, Trainer to Weightlifting," and Mink to Kono, May 13, 1966, KP.
5. "Mexico Trip 'Quite an Ordeal' for Kono Family," KP.
6. *Maui News*, April 30, 1966, and *HSB*, November 1, 1965.
7. *HSB*, January 22, 1969.
8. Tommy Kono, "Progress Report," April 23, 1966, Kono to Jorge Gilling, March 28, 1966, and Centro Deportivo Olímpico Progress Charts, April 15, 1966, KP.
9. Kono to Jorge Gilling Cabrera, KP, and *SH* 34 (September 1966).
10. Kono to Victor Copra, August 13, 1968, KP.
11. Kono to Comité Olímpico Mexicano, October 29, 1966, KP.
12. Tommy Kono, "Training Notes from the 1966 World Championships," KP.
13. Tommy Kono, "Progress Reports, January to December 1966," KP.
14. Tommy Kono, "Report, Performance of the 9 Boys of the C.D.O.M. at the XXX Mexican National Weightlifting Championships," December 30, 1966, KP.
15. Tommy Kono, "Report—Personal," December 28, 1966, KP.
16. Kono to Hoffman, March 14, 1967, KP.
17. Kono to Sáenz, April 24, 1967, and "Contrato Individual De Trabajo," August 10, 1967, KP.
18. Kono to Siegfried Perrey, July 30, 1968, KP.
19. "Recapitulation" [1967], "Servants' Accounts," and Tuition Receipt, University of the Americas, July 1, 1967, KP.
20. Kono to Hoffman, October 15, 1962, HP.
21. Russell Ogata explains that Tommy and Russell Elwell designed the knee bands by cutting neoprene "three inches below and three inches above" the knee. Tommy would then "put those things together and have them all over the apartment, and he would make those and sell those until Bob Hoffman started making them. But he did that because his knees were hurting, but again that goes back to you don't look for the excuses. You just look for the opportunities." Interview with Russell Ogata, November 12, 2016, Honolulu, Hawaii.
22. Tommy Kono, "Slim-Trim Waistband," HP.
23. Kono to Hoffman, March 14, 1967, HP.
24. Kono to Hoffman, April 27 and August 10, 1967, KP.
25. Kono to Terpak, April 14, 1967, and Kono to Hoffman, April 14, 1967, HP.
26. *SH* 29 (November 1961): 30–33.
27. *SH* 35 (June 1967): 46.
28. *SH* 36 (March 1968): 48–49.
29. Monthly Financial Statements, 1966–1971, HP.
30. Interview with Kono.
31. *SH* 45 (August/September 1977): 25–29.
32. Kono to Hoffman, January 3, 1968, HP.
33. Kono, *Championship Weightlifting*, 81.
34. *SH* 34 (November 1966): 30–31; *SH* 34 (September 1966): 38; *SH* 34 (October 1966): 46–47; and *SH* 35 (February 1967): 40–41.
35. See "Decals," *SH* 36 (February 1968): 75.
36. Kono to Hoffman, March 14, 1967, HP. Kono likely attributed the delays in his payments to York treasurer Mike Dietz who "was really tight with the money and probably cockroaching it. Nobody liked him." Author's interview with Kono. Eventually Tommy received payment of $1,529 for articles appearing from February 1967 to March 1968. Terpak to Kono, May 25, 1968, KP.
37. *SH* 35 (November 1967): 46. *SH* 35 (May 1967): 16–17; *SH* 35 (July 1967): 14–15; *SH* 36 (April 1968): 22–23; *SH* 36 (May 1968): 24–25; and *SH* 36 (July 1968): 28–29.
38. *SH* 34 (November 1966): 16–17.
39. Kono to Hoffman, July 1967, KP.
40. *SH* 35 (December 1967): 15–18 and 59–65, and "Information on Tommy T. Kono, Achievements of CDOM Boys (1966–1967), KP.
41. *SH* 35 (December 1967): insert.
42. Tommy Kono, Training Logs, Mexico, KP.
43. Kono to Hoffman, January 3, and 21, 1968, KP.
44. Kono to Victor A. Copra, August 13, 1968, KP. Privately, however, he confided to Imahara that Mateos' performance, and that of American featherweight Dan Cantore, in Los Angeles was "miserable." Although Mateos out-lifted Cantore by 10 pounds, "he walked around too much (trying to buy up everything in town) so he was sluggish." Kono to Imahara, August 7, 1968, Imahara Papers.
45. *IM* 28 (January 1969): 49.
46. *SH* 37 (January 1969): 15.
47. Freeman to Kono, November 18, 1968, KP.
48. Kono to Oscar State, January 28, 1970, KP.
49. Kono to Peter, June 19, 1968, and Perrey to Re, June 20, 1968, KP.
50. Kono to Peter, July 15, 1968, KP.
51. Kono to Perrey, July 30, 1968, and November 10, 1968, KP.
52. Perrey to Kono, December 20, 1968, KP.
53. Kono to Perrey, January 6, 1969, Perrey to Kono, January 15, 1969, and Kono to Dieter Seibold, February 19, 1969, KP.

54. Geesa to Perrey, March 3, 1969, and Theresa Mravintz to Kono, March 24, 1969, KP.

55. Inouye to Kono, April 22, 1969, and William Macomber, May 6, 1969, KP.

56. *HSB*, January 22, 1969.

57. *Stars and Stripes*, May 2, 1969, and Kono to Lippold, May 26, 1969, KP.

58. Kono to Neckermann, January 8, 1970, KP.

59. Kono to Tomas Lempart, Otto Schumann, and Wolfgang Peter, February 17, 1971, and Tommy Kono to Florence Kono, February 1, 1971, KP.

60. T. Kono, "XXXth European Weightlifting Championships," June 19–27, 1971, and "Deutsche Jr., vs Bulgarian Jr.," September 4, 1971, KP.

61. *HSB*, September 30, 1971.

62. Kono to Otto Schumann, October 10, 1971, KP.

63. Training Logs, November 7, 10, 12, and 15, 1970, KP.

64. Kono to Otto Schumann, November 14, 1971, KP. Though not normally vindictive, Tommy included a caricature of "Schumann" being crushed under a torture device labeled *Auch er kann nicht unter Druck arbeiten* (He too cannot work under pressure) in his papers.

65. Kono to Hoffman, September 9, 1969, HP. Tommy also tried to facilitate a contract between York and Adidas. Kono to Terpak, October 22, 1970, HP.

66. Kono to Hoffman, October 4, 1969, HP, and Kono, *Weightlifting*, 196.

67. Kono to Terpak, October 13, 1970, HP.

68. Terpak to Kono, November 21, 1970, HP.

69. Kono to Hoffman, May 20, 1971, HP.

70. It was not till about 1975 that Kono became aware that Bob's senility was setting in. Interview with Kono.

71. Kono to Terpak, October 19, 1971, HP.

72. Kono to Terpak, November 14, 1971, with enclosures of Oscar State to J.W. Westerhoff, January 24, 1967, and Fulton Freeman to Kono, November 18, 1968, HP.

73. You to Kono, November 23, 1971, KP.

74. Crist to Kono, January 20, 1972, and Kono to Crist, June 20, 1972, KP.

75. Crist to Johnson, December 28, 1971, and Crist to Terpak, May 5, 1972, HP.

76. Knipp to Kono, July 10, 1972, Kono to Knipp, July 21, 1972, and Knipp to Kono, August 5, 1972, HP.

77. Crist to Kono, July 20, 1972, HP, and *Long Island Press*, September 6, 1972.

78. *SH*, 40 (December 1972), 74. It is hardly surprising that Kono's report of the Olympics and departing comments to his nemesis Otto Schumann were brief and critical of the German program. Kono to Schumann, October 29, 1972, KP.

79. Crist to Rudy Sablo, September 21, 1972, and Crist to Terpak, September 22, 1972, HP, and Interview with Bob Crist, August 11, 2016, Hampton, Virginia.

80. Kono to Crist, September 19, 1972, and Kono to Young Suk Ko, September 24, 1972, KP.

81. Crist to Kono, October 19, 1972, and Stevens to Kono, October 24, 1972, KP.

82. Kono to Levin, January 8, 1989, KP.

83. Kono to Berger, November 14, 1973, KP.

84. *SH* 42 (March 1974): 5 and 80.

85. *SH* 42 (June-July 1974): 9.

86. Kono to Hoffman, February 28, 1974, HP.

87. *HA*, April 28, 1974.

88. Bob Crist, "July Newsletter," July 5, 1973, AAU No. 73-96, Crist Papers.

89. *SH* 42 (January 1974): 34.

90. Hoffman to Kono, October 7, 1973, KP.

91. *SH* 42 (February 1974): 41–42.

92. *New England Association AAU—Weightlifters' Newsletter* 22 (December 24, 1973): 1 and 4–6. In his rebuttal to the athletes' report John Terpak defended his actions as coach and explained how their grievances lacked merit. *SH* 42 (August-September 1974): 8–9.

93. See Fair, *Muscletown*.

94. Kono to Crist, March 30, 1973, KP.

95. Kono to Hoffman, February 28, 1974, HP.

96. Crist, "Coaches and Officials Clinic," July 19, 1974, AAU Notice #74-90, Crist Papers.

97. Onuma to Kono, June 5, 1975, KP.

98. "Minutes of USOC Weightlifting Committee Meeting," June 21, 1975, HP.

99. Kono to Hoffman, May 18, 1975, HP.

100. *HSB*, December 3, 1975.

101. Kono to Ogata, March 17, 1976, KP. At first, when he was "a thin asthmatic boy," he "dreamed of becoming strong," Tommy told a local reporter. "Then I wanted to someday coach the U.S. Olympic team. I took the long road to reach my goal—always with the help, training and encouragement of Dr. You." *HSB*, June 15, 1976.

102. Mark Cameron, Athletes' Report, March 2, 1976, KP.

103. "Kono optimistic after lift meet," newspaper clipping, KP.

104. Kono to David Matlin, March 8, 1976, Kono to Wilhelm, March 10, 1976, and Kono to State, April 8, 1976, KP.

105. Kono to "Lifters," April 30, 1976, and Kono to Olympic Team Candidates, June 1, 1976, KP; and "Minutes of the USOC Weightlifting Committee," June 18, 1976, Crist Papers.

106. Interview with Bruce Wilhelm, June 17, 2019, San Carlos, California.

107. Tommy Kono, "U. S. Olympic Weightlifting Team Report," October 1, 1976, HP. See also *SH* 44 (August/September 1976): 38, and *SH* 44 (October/November 1976): 10.

108. *SH* 45 (December/January 1976-77): 33.

109. To confirm Green's testimony, I asked the following: JF—"You're saying that Lee James avoided the testing by leaving?" BG—"Yes." JF—"Before he got tested?" BG—"Yes." JF—"And he was still able to claim a medal?" BG—"Now you can't do it. As soon as you lift they follow you. They grab your coat tail and walk off with you. Not then. This was the first year. They didn't have it down." Interview with Green, November 1, 2012, Dadeville, Alabama.

110. Kono, "Olympic Team Report," HP.
111. *New England & Region 1—Weightlifter's Newsletter* 39 (January 24, 1976): 17.
112. Crist to Matlin, April 7, 1976, Crist Papers.
113. Interview with Carl Miller, February 5, 2012, Santa Fe, New Mexico.

Chapter 6

1. Viktor Frankl, *Man's Search for Meaning* (Boston, 2006), xiv–xv.
2. "Employment Opportunity with The City and County of Honolulu," Recreation Specialist III (Physical Fitness) explanatory notice; Personnel Action Authorization, Department of Civil Service, November 15, 1973, and July 15, 1977; Probationary Appraisal Report, October 20, 1973; and Performance Evaluation Report, October 29, 1976, KP.
3. Interview with Mike Mizuno, November 15, 2016, Aiea, Hawaii.
4. *Ibid.*
5. Tommy Kono, "Developing Muscle Size and Strength," KP.
6. Health & P.E. Committee Minutes, December 13, 1972, KP.
7. Kono to Richard Harkins, February 5, 1973, and Kono to Crist, January 7, 1973, KP.
8. Kono to Crist, February 19, 1973, KP.
9. Kono to Tamanaha, April 29, 1973, KP.
10. Kono to Crist, June 25, 1973, KP.
11. Kono to Berger, November 14, 1973, KP.
12. *SH* 42 (October 1974): 51 and *SH* 43 (December 1974): 63.
13. See LaVerne Senyo Sasaki, *Out of the Mud Grows the Wisteria* (privately printed, 2019), 118.
14. Kono to Yamauchi, June 13, 1974, KP.
15. Interview with Kono lifting friends, November 12, 2016, Honolulu, Hawaii.
16. "Inmates Thank Tommy Kono," *Honolulu Employee Journal* (June 1975): 7.
17. "Scotty Shumann Award, 1976," KP, *Sunday Advertiser-Bulletin*, April 24, 1977, and Jimmy Carter, "Presidential Sports Award," Jogging and Weight Training, July 1977, KP.
18. Interview with Mizuno.
19. Steven Todd, to Jim Barahal, June 6, 1993, KP.
20. *HA*, November 16, 1957.
21. Interview by Michael Tsai, February 27, 2014, KP.
22. Paul Drewes, "History of the Honolulu Marathon," December 17, 2015, *KITV Island News*, http://www.kitv.com/story/30609620/history-of-the-honolulu-marathon. For a more in-depth explanation of the origins of the marathon and Tommy's role in it see Steven C. Todd to Dr. Jim Barahal, 6 June 1993, and Interview by Tsai, KP. See also *HA*, December 11, 1983.
23. Maya Avrasin, "Setting the Stage for a Special Event," *Parks and Recreation* 40 (2005), and Michael S.K.N. Tsai, *The People's Race Inc.: Behind the Scenes at the Honolulu Marathon* (Honolulu, 2016), 21.
24. Kono to Grimek, December 11, 1977, KP.
25. Jeanette Chun to the author, January 6, 2016. See also "Honolulu Marathon Association Job Description of Tommy Kono," KP.
26. Application for Mortgage Loan, International Savings & Loan Association, and Expenses per Month, February 21, 1973, KP.
27. Tommy and Florence Kono, U.S. Individual Income Tax Return, 1973, KP.
28. Disclosure Statement of Loan, April 30, 1973, KP.
29. Kono to Shoma Hotta, February 27, 1973, KP, and Florence R. Kono, "Notification of Personnel Action," September 24, 1976, KP.
30. Hubert V. Eberly to Kono, Jul 31, 1973, KP.
31. Tommy Kono, "Total Income—1974," and Tommy & Florence Kono, U.S. Individual Tax Return, 1976, KP.
32. Interview with Florence Kono and joAnn and Gary Sumida.
33. Tommy to John and Mike Kono, December 31, 1975, KP.
34. Kono to Onuma, October 13, 1975, KP, and *SH* 26 (October 1958): 16–17.
35. Tommy to John and Mike Kono, December 31, 1975, KP.
36. "In Remembrance," Funeral Service Brochure, January 30, 1976, KP.
37. Interview with Florence Kono and joAnn and Gary Sumida. Walter Imahara observes a stern demeanor was characteristic of Japanese males and usually led to discord in marriages with Caucasian females. His father was that way. Interview with Imahara, October 4, 2021, Baton Rouge, Louisiana.
38. Interview with Mark Kono, March 24, 2019, San Francisco.
39. *Ibid.*
40. *Ibid.*
41. Kono to Onuma, March 30, 1976, KP.
42. Tommy to John and Mike Kono, November 15, 1977, KP.
43. *SH* 45 (November 1977): 10 and 14.
44. Kono to John Grimek, December 11, 1977, KP, and *SH* 46 (May 1978): 42.
45. *SH* 46 (March 1978): 36.
46. *SH* 46 (March 1978): 14 and *SH* 46 (May 1978): 37.
47. *Sports Illustrated* 48 (February 27, 1978): 60–68.
48. Kono to Spitz, April 6, 1978, KP.
49. *HA*, March 13, 1983.
50. Tsai interview with Kono.
51. *HSB*, March 28, 1986.
52. *HA*, June 7, 1987.
53. Kono to Spitz, April 6, 1978, KP.
54. Kono to Ziegler, February 5, 1978, KP.
55. Kono to Spitz, April 6, 1978, KP.
56. joAnn Kono as conveyed to Sarah Fair, November 10, 2016, Aiea, Hawaii.
57. Interview with Mark Kono.
58. Kono to Spitz, April 6, 1978, KP. Aside from

his ailing knees and relative physical activity, Tommy's overall health remained good at age 47 with bodyweight of 167¾ pounds and blood pressure of 138/78. "Physical Fitness Evaluation," March 29, 1978, KP.

59. "Seller's Instructions," First Escrow Corporation, May 2, 1978, and U.S. Department of Housing and Development Settlement Statement, June 7, 1978, KP.

60. "1978," KP.

61. See Wayne W. Weber, "Certificate of Appreciation," February 1977; Theodore E. Vitori, "Letter of Appreciation," July 3, 1978; and "Performance Evaluation Report," April 24, 1979, KP.

62. Kono to Levin, May 22, 1978, KP.

63. Kono to Gunter, Happy, and Miki, June 5, 1978.

64. "Total Image," December 31, 1977.

65. *SH* 27 (March 1959): 14–15.

66. Kono to Omokawa, June 16, 1974.

67. https://www.kawasaki-net.ne.jp/kobs/files/sakkou_en.pdf.

68. https://www.bizapedia.com/hi/kio-company-inc.html.

69. Interview with Florence Kono, JoAnn Sumida, and Gary Sumida.

70. Kono to Onuma, November 8, 1977, KP.

71. Onuma to Kono, August 22, 1978, and April 16, 1979, KP.

72. Kono to Onuma, July 8, 1979, KP.

73. Ibid.

74. Onuma to Kono, September 3, 1979, KP.

75. *SH* 47 (November 1979): 39 and *SH* 49 (January 1981): 17.

76. To learn how a mawashi (loincloth) should be prepared and worn, Tommy consulted local sumo expert John Jocques who advised him that "unless the canvas is made in width of the right size it will fray." Kono to John Aronson, May 8, 1982, KP.

77. *HA*, October 31, 1979, and Kono to David Brown, November 3, 1979, and Kono to Spitz, November 14, 1979, KP.

78. Tommy Kono, "IWF Invitational Superheavyweight Championship Report, Tokyo, Japan, December 1, 1979," KP. See also "Super Lifting in Tokyo," *SH* 48 (May 1980): 33.

79. "Some Recent Achievements of Tommy Kono," 1983, KP.

80. Murray Levin, AAU Notice #80-60, *Denis Reno's Weightlifter's Newsletter* 80, December 6, 1980.

81. Nora Moore Lloyd to Kono, July 27, 1982, KP.

82. Mario J. Machado to Kono, May 6, 1982.

83. *World Weightlifting* 2 (1982), 38.

84. *HSB*, August 6, 1982.

Chapter 7

1. Kono to Wesley Barnett, February 21, 1994, KP.

2. Kono to Levin, October 16, 1981, KP.

3. Okada to Kono, December 29, 1981, KP, and *The Maui News*, January 5, 1982.

4. Kono to Okada, January 17, 1982, and Okada to Kono, February 3, 1982, KP.

5. Okada to Kono, February 21, 1982, KP.

6. *SH* 50 (August 1982): 10.

7. Interviews with Myamoto, Ogata, and DeMello, November 12, 2016, Honolulu.

8. Mike Harada, "Tribute to Tommy Kono," KP.

9. Ogata to Kono, March 24, 1982, KP.

10. "U.S. Weightlifting relocates in Colorado Springs," *USWF Newsline* 1 (April 1982): 1–2.

11. Kono to Newton, May 12 and 14, 1982, KP.

12. You to Moomaw, August 7, 1982, KP.

13. Moomaw to Anderson, April 20, 1983, KP.

14. Kono to Schmidt, August 15, 1984, KP.

15. USWF 1985 Financial Reports, United States Amateur Weightlifting Foundation, 1985, and Digest of Minutes, USWF National Convention, Board of Governors Meeting, May 6, 1985, HP. See also Peter Ueberroth, *Made in America: His Own Story* (New York, 1985).

16. Kono to Onuma, November 14, 1979, KP.

17. Berger to Kono, December 4, 1980. KP.

18. Kono to Berger (with advertisement copy), February 12, 1981, and You to Berger, May 15, 1981, KP.

19. *Parade*, July 19, 1992.

20. "Agreement," August 21, 1980, and "Exclusive Distribution Agreement," April 1, 1982, KP.

21. "Treasurer's Report from December 1981 to December 1982," KIO Company, KP.

22. Onuma to Kono, August 15, 1985, and Kono to Onuma, November 4, 1985, KP.

23. See Yoshihide Hagiwara, *Green Barley Essence* (New York, 1998), 22.

24. "T. Kono's 1983 Barley Green Biz," KP.

25. "Employee Notification of the Adjustment of Past Wages and Taxes," October 15, 1984; "Earnings and Interests" (1981); "Income" (1982); "Flo's Income and T.K.'s Income" (1983); "Individual Income Tax Return, 1981"; and "Individual Income Tax Return, 1983," KP.

26. Kono to Spitz, July 4, 1983, KP.

27. June Watanabe, "Keep the Shutterbugs Snapping," *HSB*, July 6, 1981.

28. "NPC 'Mr. Hawaii' Physique Contest Information" and "Maui Women's Bodybuilding Championships," August 7, 1982, KP.

29. "1st Annual Physiques Bodybuilding Classic," and Cathy Chang to Kono, August 26, 1983, KP.

30. Cathy Chang to AFWB Members et. al., *AFWB Newsletter* (April 1984): 3.

31. Kono to Athletic Director/Coach, February 2, 1983, KP.

32. Kono to Studio, Spa, and Gym Owners, June 8, 1983, KP.

33. Minutes of the Meeting of the Board, Hawaiian Association AAU, September 12, 1983, KP.

34. *HSB*, February 22, 1983. Kono's involvement with this booster organization was likely the result of his association with Dr. You, who

was instrumental, while a member of the Board of Regents in the early 1960s, in reviving the football program at the University of Hawaii.

35. House Resolution No. 290, March 4, 1983, House of Representatives, Twelfth Legislature, State of Hawaii.

36. Harvey Newton to Kono, March 9, 1983, KP. Although he was unable to attend the awards banquet at the Red Lion Hotel, a retrospective recognition came on May 30, 1984, with his induction into the Sacramento Athletic Hall of Fame. Dusty Miller to Kono, January 31, 1984, and Kono to Miller, February 26, 1984, KP.

37. Kono to Imahara, February 23, 1983, KP.

38. Kono to Lolotai, November 12, 1986, and "1986 Hawaii Open Olympic Weightlifting Championships Result," KP.

39. Kono to Ogata, January 11, 1987, KP.

40. Tommy Kono, "Report, 1987 Moomba Weightlifting International Tournament," March 7–8, 1987, Hawthorn, Australia, KP.

41. *Weightlifting USA* V (1987), 1.

42. Kono to Levin, April 29, 1987, KP.

43. Kono to Ajan, April 11, 1988, KP.

44. Interview with Mizuno. To appreciate Tommy's attachment to the Nuuanu YMCA, see his unpublished account on "The Nuuanu YMCA and the Glory Days of Hawaii Weightlifting," KP.

45. Kono to Nishihara, January 11, 1987, KP, and *Denis Reno's Weightlifter's Newsletter* 136 (May 16, 1987): 26.

46. Nishihara to Kono, May 5, 1987, KP.

47. "Team Hawaii, Olympic Weightlifting Recruitment Information," KP.

48. Kono to Ogata, January 11, 1987, KP.

49. Interview with Natalie Mew, February 10, 2019, Portland, Oregon. Natalie also recalls some of his favorite aphorisms. "He always told me, 'Practice doesn't make perfect. Perfect practice makes perfect.' He also preached that if you do not perform a technique correctly, you would have to repeat the correction 40 times to retrain your muscle memory." Mew to the author, February 16, 2019.

50. Kono to Board of Directors, March 26, 1986, and Kono to "Karen," October 13, 1985, KP.

51. Kono to You, December 16, 1985, KP.

52. *USA Weightlifting* 27 (Fall 2008): 18–19.

53. Kono to U.S. Women Weightlifters-Elite Group, August 14, 1987, KP.

54. "Training Camp Plan" and Kono to U.S. Weightlifting Team Members, September 14, 1987, KP.

55. Training Camp Evaluation, Team Captain Vote, KP.

56. Levin to author, November 12, 2016.

57. Telephone interview with Sibby Flowers, December 6, 2016, Knoxville, Tennessee. No less exemplary of Tommy's coaching style was his response to a query from Lynne Stoessel, who finished third in her class at the women's nationals, about controlling nervousness. Tommy advised that "you must learn to concentrate; be able to block out the audience and even the officials." Kono to Stoessel, August 8, 1987, KP.

58. In a postscript, Robin thanked Tommy for "seeing the good in John" Coffee, her local coach. "Too many people overlook him because of his appearance but he is an intelligent, caring man and I respect him greatly." Byrd to Kono, 25 September 1988. Decades later, Melanie Getz was no less grateful. "I miss our chats, talks etc. You taught me *so* much about not just wts but training and about me (as a person)." Getz to Kono, December 17, 2007, KP.

59. Kono to "Lifters," October 2, 1987, KP.

60. Kono to Kim, October 2, 1987, KP.

61. *USA Weightlifting* 25 (2006), 26. One of the American coaches who opposed Levin's initiatives was Jim Schmitz of San Francisco's Sports Palace. "He fought me at every meeting," Levin recalls, "but when the meet was over and we had that world success party he came over to me and apologized." Levin to author, November 12, 2016.

62. Kono to Team Members, November 10, 1987, KP.

63. Drechsler, "A Brief History," 19.

64. Newton to the author, January 2, 2017.

65. Newton to Kono, November 9, 1987, KP.

66. Kono to Levin, November 20, 1987, KP.

67. Kono to Byrd, October 3, 1988, and Kono to Team Members, October 27, 1988, KP.

68. Kono to Jim Schmidt, George Greenway and the Board of Directors, December 30, 1988, KP.

69. Kono to Team Members, December 14, 1988, KP.

70. Interview with John Coffee, October 2016, Marietta, Georgia.

71. Kono to Jim Schmidt, George Greenway and the Board of Directors, December 30, 1988, KP.

72. Kono to Team Members, August 4 and 9, 1989, KP.

73. Interview with Coffee.

74. *Weightlifting USA* VII, no. 5 (1989), 4.

75. "Colorado Springs Questionnaire on Training Camp," September 25–30, KP.

76. Marshall to Kono, October 12, 1989, KP. Marshall went on to place third in the 1991 world championships in Donaueschingen, Germany, but tested positive for taking stanozolol, an IOC banned substance, and was suspended from all USWF activities for two years. *Weightlifting USA* X, no. 2 (May 1992): 5.

77. Kono to Jim Schmidt, George Greenway and the Board of Directors, October 8, 1989, and "Manager's Report," October 2, 1989, KP.

78. *Weightlifting USA* VII, no. 6 (1989), 12–13.

79. *Denis Reno's Weightlifter's Newsletter* 159 (December 9, 1989): 11.

80. *Weightlifting USA* VII, no. 5 (1989), 9–15.

81. Interview with Walter Imahara, October 2, 2016, St. Francisville, Louisiana. Coping with tears presented a special problem for Tommy. "It could be from anxiety, from frustration, from happiness or for no reason at all. It is a woman's way of being able to 'let go.' You will not find this happening with the male lifters, and, unless you are prepared

for it, it will really throw you off guard when tears well in your female lifter's eyes." Kono, *Championship Weightlifting*, 63.

82. Telephone interview with Pete Miller, October 2016, Arlington, Virginia.

83. Kono to Levin, November 20, 1987, KP.

84. Interview with Harada.

85. Kono, *Championship Weightlifting*, 62–63.

86. Beth Terry, "Focus on the Future," KP.

87. Kono to Greenway, August 29, 1989, KP.

88. Kono to Greenway, October 23, 1989, and Tommy Kono, "TK Loading Master," KP.

89. Kono to USWF Board of Directors, January 17, 1989, KP.

90. Kono to Reno, May 16, 1990, KP, and *Weightlifting USA* VIII, no. 3 (1990), 10–11.

91. Kono to Jim Schmitz, George Greenway, Lyn Jones, and USWF Board of Directors, August 30, 1990, KP.

92. Kono to Mah, September 13, 1990, KP.

93. Kono to Kenneally, September 17, 1990, KP.

94. Kono to Zurek, October 7, 1990, and Zurek to Kono, October 14, 1990, KP.

95. Getz to Kono, September 7, 1990, KP.

96. Kono to USWF National Office, September 12, 1990.

97. John Saito, Jr., "Hawaii's Chad Ikei Sets Festival Record," *RAFU* newspaper clipping, KP, and *The Hawaii Herald*, November 10, 2014.

98. V. Jo Hsu, "Takes a Village: Interview with Vernon Patao," *Iron Athlete*, December 13, 2016, https://www.ironathleteclinics.com/takes-village-interview-vernon-patao/.

99. "Mr. Oahu and Mr. High School-Hawaii," April 9, 1989; "1990 Hawaii Open Weightlifting Championships," October 13, 1990; and Kono to Honorable Mazie Hirono, March 2, 1990, KP.

100. Individual Income Tax Returns for 1986 and 1987, and Performance Evaluation Report, April 5, 1988, KP.

101. Tommy to John and Mike Kono, August 19, 1987, KP. Scottish physical culturist David Webster confirmed after his 1982 visit to Hawaii that "our hero is in great shape" and "still trains three times weekly, preferably at home for when he goes to the gym he generally finds himself neglecting his personal training in order to assist others." "Posing in Paradise," *Dave Webster's World of Weights*, nd, 12.

102. Kono to Toomey, August 10, 1987, KP.

103. Kono to Onuma, March 4, 1990, KP.

104. Eugene Itogawa to Kono, August 10, 1988, KP.

105. Ishizuka to Kono, August 6, 1990, KP.

106. Kono to Rudy Riska, August 8, 1990, KP.

107. *HA*, June 11, 1991, and *HSB*, December 23, 1993.

108. "Tommy Kono Testimonial Dinner," Honolulu Japanese Chamber of Commerce, September 9, 1990; Inouye to Kono, September 9, 1990; Saiki to Kono, September 9, 1990; Waihee to Kono, September 9, 1990; Ajan to Kono, September 10, 1990; Grimek to Kono, nd; Park to Kono, nd; Yarick to Kono, nd; Peary and Mabel Rader to Kono, August 28, 1990; and Resolution, The Council of the City and County of Honolulu, July 26, 1990, KP.

109. Schwarzenegger to Kono, September 6, 1990, KP. For an explanation of Arnold's special connection with Hawaii, see *IGH* 11 (September 2009): 13–14.

110. George Bush, October 1990, KP.

Chapter 8

1. Kono to Robin Byrd Goad, November 5, 1995, KP.

2. *Weightlifting USA* 6 (1988), 1, and *Weightlifter's Newsletter* 134 (February 28, 1987): 11.

3. *Weightlifting USA* 6, no. 6, 1, and *Weightlifting USA* 8, no. 5 (1990), 5.

4. *Weightlifting USA* 9, no. 1 (1991), 14, and *Weightlifting USA* 10, no. 1 (1992), 22–23.

5. *Weightlifter's Newsletter* 157 (September 16, 1989): 4.

6. *Weightlifting USA* 9, no. 4 (1991), 2; *Weightlifting USA* 9, no. 6 (December 1991): 2; and *Weightlifting USA* 10, no. 4 (September 1992): 2.

7. *Weightlifter's Newsletter* 177 (December 14, 1991): 20–21.

8. Nick Place, "Coming Soon: Our Guarantee of Gold," *Sunday Herald* (Melbourne), December 30, 1990, cited in *Weightlifter's Newsletter* 170 (February 23, 1990): 6.

9. *Weightlifter's Newsletter* 274 (December 21, 2002): 12 and 21.

10. "Editorial," *World Weightlifting* 16 (1996/2), 2–3, and *Weightlifter's Newsletter* 199 (May 15, 1994): 15.

11. Kono to Levin, September 3, 1979, KP.

12. Drechsler to Kono, nd, and Kono to Drechsler, July 25, 1988, KP.

13. Garhammer to Hirtz and Charniga, August 28, 1988, KP.

14. Levin to Garhammer, September 29, 1988, KP.

15. Newton to Kono, February 10, 1989, KP.

16. Kono to Greenway, January 25, 1991, and Greenway to IWF Category I Referees, October 1, 1991, KP.

17. Kono to Ajan, December 17, 1991; Ajan to Greenway, March 18, 1992; and Ajan to Kono, November 23, 1992, KP.

18. *Weightlifting USA* XI, no. 3 (July 1993): 24–25.

19. Snethen to Kono, June 23, 1993, and Kono to Snethen, June 30, 1993, KP.

20. Kono to Thrush, July 8, 1993, KP.

21. "Team Selection Criteria, Oct. 15–17, 1993 USWF Board Meeting," KP.

22. *Weightlifting USA* 11 (January 1994): 12–22.

23. Tommy Kono, "International Representation," KP.

24. As an aside to Tommy, Stoessel-Ross informed him that he was continuing to have an impact. "Although you were not 'officially' copied on this letter, I wanted you to see it. Perhaps

this is where Chad [Ikei] gets his ideas from." Stoessel-Ross to Jones, July 18, 1994, KP.

25. Kono to Jones, January 13, 1991, KP.

26. Kono to Fellow Weightlifters, January 10, 1991, KP.

27. Competition Information Sheets for Chad Ikei, Phyllis Nishimoto, and Rae Nakasone, TP, and "1991 National Championships," *Weightlifting USA* IX, no. 2 (1991), 13.

28. "Coaching Production Record," February 3, 1992, KP.

29. Tseu to Kono, February 18, 1993, and Jim Schmitz to Tseu, March 27, 1993, KP.

30. Kono to Athletic Directors and Coaches, February 18, 1993, KP.

31. Kono to Henry, August 15, 1993, KP.

32. Kono to Barnett, February 21, 1994, KP. Responding to Tommy's chiding about leadership, Barnett stated that he tried to "create a positive example for everyone, but I refuse to let them be misled in telling them that all is fair and we are just not lifting enough weights to compete with other countries. I feel that if this is what the general consensus is amongst yourself and other board members, you are all being very naïve." Barnett to Kono, n.d., KP.

33. Kono to Barnett, March 20, 1994, KP.

34. Kono to Isaacs and Miyamoto, April 17, 1995, KP.

35. Kono to Johnson, July 20, 1994, KP.

36. Kono to Rentmeester, July 24, 1994, KP.

37. Kono to Smith, July 30, 1995, KP.

38. Several years later, Drechsler expressed admiration for Kono as "one of the few who are willing to stand up for what's right in the Federation and speak the truth. …. I'll always remember that when the time came to stand up to Lyn at his contract renewal, only one man stood beside me." Drechsler to Kono, November 22, 1998, KP.

39. Kono to Smith, October 16, 1995, and Kono to Drechsler, October 25, 1995, KP.

40. Kono to Oyafuso, October 30, 1996, KP.

41. Kono to Byrd-Goad, November 5, 1995, KP.

42. Kono to Polakowski, December 27, 1995, KP.

43. *Ibid.*

44. Further to solidify his political alliances, Tommy was able to room with George Greenway in Albuquerque. "I trust the man for he has high standards he lives by," he concluded. Kono to Drechsler, February 11, 1996, KP.

45. Kono to Reno, March 18, 1996, KP.

46. Schmitz to Kono, April 17, 1996, and Kono to Schmitz, April 21, 1996, KP.

47. Kono to Schmitz and Board of Directors, May 5, 1996, KP.

48. *Weightlifting USA* XIV, no. 4 (September 1996): 23.

49. *HSB*, July 27, 1996.

50. Kono also received recognition by serving as a technical official at a pre-Olympic Invitational meet in Atlanta on August 13, 1995, honoring Paul Anderson who died in 1994. Michael Gattone to Kono, March 24, 1995, KP, and *Atlanta Constitution*, August 11, 1995.

51. Kono to Hanneman, February 27, 1997, and Kono to Hughes and Sablo, March 2, 1997, KP.

52. Kono to Drechsler, March 9, 1997, KP.

53. Kono to Wilhelm, February 17, 1997, KP.

54. Kono to Reno, May 9, 1997, *Weightlifter's Newsletter* 226 (June 16, 1997): 28 and "Positive Comments on Kono Letter," *Weightlifter's Newsletter* 227 (July 25, 1997): 11.

55. Kono to Lou DeMarco, "August, September, or October" 1997, KP.

56. Levin to the USAW Leadership, Board of Directors, and USAW Members, September 24, 1997, KP.

57. Schmitz to USAW President, Board of Directors, and All USAW Members, September 18, 1997, KP.

58. Wilson to Board of Directors" and "Weightlifting's Seriously Interested," September 6, 1997, KP.

59. Barnett to Wilson, September 19, 1997, KP.

60. Derwin to Wilson, September 25, 1997, KP.

61. Sunzeri to USAW Board of Directors, September 26, 1997, KP.

62. Thrush to Kono, September 29, 1997, KP.

63. Hanneman to Kono, September 29, 1997, KP.

64. Crist to Hybl, October 2, 1997, and Kono to Hybl, October 3, 1997, KP.

65. Faeth to Hybl, October 9, 1997, KP.

66. "Report of the Board of Review" in Greenway to Levin, October 10, 1997, KP.

67. Kono to Hybl, October 18, 1997, KP.

68. Greenway to All LWC Officers, October 29, 2997, Tommy Kono, "USOTC WEIGHTLIFTING PLIGHT," and Kono to USA Board of Directors, November 2, 1997, KP.

69. Hybl to Kono, November 11, 1997, and Kono to Hybl, April 9, 1998, KP. Significantly, although likely banned from the OTC, two of the violators of IOC drug policy, Sakamaki and Paiva, competed in the 1998 national championships. *Weightlifting USA* XVI, no. 2 (June 1998): 16.

70. Tommy Kono, "USAW ELITE LIFTERS' PROGRESS," May 14, 1998, KP. Estimates for the "2000 Squad Plan" to promote high performance generated by Lyn Jones (including uniforms, competitions, and incentive bonuses) for 1997 totaled $92,000. "Lyn Jones Proposal to the USWF Board of Directors," KP.

71. Schmitz to U.S.A. Weightlifting Members, February 12, 1998, KP.

72. Kono to Michael Rinaldi, August 7, 1998, KP.

73. *Weightlifting USA* XVI, no. 2 (June 1998): 16.

74. *Weightlifting USA*, no. 3 (Fall 1998): 16.

75. *Weightlifting USA* XVII, no. 3 (June 1999): 10–11.

76. *Weightlifting USA*, no. 4 (September 1999): 2.

77. *Weightlifting USA* XVIII, no. 1 (Winter 1999/2000): 11.

78. *Weightlifting USA*, no. 3 (Summer 2000): 4.

79. Les Simonton, "Report from 2000 National

Championships, Athletes' Congress, and Board of Governors," KP.
80. Interview with Stella Herrick, September 5, 2016, Tampa.
81. Newton to Kono, 1989, KP, and Newton to author, November 25, 2019.
82. David F. Prouty, *In Spite of Us: My Education in the Big and Little Games of Amateur and Olympic Sports in the U.S.* (Brattleboro, VT, 1988), 273.
83. Telephone interview with Lou DeMarco, September 9, 2016, Warren, Ohio.

Chapter 9

1. Friedrich Nietzsche, "Maxims and Arrows," *Die Götzen-Dämmerung—Twilight of the Idols.*
2. "Team Hawaii Olympic Lifting, Sponsorship Information," and Nishimoto, Ogata, and Kono to Alex Jamile, January 11, 1995, KP.
3. Kono to Olympic Weightlifting Enthusiasts, February 26, 1995, KP.
4. Kono to Eddie Owada, June 18, 1995, KP.
5. Kono to Thrush, March 22, 1995, KP.
6. "Hawaii State Weightlifting Championships Results," March 30, 1996, and Team Hawaii, Financial Report, August 7, 1995, to August 31, 1996, KP.
7. "Weightlifting Notes from Training with Tommy Kono," KP.
8. Kono to Getz, February 16, 1997, KP.
9. *HA*, February 16, 1997; Kono to Reno, February 17, 1997; and Kono to Levin, February 17, 1997, KP.
10. Kono to Kimura, February 11, 1998, KP.
11. "Southern California Youth Weightlifting Association," www.scywa.org/staff.html.
12. Interview with Herrick.
13. Tommy Kono, "The ABC's of Olympic-Style Weightlifting," July 29–30, 2000, Auburn University, agenda in the author's possession.
14. Simonton to David Meltzer, January 16, 2016, letter in the author's possession.
15. Tommy Kono, "TK Loading Master," KP.
16. "Honolulu Marathon, Statistics, 1973–1997, "KP, and "Honolulu Marathon," http://www.digplanet.com/wiki/Honolulu_Marathon. See also Mark Osmun's early account, *The Honolulu Marathon* (New York, 1979).
17. Jeanette M. L. Chun, "A Spirit of Aloha, The 25th Honolulu Marathon, Sunday, December 14, 1997," KP.
18. Pat Bigold, "Honolulu Marathon, Interview with Dr. Jim Barahal," *RunnersWorld.com*, December 2002.
19. *HSA*, newspaper clipping, KP.
20. Chun, "Spirit of Aloha," KP.
21. "Honolulu Marathon Association Job Description of Tommy Kono," KP.
22. Kono also visited other marathons for possible ideas to incorporate into the Honolulu Marathon. See his "1991 Stockholm Marathon Report" to Barahal and the HMA Board of Directors, June 9, 1991, KP.
23. Kono to James Barahal, March 8, 1992, KP.
24. Interview with joAnn Sumida, November 9, 2019, Aiea, Hawaii. Added to Tommy's responsibilities during the marathon were additional tasks at Parks and Recreation associated with the Christmas season, including the decoration of city hall and organizing the annual employees' holiday party. "These happen to follow one after the other," he complained to George Greenway, "so I never get my Christmas cards out on time." Kono to Greenway, January 25, 1991, KP.
25. Tsai, Tommy Kono Interview.
26. Interview with Gary and joAnn Sumida, November 9, 2019, Aiea, Hawaii.
27. Drewes, "History of the Marathon."
28. Chun to Kono, George, Ishikawa Sr. and Jr., Tom, and Bicoy, October 6, 1992, KP.
29. Kono to Kevin Allen, June 17, 1996, KP.
30. Tommy Kono, "Senior Talk Outline," May 18, 1997, and February 27, 1998, KP.
31. Wayne Nishimoto to Kono, March 3, 1993, KP.
32. Kono to Drechsler, July 6, 2000, KP.
33. Eklof to Kono, October 2, 2000, and Kono to "Madam," October 9, 2000, KP.
34. Performance Evaluation Reports for Tommy T. Kono, May 8, 1993, and January 15, 1997, KP.
35. Kono to Getz, March 9, 1997, KP.
36. Tommy Kono to Mark Kono, January 2, 1994, KP.
37. Lothar Spitz to Kono, January 10, 1994, KP.
38. Harley Sumida to Tommy Kono, [1998], KP.
39. Kono to Grimek, October 8, 1996, KP.
40. Kono to Ajan, October 6, 1996, KP.
41. Kono to Grimek, January 17, 1997, KP.
42. Kono to Larry Wong, January 15, 1999, KP.
43. *Weightlifting USA* IV, no. 6 (1986), 9; *The Association of Oldetime Barbell & Strongmen*, August 2, 1990, 1; and *MuscleMag International* (February 1991): 130–31.
44. *HA*, June 11, 1994, and *HSB*, June 17, 1994.
45. Tommy Kono, "Certificate of Appreciation," KP.
46. Tamas Ajan to Weightlifting Federation of USA, January 24, 1993, and "Tommy Kono's Current Positions," April 17, 1994, KP.
47. Steve Lum, "Tommy Kono," *Hawaii Herald*, January 3, 1997.
48. *HA*, February 3, 1998; Inouye to Kono, February 3, 1998, and Akaka to Kono, February 3, 1998, KP.
49. Kono to Earl Galdeira, May 24, 1999, KP.
50. Kono to Tomei, May 9, 1998, KP.
51. Fragment Notes, nd, KP.

Chapter 10

1. Thomas Fuller, *Introductio ad Prudentiam* (Charleston, SC, 2011).

2. Interview with Darren DeMellow and Brenda Salgado, November 10, 2019, Honolulu.
3. Kono, *Weightlifting,* 186 and 191.
4. Interview with Bill and Judy Pearl, July 30, 2010, Phoenix, Oregon; Bill Pearl, *Keys to the Inner Universe* (1978); Bill Pearl, *Getting Stronger* (Bolinas, CA, 1986); and Bill Pearl, et al., *Legends of the Iron Game,* 206.
5. Arthur J. Drechsler, *The Weightlifting Encyclopedia: A Guide to World Class Performance* (Whitestone, NY, 1998), xxi.
6. Kono, *Championship Weightlifting,* 22, 41, 49, and 53.
7. Ibid., 62–63, 65, and 68–69.
8. Ibid., 91, 96, and 98.
9. Ibid., 105–6.
10. Ibid., 103–4.
11. As journalist Stephen Dinan remarked retrospectively, Bush's aides wanted him to delete it from his speech, and ESPN and Meryl Streep mocked him afterwards. "But when he used his 2004 State of the Union address to raise the issue of steroids in baseball, it boosted the issue to the top levels of politics." *Washington Times,* August 6, 2013.
12. Kono, *Weightlifting,* 114.
13. Interview with Harada.
14. Kiiha, "Tommy Kono," 10.
15. Kono, *Weightlifting,* 170.
16. "Complimentary Book List," KP.
17. Clarence Bass, "Lifting Wisdom of Tommy Kono," Ripped Enterprises, 2001, https://www.cbass.com/Kono.htm.
18. State of Hawaii Basic Business Application, 10627966, November 1, 1999. See also KIO Company, Inc., Articles of Dissolution, State of Hawaii, Department of Commerce and Consumer Affairs, March 20, 2002, KP.
19. See Book Orders; 2001 Business Related Expenses; Bank Deposits & Postage Expenses; and General Excise/Use Tax Returns for January to December 2001, KP.
20. Income & Expenses, April 14, 2003, and T.K.'s Financial Over-View, January 14, 2004, KP.
21. Interview with Leo Falasco, January 16, 2020, Waianae, Hawaii.
22. "The Importance of Healthy Knees," promotional flyer, KP.
23. Kono to "Johnson," April 2, 2006, KP.
24. 2006 Tax Purpose Reference, April 2, 2006, and 2006 Business Expenses, KP.
25. Kono to Lopez, August 21, 2003, and Lopez to Kono, August 21, 2003, KP.
26. *Milo* 11 (September 2003): 2–3.
27. Tommy Kono, "Comments on Strossen's Latest Editorial," KP.
28. Kono to Strossen, October 7, 2003, KP.
29. "My Thoughts," July 21, 27, 29, and August 7 and 9, 2004, KP.
30. Newton to Kono, May 13, 2004. KP.
31. Leo Temosheko, "2006 World Championship Results-U.S. Teams," and International Weightlifting Federation, "USA Team Classification (Senior World Championships)," June 3, 2008, KP.
32. *HSB,* September 30, 2000.
33. Steven G. Brunner to Kono, January 13, 2003, KP.
34. "Certificate of Honor," October 22, 2004; James Fang to Kono, October 13, 2004, KP; and *Nichi Bei Times,* November 8, 2004.
35. Gary Torgeson to Kono, May 23, 2005, KP.
36. *York Sunday News,* August 8, 2004.
37. *Milo* 12 (June 2004): 17 and 19.
38. Tamas Ajan to Tommy and Florence Kono, January 28, 2003, and "IWF Centenary, 1905–2005," Istanbul, March 3, 2005, KP.
39. Drechsler to Kono and Kono to Drechsler, February 8, 2002, KP.
40. Kono to Martha Elizondo, March 1, 2002, KP.
41. Tommy Kono, "Lecture Topics," January 7, 2002, KP.
42. Interview with Bill Kutzer, Sacramento, February 24, 2019.
43. On August 4, 2007, the mayor and city council of Sacramento recognized this competition by paying tribute to Tommy Kono as a "striking example of living a productive life." "Resolution Recognizing Tommy Kono," KP.
44. Interview with Paul Doherty, Sacramento, April 2019; and Megan Tornstrom DeFourny, July 1, 2005, and Angela Almanza to Doherty, KP.
45. Interview with Doherty.
46. "Jerk Workshop," March 8, 2008, KP.
47. 2008 Sacramento Weightlifting Clinic, August 9, 2008, KP.
48. "Tommy Kono 'Back to Basics' Weightlifting Clinic and Participant's Survey Form, September 26 and 27, 2009, KP.
49. Lifetime Membership, Tommy Kono, November 2008, and Certificate of Support, December 23, 2010, KP.
50. "TK Talk" in Susan Goya to Kono, May 17, 2010, KP.
51. Stalker to the author, June 8, 2017.
52. "REVELATION–November 5, 2005," with Stalker response, KP.
53. "Training Principle Concept," KP.
54. Kono, *Championship Weightlifting,* viii, xiv, 8, and 16. A poll taken in December 2019 of nine members of the East Alabama Weightlifting Club, however, indicates relative median rankings of technique (40 percent), mental (33.9 percent), and power (26.1 percent) as the principal ingredients to successful competitive weightlifting.
55. Kono, *Championship Weightlifting,* 46, 58, 81, and 98. "I like to think of myself as an amateur photographer," Tommy told Harry McLaughlin in 1964. "Some of my work from behind the Iron Curtain has appeared on front pages of Honolulu newspapers. Every time I accompany Olympic Coach Bob Hoffman to a foreign country, I end up taking photos for Strength and Health." *SH* 32 (May 1964): 16.
56. Kono, *Championship Weightlifting,* 106–7 and 187.

57. Clarence Bass, "The Mind of Tommy Kono," 2010, KP.
58. Imahara to Kono, March 23, 2007, KP.
59. See Jose Canseco, *Juiced: Wild Times, Rampant 'Roids, Smash Hits & How Baseball Got Big* (New York, 2005).
60. Interviews with Louis DeMarco, September 8 and 26, Cortland, Ohio, and Mike Conroy, February 13, 2013.
61. Interviews with Jim Schmitz, April 9, 2013, San Francisco; Wes Barnett, February 13, 2013, Colorado Springs, Colorado; and Mike Stone, October 25, 2013, Johnson City, Tennessee.
62. Interviews with Mark Rippetoe, December 12, 2012, Wichita Falls, Texas, and John Coffee.
63. Invoice, Data Reproductions Corporations, June 17, 2009, KP.
64. Hawaii Kono Company Sales, 2009, KP.
65. Kono to Drechsler, August 9, 2010, KP.
66. "Stalker's Thoughts," September 20, 2010, KP.
67. Kono to USAW Board Members, January 20, 2009, and Snethen to Ajan, January 5, 2009, KP.
68. Curry to Temoshenko, January 10, 2009, KP.
69. Schmitz to USAW Board of Directors, nd, KP.
70. Kono to USAW Board Members, January 20, 2010, KP.
71. USAW Board of Directors Minutes, March 8, 2009, https://www.teamusa.org/USA-Weightlifting/About-Us/Governance-and-Financial/Board-of-Directors/Board-Meeting-Minutes.
72. Kono to Rick Adams, October 3, 2009, KP, and USA Weightlifting Board of Directors Minutes, January 2 to July 17, 2011, https://www.teamusa.org/USA-Weightlifting.
73. Kono to Board Members, July 21, 2011, KP.

Chapter 11

1. Kono to Kei, October 15, 2008, KP. As late as the spring of 2003, however, Kono testified that he trained three times a week at the Nuuanu YMCA. "My workouts are not heavy and last about an hour. I perform 2 sets of each of 10 exercises that covers my entire body." Tyler Hass, Interview with Kono, May 5, 2003, KP.
2. "Shoulder Flexibility, Indian Clubs Swinging," KP.
3. Kono to Yukio Taketa, April 8, 2011, Al Guzman to Kono, January 12, 2012, and "Newtown Center Talk," KP.
4. Kono to Heffernan, December 29, 2010; Heffernan to Kono, nd; and *Hawai'i Athletics Strength Coaches Clinic Newsletter*, January 2012, 3, KP.
5. Whitson to Kono, October 17, 2011, KP.
6. Ricker to Kono, August 20, 2013, KP.
7. Kono to Rick Adams, October 3, 2009, KP.
8. *AOBS Newsletter. The Association of Oldtime Barbell & Strongmen* (July 2016): 2 and 12.
9. Financial Records, KP.
10. Tommy Kono, "A Gift to You for the Year 2012," KP.
11. Interview with Mark Kono. Russell Ogata remembers that "Jamie and Tommy never got along too well. Tommy's sentimental. He's not a hard ass, but he's very pragmatic about a lot of things." Interview with Ogata.
12. Interview with Florence Kono and joAnn Sumida.
13. Interview with Harada.
14. Interview with Ogata and *Ronald H. Heck, Culture and Educational Policy in Hawai'i: The Silencing of Native Voices* (New York, 1998), 137.
15. Undated newspaper clippings, KP.
16. George to the author, February 28, 2019.
17. Bilger to Kono, March 9, 2012, KP, and *The New Yorker*, July 23, 2012.
18. Rosenberg to Kono, March 1, 2012, KP.
19. Ajan to Kono, March 28, 2013, KP.
20. Kono to Kiiha, December 24, 2012, KP.
21. Interview with Doherty and Kono to Yamamoto, August 1, 2012, KP.
22. Interview with Ryan Yamamoto, April 18, 2020, Seattle.
23. Ryan Yamamoto and Suzanne Phan, *Arnold Knows Me: The Tommy Kono Story*, KVIE, 2016.
24. Interview with Yamamoto.
25. Yamamoto and Phan, *Arnold Knows Me*.
26. Edward J. Pierini, Jr., "Long Live Tommy Kono Then and Now," June 20, 2014, https://pierini-fitness.blogspot.com/2014/.
27. Kono to Kiiha, September 6, 2015, KP.
28. Kono to George, September 15, 2013, KP.
29. joAnn Kono to the author, December 6, 2016, KP.
30. Kono to George, September 15, 2013, KP.
31. Pierini, "Long Live Tommy Kono."
32. Kono to Kiiha, September 15, KP.
33. Elaine Doi, "After Visit Summary," August 1, 2011, and Kenneth Hong, "After Visit Summary," August 31, 2011, KP.
34. Ronald Ling, "After Visit Summary," November 15, 2012, and Elaine Doi, "After Visit Summary, November 15, 2012, KP.
35. Hemochromatosis, Cleveland Clinic, https://my.clevelandclinic.org/locations.
36. *The Iron Disorders Institute Guide to Hemochromatosis* (Napierville, IL, 2009), viii.
37. E.D. Weinberg, *Exposing the Hidden Dangers of Iron* (Nashville, 2004), 255 and 262.
38. *Nutrition Studies* 59 (2001), 146, and Weinberg, *Exposing the Hidden Dangers*, 255.
39. Geritol Ingredients, https://www.bing.com/images/search?q=geritol+ingredients&qpvt=geritol+ingredients&FORM=IGRE.
40. *HA*, April 27, 1951.
41. *HSB*, April 29, 1952.
42. *HA*, February 23, 1953, and December 14, 1954.
43. "Notice of Copartnership," *HA*, August 17, 1955.
44. Interview with Florence Kono and joAnn Sumida.

45. "Testimonials," *A Celebration of Life Service for Dr. Richard W. You, 1916–1995*, i–x.
46. Interview with Kawamura.
47. Interview with Ogata.
48. Interview with Wilhelm.
49. "Testimonials," *A Celebration of Life Service*, ii.
50. *HSB*, July 2, 1977.
51. *HSB*, August 9, 1977.
52. *HA*, August 22, 1979. Additionally, Tommy and Pete George filed notarized statements on You's behalf. "In the quarter of a century that I have known Dr. You," Pete states, "I am not aware of a single act performed by him that he would consider not in the best interest of his patients, community, or nation." Tommy was more effusive. In his 29-year association with Dr. You "my faith, trust, and respect for the man has never diminished. On the contrary, it has grown with time." Peter T. George, verified by Emmaline Windrath, Notary Public, First Judicial Circuit, September 15, 1977, and Tommy T. Kono, verified by Kathryn A. Sato, Notary Public, First Judicial Circuit, September 13, 1977, KP.
53. "Gustuson to Whom It May Concern," October 25, 1977, KP.
54. Interview with Darren DeMello and Brenda Salgado.
55. *HSB*, November 28, 1986, and *HSB*, March 27, 1996.
56. Interview with Harada.
57. Interview with Florence Kono and joAnn Sumida.
58. Interview with DeMello.
59. Interview with Kawamura.
60. Wilhelm elaborates that "the last time I saw him at the Nuuanu Y I could not believe it; he could barely walk. He was all stoved up. And what amazed me was with his mouth caved in. It looked like he was missing some teeth." Interview with Wilhelm.
61. Interview with Jim Schmitz.
62. Interview with Ryan Yamamoto.
63. *NikkeiWest*, December 10, 2015.
64. Tommy Kono, "To Whom It May Concern," KP.
65. Kono to Terufumi Seike, July 24, 2015, KP.
66. Interview with Wilhelm.
67. Mililani Memorial Park Mortuary, April 28, 2016, and Funeral Program, May 23, 2016.
68. Crypt Inscription, National Memorial Cemetery of the Pacific. According to Sarah Fair, Flo explained to her that the inscription "Because You Loved Me" was one of the choices the engravers give people to use, and she chose it because early on, she left and went to New York and Tommy came and got her. Conversation with Sarah Fair, November 12, 2016.
69. "A Memorial Resolution By the Honorable Kevin McCarty, 7th Assembly District, the Honorable Ken Cooley, 8th Assembly District, and the Honorable Richard Pan, 6th Senatorial District Relative to memorializing Tamio 'Tommy' Kono, Members Resolution No. 1181," April 24, 2016; Ernest Y. Martin, Council Chair and Presiding Officer, "In Memoriam With Deepest Sympathy," May 23, 2016; Doris O. Matsui, *Congressional Record*, 114th Congress, Second Session, July 26, 2016; and Kevin Johnson, Mayor, "Resolution Recognizing Tommy Kono Day, July 26, 2016, KP.
70. 7th Annual Sacramento Sports Hall of Fame Induction Celebration, January 26, 2019, Thunder Valley Casino Resort program, and "SSHOF Speech by Mark Kono," KP.

Epilogue and Conclusion

1. J.C. Herz, *Learning to Breathe Fire: The Rise of Crossfit and the Primal Future of Fitness* (New York, 2014), 139.
2. *HSB*, July 16, 1986.
3. Kono, *Championship Weightlifting*, v.
4. Kono to Whom It May Concern, September 13, 1977, KP.
5. *HSB*, May 29, 1979. When Dr. You was on the verge of death, Tommy made a special plea to Arnold Schwarzenegger to compose a message to be read at his service. "Doc has done so much for so many persons. His interest was in all different sports but in particular he had a great love for bodybuilding and weightlifting. It would mean so much to have something written by someone as well-known like yourself." Kono to Schwarzenegger, November 8, 1995, KP.
6. Sports writer Carl Machado characterized You as a physician and surgeon with "a tremendous practice" and "as modest as one begging for business." *Hawaii Catholic Herald*, April 18, 1952.
7. "They tell me that this year's 'Mr. America' [Jim Park] is a vitamin and high protein guy," chuckled York feature writer Harry Paschall. Maybe eventually we will come to a point where we can pile on the lumps by just inhaling iron pills instead of using them." *SH* 20 (November 1952): 17.
8. *HA*, October 23, 1955.
9. *HA*, March 11, 1956.
10. *HA*, December 5, 1965.
11. *HSB*, July 12, 1992, and *HSB*, April 27, 2016.
12. Interview with Yamamoto.
13. Victor Hugo, *Les Misérables* (New York, 2008), 372.
14. Kono to Kenji Onuma, August 7, 1974, KP; *HA*, August 4, 1983; and *HSB*, January 10, 1980.
15. Imahara and Meltzer, *Book of Remembrance*, 2, 28–29, 39, and 48.
16. Imahara to Warren Perrin, November 18, 2020, Lafayette, Louisiana.
17. Seb Ostrowicz, *The Greatest Weightlifters of All Time* (Studley, UK, 2018), 5 and 175.
18. Interview with Harada.
19. Interview with Kawamura.
20. Interview with Harada.
21. "Olympic Champion Tommy Kono, World Champion, Olympic Weight Lifter," KP.
22. Conversations with Florence Kono and joAnn Sumida recorded by Sarah Fair, November 12, 2016.

23. This pattern of behavior coincides with the contention of Stephen Fugita and David O'Brien that "the persistence of Japanese American ethnicity stems from elements in traditional Japanese culture" and that "Japanese Americans may readily adopt 'American ways' and 'fit in' without losing a basic sense of their peoplehood." Fugita and O'Brien, *Japanese American Ethnicity*, 5 and 101.

24. Interview with Florence Kono, joAnn Sumida, and Gary Sumida.

25. Kono to Cox, October 25, 1996, KP.

26. Drechsler, "Celebrating Lives."

27. Interview with Harada.

28. *HSB*, July 12, 1992.

29. "Tom Kono, Las Vegas, December 2, 1977, KP.

30. Kono, *Championship Weightlifting*, 2 and 105.

31. *SH* 37 (July 1969): 20. According to Tommy, "Pete never stressed diet, technique or his training program although these are basic, elemental parts of becoming a champion. His emphasis was the importance of a positive mental attitude." Kono, *Weightlifting*, 205.

32. Émile Coué, *Self Mastery Through Conscious Autosuggestion* (New York, 1922), 17, 28, and 32.

33. Kono, *Championship Weightlifting*, 20 and 36. George confirms that Larry Barnholth "often mentioned Emil Coue [sic]" and that Pete, in turn, discussed Coué's ideas with Tommy. George to the author, February 6, 2017.

34. Kono to Teegarden, June 26, 1950, KP.

35. Peale, *Power of Positive Thinking*, 8, 15, 39, 56, and 211.

36. George to the author, January 31, 2017.

37. Norman Vincent Peale, "Never Let Anything Get You Down," newspaper clipping, KP.

38. Ezra Bowen, "Think and Lift," *Sports Illustrated* 1 (December 20, 1954): 28.

39. In 1971, Tommy told Bob Hoffman that "I read this book about 15 years ago and I've used many of its principles as my guideline." Kono to Hoffman, May 20, 1971, HP. Tommy later confided to Russ Ogata that Hill's book was "an old time favorite of mine." Kono to Ogata, January 11, 1987, KP.

40. Hill, *Think & Grow Rich*, 31, 116, 111 and 39–40.

41. George to the author, January 31, 2017.

42. Kono, *Weightlifting*, 186. Although it relates more to interpersonal relations than individuals Tommy was also influenced by the gospel of success imparted by Dale Carnegie in *How to Win Friends and Influence People* (New York, 1936).

43. Tommy Kono, "The Advantage of Disadvantage," March 3, 1953, KP.

44. Kono, *Championship Weightlifting*, 177.

45. Pete George, "Recollections of Tommy Kono," November 12, 2016, transcript in the author's possession.

46. Drechsler to Kono, "Facts of Life," November 22, 1998, KP.

47. James Michener, "Introduction," *Years of Infamy: The Untold Story of America's Concentration Camps* (Seattle, 1996), 31.

48. A. Grove Day, "America's Mightiest Little Man," *Coronet* 48 (July 1960): 110.

49. Donna K. Nagata, Jacqueline H.J. Kim, and Kaidi Wu, "The Japanese American Wartime Incarceration: Examining the Scope of Racial Trauma," *American Psychologist* 74 (January 2019): 9.

50. Harry H.L. Kitano and Akemi Kikumura, "The Japanese American Family," in Russell Endo, Stanley Sue and Nathaniel N. Wagner, *Asian-Americans: Social and Psychological Perspectives* 2 (1980), 3.

51. Edwin O. Reischauer, *The Japanese* (Cambridge, MA, 1978), 152 and 217.

52. LaVerne Sasaki, who conducted Tommy's funeral, admits that "a Buddhist is difficult to pin down....that person can be Buddhist/Christian/Jew/Taoist/Hindu/American Indian/Agnostic/Heathen at the same time. Tommy was probably that way." Sasaki to the author, June 28, 2020.

53. Interview with Kono.

54. Interview with Imahara.

55. Imahara and Meltzer, *Book of Remembrance*, 55.

56. Sumida to the author, January 15, 2017.

57. D.T. Suzuki, *Zen Buddhism*, ed. William Barrett (Garden City, NY, 1956), 10. In "Zen for the West," William Barrett concurs that Zen desires "facts as living and concrete," a kind of radical intuitionism whereby "thinking and sensing live, move, and have their being within the vital medium of intuition." Nancy Wilson Ross, *The World of Zen: An East-West Anthology* (New York, 1960), 347–48. Barbara Gail Montero, however, regards Zen as too reliant on the unconscious state of mind or what she calls the "just-do-it principle" and not on consciousness or "cognition-in-action-principle." Montero, *Thought in Action: Expertise and the Conscious Mind* (New York, 2016), 9.

58. Kono, *Championship Weightlifting*, 105–6. Not unlike Tommy's sense of getting "in the zone" is Mihaly Csikszentmihalyi's concept of "flow" as a way of tapping into ultimate human potential. ... Optimal experience is thus something we must *make* happen." It is achieved through "control over one's inner life" which enables a person to "concentrate attention on the task at hand and momentarily forget everything else." Csikszentmihalyi, *Flow*, 3 and 6.

59. *Time* 75 (June 27, 1960): 69.

60. Arthur Drechsler, "Tommy Kono—A Weightlifter's Weightlifter," *USA Weightlifting*, April 27, 2016.

61. Interview with Mel Miyamoto, November 12, 2016, Honolulu, Hawaii.

62. Kono, *Championship Weightlifting*, 105–6.

63. Kono to Getz, February 16, 1997, KP.

64. Tommy Kono, "To Whom It May Concern," Note to his friends, KP.

65. A 2002 biographical entry for the Japanese

Cultural and Community Center of Northern California states that "from his pre-teen days, Kono remembers his parents talking with friends from the 'old country.' Two words that deeply impressed him were 'shikata-ganai' and 'arigatai.' ... It is being thankful for even a crooked bar or a broken up platform to lift on. The fact that you have some equipment, any equipment, to train with is better than having nothing." Kathleen Barrows to Kono, September 20, 2002, KP.

Bibliography

Archives

Civil Archives Division, National Archives
Bob Crist Papers
Department of Commerce, Bureau of the Census
Bob Hoffman Papers
Walter Imahara Papers
Tommy Kono Papers
John Ziegler Papers

Interviews

Wes Barnett
Isaac Berger
John Coffee
Mike Conroy
Edward Coyle
Lou DeMarco
Darren DeMello
Paul Doherty
Clyde Emrich
Leo Falasco
Sibby Flowers
Pete George
Ben Green
Gary Gubner
Mike Harada
Stella Herrick
Gloria Imagire
Gary Kawamura
Osmo Kiiha
Florence Kono
Tommy Kono
William Kutzer
Murray Levin
Carl Miller
Pete Miller
Brian Miyamoto
Mel Miyamoto
Harvey Newton
Russell Ogata
Bill Pearl
Judy Pearl
Joe Puleo
John Pulskamp
Louis Riecke
Mark Rippetoe
Brenda Salgado
Jim Schmitz
Mike Stone
Gary Sumida
joAnn Sumida
Hirofumi Tanaka
Chuck Vinci
Bruce Wilhelm
Ryan Yamamoto

Books & Articles

"Association of Oldetime Barbell and Strongmen." *MuscleMag International* (February 1991).
"Athletes' Report." *SH* 42 (August–September 1974).
"Atlas Come to Life." *Time*, June 27, 1960.
Baker, Gene. "We and They." *Weightlifting USA* 6 (1988).
Barnholth, Lawrence. *Secrets of the Squat Snatch*. Akron, OH: American College of Modern Weight Lifting, 1950.
Bass, Clarence. "Lifting Wisdom of Tommy Kono." *Ripped* (Clarence Bass Enterprises), 2001, https://www.cbass.com/Kono.htm.
"The Big Tomato." *Midtown Monthly,* March 11, 2011, http://www.midtownmonthly.net/life/the-big-tomato/.
Bigold, Pat. "Honolulu Marathon, Interview with Dr. Jim Barahal." *RunnersWorld.com*, December 2002.
_____. "Olympic Flashback, The World's Strongest Man." *HSB*, September 30, 2000.
Billingsley, Mark. "The Strength to Succeed." *The Sacramento Bee*, February 24, 2005.
Bloom, Alfred. "Shin Buddhism in America," in Charles S. Prebish and Kenneth K. Tanaka, eds. *The Faces of Buddhism in America*. Berkeley: University of California Press, 1998.
Bowen, Ezra. "Think and Lift." *Sports Illustrated* 1 (December 20, 1954).
Cady, Mike. "Editorial." *Weightlifting USA* 16, no. 3 (Fall 1998).
Canseco, Jose. *Juiced: Wild Times, Rampant 'Roids, Smash Hits & How Baseball Got Big*. New York: HarperCollins, 2005.
Carnegie, Dale. *How to Win Friends and Influence People*. New York: Simon & Schuster, 1936.

Bibliography

Catlin, Oliver. "USAW's Super Lifters Say, 'Up, with the Records' and Away Up." *Weightlifting USA* 17, no. 3 (June 1999).

"Chest Drive Launched!" *Maui News*, September 6, 1965.

"Cioroslan Diagnoses Resident Athlete Abilities." *Weightlifting USA* 10, no. 1 (1992).

Coster, Charles. "Echoes from Munich." *SH* 24 (June 1956).

Coué, Émile. *Self Mastery Through Conscious Autosuggestion*. New York: Malkan, 1922.

Csikszentmihalyi, Mihaly. *Flow: The Psychology of Optimal Experience*. New York: Harper, 1990.

Daniels, Roger. *Prisoners Without Trial: Japanese Americans in World War II*. New York: Hill and Wang, 1993.

Day, A. Grove. "America's Mightiest *Little* Man." *Coronet* 48 (July 1960).

DeCoste, Jim. "Weightlifting After the Cold War." *Denis Reno's Weightlifter's Newsletter* 177 (December 14, 1991).

Derwin, Brian P. "President's Report." *Weightlifting USA* 12, no. 4 (September 1999).

Drechsler, Arthur. "A Brief History of Women's Weightlifting." *USA Weightlifting* 27 (Fall 2008).

———. "Tommy Kono—A Weightlifter's Weightlifter." *USA Weightlifting* (April 27, 2016).

———. *The Weightlifting Encyclopedia: A Guide to World Class Performance*. Whitestone, NY, 1998.

Drewes, Paul. "History of the Honolulu Marathon." December 17, 2015. *KITV Island News*, http://www.kitv.com/story/30609620/history-of-the-honolulu-marathon.

Drinnon, Richard. *Keeper of Concentration Camps: Dillon S. Myer and American Racism*. Berkeley: University of California Press, 1987.

Duus, Masayo. *Unlikely Liberators: The Men of the 100th and 442nd*. Honolulu: University of Hawaii Press, 1987.

Easterwood, Jim. "Kono Accepts German Offer." *HSB*, January 22, 1969.

Elleman, Bruce. *Japanese-American Civilian Prisoner Exchanges and Detention Camps, 1941–45*. London: Routledge, 2006.

Fair, John D. "The Ethnicity of Ohio's Strength Culture." *Ohio History* 117 (2010).

———. *Muscletown USA, Bob Hoffman and the Manly Culture of York Barbell*. University Park: Pennsylvania State University Press, 1999.

———. "The Tragic History of the 'Military Press' in Olympic and World Championship Competition, 1928–1972." *The Journal of Sport History* 28 (Fall 2001).

Fejer, Ferenc. "All-time Ranking List According to Medal Points." *World Weightlifting* 2 (1982).

Frankl, Viktor. *Man's Search for Meaning*. Boston: Beacon, 2006.

Frizzell, Pat. "Sports Patter." *Sacramento Union*, July 2, 1961.

Fugita, Stephen S., and Fernandez, Marilyn. *Altered Lives, Enduring Community: Japanese Americans Remember Their World War II Incarceration*. Seattle: University of Washington Press, 2004.

Fugita, Stephen S., and O'Brien, David. *Japanese American Ethnicity, the Persistence of Community*. Seattle: University of Washington Press, 1991.

Fullard-Leo, E. "Amateur Athletics." *The Honolulu Advertiser*, October 23, 1955.

Fuller, Thomas. *Introductio Ad Prudentiam: Or, Directions, Counsels, and Cautions, Tending to Prudent Management of Affairs in Common Life*. Charleston, SC: Nabu, 2011.

Gee, Bill. "Olympic Coach Picks Bulgaria." *HSB*, June 15, 1976.

———. "Tommy Kono Named U.S. Olympic Weightlifting Coach." *HSB*, December 3, 1975.

George, Peter. "Mental Attitude of the Champion." *SH* 37 (July 1969).

———. "Tommy Kono: Greatest Weightlifter of All Time." *Iron Game History* 14 (July 2017).

Go for Broke. Metro Goldwyn Mayer film (1951).

Goss, Kim. "Chester Teegarden." *Weightlifting USA* 7, no. 6 (1989).

Hagiwara, Yoshihide. *Green Barley Essence*. New York: McGraw-Hill, 1998.

Hammer, Armen. "Weightlifting Legend Tommy Kono Passes Away at 85." *FloElite*, April 25, 2016.

Hasse, Bob. "1957 World Weight Lifting Championships." *SH* 26 (March 1958).

Heck, Ronald H. *Culture and Educational Policy in Hawai'i: The Silencing of Native Voices*. New York: Routledge, 1998.

Herz, J.C. *Learning to Breathe Fire: The Rise of Crossfit and the Primal Future of Fitness*. New York: Three Rivers, 2014.

Hill, Napoleon. *Think & Grow Rich*. Cleveland: Ralston, 1937.

Hise, Bob. "Jr. Nationals and 'Jr. Mr. America.'" *Iron Man* 12/1 (June-July 1952).

———. "This Is Your Life—Tommy Kono." *Iron Man* 20 (July 1960).

Hoffman, Bob. "About the BH Knee and Waist Bands." *SH* 35 (June 1967).

———. "Functional Isometric Contraction: The Bill March Story." *Amateur Athlete* (April 1962).

———. "The Most Important Article I Ever Wrote." *SH* 29 (November 1961).

———. "The 1952 National Sr. Championships." *SH* 20 (October 1952).

———. "1976 Olympic Weightlifting Results." *SH* 44 (October/November 1976).

———. "1973 World Championships." *SH* 42 (January 1974).

———. "The Philadelphia Story." *SH* 24 (September 1956).

———. "Report from Stockholm." *SH* 27 (February 1959).

———. "Rome Report XVII Olympiad." *SH* 29 (February 1961).

———. "Senior Nationals & Olympic Tryouts Report." *SH* 28 (October 1960).

———. *Weight Lifting*. York: Strength & Health, 1939.

———. "Who Is the World's Best Weightlifter?" *Strength & Health* 29 (April 1961).

Hogan, Carol. "Clinic Has Made Strides." *HA*, March 13, 1983.

Hollan, Timothy J. *The German-Americans and World War II: An Ethnic Experience.* New York: Peter Lang, 1996.

Horine, Conrad. "The Strongest Man in the World Competition." *SH* 45 (November 1977).

Hosokawa, Bill. *Nisei: The Quiet Americans.* Boulder: University Press of Colorado, 2002.

House Resolution No. 290, March 4, 1983, House of Representatives, Twelfth Legislature, State of Hawaii.

Howard, John. *Concentration Camps on the Home Front and Japanese Americans in the House of Jim Crow.* Chicago: University of Chicago Press, 2008.

Hsu, V. Jo. "Takes a Village: Interview with Vernon Patao." *Iron Athlete*, December 13, 2016, https://www.ironathleteclinics.com/takes-village-interview-vernon-patao/.

Ichihashi, Yamato. *Japanese in the United States: A Critical Study of the Problems of the Japanese Immigrants and Their Children.* Stanford: Stanford University Press, 1932.

Imada, Lee. "Maui's Brian Okada Is Lifting Maui on Map." *Maui News*, January 5, 1982.

Imahara, Walter M., and Meltzer, David E., eds. *Book of Remembrance for Tommy Kono.* Mesa, AZ: privately printed, 2017.

The Iron Disorders Institute Guide to Hemochromatosis. Napierville, IL: Cumberland House, 2009.

"Ishikawa Was Olympic Lifter." *HA*, November 30, 2008.

Ito, Monte. "He'll Be Doing What He Loves." *HA*, December 5, 1965.

_____. "Tommy Kono Does It Again!" *HA*, 1957.

Kendis, Kaoru Oguri. *A Matter of Comfort: Ethnic Maintenance and Ethnic Style Among Third Generation Japanese Americans.* New York: AMS, 1989.

Kiiha, Osmo. "George Brothers." *Iron Master* 6 (April 1991).

_____. "Tommy Kono." *Iron Master* 5 (December 1990).

Kirkley, George. "Sensational Olympic Lifting." *Iron Man* 28 (January 1969).

Klemens, Bruce. "Senior Nationals." *SH* 50 (August 1982).

Kono, Tommy. "ABC of Weightlifting." *SH* 37 (October 1969).

_____. *Championship Weightlifting: Beyond Muscle Power, the Mental Side of Lifting.* Honolulu: Hawaii Kono, 2010.

_____. "Cindy Wyatt Wants to Be a Champion." *SH* 30 (November 1962).

_____. "Food Supplements—An Essential Part of an Athlete's Diet." *SH* 34 (September 1966).

_____. "A Major Breakthrough in the Field of Weight Training." *SH* 35 (June 1967).

_____. "Manuel Mateos, Mexico's Mighty Mite." *SH* 34 (November 1966).

_____. "Medals in Manchester." *Weightlifting USA* 7, no. 6 (1989).

_____. "The Snatch in Relation to the Clean & Jerk." *SH* 34 (October 1966).

_____. "Tommy Kono's Training Methods." *SH* 25 (December 1956).

_____. *Weightlifting, Olympic Style.* Honolulu: Hawaii Kono, 2001.

"Kono Only American Lifter to Make Trip to Moscow." *HSB*, March 6, 1958.

"Kono QB Club's Top Sportsman." *HSB*, February 22, 1983.

"Kono Right at Home in Mexico Olympic Center." *Maui News*, April 30, 1966.

"Kono to Give AAU a Lift." *Long Island Press*, September 6, 1972.

Kono to Reno, May 9, 1997. *Weightlifter's Newsletter* 226, June 16, 1997.

"Kono Welcomes Elwell as Health Center Aide." *Maui News*, June 17, 1964.

Kwon, Bill. "He's the Greatest, That's All." *HSB*, August 6, 1982.

LaGumina, Salvatore J. *The Humble and the Heroic, Wartime Italian Americans.* Youngstown, NY: Cambria, 2006.

Lambert, Mike. "World's Strongest Men." *SH* 50 (October 1982).

Lee, Bobbie. "Lifters Commit to Year-Round Training." *Weightlifting USA* 9, no. 1 (1991).

Levin, Murray. AAU Notice #80–60. *Denis Reno's Weightlifter's Newsletter* 80 (December 6, 1980).

_____. "20th Anniversary of Women in Weightlifting." *USA Weightlifting* 25 (2006).

Litsky, Frank. "Tommy Kono, Weight-Lifting Champion Raised in Internment Camp, Dies at 85." *The New York Times*, April 29, 2016.

Lotchin, Roger W. *Japanese American Relocation in World War II: A Reconsideration.* Cambridge: Cambridge University Press, 2018.

Lum, Steve. "Tommy Kono." *The Hawaii Herald*, January 3, 1997.

Maeda, Wayne. *Continuing Traditions: Japanese Americans, Story of a People—1869 to 1992.* Sacramento: Sacramento Regional Japanese American Exhibit Committee, 1992.

Maki, Mitchell T., Kitano, Harry H.L., and Berthold, S. Megan. *Achieving the Impossible Dream: How Japanese Americans Obtained Redress.* Urbana: University of Illinois Press, 1999.

Maraniss, David. *Rome 1960: The Olympics That Changed the World.* New York: Simon & Schuster, 2008.

Markson, Robert J. "Cold War Slips Into Story of a Remarkable Athlete." *Sacramento Bee*, n.d., 1954.

Matsumoto, Toru. *Beyond Prejudice.* New York: Arno, 1978.

McLaughlin, Harry. "The Real Life Story of Tommy Kono." *SH* 32 (May 1964).

Michener, James. "Introduction." Weglyn, *Years of Infamy* 27–31.

Miller, Ann. "A Real Heavy Weight." *HSB*, July 12, 1992.

Miller, Carl. "First USA Weightlifting Coordinator Suggests Improvements in USA Weightlifting Programs." *Denis Reno's Weightlifter's Newsletter* 134 (February 28, 1987).

Mitsukado, Andrew. "Hour of Decision for Kono." *HA*, May 12, 1963.

Montero, Barbara Gail. *Thought in Action: Expertise and the Conscious Mind*. New York: Oxford University Press, 2016.

Morais, Dominic G., and Todd, Jan. "Lifting the Iron Curtain, Paul Anderson and the Cold War's First Sport Exchange." *Iron Game History* 12 (February/March 2013).

Nagata, Donna K. *Legacy of Injustice: Exploring the Cross-generational Impact of the Japanese American Internment*. New York: Plenum, 1993.

Nelson, Deb. "Tommy Kono." *Weightlifting USA* IV, no. 6 (1986).

Nelson, R.L. "Iron and Colorectal Cancer Risk: Human Studies." *Nutrition Studies* 59 (2001).

Niiya, Brian. "The Nuuanu YMCA and the Glory Days of Hawaii Weightlifting." *The Hawaii Herald, Hawaii's Japanese American Journal* 20, no. 17 (September 3, 1999).

"1973 World Weightlifting Championships— Report by the United States Team." *New England Association AAU—Weightlifters' Newsletter* 22 (December 24, 1973).

Official Score Book-1957, AAU National Senior Weight-Lifting Championships and Mr. America Competition. Daytona Beach, Florida, June 22–23.

Okihiro, Dr. Michael Okihiro. "Chad Ikei Paying It Forward." *The Hawaii Herald*, November 10, 2014, https://www.thehawaiiherald.com/2014/11/10/chad-ikei-paying-it-forward/.

"Olympic Journey of American Weightlifting Legend Kono Began in WWII Internment Camp." *Nikkeiwest*, December 10, 2015.

Osmun, Mark. *The Honolulu Marathon*. New York: J.B. Lippincott, 1979.

Ostrowicz, Seb. *The Greatest Weightlifters of All Time*. Studley, UK: Powerful Ideas, 2018.

Paschall, Harry. "Behind the Scenes." *SH* 20 (November 1952).

_____. "Nat. Lifting Championships." *Iron Man* 10 (May/June 1950).

Peale, Norman Vincent. *The Power of Positive Thinking*. New York: Prentice-Hall, 1952.

Pearl, Bill. *Getting Stronger*. Bolinas, CA: Shelter Publications, 1986.

Personal Justice Denied: Report of the Commission on Wartime Relocation and Internment of Civilians. Seattle: University of Washington Press, 1997.

"Pete George-Wonder Boy and Larry Barnholth's ACMWL Gym." *Iron Man* 9 (March 1949).

Petersen, William. "Success Story, Japanese-American Style." *The New York Times Magazine*, January 9, 1966.

Pierini, Edward J., Jr. "Long Live Tommy Kono Then and Now." June 20, 2014, https://pierini-fitness.blogspot.com/2014/.

Polakowski, Chris. "Eastern Lifters Sustain 'Hammer Time' at Camp." *Weightlifting USA* 8, no. 5 (1990), 5.

"Positive-Thinking Kono Says the Mind Plays Large Role." *York Dispatch*, August 6, 1960.

Prebish, Charles S., and Tanaka, Kenneth K., eds. *The Faces of Buddhism in America*. Berkeley: University of California Press, 1998.

Prouty, David F. *In Spite of Us: My Education in the Big and Little Games of Amateur and Olympic Sports in the U.S.* Brattleboro, VT: Velo-news, 1988.

Quinn, Joe. "Kono Named to Coach German Weightlifters." *Stars and Stripes*, May 2, 1969.

Rader, Peary. "Final Olympic Tryouts." *Lifting News* 11 (December 1964).

_____. "Intense Competition Sparks Olympic Tryouts at World Fair in New York City." *Lifting News* 11 (October 1964), 4–6.

_____. "1952 National Weight Lifting Championships." *Lifting News* 12/2 (August-September 1952).

Reischauer, Edwin O. *The Japanese*. Cambridge: Harvard University Press, 1978.

Reno, Denis. "Women's World Weightlifting Championships." *Denis Reno's Weightlifter's Newsletter* 159 (December 9, 1989).

"Resolution." The House of Representatives of the State of Hawaii. October 22, 1959, H.R. No. 101.

Rinehart, Mary Ann. "Elite Women Establish Personal Records." *Weightlifting USA* 7, no. 5 (1989).

_____. "Suleymanoglu Demonstrates Technique in Colorado Springs." *Weightlifting USA* 6, no. 6 (1988).

Rogers, Adam. "Zen and the Art of Olympic Success." *Newsweek*, July 22, 1996.

Ross, Nancy Wilson. *The World of Zen: An East-West Anthology*. New York: Vintage, 1960.

Sasaki, LaVerne Senyo. *Out of the Mud Grows the Wisteria*. Privately printed, 2019.

Scheuring, Ian. "Olympic Gold Medalist, Legendary Weightlifter Tommy Kono Dies." *Hawaii News Now*, April 24, 2016.

Schmitz, Jim. "President's Message." *Weightlifting USA* 9, no. 4 (1991), 2.

Schudel, Matt. "Tommy Kono, Two-time Olympic Champion Weightlifter, Dies at 85." *The Washington Post*, May 1, 2016.

Seip, Jim. "York's Gold: Greatest Olympian Found America's Strength Here." *York Sunday News*, August 8, 2004.

Shuman, Frand. "World's Strongest Men." *SH* 47 (November 1979).

Sigall, Bob. "Tommy Kono." *Health and Strength* (October 2015): 19.

Spickard, Paul. *Japanese Americans: The Formation and Transformations of an Ethnic Group*. New Brunswick: Rutgers University Press, 2009.

Strossen, Randall J. "The Arnold Expo: The Woodstock of the Weight World." *Milo* 12 (June 2004).

"Super Lifting in Tokyo." *SH* 48 (May 1980).

Suzuki, D.T. *Zen and Japanese Culture*. Princeton: Princeton University Press, 2010.

Taketa, Henry. "Kono's Is Alger Story." *Pacific Citizen*, December 19, 1952.

Takezawa, Yasuko I. *Breaking Silence: Redress and Japanese American Ethnicity*. Ithaca: Cornell University Press, 1995.

Tanaka, Wayne. "Maui Welcomes Tommy Kono." *Maui News*, May 2, 1964.

"Testamonials." *A Celebration of Life Service for Dr. Richard W. You, 1916–1995.*

Thomas, Dorothy Swaine. *The Spoilage.* Berkeley: University of California Press, 1946.

Todd, Terry. "The Jovial Genius of Dr. John Ziegler." *SH* 33 (October 1965).

"Tommy Kono (1930–2016) Olympian Was Worth His Weight in Gold." *Daily Express* (London), May 7, 2016.

"Tommy Kono to Coach Mexican Weightlifters." *HSB*, November 1, 1965.

Totten, Leo. "U.S. Finishes Fifteenth at 59th World Championships." *Weightlifting USA* 7, no. 5 (1989).

Tsai, Michael S.K.N. *The People's Race Inc.: Behind the Scenes at the Honolulu Marathon.* Honolulu: University of Hawaii Press, 2016.

Tsuda, Takeyuki. *Japanese American Ethnicity: In Search of Heritage and Homeland Across Generations.* New York: New York University Press, 2016.

"Tule Lake." *Life* 16, March 20, 1944.

Tymn, Mike. "Kono: U.S. Weightlifters Need to Set Higher Goals." *HA*, March 31, 1984.

Ueberroth, Peter. *Made in America: His Own Story.* New York: William Morrow, 1985.

"United States National Weightlifting Records, November 29, 1957." *SH* 26 (April 1958).

USAW Board of Directors Minutes, March 8, 2009, https://www.teamusa.org/USA-Weightlifting/About-Us/Governance-and-Financial/Board-of-Directors/Board-Meeting-Minutes.

USA Weightlifting Board of Directors Minutes, January 2 to July 17, 2011, https://www.teamusa.org/USA-Weightlifting.

Van Cleef, Ray. "Strongmen the World Over." *SH* 20 (July 1952).

"Walking Clinic Fills an Exercise Need." *HSB*, March 28, 1986.

Watanabe, June. "Keep the Shutterbugs Snapping." *HSB*, July 6, 1981.

Weglyn, Michi Nishiura. *Years of Infamy: The Untold Story of America's Concentration Camps.* Seattle: University of Washington Press, 1996.

Weinberg, E.D. *Exposing the Hidden Dangers of Iron.* Nashville: Cumberland House, 2004.

Wildie, Kevin. *Sacramento's Historic Japantown: Legacy of a Lost Neighborhood.* Charleston, SC: History Press, 2013.

"XIX Junior World Championships." *Weightlifting USA* XI, no. 3 (July 1993).

Yarick, Ed. "Final Olympic Tryouts." *Iron Man* 16 (January 1957), 12–13.

———. "This Is Your Story, Tommy Kono—Olympic Champion." *Iron Man* 12 (May 1953).

Yoo, David. *Growing Up Nisei: Race, Generation, and Culture Among Japanese Americans of California, 1924–49.* Urbana: University of Illinois Press, 2000.

Zalburg, Sanford. "Tommy Kono Regained Health by Weight-Lifting." *HA*, March 11, 1956.

Index

AAU Executive and Foreign Relations Committee 52
AAU Sullivan Award 66–67, 72, 81, 200, 233
AAU Weightlifting Committee 105
Abadjiev, Ivan 155, 191, 201
Adams, Rick 257
Adidas 102, 249
Ajan, Tamas 5, 140, 142, 144, 152, 157, 163, 182, 189, 195, 202, 208, 252–53, 255–57
Akaka, Daniel 183, 255
Ala Moana Shopping Center 138
Alanis, Mauro 92, 98
Alexeev, Vasili 139, 158, 185, 187
All-American Weightlifting Team 35
Allen, Kevin 255
Almanza, Angela 256
Aloha State Games 152, 183
Aloha Tower Marketplace 173
Al-Zubaida, Hussain 49
Amateur Sports Act of 1978 136
America Cup 132
America on Trial 5
American College of Modern Weightlifting 25, 226
American Federation of Women Bodybuilders 139
American Open 159
American Psychologist 259
American Samoa 140
American Specialist Program 99
American System of Training 187, 199
American Weightlifting Association 156
Americanization 7–8
Amfac Inc. 214
Anderson, Eileen 136
Anderson, Paul 42, 45–52, 60, 64, 75, 243, 254, 264
Arigatai 175, 228, 230–31, 238, 260

Arnold Knows Me 208–9, 216–18, 221, 257
Arnold Sports Festival 191, 194, 197, 208
Aronson, John 251
Ashman, Dave 1
Asian American History Month 209
Asian American Movement 237
Asian American Voluntary Action Center 132
Asian Pacific American Leadership Award 194
Association of Oldetime Barbell & Strongmen 183, 255
asthma 17, 121, 180
Athletes in Action 105
Athletic Journal 95
Atlas, Charles 17
Auburn University 175
Auerbach, Stuart 246
Aurelius, Marcus 1, 231
Australian Weightlifting Federation 141
Avrasin, Maya 250

Bad Godesberg 100
Baghdad 48
Bailey, Ed 37
Baker, Chris 240, 242
Baker, Gene 153, 156, 261
Balik, John 153
Bannister, Roger 226
Barahal, Jim 176–78, 250, 255, 261
Barley Green 130, 138
Barnett, Wes 2, 160, 163, 164, 165, 167–68, 201, 251, 257, 261
Barnholth, Larry 25, 40, 226–27, 230, 259, 264
Barrett, William 259
Barrows, Kathleen 260
Bass, Clarence 2, 105, 189, 256–57, 261
Baszanowski, Waldemar 133
Bates, Frank 110
Baumgartner, Bruce 208

Bednarski, Bob 75, 96, 145
Beirut 46
Berger, Isaac 2, 60, 62, 65–66, 70, 107–8, 117, 131–32, 137, 140, 142–43, 224, 245–46, 229–51, 261
Bergin, William 242
Berlin 31–32, 94
Berry, Mark 25
Berthold, S. Megan 238
Better Nutrition 44
Beyond Prejudice 5
Biblical heroes 96
Bigler, Sam 111
Bigold, Pat 183, 194, 255, 261
Bilger, Burkhard 208
Blake, Ryan 2
Bloom, Alfred 238, 261
Bloom, Don 239
Bochenek, Jan 67
bodybuilding 1, 18–19, 21, 23, 25, 36, 37, 40–41, 57, 73, 77, 84, 115–16, 139, 142, 146, 152–53, 159, 186, 204, 209, 221, 223, 241, 251, 258
Bodytribe Fitness 205
Boff, Vic 69, 189
Bogdanovsky, Fyodor 61, 67
Bombay 50
Boston Marathon 119, 212
Botev, Stefan 155
Boulos, Antoine 41
Bowen, Ezra 259, 261
Boy Scout Jamboree 70
Boys Life 106
Bradford, Jim 1, 48, 246
Bragg, Paul 85
Brewer, Bill 42
Brignolo, George 24, 28
Brock, Alvin 64
Brown, David 251
Brown, Francis Hyde L'i 183
Brown, Shelly 2
Brummel, Valeri 200
Brundage, Avery 68
Brunner, Steven G. 256
Bryant, Bear 201
Buddhaheads 8

267

Buddhism 6, 8, 10, 14, 17, 20, 32, 64, 88, 117, 121–23, 174–75, 189, 217, 228–30, 238, 243–44, 259, 261, 264
Bulganin, Nikolai 50
Bulgarian System of Training 147, 154, 161, 174–75, 186–88, 191–92, 199, 201–2
Bulgo, Joe 82–83, 85
Bulletin, California Weight Lifters Association 241
Burdick, Eugene 244
Burg, William 239
Burns, James 214
Bush, George Herbert Walker 152
Bush, George W. 5, 188
Business and Professional Women of Honolulu 136

Cabrera, Jorge Gilling 248
Cady, Mike 168, 261
Caesar, Willie 212
Cairo 46
Caitlin, Oliver 168
Calcutta 50–52
Caldwell, Dan 110
California Packing Corporation (CPC) 14
California State Assembly 29
California State Championships 28
Cameron, Ken 36
Cameron, Mark 110–12, 132, 249
Canseco, Jose 201, 261
Cantore, Dan 110–11, 248
Capsouras, Frank 108
Carnegie, Dale 259, 261
Carter, Jimmy 119, 250
Caulkins, Tracy 152
Cayetano, Ben 183
Cayeux, Robert 34, 187, 243
CBS Sports Spectacular 125
Central American Games 234
Centro Deportivo Olímpico Mexicano (CDOM) 94, 248
Cerda, René de la 91, 248
Championship Weightlifting 97, 107, 169, 198–99, 201–2, 219, 226, 245, 248, 253, 259, 263
Chang, Cathy 139, 251
Changmei, Han 148
Charniga, Bud 156, 253
Chicago International Amphitheatre 64
Chinese Exclusion Act 13
Christensen, John 219
Christian Science Monitor 19
Christianity 6, 19, 70, 105–6, 122, 247, 259
Christiansen, Karen 173
Chun, Jeanette 120, 176–77, 179, 190, 250, 255

Chun, Ronald 179
Cioroslan, Dragomir 154, 162, 167, 191–192, 196, 202–3, 262
cirrhosis of the Liver 1, 211, 215, 217
City/County of Honolulu 217
Civil Liberties Act of 1988 152
Civil Rights Movement 5, 10
Clark, Bill 189
Cleveland, Dick 213
Cleveland, Gary 2, 87, 164, 189
Cleveland Clinic 211, 257
Clinton, Bill 5
Coates, George 237
Coates, Tuesday 237
Cody, Louisa 14, 239
Cody, William (Buffalo Bill) 14, 239
Coffee, John 2, 146, 147, 202, 252, 257, 261
Cohen, Howard 2, 162, 166
Cold War 7–9, 26, 50, 52, 99, 155, 225–26, 243–44, 263–64
Coleman, Ronnie 204
collapsible abdominal-slant board 131
Collazo, Thomas 64
Colley, Collenne 146–47
Cologne 100
Columbu, Franco 117, 124
Comité Olímpico Mexicano 98, 248
Community Chest 85
Community Fitness Committee City 118
Communism 100
Concentration Camps on the Home Front 5
Concussion 211
Connolly, Harold 132–33
Conroy, Mike 2, 201, 257, 261
Cooley, Ken 258
Copenhagen 32, 43, 87
Copra, Victor 248
Coué, Émile 226–27, 230, 259, 262
Country Power 190–91
Cox, Pamela You 224
Coyle, Edward 2, 261
Crabbe, Buster 151, 183
Creighton University 53
Crist, Bob 2, 105–6, 108–9, 113, 116, 125, 166, 249–50, 254, 261
Crowther, Rebecca 2
Csikszentmihalyi, Mihaly 55, 244, 259, 262
Curry, Nicholas 203, 257
Cutler, Jay 204
Cypher, Marty 141, 144
Cyr, Louis 39

Daniels, Roger 13, 237, 239, 262
Danube Cup 104
Data Reproductions 190, 257

Davis, John 30, 38, 44, 108, 133, 139, 141, 158, 188, 237, 242
Day, A. Grove 246, 259, 262
DeCoste, Jim 155, 262
DeFourny, Megan Tornstrom 256
Dellinger, Jan 2
DeMarco, Lou 2, 9, 27, 169, 186, 199, 201, 221–22, 240, 242, 246–47, 254–55, 257, 261
DeMartini, Chris 167
DeMello, Darren 2, 135, 185, 215–16, 251, 256, 258, 261
DeMillo, Joan 125
Denver Marathon 178
Department of Motor Vehicles (California) 23, 36
Derwin, Brian 162, 164–69, 254, 262
Detroit Lions 71
Detroit Masonic Temple 65
Detroit Tigers 71
Dietz, Mike 97, 103, 248
Dinan, Stephen 256
Ditka, Mike 247
Doherty, Paul 2, 197–98, 208–9, 256–57, 261
Doi, Elaine 210–11, 257
Downs, Hugh 247
Downtown Athletic Club 151, 183
Drechsler, Arthur 2, 145, 156, 161–62, 164, 180, 186, 196, 199, 202, 206, 221, 225, 228, 230, 252–57, 259
Drewes, Paul 119, 250, 255, 262
Drinnon, Gary 111
Drinnon, Richard 239
Drug Enforcement Administration 75
Dube, Joe 2, 145
Duganov, Yury 46
Duus, Masayo 8, 238, 262

Earnest, Keith D. 246
East Alabama Weightlifting Club 3, 175, 256
East European System 161, 187–88
Easterwood, Jim 100, 262
Eberly, Hubert V. 250
Edwards, Ralph 67–68
Edwards, Roy 189
Eiferman, George 182
Eisenhower, Dwight 68
Eklof, Bo 181, 255
Elizondo, Martha 196, 256
Elleman, Bruce 15, 239, 262
Elwell, Russell 84, 247–48
Emrich, Clyde 1, 2, 31–33, 35, 44, 48–49, 242, 244, 261
encephalopathy 1, 211
Endo, Russell 259
Enryo 238

European Weightlifting
 Championships 249
Excellence 2000 Award 183

Faeth, Karl 110, 166–67, 254
Fair, Sarah 3, 127, 241, 250, 258
Falasco, Leo 2, 190–91, 256, 261
Fang, James 256
Farrington High School 56, 140
Fasi, Frank 106
Fay, J.L. 247
Fejer, Ferenc 132, 262
Fernandes, William 246
Fernandez, Marilyn 7, 238
Ferris, Dan 62
5-A-Day-Coalition 183
Flowers, Sibby 2, 144, 252, 261
Folies Bergère 242
Ford, Gerald 5
Ford, Glenda 146
Foreman, George 152
Fort Mason 28
Fort Ord 27–28
Forte, Osvaldo 45
442nd Japanese American Regiment 7
Fox, James 168
Frankfurt 31
Frankl, Viktor 114, 250, 262
Freeman, Fulton 99, 104, 249
Frizzell, Pat 79
Fugita, Stephen 6–7, 259, 262
Fuhrman, Diana 146–47
Fujii, Tad 55–56, 64, 245
Fujioka, Tad 17, 68, 221
Fukuda, Richard 130, 138
Fullard-Leo, E. 56, 262
Fuller, Thomas 185

Gable, Dan 208
Galdeira, Earl 255
Gallman, Waldemar 49, 133
Gaman 6, 17, 238
Garfield, Charles 143
Garhammer, John 147, 150, 156
Gattone, Michael 254
Gee, Bill 118
Geesa, Martha 100
Gentlemen's Agreement of 1907 13
George, George 2
George, Jim 2, 48–49, 51, 59, 72, 75, 156, 161, 224, 244, 246
George, Pete v, 2, 25–26, 30, 34, 44, 48, 55, 59–60, 73, 80, 82–83, 132–33, 135, 142, 145, 151, 156, 158, 161, 163, 173, 179, 182, 186, 207–8, 210, 216, 219, 221–22, 224, 226, 230, 237, 241–42, 258–59, 261, 264
Geritol 212, 257
German Americans 5, 237
German Sports Federation 99

German Weightlifting Federation 99
Gettysburg College 154
Getz, Melanie 146, 150, 174, 181, 230, 252
Giller, Richard 25
Giordano, Bob 203
Glossbrenner, Herb 237
"Go for Broke" 5–10, 80, 117–18, 174, 262
Goad, Robin Byrd 2, 144–46, 161, 164, 253–54
Golden Age of Weightlifting 97, 219
Gold's Gym 151
Gough, Tom 168
Goya, Susan 256
Green, Ben 2, 112, 147, 261
Greenfield, George 25
Greenstein, Harry 69
Greenstein, Joseph 69
Greenstein, Leah 69
Greenway, George 153, 157, 165, 252–55
Grimek, John 25, 27, 72, 74, 77, 120, 152, 182, 194, 222, 244, 250
Grimm, Travis 167
Grippaldi, Phil 109–12
Grose, Peter 243
Gubner, Gary 2, 78, 246, 261
Gustuson, Donald 215
Guzman, Al 257

Hagiwara, Yoshihide 138, 251, 262
Hall, Gary 208
Halluin 34
Hamilton, Scott 152
Hanneman, Larry 163–64, 166
Hansen, Carl 52
Hara, Ben "Ace" 17, 68
Harada, Mike 135, 148, 188, 207, 215–16, 223, 225
Hardesty, Dan 246
Harkins, Richards 250
Hass, Tyler 257
Hasse, Bob 62
Hassle Free Barbell Club 197
Hatfield, Fred 132
Hawaii Airlines 173
Hawaii Association of the AAU 139, 210
Hawaii Athletic and Physical Culture Association 53
Hawaii Food Bank 180
Hawaii Herald 183, 253, 255, 263, 264
Hawaii Nostalgia 180
Hawaii Open 140, 252–53
Hawaii Sports Hall of Fame 183, 220
Hawaii State Health Department 183

Hawaii State Weightlifting Championships 255
Hawaiian AAU Long Distance Running Committee 119
Hawaiian AAU Weightlifting Committee 37
Hawaiian House of Representatives 139
Hawaiian Senate 100
Hayashi, Ann Kiyumura 194
Hayworth, Rita 37
Health and Strength 189, 237, 242, 245, 264
Heck, Ronald H. 262
Heffernan, Tommy 205
Heidelberg 32, 34–35, 242
hemochromatosis 211, 213, 257
Henry, Mark 75, 160
Henry, Sid 2
hepatic encephalopathy 1, 211
Hepburn, Doug 42
Herrick, Richard 175
Herrick, Stella 2, 169, 175–76, 255, 261
Herz, J.C. 219, 258, 262
Hi-Proteen 39, 61, 72, 74
Hickam Air Force Base 120, 128, 138
Hill, Jack, Jr. 97
Hill, Napoleon 9, 143–44, 227, 231, 238
Hilligenn, Roy 37–38
Hirono, Mazie 253
Hiroshima 13, 205, 239
Hirtz, Tom 156
Hise, Bob 28, 68, 124, 156
Hixson, Walter L. 243
Hoder, Al 107
Hoffman, Bob 9, 17, 25–27, 38–39, 44, 47, 53, 68–69, 84, 94–96, 110, 129, 153, 194, 206, 219, 246, 248, 256, 259, 261
Hoffman Formula 38
Hoffman Liver Tablets 98
Hogan, Carol 126
Hogue, Bob 241
Holbrook, Tom 108
Holiday, Dwight 213
Hollan, Timothy J. 237, 262
Hollander, Paul 244
Holovcek, Ed 36, 77
Hong, Kenneth 210, 257
Honolulu Advertiser 38, 56, 62, 174, 24, 262
Honolulu Department of Parks and Recreation 104, 106, 109, 114–16, 136, 139, 151, 174, 177, 181, 224
Honolulu Marathon 119–20, 125–26, 132, 162, 176–79, 182, 190, 206, 210, 250, 255, 261, 264–65
Honolulu Marathon Hall of Fame 179

Honolulu Quarterback Club 119, 175, 183
Honolulu Sertoma Club 119
Honolulu Sporting Goods (Honsport) 128, 130
Honolulu Star-Advertiser 1
Honolulu Star-Bulletin 37–38, 100, 118, 133, 194, 212, 219, 242
Horner, Atlee 243
Horvath, Barton 244
Hosley, David 209
Hosokawa, Bill 7, 19
Hosokawa, Robert 19
Hotta, Shoma 250
Howard, John 237, 263
Hsu, V. Jo 253, 263
Hu, Ulululaulani 246
Hughes, Jack 163
Hugo, Victor 221, 258
Hussey, Dane 110
Huszka, Mike 144
Hutton, E.F. 196
Hybl, William 166–67, 254

Ichihashi, Yamato 6, 238, 263
Ichinoseki, Shiro 247
Ikei, Chad 150, 159–60, 253–54, 264
Imada, Lee 134
Imagire, Gloria 2, 261
Imahara, Walter v, 2, 96–97, 140, 148, 186, 190, 199–200, 222, 229, 237, 250, 252, 257–259, 261, 263
Incentive Plan for 2000 66, 163
Independence Day Physical Fitness Festival 131, 139
Inouye, Daniel 100, 152, 183, 249, 253, 255
International Olympic Committee 183
International Olympic Lifter 237
International Weightlifting Congress 52
International Weightlifting Federation 5, 77, 132, 139–40, 142, 144, 156–57, 182, 193, 195–96, 203, 208, 222
International Weightlifting Hall of Fame 183
Inukai, Harry 239
Ireland, Dr. Richard 123
Iron Athlete 253, 263
Iron Disorders Institute 211, 257, 263
Iron Man 25, 28–29, 40–41, 45, 107, 153, 192, 240, 262–65
Iron Master 237, 263
Isaac, Bobby 247
Isaacs, David 160
Ishibashi, Herbert 139
Ishikawa, Emerick, Jr. 179

Ishikawa, Emerick, Sr. 16, 37, 53, 56, 82–83, 118, 179, 182
Ishizuka, Karen 151
isometric contraction 74–75, 95–96, 262
Issei 6–8, 13, 239
Istanbul 195–96
Italian Americans 5, 237, 263
Ito, Masayuki 130
Ito, Monte 62, 221, 263
Itogawa, Eugene 253
IWF Centenary 196, 256
IWF Executive Board 202–3
IWF Invitational Superheavyweight Championship 132, 251
IWF Magazine 237

JACL 19, 27, 237
James, Lee 110–12, 249
Jamile, Alex 255
Japan 6–8, 13, 15, 62, 74, 76, 93, 99, 109–10, 124, 129–31, 134, 137–38, 149, 176, 179, 197, 217, 220, 222–23, 234, 238–40, 243, 251
Japan Deep Hole Boring 129
Japanese American National Museum 151
Japanese American Sports Hall of Fame 194
Japanese Americans 5, 174, 183, 204, 221, 228–29
Japanese Chamber of Commerce 152
Japanese Cultural and Community Center of Northern California 260
"Japantown" 15
Jeep Eagle Aloha Bowl 152
Jocques, John 251
Johnson, Arlys 146, 161
Johnson, Clarence 44, 46, 52
Johnson, Kevin 258
Johnson, Rafer 151
Johnson, Van 237
Jones, Arthur 199
Jones, Lyn 158, 161–62, 164, 168, 196
Jones, Shirley 101
Joyner, Florence Griffith (Flo Jo) 147
Judo 17, 147, 149, 240
Junior National Championships: 1952, Oakland 28
Junior Olympic Weightlifting Training Camp 125
Junior World Championships: 1993, Cheb 157

Kabul 49, 52
Kahanamoku, Duke 151–52, 183
Kailajarvi, Jaakko 77

Kaiser High School 150
Kaiser Hospital 214
Kamura, Kris 175
Kanoa, Melchor Miles 181
Kapiolani Park 120, 126, 131, 135, 139, 179
Karlsrhe 33
Kashiwagi, Hiroshi 16
Kasyanov, V.M. 57, 240, 245
Kawamura, Gary 2, 56, 118, 143, 159, 174–75, 213, 215–216, 223, 245, 258, 261
Kawashima, Dot 130
Kawashima, Mitsuo 82–83, 130–131, 151
KCRA 68
Keiki Asthma Fair 180–81
Kelly, John, Sr. 152
Kendis, Kaoru 9, 238, 263
Kenneally, Lauren 150, 253
Khrushchev, Nikita 50
Kiiha, Osmo 2, 18, 61, 189, 208, 210, 237, 240–43, 245–246, 256–57, 261, 263
Kikumura, Akema 228
Kim, Jacqueline 228, 252, 259
Kim, Suzanne 145, 252
KIO Company 124, 129–131, 137–138, 189–90, 224, 251, 256
Kirkley, George 98, 263
Kitamusa, Ichiro 239
Kitamusa, Ohata Oiji 239
Kitano, Harry H.L. 228, 238, 259, 263
Klamath Falls Naval Air Station 17, 240
Klemens, Bruce 2, 140–41, 166, 195, 263
Knipp, Russell 96, 105, 109, 124, 249
Ko, Young Suk 104, 106, 249
Kokoro 17
Konno, Evelyn 213
Konno, Ford 132, 212
Kono, Fannie 205
Kono, Florence 3, 61, 81–82, 85, 96–97, 101, 106–108, 124, 127–28, 130, 132, 138, 140, 151, 177, 181, 191, 207, 212, 216, 224–25, 247, 249–51, 256–59, 261
Kono, Frank (Yoshio) 14–15, 20, 206
Kono, Ishimi (Ohata) 14–15, 24, 27, 223, 239
Kono, Jamieson 82, 92, 122, 124, 127, 138, 181, 206–7, 225, 247
Kono, John (Twao) 14–15, 20, 78, 83, 206, 244, 247, 250, 253
Kono, Kanichi 13–15, 20, 68, 121, 223, 239, 243–244
Kono, Keizo 13
Kono, Mark 3, 17, 68, 122–127,

Index

Kono, Tommy (*continued*)
138, 181, 207, 218, 225, 241, 245, 250, 255, 257–258

Kono, Mike (Tadao) 14–15, 20, 83, 206, 210, 244, 247, 250, 253

Kono, Miriam 181

Kono, Tom T. 240

Kono, Tommy:
Americanization 8–9, 19, 20, 29–30, 34, 36, 55; *Arnold Knows Me* 208–9, 216–18, 221, 230–31; Bob Hoffman's influence 28–29, 39, 44–50, 57, 59, 61, 72, 74, 219–20; Buddhist influences 6–8, 10, 17, 32, 217, 229–31; business ventures 74, 94–96, 128–32, 137–38, 190–91; Dr. Richard You's influence 37, 41, 53–55, 57–61, 70, 73, 76, 211–15, 220; early competitions 21–22, 24–25, 27–29; early weightlifting experiences 16–19; employment 23, 36; family life 120–24, 127–28, 181–82, 206–8, 223–26; goodwill tours 45–53; health issues 5, 17, 24, 27, 50, 52, 61, 70, 73; hemochromatosis 1, 210–18; high school and college days 20–23; Honolulu Marathon 119–20, 176–81; Honolulu Parks and Recreation 114–119; the idea man 94–97, 114–16; influence of Chester Teegarden 23–24; Japanese and family origins 13–15; knee ailments 70–71, 76, 182, 204; Korean War impact 27–28, 31–36; local, national and international accolades 5, 29, 45, 54, 62, 64, 67–68, 118–19, 132–33, 151–52, 183–84, 193–96; Louis Riecke competition 1, 65, 74–75; marriage and Maui 81–88; mind over matter 9, 25–26, 34, 39–40, 45, 62, 66, 70, 75, 222–23, 226–29; The Nuuanu YMCA Training 55–56; Olympic and world championships 29–31, 38–39, 44, 59–62, 65–67, 70–73, 76; Olympic coaching 91–94, 97–102, 107–13, 144–49; Pan American Games 45, 66, 75; patriotism 7–9, 29–30, 34, 53, 63, 70; performance-enhancing drugs 72, 75–76, 201–2; Philadelphia story 24–26; physique triumphs 40–42, 48, 56, 77; public service 31–36, 62, 68, 70–71, 116–19, 124–27, 134–43, 149–51, 158–61, 173–81, 196–98, 204–6; Shikata-Ga-Nai and Arigatai 19, 32, 151, 175, 230; Tommy's books 185–91, 198–202; Tule Lake encampment 5–6, 15–19, 70; weightlifting politics 153–58, 161–69, 191–93, 202–3; York aspirations 94–97, 102–7

Kono Classic 206, 208
Kono Company 190
Kono, Yamagata Akino 13
Kono-mama 6
Korean War 8, 27–28, 175, 217
Koszewski, Zabo 28, 36, 77
Kowalski, Tommy 64
Krauss, Bob 63
Kuniyoshi, Edwin 16
Kurinov, Alexander 71, 73, 76
Kutzer, William 196–97, 256, 261
KVIE 209, 257

LaGumina, Salvatore J. 237, 263
LaLanne, Jack 151
Lear, John 110
Lederer, William J. 244
Lee, Sammy 35, 117, 132, 152, 194
Legacy of Injustice 5
Lempart, Tomas 249
Lenz, Henry 28
Leong, Timmy 82, 151, 182
Levin, Murray 2, 65, 107, 125, 128, 132, 134, 141, 144–45, 148, 153, 156, 162, 165–67, 174–75, 249, 251–55, 261, 263, 294
Life magazine 106
Lincoln School 20, 240
Ling, Ronald 211
Lippold, Walter 100, 249
Little Olympics (Mexico City) 97
Lloyd, Nora Moore 251
Lolotai, Al 140
Lomakin, Trofim 45
Long Distance Running Committee 119
Long Island Press 249, 263
Lopez, Laurie 191, 256
Lotchin, Roger 238, 263
Lowe, Fred 108, 111
Loyola Marymount University 136
Lum, Steve 255
Lynn, Sherri 181

MacFadden, Bernarr 16
Machado, Carl 258
Machado, Mario J. 251
Mack Trucks 139–40
Mackey Yanagisawa Lifetime Achievement Award 152, 183
McCarty, Kevin 258
McClellan Air Force Base 20
McCormick, Pat 35, 117

McKinley High School 37, 42, 117, 139
McKinney, James 68
McLaughlin, Harry 263, 256
Macomber, William 249
McQueen, Red 66
McRae, Tim 168
Macy, Jeff 164
Madison Square Garden 65
Maeda, Wayne 239, 263
Mah, Jackie 150
Maki, Mitchell T. 238, 263
Mandalay 51
Mang, Rudolf 101
Mannheim 35, 103, 122
Maraniss, David 246, 263
Marathon Association 177, 190, 206, 250, 255
March, Bill 70, 74–75, 77–78, 80, 262
Marcyan, Walt 125
Marshall, Karyn 145–48, 252
Marshall, Peter 147
Martin, Ernest Y. 258
Martin, Louis 78
Maryland Penitentiary 71
Mason, Max 194
Masumoto, David Mas 238
Mateos, Manuel 92, 97–98, 248, 263
Matlin, David 111, 113, 249–50
Matsui, Doris O. 258
Matsumoto, Toru 237, 263
Matsunaga, Val 246
Matsuzawa, B.M. 55
Mattos, Jodie 2
Maui Health Center 84–85, 91, 128, 247
Maui News 247–48, 251, 262–64
Maui Women's Bodybuilding Championships 139
Maung, Tun 41, 50
Medina, Miguel 98
Meiji Restoration Act of 1868 |13
Melaleuca 130, 215
Meltzer, David 2, 177, 237–38, 241, 245, 255, 258–59, 263
Menehune Water Company 177
Metz, William 42
Mew, Natalie 2, 143
Mexico National Championships 91–92, 98
Michener, James 15, 228, 239, 259, 263
Midtown Monthly 261
Mihajlovic, Vladan 242
Miki, George 237, 251
Mililani Memorial Park and Mortuary 217, 258
Miller, Ann 88, 221, 225
Miller, Carl 2, 106–8, 112–13, 153, 161, 250, 261, 263

Index

Miller, Dusty 252
Miller, Pete 2, 148, 253
Miller, Vernon 245
Milo 160, 189, 191–92, 256, 264
Minidoka 19
Miniversal 137
Mink, Patsy 91, 248
Misaka, Wat 194
Miss Fourth of July 139
Mr. America 37, 77, 148, 182, 194, 245, 247, 258, 262, 264
Mr. California 36
Mr. Hawaii 117, 139
Mr. High School-Hawaii 139, 253
Mr. Iron Man 40–41, 233
Mr. Olympia 139, 204
Mr. Universe: 1955, Munich 48; 1956, Virginia Beach 52; 1957, Tehran 233; 1959, Warsaw 67; 1961, Vienna 75, 77, 196, 209
Mr. Waikiki 139
Mr. World: 1954, Roubaix 41, 233
Mitsukado, Andrew 64, 78–79, 105, 244, 263
Mixon, Christopher 2
Miyake, Yoshinobu 188, 247
Miyamoto, Brian 2, 135, 140, 142, 216, 261
Miyamoto, Mel 2, 160, 197, 216, 230, 254, 259, 261
Mizuno, Mike 2, 114–16, 119, 142, 148, 250, 252
Moanolua Clinic and Medical Center 210
Mobium Corporation 132
Mochitsuki 123
Model Minority 9
Montero, Barbara Gail 259, 263
Moomaw, Donn 236, 251
Moomba Weightlifting Tournament 141, 252
Morais, Dominic 243, 263–64
Morita, Pat 239
Morris, Bob 154, 167
Morrissey, E.J. 240
Moscow Invitational Meet: 1955 45, 62–64; 1958 62–64, 263; 1961 74–76, 200, 246; 1962 77–78
Mottainai 238
Mravintz, Theresa 249
Murray, Jim 45
Muscle Beach 27
Muscle Builder 69
MuscleMag International 255, 261
Muscular Development 96, 107, 247

Nagashima, Euphemia 151, 181
Nagata, Donna K. 228, 237, 259, 264

Nahan, Stu 68
Nakano, Lane 237
Nakasone. Rae 159, 254
Napier, Jim 110
National Amateur Body-Builders' Association (NABBA) 77
National Archives 239, 244, 261
National Junior Championships 28, 162, 193
National Memorial Cemetery of the Pacific 217, 219, 258
National Physical Education School 99
National Sports Festival 156
National Weightlifting Championships: 1950, Philadelphia 2, 24–26, 230; 1951, Los Angeles 27–28; 1952, New York 29, 53, 173; 1953, Indianapolis 38; 1954, Los Angeles 43–44, 243; 1955, Cleveland 45; 1956, Philadelphia 56–57; 1957, Daytona Beach 61; 1958, Los Angeles 129; 1959, York 66; 1960, Cleveland 70–71, 246; 1961, Los Angeles 76; 1962, Detroit 71, 78; 1963, Harrisburg 1, 8, 62, 79–80, 188, 247; 1964, Chicago 86; 1965, Los Angeles 87–88; 1972, Detroit 105; 1973, Williamsburg 108–9; 1974, York 117; 1975, Culver City 110, 121; 1977, Culver City 96; 1987, Livonia 142; 1991, Blaine 159; 1995, Guanzhou 162; 1996, Shreveport 162; 1997, Blaine 163; 2000, Frederick 169
Nautilus 131, 199
NBC News 1
Neckerman, Josef 100
Nehru, Jawaharlal 50
Nelson, Deb 183, 264
Nelson, R.L. 211, 264
New Delhi 50
New York Marathon 162
New York Times 1, 63, 70, 238, 263–64
New York World's Fair 86
New Yorker 208, 257
Newsom, Gavin 194
Newton, Harvey 2, 136, 142, 153, 156–57, 193, 252–53, 255–56, 261
Newtown Estates Community Association 205
Nichi Bei Times 256
Nicoletti, Victor 28, 36
Nielsen, Roger 151
Nietzsche, Friedrich 173, 255
Niiya, Brian 2, 16, 240, 242, 264

NikkeiWest 217, 258, 264
Nikulin, Alexander 242
Nippon High Speed Boring 130, 138
Nisei 5–9, 19, 21, 31, 228, 238–40, 263, 265
Nishihara, Kenny 142, 252
Nishimoto, Phyllis 159, 173, 254–55
Nishimoto, Wayne 255
Nixon, Richard 47, 52, 68, 244
Noguchi, Kinya 245
Nomura, Harriet 81
Nomura, Mildred 213
Northern California Championships 24, 27, 40
Nutrition Review 211

Oahu Open 56
Oak Park Athletic Club 27
Obama, Barack 207
O'Brien, David 6, 259
O'Brien, Parry 67, 132
Ogata, Russell 2, 56, 110, 135–36, 141–42, 173, 207–8, 213, 216, 240, 245, 248–49, 251–52, 255, 257–59, 261
Ohio History 237, 262
Okada, Brian 134–35
Okage-sama-de 238
Olympic Games: 1948, London 17, 29, 34, 44, 55, 80, 83, 173–74, 237, 242; 1952, Helsinki 13, 28–32, 34–35, 43, 53, 104, 188, 212–13, 228, 237, 242; 1956, Melbourne 52, 55, 59–61, 119, 128–29, 209, 213, 237, 246; 1960, Rome 70–72, 74, 209, 230, 246, 262; 1964, Tokyo 79, 87; 1968, Mexico City 91; 1972, Munich 99, 106; 1976, Montreal 110, 112, 121, 123, 141, 149, 244; 1980, Moscow 132; 1984, Los Angeles 132, 136–37; 1988, Seoul 142–43, 151, 153 1992, Barcelona 150–51, 154–55; 1996, Atlanta 150, 158, 160, 163, 168, 182–83; 1998, Nagano 175, 181; 2004, Athens 192; 2012, London 208; 2016, Rio de Janeiro 209
Olympic Training Center 135–36, 142–43, 147, 149–50, 153–54, 156–60, 167–68, 174, 179, 192, 196, 202–3,
Olympic Trials 118, 163, 175, 230
Omokawa, Owao "Ban-san" 129–30, 138, 251
Omori, Pat 109, 117–18
O'Neill, Sheila 240
Onuma, Kenji 110, 121, 128–32, 137–38, 151, 223, 249–51, 253, 258

Index

Orlof, Marty 40
Oshima, Mike 7
Osmun, Mark 255, 264
Ostrowicz, Seb 222–23, 258, 264
Ouchi, Hitoshi 247
Outrigger Canoe Club 173
Owada, Eddie 255
Oyafuso, Wayne 161, 254

Pacheco, Felipe 92
Pacific Citizen 8, 27, 29
Pacific Coast AAU 35
Pacific Coast Championships 23–24, 37, 43
Pacific Islands Power Lift Championships 117
Pahlavi, Mohammad Reza 46–47
Paiva, Charles 167
Palinski, Ireneusz 78
Palumbo-Liu, David 238
Pan, Richard 258
Pan American Airways 139
Pan American Games: 1955, Mexico City 45, 53; 1959, Chicago 66; 1963, Sao Paulo 78–79; 1967, Winnipeg 75, 94, 97–98, 168
Panini America 208
Park, Jim 77, 258
Park, Reg 56, 77, 152, 183
Paschall, Harry 25, 34, 258, 264
Pateo, Vernon 140, 159, 173, 215
Patera, Ken 187
PBS 209
Peale, Norman Vincent 9, 227, 231
Pearl, Bill 36, 77, 125, 185–86, 237, 256, 261, 264
Pearl, Judy 185, 256, 261
performance-enhancing drugs 9, 72, 75–76, 78, 88, 112, 188, 201
Perrey, Siegfried 99–100, 248–49
Perrin, Warren 258
Peter, Wolfgang 99, 249
Petersen, William 6, 8–9, 238, 264
Phan, Suzanne 209, 216, 257
Pharmaceuticals Inc. 212
Pierini, Edward 210, 257, 264
Pirosh, Robert 237
Pisarenko, Anatoly 223
Pitman, Joe 1, 25, 27, 29, 46–47
Place, Nick 253
Plukfelder, Rudolf 77–78
Polakowski, Chris 154, 162, 254, 264
Poole, Harold 247
Potter, Don 64
"Powerhooks" 190
Power Pit 206

Powers, Stefanie 247
Prebish, Charles S. 238, 261, 264
President's Council on Physical Fitness 117–18
Prisoners Without Trial 5
Prize of Moscow Tournament: 1958 63; 1961 74, 200; 1962 77
Prouty, David 169, 255, 264
Puddington, Arch 243
Puleo, Joe 2, 87, 96, 109, 164, 246, 261
Pulskamp, John 2, 246, 261

Quality Training 186, 199

Rader, Mabel 144, 152–53
Rader, Peary 29, 45, 67, 71, 87, 153, 192, 253, 264
RAFU 253
Rangoon 50
Re, Edward 99
Reagan, Ronald 5, 152
record breakers: 1977, Las Vegas 125; 1978, Las Vegas 128; 1983 Allentown 125, 128, 139
Redding, Serge 187
Reeves, Steve 77, 151
Region V AAU Powerlifting Championships: and Mr. Teenage Physique Contest 116
Regos, Laszlo 205
Reischauer, Edwin 229, 259, 264
Reno, Denis 2, 113, 146–48, 150, 162, 164, 173–74, 189, 251–55, 262–64
Rentmeester, Lea 161, 284
Rethwisch, Gus 139
Reville, Rex 37
Rezadadeh, Hossein 195
Ricker, Kat 205, 257
Riecke, Louis 1–2, 65, 74–75, 80, 246–47, 261
Rigert, David 176
Rigoulot, Charles 34
Rim of the Pacific Marathon 119
Rinaldi, Michael 254
Rippetoe, Mark 2, 202, 257, 261
Riska, Rudy 253
Robbins, Jim 239
Robert, Leo 77
Robin, Arthur 48, 77
Rodriguez, Andrew 2
Rogers, Adam 91, 264
Roosevelt, Franklin 6, 19
Rosenberg, Zachary 208, 257
Ross, Clarence 37, 125
Ross, Nancy Wilson 259, 264
Rotaishi, Tanouye Tenshin 229
Roubaix, France 41
Royal Hawaiian Hotel 60

Royal Hawaiian Shopping Center 173
Ruiz, Robin 167
"Run America Run" 128

Sablecky, Christine 181
Sablo, Rudy 105, 110–12, 162, 164, 183, 249, 254
Sacramento 14, 16, 20, 30, 39, 47, 53–55, 67–68, 79, 81, 85, 121, 125, 132, 150, 196–98, 206, 209–10, 217, 223, 226, 239, 256
Sacramento Assembly Center 15
Sacramento Athletic Club 241
Sacramento Athletic Hall of Fame 252
Sacramento Bee 1, 239–41, 243, 261, 263
Sacramento City College 194
Sacramento Classic 209
Sacramento High School 20, 79, 184, 197, 209
Sacramento History Center 151
Sacramento Junior College 21, 240
Sacramento Memorial Lawn Cemetery 243–44
Sacramento Regional Japanese American Exhibit Committee 263
Sacramento Sports Hall of Fame 151, 218, 245, 258
Sacramento State University 196
Sacramento Unified School District 240
Sacramento Union 26, 30, 241–243, 245–47, 262
Sacramento Weightlifting Clinic 256
Sáenz, Dr. Josué 94, 98, 248
Saiki, Patricia 152, 253
St. Anthony's High School 85
St. Cyr, Philip 113
St. Francis Hospice 217
St. Moritz 101
Saito, John, Jr. 253
Sakamaki, Catherine 173, 175
Sakamaki, John 175
Sakamaki, LeGrand 159, 167, 173, 175, 254
Sakata, Harold 55–56, 82–83, 118, 132, 214, 242, 244
Salgado, Brenda 2, 185, 256, 258, 261
San Diego State University 194
San Francisco Chronicle 13
San Francisco Examiner 13
Sansei 10, 228
Santiago, Jose 167
Saruwatori, Tamaki 14
Sasaki, LaVerne 2, 17, 217, 240, 250, 259, 264

Sato, Cathryn A. 258
Sato, G. 6
Satori 6
Scaff, Dr. Jack 1, 125–26
Schemansky, Norbert 2, 30, 38, 44, 69, 78, 140, 142, 160–61, 175, 224, 237, 246
Schmitz, Jim 2, 136, 142, 154, 163, 165–66, 168, 201, 203, 216, 252–54, 257–58, 261, 264
Schnell, Josef 104, 137, 176
Schodl, Gottfried 242
Schouten, Greg 167
Schultz, Jaime 2
Schumann, Otto 101–2, 249
Schwarzenegger, Arnold 77, 117–18, 152, 190, 194–97, 208–09, 253, 258
Scott, Larry 139
Scotty Shumann Award 119, 250
Scout-O-Rama 85
Secrets of the Squat Snatch 25, 134
Seibold, Dieter 248
Seike, Terufumi 258
Seki, Sherman 2
senior citizens 126, 180, 198, 204
Shakley 130
Shealy, Robert 28
Shepard, Jeremy 3
Shepatin, Giselle 146
Sheppard, Dave 43–44, 46–47, 142, 161
Sherman, Eddie 67
Shiatsu 177
Shikataganai 6, 217, 228, 230–31
Sigall, Bob 237, 264
Simonton, Les 3, 169, 176, 254–55
Sinatra, Frank 132
Singley, Elmer 27
Sisto, Walter 167
Skinner, Kelly 203
Skinner Company 14, 239
Slater, Cindy 2
Slim-Trim Waistband 95–96, 248
Smalcerz, Zygmunt 209
Smith, Bill 174
Smith, Dick 112, 161–62, 175, 254
Snethen, Dennis 157, 162, 202–3, 253, 257
Sojourner Syndrome 13
Southern California Youth Weightlifting Association 175, 255
Sowell, Thomas 207–8
Spassov, Angel 154
Spellman, Frank 2, 29, 40, 43, 243
Spickard, Paul 6, 237–38, 264

Spitz, Ewald 102–3
Spitz, Lothar 101, 125–27, 132, 138, 250–51, 255
Spitz, Mark 208
Spitz, Otto 102–3
The Spoilage 5
Sports Illustrated 95, 125, 227, 240, 250, 261
Sports Palace 142, 144, 252
Sportsman of the Year 66, 139
Stalker, Douglas 2, 199, 202, 256–57
Stanczyk, Stan 28, 40, 43–44, 46–47, 79, 156, 158, 242
Stanford University 6
Stanko, Steve 69
Stark, Al 110
Stark Center for Physical Culture & Sports 2–3, 69, 205, 219
Starr, Bill 96, 192
Stars and Stripes 100, 249, 264
State, Oscar 34, 104, 110–11, 248–249
Stefan, Jacob 108
Stenzil, Decia 164
Stepanov, Vasily 59
Stern, Betty 125
Stern, Leo 125
Steve Reeves Award 151
Stevens, Jim 107
Stewart, Warren J. 241
Stinger, Cindy 209–10
Stoessel-Ross, Lynne 146, 158, 252–254
Stone, Mike 2, 147, 201
Stranahan, Frank 183
Strength & Health 1, 18, 25, 28–29, 39, 45–46, 52, 58, 69, 77, 82, 95–97, 107–108, 110, 129, 153, 164, 186, 192, 220, 226
Strength & Health League 135
Strossen, Randy 189, 191–92, 194, 196, 256, 264
Sue, Stanley 259
Suggs, Tommy 96
Suleymanoglu, Naim 153–55, 264
Sumida, Gary 3, 121–22, 179, 181, 229–30, 247, 250–51, 255, 259, 261
Sumida, Harley 181, 255
Sumida, joAnn (Kono) 3, 92, 121–24, 127, 130, 138, 179, 181, 207, 209, 215, 224–25, 247, 250–51, 255, 257–58, 261
SUNY Plattsburgh 112
Sunzeri, Jeff 166, 254
Suzuki, Daisetz 6, 230, 238, 259, 264
Svinth, Joseph R. 244–45

Takano, Bob 149–50
Taketa, Yukio 257

Takezawa, Yasuko I. 239, 264
Talluto, Pete 92
Tam, Eddie 84
Tamanaha, Dwight 117, 250
Tamanaha, Norman 119, 212
Tanaka, Hirofumi 2, 10, 238, 261
Tanaka, Kenneth K. 238, 264
Tanaka, Richard Koichi 237
Tanaka, Wayne 87, 264
Tarzan 62
Team Hawaii 142, 159, 173, 252, 255
Team Sacramento 196
Team USA 198
Ted Mack Amateur Hour 212
Teegarden, Chester 23–27, 79, 240–41, 259, 262
Tehran 46
Temosheko, Leo 193, 203, 256
Terlazzo, John 247
Terpak, John 44, 46–48, 65, 95, 103–5, 110, 124, 132–33, 229, 248–49
Territorial Weightlifting Championships 38, 57
Terry, Beth 149, 253
Thomas, Dorothy 237, 265
Thomas, Julie 2
Thompson, William 106–7
Thompson Vitamins 105–6
Thornley, Richard, Jr. 237
Three Year Swim Club 174
Thrush, John 158, 162, 166, 173, 253–55
Thunder Valley Casino Resort 258
Time 71
Title IX 144
T.K. Knee Band 95–96
TK Loading Master 149, 253
Todd, Jan 2–3, 243, 264
Todd, Steven 119, 250
Todd, Terry 2–3, 5, 132, 246, 265
Tom, Richard 56, 82–83, 118, 179, 182
Tomei, Gloria DePrato 184, 255
Tomita, Richard 37, 64, 83, 118, 182, 242
Tommy Kono (Open) Classic 197
Toomey, Bill 117, 151
Torgeson, Gary 256
Total Image 128, 130
Toth, Geza 77
Totten, Leo 154, 161
Trans World International 132
Tri-State High School 240
Tsai, Michael S.K.N. 119, 242, 244, 250, 255–65
Tseu, Dr. Lawrence 159, 254
Tsuda, Takeyuki 6–8, 238, 265
Tulare Assembly Center 16

Index

Tulare News 240
Tule Lake Internment Camp 5, 13, 15–19, 70, 148, 152, 173, 220–21, 223, 228
Tulean Dispatch 17, 239–40
Turnund Sportverein 100
Twenty-One 212

Ueberroth, Peter 137, 251, 265
Ugly Americans 51
Uhalde, Dan 23, 25
Ultra II Diet 130
Underdahl, Joseph 241
Union Pacific Railroad 14
United Press International 243
United States Amateur Weightlifting Foundation 251
United States Army 27
United States Census 1910, 239
United States Cycling Federation 169
United States House of Representatives 67, 217
United States Olympic Committee 116, 131, 166–67, 175, 198, 202–3
United States Olympic Hall of Fame 152–53
United States Pan Asian American Chamber of Commerce 183
United States State Department 46, 51–53, 94, 99–100, 132
United States Weightlifting Committee 110
United States Weightlifting Federation 65, 136, 139–40, 156–57
Universal Gym 137
University at Buffalo 82
University of Alabama 201
University of Arkansas 244
University of Delaware 199
University of Hawaii 53, 82, 120, 213, 215, 252, 265
University of Hawaii Strength and Conditioning Coaches Clinic 205
University of Texas 3, 10, 219, 238–39
University of the Americas 248
USA Weightlifting 144–51, 164–69, 189, 192–93, 196, 201–4, 224
USAW Board of Directors 202, 257
USIA 49–50, 244
USOC Development Center 165

Van Cleef, Ray 25–26, 28, 61, 68–69, 71, 265
Venable, Stewart 198
Veres, Gyozo 78

Vietnam War 10
Villaflor, Ben 213
Vinci, Chuck 2, 46–51, 60, 72, 142, 237, 244, 246, 261
Vitori, Theodore E. 251
Vorobiev, Arcady 40, 98, 132

Wagner, Dr. John 126
Wagner, Nathaniel N. 259
Waihee, John 152, 253
Waikiki Beach 37
Walker, Sam 111
War Relocation Authority 6, 8, 15, 239
Ward, Philip R. 239
Ward Warehouse 173
Waseda University 110, 129
Washington Post 1, 246
Washington Redskins 140
Watanabe, Gary 128, 130
Watanabe, June 251, 265
Weber, Wayne W. 251
Weglyn, Michi Nishiura 237, 265
Weider, Joe 69, 102, 104, 107, 130
Weightlifting Olympic Style 107, 169, 186, 189–90, 196, 202, 217, 226, 241–42
Weightlifting USA 163, 183, 241, 168, 252–55, 261–65
Weinberg, E.D. 211, 257, 265
Weir, Tom 105–106
Werksan Barbell 197
Wesley Weightlifters 157
West, Mae 42, 194
West German Olympic Committee 100
Westerhoff, J.W. 249
What's My Line 212
Whitson, Michael 204–5, 257
Whittier College 175
Wildie, Kevin 238, 240, 265
Wilhelm, Bruce 2, 110–13, 164, 213, 216–17, 249, 254, 258, 261
Wilkes, Corey 167
Willis, Tim 202
Willoughby, David 244
Wilson, Don 136–137, 165, 168, 254
Windrath, Emmaline 258
Winter Olympics: 1998, Nagano 175, 181
Wolford, Monte 36
Women's National Weightlifting Championship: 1981, Waterloo 144
Women's World Weightlifting Championship: 1987, Daytona Beach 144–45; 1988, Jakarta 145–46; 1989, Manchester 145, 147, 263; 1990, Sarajevo 149–50
Wong, Larry 255
Wood, Hal 108

World Age Group Games 128
World Sports Medicine and Health Clinic 215
World War II 5, 7, 9, 45, 53, 55, 85, 117, 152, 237–39, 262
World Weightlifting Championships: 1950, Paris 27; 1953, Stockholm 38, 40, 81, 188; 1954, Vienna 41, 44, 69, 77; 1955, Munich 48, 50, 70, 244, 262; 1957, Tehran 61–62, 71, 245; 1958, Stockholm 65–66; 1959, Warsaw 66–67, 70, 71; 1961, Vienna 76, 152, 196, 209; 1962, Budapest 78; 1963, Stockholm 75, 80–81; 1966, East Berlin 94; 1969, Warsaw 145; 1971, Lima 101, 187; 1973, Havana 108; 1983, Moscow 136; 1989, Athens 148; 1991, Donaueschingen 157, 252; 1993, Melbourne 155, 158; 1994, Istanbul 163; 1995, Guangzhou 162; 1997, Chiang Mai 168; 1998, Lahti 168; 1999, Athens 168; 2006, Santo Domingo 193
World's Strongest Man Competition: 1977, Hollywood, CA 124; 1978, Hollywood, CA 128; 1979, Hollywood, CA 131–32; 1980, Great Gorge, NJ 132–33; 1982, Valencia, CA 132
WRA 237
Wright, Ken 27
Wright, Dr. Russell 71
Wu, Ellen 238
Wu, Kaidi 228, 259
Wyatt, Cindy 82, 263

X-D-R (exercise-diet-rest) Training System 54, 214

Yahoo Sports 1
Yamaguchi, Kristi 194
Yamamoto, Ryan 208–9, 216, 221
Yamauchi, John 109, 117–18, 250
Yarick, Alyce 152
Yarick, Ed 23, 28, 34, 36, 38, 40, 59, 125, 241, 253, 265
Years of Infamy 5
YMCA: Berkeley 24, 27, 40–41; Chicago 222; Los Angeles 24, 27; Nuuanu 2, 38, 54–56, 64, 70, 74, 82, 115 117–19, 135, 139, 142–43, 150, 160, 173–74, 185, 188, 197–98, 205, 215–16, 240, 242, 252, 258, 264; Sacramento 21–22, 67–68, 233, 245; San Jose 22, 28, 40, 189, 240; Tokyo 55; Waynesboro 1; York 222

Yogi, Yoshi 142, 150, 159, 215
Yonomine, Wally 194
Yoo, David 8, 20, 238–40, 265
York Athletic Club 61, 220
York Athletic Company 54
York Barbell Club 25, 95–96, 103–4, 109, 125, 128, 159, 189, 194, 212, 215, 222
York Dispatch 1, 70, 264
York Health Center 220
York Health Food Store 54
York International Building 220
York Invitational Weightlifting Meet 220
York XDR Club 220
Yoshioka, Tom 37, 56
You, Dr. Richard 37, 41, 53–59, 60, 64, 70–71, 73, 75–76, 78, 81–84, 93, 104, 106, 114, 119–21, 130, 136–37, 143, 205, 211–15, 220–21, 224, 244, 246, 251, 258, 264
Young Laundry and Dry Cleaning 177
Yuen, Jann 220

Zalburg, Sanford 221, 265
Zatopek, Emil 119
Zen 6–7, 88, 91, 174, 189, 199–200, 204–5, 225, 229–31, 238, 259
Ziegelhausen 34
Ziegler, Dr. John 44, 72, 74–75, 80
Ziegler, Otto 126
Zurek, Stephanie 150, 253
Zweibrucken 31

www.ingramcontent.com/pod-product-compliance
Lightning Source LLC
Chambersburg PA
CBHW060337010526
44117CB00017B/2866